Risk Assessment in Litigation
Conditional Fee Agreements,
Insurance and Funding

Dedication

To Caroline

and

To Nicholas

Risk Assessment in Litigation
Conditional Fee Agreements,
Insurance and Funding

David J Chalk
Principal Lecturer, Anglia Polytechnic University
Consultant Head of Risk Assessment at Litigation
Protection Ltd

Butterworths
London, Edinburgh, Dublin
2001

United Kingdom	Butterworths, a Division of Reed Elsevier (UK) Ltd, Halsbury House, 35 Chancery Lane, LONDON WC2A 1EL and 4 Hill Street, EDINBURGH EH2 3JZ
Australia	Butterworths, a Division of Reed International Books Australia Pty Ltd, CHATSWOOD, New South Wales
Canada	Butterworths Canada Ltd, MARKHAM, Ontario
Hong Kong	Butterworths Hong Kong, a division of Reed Elsevier (Greater China) Ltd, HONG KONG
India	Butterworths India, NEW DELHI
Ireland	Butterworth (Ireland) Ltd, DUBLIN
Malaysia	Malayan Law Journal Sdn Bhd, KUALA LUMPUR
New Zealand	Butterworths of New Zealand Ltd, WELLINGTON
Singapore	Butterworths Asia, SINGAPORE
South Africa	Butterworths Publishers (Pty) Ltd, DURBAN
USA	Lexis Law Publishing, CHARLOTTESVILLE, Virginia

© Reed Elsevier (UK) Ltd 2001

A CIP Catalogue record for this book is available from the British Library.

ISBN 0-406-93915-2

9 780406 939159

Typeset by Columns Design Ltd, Reading, England
Printed by Printed and bound in Great Britain by Butler & Tanner Ltd, Frome, Somerset

Visit Butterworths LEXIS *direct* at www.butterworths.com

Foreword

Conditional Fee Agreements are not only a different way of financing litigation; they require litigation to be conducted by lawyers in an entirely different way.

With CFAs, lawyers have crossed from being professional but financially disinterested advisors to be co-adventurers with the client in the commercial risks and return of disputed claims. Lawyers are no longer paid 'win, lose or draw.' With Conditional Fee Agreements the payment of legal costs depends on the success lawyers can achieve in the case for the client. That is a major sea change for the legal profession and presents new and significant challenges.

A CFA does not alter the solicitor's duties to his client and the Solicitors' Costs Information and Client Care Code applies to conditional fees as it applies to any other basis of charging. However, in many cases, lawyers will now work with 'funders' of litigation, who could be trade unions or insurers. To work successfully in a world where cases are financed under CFAs lawyers need a new approach, new skills and to provide a higher level of service to the client. These massive challenges are in addition to the need to get to grips with the common law and the rules under which Conditional Fee Agreements must operate.

However these challenges are nothing new. All professionals, at one time or another, have to face situations where they have a duty of care to their client and must manage any obligations they have to a third party. Any lawyer who takes a case on legal aid has to manage duties to the court, the client and the Legal Services Commission. Conditional Fee Agreements introduce new relationships but lawyers should be well equipped with the skills needed to manage these complex situations.

David Chalk's book is a welcome addition to the legal library because it addresses the complex web of legal relationships under CFAs in a comprehensive and authoritative manner, and gives a guide to the duties owed to all the parties in the relationships created by the different methods of financing litigation.

I am confident this book will be of immense use to both practitioners and those who fund and commission legal work under CFAs.

David Lock, MP
Parliamentary Secretary, Lord Chancellor's Department
1 June 2001

Preface

This book is in large measure the result of a research project funded by the European Social Fund with the generous match funding of Blake Lapthorn Solicitors and Litigation Protection Limited. That project attempted to discover how litigators do, or might, assess risk. The work was carried out in the context of conditional fee agreements but it is apparent that the discipline of risk assessment in litigation is by no means confined to that context.

The book therefore brings together the main points of focus in the modern world of litigation, namely CFAs, insurance, funding and risk. The aim in particular is to get the idea of risk assessment onto the agenda by suggesting aims and methods. Additionally the world of insurance in the context of litigation is presented as recognition of the fundamental role it now plays, as does the provision of funding. The reforms in the funding of litigation have taken little more than five years to reach the point now where significant opportunities have been created across the whole spectrum of litigation. Necessarily the statutory regime has increased in complexity and the approaches which individual legal practitioners are able to take have increased markedly. There is no single type of funding arrangement, even if one confines the search to CFAs. I have attempted therefore to resist any temptation to favour one approach over another and have instead sought to provide the materials needed to support a thoughtful decision process.

There is still more change to come and there must surely never be an absolutely opportune moment to publish a book of this nature. In particular removal or at the very least serious pruning of the indemnity principle is expected in the near future. In the personal injury field it is expected that the Court of Appeal will consider the statutory provisions relating to the recoverability of success fees and insurance premiums. Inevitably therefore there will be a need to ensure that important changes are taken into account when making reference to the material within these pages.

The law is as at 1 May 2001.

David Chalk
Arundel

Acknowledgments

The opportunity to write this book has arisen from the European Social Fund Project –Risk Assessment in Litigation and accordingly I express my sincere thanks to all who supported that project, the match funders, the many practitioners who without exception willingly discussed risk, the great many practitioners who subsequently attended workshops and generously contributed their experiences and to my colleagues at Anglia Law School for putting up with my absence. I am pleased also to be able to acknowledge the personal support throughout that project of David Higham and Brian Raincock.

During the process of writing this book I have been grateful for the help of so many people who have cheerfully discussed points of law or practice. In particular colleagues at Litigation Protection Limited have been of enormous help and have made an academic feel most welcome in the commercial world. Thanks also to His Honour Judge Michael Cook, Senior Costs Judge Peter Hurst and Peter Birts QC all of whom have found time in their heavy commitments to provide help. I am grateful also for the guidance of the reviewers of the proposal and the proofs. I have also been supported by the officials at the Lord Chancellor's Department throughout the period of the project and the writing of the book. The Parliamentary Secretary has been supportive of both the project and this book and has generously contributed the Foreword for all of which I am most grateful.

The publishing and editorial team at Butterworths have been a tower of strength and the epitome of patience and in particular I thank the Publisher and especially the Editor whose task it has been to keep me on track, a task which has been discharged with the utmost care.

Finally thank you to my wife and son, to whom the book is dedicated, for their love and tolerance.

CONTENTS

PART 8   COSTS ORDERS AGAINST THIRD
          PARTIES

PART 9   RISK ASSESSMENT

PART 10   CASE STUDIES

Each case study will have applications of the methods of risk assessment and a commentary on the factors relevant to that field of litigation

PART 11   NON-MONEY CLAIMS

PART 12   QUESTIONS AND ANSWERS

APPENDICES

TABLE OF STATUTES

References in this Table are to paragraph number. Where a paragraph number appears in **bold** this indicates that the statute is set out in part or in full. References in *italic* indicate material contained in the Appendices and the page at which it appears.

Table of Statutes

TABLE OF STATUTORY INSTRUMENTS

References in this Table are to paragraph number. Where a paragraph number appears in **bold** this indicates that the provision is set out in part or in full. References in *italic* indicate material contained in the Appendices and the page at which it appears.

TABLE OF PRACTICE DIRECTIONS

References in this Table are to paragraph number. Where a paragraph number appears in **bold** this indicates that the provision is set out in part or in full. References in *italic* indicate material contained in the Appendices and the page at which it appears.

TABLE OF CASES

S

T

V

W

Part 1

The Regulation of Litigation Funding

Chapter 1

The Common Law

MAINTENANCE AND CHAMPERTY

Introduction

1.1   The Common Law doctrines of maintenance and champerty have been traced back[1] to at least[2] the Statute of Westminster of 1275 and until 1967 they gave rise to criminal and civil liability. A definition for modern purposes can be found in *Trendtex Trading Corpn v Crédit Suisse*—

> '[Maintenance] may be defined as the rendering by one person, improperly, of assistance to another in prosecuting or defending proceedings in which the person so rendering the assistance has no legitimate interest. Champerty was merely an aggravated form of maintenance and was constituted by an agreement between maintainer and the maintained for the division of the proceeds of the suit.[3]'

The Law Commission considered the doctrines in 1966[4], and recommended the abolition of the criminal and tortious liability. Effect was given to that recommendation by ss 13 and 14 of the Criminal Law Act 1967[5], but the doctrines were preserved in so far as they might affect the legality of a contract[6].

---

1   1919 35 LQR 50, Winfield.
2   Lord Mustill stated in *Giles v Thompson* [1993] 3 All ER 321 at 350, that the doctrines are so old that their origins can no longer be traced.
3   [1981] 3 All ER 520 per Oliver LJ at 749.
4   *Proposals for the Reform of the Law relating to Maintenance and Champerty* (Law Com no 7, November 1966).
5   Section 13 abolished the offence of maintenance including champerty. Section 14(1) abolished tortious liability for maintenance and champerty.
6   Section 14(2) provides—
    'The abolition of criminal and civil liability under the law of England and Wales for maintenance and champerty shall not affect any rule of that law as to the cases in which a contract is to be treated as contrary to public policy or otherwise illegal.'

1.2   The doctrines continued to have a potential importance, therefore, where a contract might commit the mischief which maintenance and champerty was designed to outlaw. The Law Commission[1] in recommending the retention of the effect on contracts, reviewed the role of champerty and maintenance—

> '16. There is, however, one field in which that particular species of maintenance—champerty—plays an effective role. There is a substantial

body of case law to the effect that champertous agreements (including in this context "contingency fee" agreements) are unlawful as contrary to public policy; see, eg *Laurent v Sale & Co* ([1963] 2 All ER 63, [1963] 1 QB 232). This rule has an important bearing upon the practice of solicitors. For instance, section 65 of the Solicitors Act 1957 reflects the rule when it declares that nothing in the Act is to be treated as giving validity to "(a) any purchase by a solicitor of the interest, or any part of the interest, of his client in any action, suit or other contentious proceeding; or (b) an agreement by which a solicitor retained or employed to prosecute any action, suit or other contentious proceeding stipulates for payment only in the event of success in that action, suit or proceeding." And it is clear that a client can apply pursuant to section 61 of the Act to set aside a champertous agreement made with his solicitor for the conduct of litigation.

17. This rule of public policy has many implications for solicitors. The following are important:—"(*i*) 'Contingency fee' agreements are unlawful: see, eg *In re a Solicitor* ([1912] 1 KB 302, [1911–13] All ER Rep 202). (*ii*) A solicitor cannot recover from professional indemnity insurers loss arising from his having entered into an agreement in fact champertous: *Haseldine v Hosken* ([1933] 1 KB 822, [1933] All ER Rep 1). (*iii*) A solicitor who has made, or knowingly participates in the furtherance of, a champertous agreement is not entitled to enforce a claim for costs: *Re Trepca Mines Ltd (No 2)* ([1962] 3 All ER 351, [1963] Ch 199)—in which the earlier authorities are referred to. This aspect is important to an English solicitor asked to act for parties resident in a jurisdiction where litigation on a contingency fee basis is lawful—eg the United States of America or some of the Common Market countries. (*iv*) A solicitor who is conducting his client's litigation on a champertous basis may find himself ordered by the court to pay the other side's costs: *Danzey v Metropolitan Bank of England and Wales* ((1912) 28 TLR 327)".'

Prior to that report and the abolition of the criminal and tortious liability, the origins and purposes of the doctrines were given judicial consideration by Dankwerts J[2] in the context of the funding of litigation. The common interests of members of an association which had as an aim the prevention of pollution to rivers and those of a riparian owner were recognised as sufficient justification for the funding an action against an alleged polluter of a river. The essence of the doctrines since before that time had become the acceptance of justifications for what would otherwise have been unlawful interference in the administration of justice—

'The doctrine of maintenance, which appears in the Year Books, and was discussed briefly by Lord Loughborough in *Wallis v Duke of Portland*[3], and more elaborately by Lord Coleridge, CJ, in *Bradlaugh v Newdegate*[4], does not appear to me to be founded so much on general principles of right and wrong or of natural justice as on considerations of public policy. I do not know that, apart from any specific law on the subject, there would necessarily be anything wrong in assisting another man in his litigation. But it seems to have been thought that litigation might be increased in a way that would be mischievous to the public interest if it could be encouraged and assisted by persons who would not be responsible for the consequences of it, when unsuccessful. Lord Loughborough, in *Wallis v Duke of Portland*, says that the rule is, "that parties shall not by their countenance aid the prosecution of suits of any kind, which every person must bring upon his own bottom, and at his own expense". But the law from the earliest times has countenanced some relaxation of the utmost strictness of that rule; and some particular cases have been specifically allowed as constituting excuses for that interference in the suit of another which would otherwise have amounted to maintenance.[5]'

The search for a comprehensive definition and list of exceptions was, however, regarded as futile by Fletcher Moulton LJ in *British Cash and Parcel Conveyors Ltd v Lamson Store Service Co Ltd*—

'I doubt whether any of the attempts at giving definitions of what constitutes maintenance in the present day are either successful or useful. They suffer from the vice of being based upon definitions of ancient date which were framed to express the law at a time when it was radically different from what it is at the present day, and these old definitions are sought to be made serviceable by strings of exceptions which are neither based on any logical principle nor in their nature afford any warrant that they are exhaustive. These exceptions only indicate such cases as have suggested themselves to the mind of the court, and it is impossible to be certain that there are not many other exceptions which have equal validity.[6]'

1   See note at 4 para **1.1** above.
2   *Martell v Consett Iron Co Ltd* [1954] 3 All ER 339; affd [1955] 1 All ER 481, CA.
3   (1797) 3 Ves 494.
4   (1883) 11 QBD 1 at 11, where the following justifications were stated—
     'A master for a servant or a servant for a master; an heir; a brother; a son-in-law; a brother-in-law; a fellow commoner defending his rights of common; a landlord defending his rights of common; a rich man giving money to a poor man out of charity to maintain a right which he would otherwise lose.'
5   *Alabaster v Harness* [1895] 1 QB 339 at 342.
6   [1908] 1 KB 1006 at 1013.

1.3   Recourse to maintenance and champerty nonetheless continued throughout the twentieth century. In *Giles v Thompson*[1] the House of Lords was called upon to consider it in relation to the provision of hire cars to persons who had suffered damage to their own cars through no fault of their own. The argument in maintenance terms arose because the hire company did not seek payment for the hire but sought to recover the costs from the driver at fault and if necessary to do so through litigation. Steyn LJ in the Court of Appeal had reviewed the history of the doctrines enabling Lord Mustill to express a conclusion as to the modern position—

'In practice, they have maintained a living presence in only two respects. First, as a source of the rule, now in the course of attenuation, which forbids a solicitor from accepting payment for professional services on behalf of a plaintiff calculated as a proportion of the sum recovered from the defendant. Secondly, as the ground for denying recognition to the assignment of a "bare right of action". The former survives nowadays, so far as it survives at all, largely as a rule of professional conduct, and the latter is in my opinion best treated as having achieved an independent life of its own.[2]'

Maintenance, therefore, was to be regarded as the wanton and officious intermeddling with the disputes of others where the assistance rendered is without justification or excuse. Champerty however was still seen in a different light and as being concerned with the provision of legal advice in return for a share of the proceeds. It is this continued role for the ancient doctrines which has given rise to modern case law in the context of the funding of litigation through fee arrangements with legal representatives[3]. The independent life enjoyed by the assignment line of cases has particular relevance in the context of insolvency[4].

1   [1993] 3 All ER 321.
2   Ibid at 351. (The decision of the House of Lords in *Dimond v Lovell* [2000] 2 All ER 897 has no bearing on the matters dealt with in *Giles v Thompson*).
3   See para **1.10** below.
4   See para **1.21** below.

The modern case law

1.4   The position of funding agreements between clients and their legal representatives and of the assignment of actions are dealt with separately[1] as lines of authority deriving from the doctrines of maintenance and champerty. There is considerable case law outside of these contexts instructive as to the continued breadth of the common law and the effects which maintenance and champerty can have on litigation.

1   See paras **1.10f** and **1.21f** respectively.

1.5   Steyn LJ in *Giles v Thompson*[1] in reviewing the modern cases from *Martell v Consett Iron Co Ltd*[2] to *Re Trepca Mines Ltd (No 2)*[3] concluded that they were harmonious in the public policy which they sought to implement, namely the protection of the integrity of public civil justice. In *Re Trepca Mines (No 2)* Lord Denning MR set out the fears underlying this policy—

> 'The reason why the common law condemns champerty is because of the abuse to which it may give rise. The common law fears that the champertous maintainer might be tempted, for his own personal gain, to inflame the damages, to suppress evidence, or even to suborn witnesses. These fears may be exaggerated; but, be that so or not, the law for centuries has declared champerty to be unlawful, and we cannot do otherwise than enforce the law; and I may observe that it has received statutory support, in the case of solicitors, in S 65(1)(a) and (b) of the Solicitors Act 1957.[4]'

As for any process of development of the common law policy, Lord Roskill took the view the cases in the twentieth century adopted a more liberal attitude towards the supporting of litigation by a third party than had previously been the case. In *Martell v Consett*, Dankwerts J observed that 'unless the law of maintenance is capable of keeping up with modern thought, it must die in a lingering and discredited old age'[5]. This view was restated in *Hill v Archbold*[6] where the same judge stated that public policy is not fixed and immutable and must be altered by the passage of time. In that case it was the funding of a litigant by a trade union which was called into question but the Court of Appeal had no difficulty in recognising that the public policy behind the law of maintenance had moved on—

> 'Much maintenance is considered justifiable today which would in 1914 have been considered obnoxious. Most of the actions in our courts are supported by some association or other, or by the State itself. Very few litigants bring suits, or defend them, at their own expense. Most claims

by workmen against their employers are paid for by a trade union. Most defences of motorists are paid for by insurance companies. This is perfectly justifiable and is accepted by everyone as lawful, provided always that the one who supports the litigation, if it fails, pays the costs of the other side.[7]'

1 [1993] 3 All ER 321.
2 [1954] 3 All ER 339.
3 [1962] 3 All ER 351.
4 Ibid at 355f–355g.
5 Ibid note 2 at 347a.
6 [1967] 3 All ER 110.
7 Ibid, per Lord Denning at 112.

1.6 The *Trendtex*[1] decision throughout its passage through the courts produced significant statements of the modern law. Trendtex had an action against the Central Bank of Nigeria (CBN), lacked funds to pursue it and owed substantial sums to Credit Suisse. By agreement Credit Suisse guaranteed Trendtex's costs and took an assignment of all claims against CBN. Credit Suisse was also given power under the agreement to bring actions in the name of Trendtex. Credit Suisse had a legitimate interest having financed the original transaction which was now the subject of the litigation and being owed substantial sums stemming from that transaction. There was therefore justification in the arrangement in favour of Credit Suisse. The Court of Appeal was prepared to accept that not only was Credit Suisse maintaining the action but it was also to participate in the proceeds. Oliver LJ confronted the distinction between maintenance and champerty and concluded that Credit Suisse had justification for each—

'I am unable to follow why, once it is established that there is sufficient interest in a third party to justify his supporting another's action, that interest should not equally justify his participating in the proceeds of the action, for instance, by taking a charge on such proceeds for what is due to him and for expenses incurred in supporting the litigation.

All the authorities concur in pronouncing that champerty is merely a species of maintenance , and it is clear from *Clegg v Bromley*[2] that the mere agreement to participate in the proceeds of an action without maintaining it does not constitute champerty. If, therefore, the supporting of the action is itself justified by a sufficient interest in the person lending support, so that he does not (or did not prior to 1967) commit the offence of maintenance, the fact that he participates in the proceeds cannot logically render him guilty of an offence which, by definition, depends on his also being guilty of maintenance.

In my judgment, the quality of interest required to justify an agreement which is otherwise champertous is no different from that required to justify an agreement which is otherwise void for maintenance.[3]'

1 *Trendtex Trading Corpn v Crédit Suisse* [1980] 3 All ER 721, CA affd [1981] 3 All ER 520, HL.
2 [1912] 3 KB 474.
3 Ibid note 1 at 753c–753g.

1.7 In the House of Lords the decision rested on the provision in the agreement between Trendtex and Credit Suisse that the latter could re-assign to a third party which would not have any justifiable interest in the litigation. On this basis the House declared the agreement to be void. Lord Wilberforce viewed the possibility of Credit Suisse selling the action as being one likely to lead to profit for the buyer and possibly by Credit Suisse itself and that involved trafficking in litigation. Looking at the totality of the transaction the introduction of the third party rendered the agreement void as being a step towards the sale of a bare cause of action to a third party who had no genuine commercial interest in the claim.

The role of insurers in the funding of litigation was well established and indeed commonplace at the time of the decision in *Hill v Archbold*[1] but more recently that role has been challenged on grounds of maintenance. In *Murphy v Young & Co's Brewery plc*[2] the claimant, funded under a legal expenses insurance policy, lost the claim and was liable for costs. The limit of indemnity in the policy of insurance was significantly below the costs claimed by the successful defendant. That defendant sought to recover full costs from the insurer in excess of the insured sum. The Court of Appeal held that the insurer in such cases was not to be regarded as an unlawful maintainer provided, as was the case on the facts here, that the insurer had no interest in the outcome of the case and had not intervened nor exercised control over the conduct of the litigation.

1   [1967] 3 All ER 110 and see above para **1.4**.
2   [1997] 1 All ER 518.

1.8   The position of a liability insurer rather than a legal expenses insurer may prove to be sufficiently close to the outcome of the litigation to render the insurer liable for costs in excess of the limit of indemnity. In *TGA Chapman Ltd v Christopher*[1] the defendant's insurers had unsuccessfully contested both liability and quantum. The claimant's costs brought the total claim to a figure well in excess of the limit of indemnity under the defendant's policy. The Court of Appeal upheld the award of costs over and above the policy limit. The decision in *Chapman* has been recently applied again to hold a liability insurer responsible for costs in excess of the policy cover. In *Monkton Court Ltd (t/a CATS) v Perry Prowse (Insurance Services) Ltd*[2] at first instance, reliance was placed upon five factors identified in *Chapman*—

(1)   the insurers determined that the claim would be fought;
(2)   the insurers funded the defence of the claim;
(3)   the insurers had the conduct of the litigation;
(4)   the insurers fought the claim exclusively to defend their own interests; and
(5)   the defence failed in its entirety.

These factors had earlier been considered by Thomas J[3]. On the facts it was found that the action was controlled by the insurer with the predominant (though not exclusive) aim of defending its interests. The defendant had ceased trading during the course of the case and in any event under the insurance was only liable to pay an excess limit of £2,500[4]. The insurer was held liable for the costs (an order under s 51(1) of the Supreme Court Act 1981) including for the period after the insurer had withdrawn cover and the instructed solicitors had come off the record.

1   [1998] 1 WLR 12.
2   [2000] 1 All ER (Comm) 566.
3   *Citibank NA v Excess Insurance Co Ltd* [1999] Lloyd's Rep IR 122. See also *Gloucestershire Health Authority v M A Torpy and Partners Ltd (t/a Torpy & Partners)* [1999] Lloyd's Rep IR 203 which held that a clause in an insurance policy indemnifying costs incurred in defence of a claim did not cover the costs which the insured was ordered to pay to the other side. On the facts there, however, the interests of the defendant were being pursued, albeit in tandem with the interests of the insurer.

4   See also *Pendennis Shipyard Ltd v Magrathea (Pendennis) Ltd* [1998] 1 Lloyd's Rep 315 where the
    defendant company was insolvent. There is a difficulty where, as in *Pendennis* and *Chapman*
    and *Monkton*, the defendant is insured but is personally as a matter of practicality not
    defending their own interest. (It had been argued in *Monkton* that the defendant had an
    interest in defending its professional reputation but there was no evidence of instructions to
    defend on this basis and in any event the defendant had ceased trading). The difficulty is
    that the insurer will be seen to be defending the action for its own interests and in so doing it
    will be unable to plead the limit of indemnity in the policy on the issue of costs.

1.9   The Court of Appeal has recently considered again the recoverability of
costs from an unsuccessful defendant's liability insurer. In *Cormack v
Washbourne (formerly trading as Washbourne & Co)*[1] the position was
summarised as being that an insurer taking a subrogated claim will always
be liable for costs as being for practical purposes the claimant, an insurer of a
defendant where there is no limit of cover pays costs as part of the cover.
Where however, the defendant's insurance policy does have a limit of cover,
the court has a discretion to award costs even though the total claim will then
exceed the limit of cover. This was a professional indemnity case where the
policy gave control of the litigation to the insurer which instructed solicitors
to defend the claim. Auld LJ held that in the context of s 51 the discretion to
order a non-party to pay costs should only be exercised where the
circumstances of the case are sufficiently exceptional to warrant it. On the
facts the trial judge had concluded that the defendant had a continuing
substantial interest in his defence and in avoiding all liability in order that
he may obtain insurance in subsequent years. The Court of Appeal whilst
applying a test of exceptionality emphasised that this was not a rigid test,
accepted that a predominance of the insurer's interest may suffice but that a
balance of interests was shown to have occurred and that this was not a case
where exceptionally an order should be made. Of some importance also was
the finding that a failure to disclose that the defendant's limit of indemnity
was being neared during the course of the litigation did not constitute
exceptionality.

1   [2000] 15 LS Gaz R 39, CA.

Legal representatives

1.10   The impact of maintenance and champerty on the role of lawyers in
litigation has been the subject of considerable case law, much of it in the
1990s, once Parliament had made it clear that conditional fee agreements
were to become lawful[1]. The traditional approach was summed up in the
Trendtex case—

> 'Champerty is a species of maintenance; but it is a particularly obnoxious
> form of it. It exists when a maintainer seeks to make a profit out of another
> man's action, by taking the proceeds of it, or part of them, for himself.
> Modern public policy condemns champerty in a lawyer whenever he seeks
> to recover not only his proper costs but also a portion of the damages for
> himself, or when he conducts a case on the basis that he is to be paid if he
> wins but not if he loses.[2]'

Lord Denning had twice earlier addressed this point with the same degree
of disapproval in *Wallersteiner v Moir (No 2)*[3] and in *Re Trepca Mines*[4]. In the
former, reference was made to Lord Esher MR in *Pittman v Prudential Deposit
Bank Ltd*[5]—

'In order to preserve the honour and honesty of the profession it was a rule of law which the court had laid down and would always insist upon that a solicitor could not make an arrangement of any kind with his client during the litigation which he was conducting so as to give him any advantage in respect of the result of that litigation.[6']

Lord Denning rejected the argument that the Criminal Law Act 1967 had removed the only reason for not allowing such arrangements[7] by abolishing the criminal offences. There were policy reasons as explained by Lord Esher why arrangements of this kind were still to be outlawed. Wallersteiner was a minority shareholder action brought by Moir who argued that derivative actions should be seen as an exception to the prohibition of champertous fee arrangements. Lord Denning was prepared to recognise such an exception but he was not supported by Buckley and Scarman LJJ. Buckley LJ regarded an arrangement that the lawyer be paid only in the event that the litigation succeeds as being maintenance. Where there was remuneration as a proportion of recoveries then there was also champerty. It was not for the court to provide an exception. In *Trepca Mines* an agreement gave a third party exclusive power to conduct the litigation with a 25% share of the proceeds. The third party later challenged the solicitor's bill on the basis that the solicitor was an accessory to an unlawful and champertous agreement. Lord Denning made clear why champerty was condemned[8] and held that it applied to proof in a liquidation just as much as to suits or actions. The solicitor knew that the litigation was being funded under a champertous agreement but was not a party to it. The court held that this was not sufficient to debar a solicitor from recovering his costs. Had the solicitor drafted the champertous agreement, or had he ensured that the agreement was carried out with regard to the distribution of the proceeds, then he would be acting unlawfully and could not recover his costs. On the facts it was held that the solicitor had acted to ensure the interests of the party to the champertous agreement and he was not able to recover costs. This case preceded the Criminal Law Act 1967 and parts of the judgments talk in terms of criminal accessories. However, it is nonetheless a clear statement of the public policy prevailing a that time which was to become significant in the case law 30 years later.

1   See Chapter 3 below.
2   [1980] 3 All ER 721 at 741f–741g per Lord Denning.
3   [1975] 1 All ER 849.
4   [1962] 3 All ER 351.
5   (1896) 13 TLR 110.
6   Ibid at 111.
7   Lord Denning referred to all such arrangements as 'contingency fees', a phrase which is now used to refer to an arrangement to take a percentage of damages.
8   See note 2 above.

1.11   *Re Trepca Mines*[1] showed that an indirect association with champerty could be fatal in terms of the recovery of costs. In *Aratra Potato Co Ltd v Taylor Joynson Garrett*[2] the High Court found that a retainer fee arrangement which provided for a discount on the normal fee where cases failed was an agreement for fees dependent upon the outcome of the case and was, therefore, champertous. This was a decision made after the passing, but before the bringing into force, of the Courts and Legal Services Act 1990 (CLSA 1990)[3], which provides for conditional fee agreements. Garland J referred to Lord Denning in *Wallersteiner*[4]—

'Even if the sum was not a proportion of the amount recovered, but a specific sum or advantage which was to be received if he won but not if he lost, that, too, was unlawful: see *Pitman v Prudential Deposit Bank Ltd* (1896) 13 TLR 110 per Lord Esher MR. It mattered not whether the sum to be received was to be his sole remuneration, or to be an added remuneration (above his normal fee), in any case it was unlawful if it was to be paid only if he won, and not if he lost.[5]'

Further support for this view was taken from the Solicitors' Practice Rules[6] and from the Solicitors Act 1974, s 59[7] although the rules at the time did not refer to fees other than as a share of proceeds and the Act is in the negative form of not itself giving validity to such arrangements. Reliance was further placed on the judgment in *Trendtex* where Lord Denning[8] included as champertous any fee arrangement where the legal representative is to be paid if he wins but not if he loses. *Aratra Potato* also decides that irrespective of whether a champertous agreement is to be regarded as void, voidable or unenforceable, fees cannot be recovered under it nor by quantum meruit[9]. Money already paid under the agreement was, however, not repayable[10]. An argument based on severance of the offending words of the retainer failed on the facts as being an attempt at unilateral rectification.

1 [1962] 3 All ER 351.
2 [1995] 4 All ER 695. This case was overruled in *Thai Trading Co v Taylor* [1998] 3 All ER 65, a decision which has since been doubted. The decision in *Aratra* expresses the policy which cases doubting *Thai Trading* continue to uphold.
3 See generally Chapter 3 below. Garland J considered that a retainer agreement was not within s 58 at all—[1995] 4 All ER 695 at 703. This view is borne out by the introduction of Collective CFAs. See Chapter 9.
4 [1975] 1 All ER 849.
5 [1975] 1 All ER 849 at 860.
6 At the time (1987) Rule 8(1) provided—
    'A solicitor who is retained or employed to prosecute any action, suit or other contentious proceeding shall not enter into any arrangement to receive a contingency fee in respect of that proceeding.'
    The definition of 'contingency fee' was given in a commentary—
    'Any arrangement whereby a solicitor is to be rewarded in the event of success by a share in the proceeds or the subject matter of the action amounts to a contingency fee arrangement. This is so, even if the agreement further stipulates a minimum fee in any case, win or lose.'
    It was not until the 1993 edition of the rules that reference was made to a fee payable only in the event of success.
7 Section 59(2) provides—
    'Nothing in this section or in sections 60 to 63 shall give validity to ... (b) any agreement by which a solicitor retained or employed to prosecute any action, suit or other contentious proceeding, stipulates for payment only in the event of success in that action, suit or proceeding ...'.
8 [1980] 3 All ER 721 at 741—see para **1.10** above.
9 [1995] 4 All ER 695 at 708–709.
10 Supra at 709–710. 'The better rationale is that the champertous agreement is unenforceable rather than void or voidable.' at 710D.

1.12   The decision of the Court of Appeal in *Thai Trading Co v Taylor*[1] departs from the traditionally hostile approach to the funding arrangements of lawyers. The decision led to an amendment of the Solicitors' Practice Rules and to the Code of Conduct of the Bar to permit both professions to enter into agreements which would have been champertous. The decision has been followed and doubted and distinguished but has not been overruled. It is likely that a significant number of funding agreements were made in reliance upon the decision and its incorporation into the professional rules. It is also likely that a challenge will be made in the future in respect of such an agreement made outside of the statutory scheme at a time when *Thai Trading* was thought to be good law. The decision, therefore, warrants further consideration.

1   [1998] 3 All ER 65.

1.13   The facts of this decision were simple. The defendant was sued for the price by the supplier of a bed which the defendant claimed was not of the contractual standard. The defendant was represented by her solicitor husband. The supplier of the bed failed in their action and costs were (in part) ordered against them. The supplier's case to avoid paying those costs was dealt with in the Court of Appeal by reference to three main arguments: The indemnity principle[1], The Solicitors' Practice Rules and Champerty. The facts as found by the trial judge were that there was no express agreement between the defendant and her husband but that there was an understanding that she would not pay costs if the case lost.

Indemnity principle—

Millett LJ seems to adopt the trial judge's view that even if there was an express agreement that costs would only be paid in the event of winning, the defendant would be entitled to an indemnity from the claimant in the event which actually happened (winning) even though in a different event which had not happened (losing) the defendant would have had no liability.

Practice Rules—

Referring to *Picton Jones & Co v Arcadia Developments Ltd*[2] Millett LJ held that a professional rule which prohibits a particular practice does not of itself make the practice contrary to law.

Champerty—

Referring first to maintenance Millet LJ said—

> 'The language and the policy which it describes are redolent of the ethos of an earlier age when litigation was regarded as an evil and recourse to law was discouraged. It rings oddly in our ears today when access to justice is regarded as a fundamental human right which ought to be readily available to all.[3]'

It was not contended that there was unlawful maintenance—Mr Taylor had a legitimate interest in the outcome of the case both as the defendant's husband and as her employer.

As to champerty, having referred to authority, Millett LJ took particular exception to the decision in *Aratra Potato*[4] the result of which he thought revealed that something had gone badly wrong with the law. His Lordship provided three propositions—

> 'First, if it is contrary to public policy for a lawyer to have a financial interest in the outcome of a suit this is because (and only because) of the temptations to which it exposes him. At best he may lose his professional objectivity; at worst he may be persuaded to attempt to pervert the course of justice. Secondly, there is nothing improper in a lawyer acting in a case for a meritorious client who to his knowledge cannot afford to pay his costs if the case is lost (see *Singh v Observer Ltd (note)* [1989] 3 All ER 777 and

A Ltd v B Ltd [1996] 1 WLR 665). Not only is this not improper; it is in accordance with current notions of the public interest that he should do so. Thirdly, if the temptation to win at all costs is present at all, it is present whether or not the lawyer has formally waived his fees if he loses. It arises from his knowledge that in practice he will not be paid unless he wins.

Accordingly, either it is improper for a solicitor to act in litigation for a meritorious client who cannot afford to pay him if he loses, or it is not improper for a solicitor to agree to act on the basis that he is to be paid his ordinary costs if he wins but not if he loses. I have no hesitation in concluding that the second of these propositions represents the current state of the law.[5']

1 See below para **1.36**.
2 [1989] 1 EGLR 43 where the rules in question were those of the RCIS.
3 [1998] 3 All ER 65 at 69j.
4 [1995] 4 All ER 695. Oliver LJ in the *Crédit Suisse* case had taken the view that there can be no champerty if there is not first maintenance. See para **1.6** above.
5 [1998] 3 All ER 65 at 69. Millett LJ concluded that *Aratra Potato* had been wrongly decided—at 73.

1.14 A narrower basis for Millett LJ's decision concerned the consequences of a finding that the arrangement between the Taylors was unlawful. Even if it was, it was held that because the agreement gave no entitlement to more than the ordinary fee, there was nothing unlawful in the obligation to pay proper costs if the case wins. If anything was unlawful it was the reduction to nil if the case lost. Severance here was being entertained even though it had been rejected in *Aratra Potato* which Millett LJ now held to have been wrongly decided. Millett LJ does not explore the effect of severance and it is submitted that the result would have been just as much the unilateral rectification not permitted in *Aratra Potato*. If the agreement not to pay in the event of losing is severed the remaining agreement would appear to mean that there is a liability to pay for the services if the case loses—somewhat of a contradiction to the understanding of the parties. It is difficult to see this part of the judgment as being sufficient to dispose of the case since Millett LJ continues to refer to the arrangement at least in part as being not unlawful—a reference to champerty. Had it been held that the agreement was unlawful even as to payment of the normal fee in a win then the question of severance would of course not have arisen. Severance was only possible because part of the agreement at least was lawful—a decision based upon a view of champerty not held by the court in *Aratra Potato*.

As for the passage of the CLSA 1990, Millett LJ takes the view that the Act was needed in order to make lawful an increase over normal fees if a case wins. It was not needed in order to legitimate a solicitor acting for clients without means.

The sum of this judgment is that the understanding between the Taylors did not offend the indemnity principle, that although it was a breach of the professional rules that did not make it unlawful, and that the public policy behind champerty having moved on, the arrangement was not unlawful under that heading either.

It is important to consider the basis for Millett LJ's decision because it has been doubted in subsequent cases and is likely to be called into question in the future. It was however followed before the decision had been reported. In *Bevan Ashford (a firm) v Geoff Yeandle (Contractors) Ltd*[1], Sir Richard Scott V-C relied upon the decision in *Thai Trading* in considering a conditional fee agreement between a solicitor and counsel under which counsel was to receive no fee if the case lost but an increase on normal fees of 50% if the case won. There was also a CFA between the solicitor and client with no uplift in the case of winning. The agreements related to arbitration proceedings which were not included in the statutory regime. Scott V-C held that the law of maintenance and champerty did apply to arbitrations. Reference was made to decisions where champerty had been held not to apply outside of litigation[2]. It was held however, that arbitration is a form of litigation and the policy behind champerty was as valid in arbitration as in court proceedings. It was necessary then to determine whether the agreements were champertous. Relying on *Thai Trading* it was clear that the solicitor/client CFA was not champertous. It was equally clear that *Thai Trading* did not provide such a clear answer with respect to the solicitor/counsel agreement.

1 [1998] 3 All ER 238.
2 *Jeremy Pickering (t/a City Agents) v Sogex Services (UK) Ltd* [1982] 1 EGLR 42—challenges to rating assessments; *Picton Jones v Arcadia Developments Ltd* [1989] 1 EGLR 43—obtaining planning permission. See also *Cannonway Consultants Ltd v Kenworth Engineering Ltd*—(1997) ADLRJ 95—a decision of 1994 from Hong Kong which Scott VC did not find assisted him.

1.15   Scott V-C referred then to a general statement concerning the development of champerty made in *Thai Trading* by Millett LJ having considered the reasoning in *Aratra Potato*—

'... the absurdities to which such reasoning is capable of leading were dramatically exposed ... If this is the law then something has gone badly wrong. It is time to step back and consider the matter afresh in the light of modern conditions.[1]'

The absurdity which the application of champerty was likely to lead to in *Bevan Ashford* was that the CFA would have been lawful in court proceedings but not in arbitration. Scott VC found this to be sufficient to conclude—

'... if a conditional fee agreement relating to a particular cause of action is sanctioned for proceedings in court by S 58 of the 1990 Act and by the 1995 order and the 1995 regulations, the conditional fee agreement is free from any public policy objection in relation to arbitration proceedings in pursuance of that cause of action.[2]'

The significant difference between *Thai Trading* and *Bevan Ashford* is that whilst the latter appears to be more radical than the former in that it accepts that there will be an uplift in fees in the event of a win, it is far narrower than *Thai Trading*. The CFAs in *Bevan* complied in all respects with the 1990 Act— that was by far the case in *Thai Trading* where if the facts were to recur today they would clearly not comply with the statute. *Bevan* decides that the policy behind champerty cannot go as far as outlawing in arbitration what Parliament has permitted in court—*Thai Trading* held that champerty did not outlaw what Parliament had not permitted. It is open for a later court to follow *Bevan Ashford* on the champerty point with regard to arbitration without approving the decision in Thai itself. However, later cases have raised the further difficulty that such agreements were contrary to the Solicitors' Practice Rules[3]. This point was not considered in *Bevan Ashford*.

1 [1998] 3 All ER 65 at 72.
2 [1998] 3 All ER 238 at 248.
3 See below paras **1.16** and **1.17** and Chapter 2 especially para **2.8**.

1.16 Millett LJ had overruled the High Court decision in *British Waterways Board v Norman*[1] which was a case concerned with the power to award costs under the Environmental Protection Act 1990 (EPA 1990). It was in a subsequent High Court case under that Act that *Thai Trading* was first put in doubt. In *Hughes v Kingston upon Hull City Council*[2] the facts were almost identical to those in *BWB v Norman*. Solicitors acting for a complainant under the EPA 1990 were found as fact at first instance not to have intended to charge their client if the case lost and that they were aware that the client was impecunious. The stipendiary magistrate had approached the question on the basis of public policy and the decision in *BWB v Norman*[3]. Rose LJ approached the case from the Solicitors' Practice Rules which at the time prohibited contingency agreements[4]. Rose LJ relied upon *Swain v Law Society*[5] as binding authority that the rules were subordinate legislation and that an agreement in breach of the rules meant that the agreement was unlawful. The decision in *Thai Trading* had not considered *Swain* and Rose LJ held that that decision did not alter the effect of a breach of the rules. There is little in the judgment, therefore, concerned with champerty and the views on that expressed by Millett LJ in *Thai Trading*, although Rose LJ did not reject the argument that the non-citation of Swain wholly undermined the basis of Millett LJ's analysis.

1   (1993) 26 HLR 232.
2   [1999] 2 All ER 49.
3   Where McCowan LJ held that the solicitors had never intended to seek costs from the complainant and therefore under the indemnity principle they could not recover costs from the losing respondent. It was further held in *BWB v Norman* (note 1 above) that the agreement was for a contingency fee and was unlawful as being against public policy.
4   Rule 8 referred to contingency fees, a phrase widely defined in Rule 18—see para **1.11** note 7. For the current rules see Chapter 9 .
5   [1982] 2 All ER 827.

1.17 The status of the Solicitors' Practice Rules has twice been considered since *Hughes*. In *Mohamed v Alaga & Co (a firm)*[1] the Court of Appeal was concerned with Rule 7 which prohibited fee-sharing arrangements. The leading judgment was given by Lord Bingham of Cornhill CJ who held that *Swain v Law Society* [2] was authority for the proposition that the rules had the force of secondary legislation and that an agreement in breach of those rules was unenforceable. The decision in *Thai Trading* was not considered. In a more recent decision of the Court of Appeal the status of the rules was again held to be that of subordinate legislation, this time with respect to Rule 8 on contingency fees. In *Awwad v Geraghty & Co (a firm)*[3] in a libel action a solicitor had orally agreed to charge one fee in the event of a win and a lower fee if the case lost. That agreement was made in 1993, before the implementation of the 1990 Act, and had to be seen against Rule 8 as it existed at that time[4]. It was held that the agreement was unlawful. The leading judgment was given by Schiemann LJ at the invitation of Lord Bingham of Cornhill CJ. After extensive quotation from the judgment of Mustill LJ in *Thai Trading*[5] Schiemann LJ said that it was manifestly unfortunate that *Swain v Law Society* had not been cited in *Thai Trading* and that neither *Thai Trading* nor *Hughes v Kingston upon Hull*[6] had been cited in *Mohammed v Alaga*. His Lordship went on to say that the criticism of *Thai Trading* in *Hughes* was justified and that the court was not bound to follow *Thai Trading* nor *Mohamed v Alaga*[7]. In going then to consider the lawfulness of such agreements as at 1993, when the agreement in *Geraghty* was made, although Schiemann LJ has accepted that the agreement was contrary to a professional rule, and if the approach in *Mohammed* was to be taken that would have decided the case, his Lordship seems to take the view that the issues arising from champerty require consideration. That said, the conclusion is that public policy in 1993 was that expressed in 1975 by Lord Denning in *Wallersteiner v Moir (No 2)*[8]. Having reached the conclusion that such an agreement as was made in Geraghty was unlawful, it was possible to reject an argument that Rule 8 was ultra vires in attempting to outlaw a lawful act. This emphasises that the real basis of the decision in *Geraghty* is the status of Rule 8 and not the modern law of champerty. Had the court not followed *Mohammed* as to the effect of Swain it would have been necessary to deal with the views of the court in *Thai Trading* as to the modern law of champerty. In following *Mohammed* it was open to the court to move away from *Thai Trading* by the same means adopted by the High Court in *Hughes*.

1 [1999] 3 All ER 699.
2 [1982] 2 All ER 827.
3 [2000] 1 All ER 608.
4 Rule 8 in 1993 provided—
  'A solicitor who is retained or employed to prosecute any action, suit or other contentious proceedings shall not enter into any arrangement to receive a contingency fee in respect of that proceeding.'
  'Contingency fee' is defined in Rule 18 as—
  '... any sum (whether fixed, or calculated either as a percentage of the proceeds or otherwise howsoever) payable only in the event of success in the prosecution of any action, suit or other contentious proceeding.'
  Rule 8 has since been amended, once to incorporate CLSA 1990, s 58 and once to incorporate *Thai Trading*—see below Chapter 2.
5 [1998] 3 All ER 65.
6 [1999] 2 All ER 49.
7 [2000] 1 All ER at 622C.
8 [1975] 1 All ER 849. See above paras **1.10** and **1.11**.

1.18   The significance of *Swain* and the effect of the Solicitors' Practice Rules for the legality of fee agreements cannot be overestimated. It is regrettable that the decision in *Bevan Ashford* was not considered in *Mohammed* nor in *Geraghty*. The decision in *Geraghty* clearly calls into question the correctness of *Thai Trading*, upon which *Bevan Ashford* relies, on the basis of the effect of a breach of the professional rules. It is regrettable also that the Rule 8 point was not considered in *Bevan Ashford* itself. If *Geraghty* is correct as to the status of Rule 8 then *Bevan Ashford* is wrongly decided on that point alone. This leads to the extraordinary situation that the solicitor/client agreement in *Bevan Ashford* is clearly unlawful whereas the solicitor/counsel agreement breaches the professional rules of both parties but only the solicitor's breach is unlawful[1]. The continuing importance of *Bevan Ashford* is, therefore, that it deals with arbitration before the 1990 Act was amended to include this in the statutory scheme. Any CFA relating to arbitration made before 1 April 2000 relies upon *Bevan Ashford* for its validity.

1 Unless it can be argued that a breach of the Code of Conduct of the Bar is also a breach having the effect of a breach of subordinate legislation. (The Code of Conduct was amended shortly after the agreement made in *Bevan Ashford*.)

1.19   It is submitted that *Swain v Law Society*[1] is not authority for the proposition for which it has been relied upon. The question for decision in *Swain* was whether the Law Society's chosen compulsory insurance scheme for professional negligence gave rise to a right in members of the Law Society to participate in the commission paid to it. Only Lord Brightman refers to the Rules as having the force of secondary legislation. He does so in refuting the argument that for the scheme to provide an indemnity for the non-party membership of the Law Society it was necessary that a trust be constituted and if that be the case then the members were entitled to an account of the commission. Lord Brightman agrees with Lord Diplock that the insurance scheme was enforceable as a matter of public law without any need for a private law mechanism such as a trust. His Lordship summarised that position—

> 'It was urged before us that in the absence of a trust, a solicitor who was intended under the terms of the master policy to be insured would have no legal remedy against the insurers for refusing to insure him; … My Lords, I find this reasoning unconvincing. This is a statutory indemnity scheme. The rules have the force of a statute, and the form of the master policy and the form of the certificate of insurance have statutory authority, just as much as if the rules, master policy and certificate were set out in a schedule to the Act.[2]'

Lord Diplock referred in depth to the fact that the insurance scheme was set up under powers vested in the Law Society which it exercised in a public capacity and he did so in reaching a decision which did not depend upon private law. The main case cited to their Lordship's House concerned privity of contract since that was the main thrust of the challenge to the Law Society[3]. It may also be significant that the indemnity rules were created under s 37 of the Solicitors Act 1974, a section which Lord Brightman clearly considered to be part of a special group[4] enacted in the interests of the public. Rule 8 is created under s 31 of the 1974 Act. It is submitted that the meaning attributed to the words of Lord Brightman and the opinion of Lord Diplock in the subsequent cases, beginning with *Hughes v Kingston upon Hull City Council*[5] and culminating in *Geraghty*[6], are far removed form the context of *Swain* and were not intended to have the effect which they are now being given.

1   [1982] 2 All ER 827.
2   Ibid at 840d–840f.
3   *Beswick v Beswick* [1967] 2 All ER 1197; Cited also were *Morgan v Palmer* (1824) 2 B & C 729 (unlawful exactment) and *Skinners' Co v Irish Society* (1845) 12 Cl & Fin 425 (trusts). See also *Picton Jones v Arcadia Developments Ltd* [1989] 1 EGLR 43 (status of the professional rules of the RICS).
4   The group consists of ss 35, 36 and 37; Lord Brightman said—
     '… the principal purpose of s 37 was to confer on the Law Society the power to safeguard the lay public … This is underlined by the position of s 37, which is one of a group of three sections, the other two of which are plainly enacted in the interests of the lay public.'
5   [1999] 2 All ER 49.
6   [2000] 1 All ER 608.

1.20   A further complication arises given the changes made to Rule 8 during the period 1990 to 1998. Rule 8 was amended to reflect the implementation in 1995 of s 58 of the CLSA 1990 so that agreements complying with the Act were not a breach of the Rule. Following *Thai Trading*, Rule 8 was again amended to its current form. The difficulty with holding that the Rule is itself secondary legislation is that it is not susceptible to speedy amendment and until amended it would render unlawful an act which either Parliament has declared lawful or the common law has declared to be not unlawful. It is further difficult to accept that the Law Society Rule is doing anything other than following changes in the law. The result however is that funding agreements must have complied with the version of Rule 8 existing at the time the agreement was made even though complying with the statutory scheme under the 1990 Act or relying on *Thai Trading* or *Bevan Ashford*. It is beyond doubt that many agreements were made which did not take account of this double requirement.

The assignment cases

1.21 Lord Mustill in *Giles v Thompson*[1] asserted that maintenance and champerty survived into the late twentieth century as a ground for denying the assignment of a 'bare cause of action'[2]. The case law is considerable in this area and is of some importance in the field of insolvency[3] where the intervention of statute has produced its own line of authority albeit based upon notions of maintenance and champerty.

1 [1993] 3 All ER 321.
2 Ibid at 351.
3 See for example (1996) 112 LQR 560, (1998) 114 LQR 207 and 563. See also Campbell 27 ABLR 142.

1.22 Three routes by which one person may seek to benefit from another's current or future litigation were outlined in *Re Oasis Merchandising Ltd (in liquidation), Ward v Aitken*[1]—

(1) the transfer of property carrying with it a right of action[2];
(2) the assignment of a bare cause of action[3]; and
(3) the assignment of the damages that may be awarded in an action. The first and third are lawful, the second is not[4].

1 [1997] 1 All ER 1009.
2 *Camdex International Ltd v Bank of Zambia* [1996] 3 All ER 431.
3 *Trendtex Trading Corpn v Crédit Suisse* [1981] 3 All ER 520.
4 *Glegg v Bromley* [1912] 3 KB 474 where the action was for slander (a personal action) and thus only the proceeds or fruits of the action were assigned.

1.23 The assignment of a 'bare right of action' has long been seen as a clear example of both maintenance and champerty[1] since there can be little doubt that an assignee will not only maintain the action but seek to profit by it. However, an early distinction was made between the assignment of a bare right of action and the assignment of property of some other kind where attached to it was an incidental right of action[2]. The notion of an 'undisputed debt' was also arrived at as an example of property capable of being assigned[3]. Nonetheless, the plethora of cases with apparently differing views as to what category the facts fall into led Oliver LJ in the *Trendtex* case to disclose 'a growing sense of bewilderment at the apparent contradictions'. Even the distinction between personal actions and non-personal came to be difficult to make with claims for breach of contract at times being held to be personal and not assignable[4]. By the Supreme Court of Judicature Act 1874 debts became segregated from other contractual rights and were expressly assignable. The contradictions evident in the mass of case law led Oliver LJ in the *Trendtex* case to rationalise them as showing a dichotomy between personal non-assignable contracts and claims to enforce proprietary rights.

1 *Prosser v Edmonds* (1835) 1 Y & C Ex 481. See Bailey *Assignment of Debts in England from the Twelfth to the Twentieth Century* (1932) 48 LQR 547.
2 *Dawson v Great Northern and City Railway Co* [1905] 1 KB 260.

3 *Fitzroy v Cave* [1905] 2 KB 364. *Camdex International v Bank of Zambia* [1996] 3 All ER 431 rejects the distinction between disputed and undisputed debts.
4 *May v Lane* (1894) 64 LJQB 236 and see the review of the case law in the judgment of Oliver LJ in *Trendtex Trading Corpn v Crédit Suisse* [1980] 3 All ER 520 at 721. The benefit of a contract before a breach was, however, assignable as property—see *Torkington v Magee* [1902] 2 KB 427.

1.24 The distinction between so called 'bare rights of action' and property rights, whilst fully supported by the case law[1], is most likely to be explained in terms of a reluctance to impose the consequences of champerty in all but the most unpalatable of cases. Given such a distinction and given the consequences of finding a case falls into one as opposed to the other, as can be expected a vast body of case law developed in attempting to determine what did or did not constitute a right of property and what a bare right of action. At the time of *Prosser v Edmonds*[2] actions in the law of tort were synonymous with an interference with personal rights and accordingly came to be blanketed as non-assignable. A debt or liquidated damages claim was however seen as assignable property[3]. To add to the complexity, a right in contract which was attached to property was assignable along with the property[4]. The modern distinction between assigning the bare right of action and assigning merely the prospective fruits of the action was accepted at least as early as 1912[5].

1 Thus assignment of bare rights was seen as champertous in *Glegg v Bromley* [1912] 3 KB 474 whilst an assignment of a right to compensation with regard to property was acceptable in *Dawson v Great Northern and City Rly Co* [1905] 1 KB 260.
2 (1835) 1 Y & C Ex 481.
3 *Fitzroy v Cave* [1905] 2 KB 364.
4 *Ellis v Torrington* [1920] 1 KB 399 where Scrutton LJ said that the assignee was not guilty of maintenance or champerty because he was not buying in order to obtain the cause of action but in order to protect the property which he had bought, at 412–413. See also *Williams v Protheroe* (1829) 5 Bing 309 sale of customary hereditaments with assignment of action against tenants for rent due.
5 *Glegg v Bromley* supra note 1.

1.25 Nonetheless, the champertous nature of an assignment of a bare cause of action was accepted in the *Trendtex*[1] case as still representing the law with all the fine distinctions that that implies. Lord Roskill in *Trendtex*[2] reviewed the assignment cases in the light of modern conceptions of maintenance and champerty and concluded that the law had become more liberal in its approach to the circumstances in which it would recognise the validity of an assignment of a cause of action. His Lordship concluded—

'The court should look at the totality of the transaction. If the assignment is of a property right or interest and the cause of action is ancillary to that right or interest, or if the assignee had a genuine commercial interest in taking the assignment and in enforcing it for his own benefit, I see no reason why the assignment should be struck down as an assignment of a bare cause of action or as savouring of maintenance.[3]'

1 [1981] 3 All ER 520.
2 Ibid.
3 Ibid at 531e.

1.26 The recent case law in this area is almost exclusively found in the field of insolvency where statute has long intervened[1]. The Insolvency Act 1986, Schs 4 and 5, are the current statutory provisions giving power to a liquidator or trustee in bankruptcy to sell[2] the property of the insolvent. 'Property' is defined widely in s 426 as—

'money, goods, things in action, land and every description of property wherever situated and also obligations and every description of interest ....'.

Disposing of bare causes of action is clearly within the powers thus bestowed[3]. In the context of insolvency, assigning the cause of action but with a right to share in the proceeds can provide in some cases the only means of realising the property[4].

1   Since the Bankruptcy Act 1869 and the Companies Act 1862 assignment of a bare cause of action has been permitted. The provisions of the Insolvency Act 1986 are the modern equivalent.
2   In *Weddell v JA Pearce & Major (a firm)* [1987] 3 All ER 624 and *Grovewood Holdings plc v James Capel & Co Ltd* [1994] 4 All ER 417 it was held that an assignment in return for funding of the litigation and a share in the proceeds constituted a 'sale' for the purposes of the statutory power. In the latter case however, sale of the fruits of the action alone was held not to be within the insolvency exemption from maintenance and champerty.
3   *Seear v Lawson* (1880) 15 Ch D 426. In *Ramsey v Hartley* [1977] 2 All ER 673, the Court of Appeal, having reviewed authority going back more than a century, held that a trustee was able to assign a bare right of action. See also *Stein v Blake* [1995] 2 All ER 961. In *Quofax Ltd v Larcombe* (6 June 1996, unreported) it was held that a receiver had power to sell a bare cause under s 42(1) of the Insolvency Act 1986.
4   *Guy v Churchill* (1888) 40 Ch D 481 (bankruptcy). In *Bang & Olufsen UK Ltd v Ton Systeme Ltd* [1993] CA Transcript 834 CA such a sale by a liquidator was regarded as an exercise of a statutory power not governed by maintenance and champerty.

1.27   In *Grovewood Holdings plc v James Capel & Co Ltd*[1] Lightman J distinguished between an assignment of the whole claim (which is within the statutory power of sale) and the assignment of a share of the proceeds which was held not to be within the insolvency exception to maintenance and champerty. A stay of proceedings was granted[2]. In *Re Oasis Merchandising*[3] the Court of Appeal agreed with Robert Walker J's comment that he had considerable difficulty with the judgment in *Grovewood*. The *Oasis* case itself decided that an action which can only be brought by the office holder was not 'property' of the insolvent and therefore an assignment was not within the statutory exemption from maintenance and champerty. This was a wrongful trading action and the decision to stay the proceedings on the grounds of champerty was upheld by the Court of Appeal[4]. The very broad powers given in Sch 4 of the Insolvency Act 1986 were not capable of authorising an unlawful act of champerty.

1   [1994] 4 All ER 417 and see note 2 above at para **1.26**.
2   The potential under the agreement for a sub-assignment to an anonymous third party heavily influenced the granting of a stay in circumstances where a third party costs order would have been ineffectual.
3   [1997] 1 BCLC 689. See Walters (1996) 112 LQR 560 and Capper (1998) 114 LQR 563.
4   See also *Re Ayala Holdings* [1996] 1 BCLC 467 where at first instance it was held that an action under s 127 of the Insolvency Act 1986 for transaction at an undervalue could not be assigned.

1.28   *Grovewood* provided difficulty in a further decision of the Court of Appeal in *Abraham v Thompson*[1] where Millet LJ preferred *Martell v Consett Iron Co Ltd*[2] and did not accept the reasoning in *Grovewood*. The approach to be taken was to look to the power under s 51 of the Supreme Court Act 1981 to order costs against a third party and to wait therefore until the end of the case to deal with any third party involvement. It was held also that there was no power to order disclosure of the identity of a funder until the time came for the exercise of the power to order such a party to pay costs.

1 [1997] 4 All ER 362. The court had no jurisdiction to order a stay of proceedings unless there was an abuse of the process of the court. In *Stocznia Gdanska SA v Latreefers Inc* [2000] All ER (D) 148, the Court of Appeal held that the fact that a funding arrangement might be against public policy and therefore unenforceable between the parties, was by itself no reason for regarding the proceedings to which it related or their conduct as an abuse. See also *Faryab v Smyth* [1998] CLY 411 where in the absence of abuse of process the Court of Appeal refused an application for a dismissal of appeal on grounds of champerty.
2 [1954] 3 All ER 339.

1.29   The House of Lords in *Norglen*[1] had to consider an assignment of an action in circumstances where the claimant companies had gone into liquidation after the commencement of proceedings. The assignees were directors of the company, with a beneficial interest in the outcome of the case and personal circumstances such that they would qualify for legal aid. The assignment was challenged by the defendants on the basis that there was an abuse. It was held that a liquidator had power to make such an assignment which was not invalidated even where the conduct of the liquidator was challenged by creditors. It was further held that the assignees were entitled to be substituted as claimants with any abuse of the legal aid scheme purely a matter for the Legal Aid Board. The Court of Appeal had held that there was no jurisdiction to make an order for security for costs against the directors as individuals. The House of Lords upheld that decision.

1 *Norglen Ltd (in liquidation) v Reeds Rains Prudential Ltd; Circuit Systems Ltd (in liquidation) v Zuken-Redac (UK) Ltd* [1998] 1 All ER 218.

1.30   As to the power of a liquidator to assign a cause of action Lord Hoffmann said—

'The position of liquidators and trustees in bankruptcy is however quite different. The courts have recognised that they often have no assets with which to fund litigation and that in such a case the only practical way in which they can turn a cause of action into money is to sell it, either for a fixed sum or a share of the proceeds, to someone who is willing to take the proceedings in his own name.'[1]

His Lordship quoted from *Ramsey v Hartley*[2]—

'Now the sale of a cause of action by a trustee can only be effected by an assignment. It vests in the trustee in the first place because it is deemed to have been duly assigned to him … The legal process by which it gets to him must operate to vest it in the person to whom he sells it. If this were not so, such a cause of action would be of no value to the creditors unless the trustee himself tried to enforce it. To do so, unless success was assured, would require the expenditure of money which would otherwise be available for distribution among the creditors. To assign the cause of action for good consideration to another person who was willing to try to enforce it could be a sensible way of disposing of the bankrupt's assets.'[3]

1 *Norglen Ltd (in liquidation) v Reeds Rains Prudential Ltd; Circuit Systems Ltd (in liquidation) v Zuken-Redac (UK) Ltd* [1998] 1 All ER 218 at 224.
2 [1977] 2 All ER 673.
3 Ibid, per Lawton LJ at 698.

1.31 The legal aid point was dealt with simply on the basis that the Legal Aid Board had power[1] to reject the application of the directors. It was noted that the Lord Chancellor had, since the granting of legal aid in the cases being considered, made further regulations[2] expressly to deal with applications in circumstances such as those applying to this appeal. Accordingly the validity of the assignment itself could not be questioned on the basis that its purpose was to exploit the legal aid scheme.

1   Legal Aid Act 1988, s 15(3)(a).
2   Civil Legal Aid (General) (Amendment) (No 2) Regulations 1996, SI 1996/1257.

1.32 A further variation in the funding of insolvency litigation occurred *Re Exchange Travel (Holdings) Ltd (in liq.) (No 3), Katz v McNally*[1]. A preference action under Insolvency Act 1986, s 239 was funded by a wholly owned subsidiary of the company. The subsidiary was also a major creditor of the company and was itself insolvent. The subsidiary agreed to indemnify the company for the costs of the action in return for a first charge over any recoveries. The issue for the Court of Appeal was whether the recoveries had to be distributed *pari passu* to all the creditors or whether they could be used to reimburse the costs of the action. It was held that the right of a liquidator to take an indemnity against the costs of performing his duty could not be challenged. The subsidiary was to be subrogated to the position of the liquidator re the indemnity. Significant to the decision that there had been no abuse of the process of the court were the facts that the subsidiary had played no part in the litigation beyond funding it and the liquidator had not sold the fruits of the action.

1   [1997] 2 BCLC 579. Phillips LJ took the unusual step of expressly stating that is observations were not the ratio decidendi of the case. Morritt LJ accepted that a right in a liquidator to bring s 239 proceedings (preferences) was not property of the company at the commencement of the winding up capable of being sold by the liquidator. His Lordship said that that did not mean that the recoveries did not become assets in the hands of the liquidator out of which the costs and expenses of the liquidation may be paid. *Oasis Merchandising* [1997] 1 BCLC 689 was viewed as a case dealing only with the matter of whether the action was property of the company at the commencement of the winding up. The decision in *Re M C Bacon (No 2)* [1991] Ch 127 would in this respect be doubted were a final decision on the matter required.

1.33 The position of a liquidator bringing statutory actions under the Insolvency Act 1986 continues to cause difficulty with regard to the funding of the action. In *Lewis v IRC*[1] the Court of Appeal considered whether a liquidator could recoup out of the assets of the company as an expense of the liquidation, the costs of such litigation, whether or not successful, including any costs which he may be ordered to pay. The IRC as one of four preferential creditors challenged the decision of the High Court[2] in favour of those costs being recouped. The Court of Appeal held, applying *Mond v Hammond Suddards (a firm)*[3], that the liquidator had no automatic entitlement to recoup the costs of such litigation, whether successful or unsuccessful. The decision and reasoning in *Re M C Bacon (No 2)*[4] was expressly approved. The recovery of costs therefore rests in the discretion of the court, although the Court found difficulty in determining the source of such a discretion. On the assumption that there was a discretion Peter Gibson LJ said—

> 'It is appropriate to be cautious where the court is asked to provide for the liquidator's costs out of the assets even if the litigation ultimately proves unsuccessful, particularly where the preferential creditors who would

otherwise be paid a dividend oppose the use of the Company's money for that purpose.[5]'

1   [2000] 46 LS Gaz R 39, CA.
2   *Re Floor Fourteen Ltd* [1999] 2 BCLC 666. The liquidator had applied to the High Court for an order that the realised funds of the company could be used to commence the litigation. The order was granted.
3   [2000] Ch 40.
4   [1991] Ch 127.
5   The combination of a CFA with an insurance policy where the premium is funded or deferred may provide a means whereby such litigation can be funded without recourse to the assets. The risk for the liquidator would be in the insolvency of an unsuccessful defendant who fails to meet a costs order.

THE MEANING OF CONTENTIOUS BUSINESS

1.34   Section 87(1) Solicitors Act 1974—

'"contentious business" means business done, whether as solicitor or advocate, in or for the purposes of proceedings begun before a court or before an arbitrator ...[1], not being business which falls within the definition of non-contentious or common form probate business contained in [section 128 of the Supreme Court Act 1981];[2].

1   In definition 'contentious business' words omitted repealed by the Arbitration Act 1996, s 107(2), Sch 4.
2   In definition 'contentious business' words 'section 128 of the Supreme Court Act 1981' in square brackets substituted by the Administration of Justice Act 1985, s 8 and Sch 1, para 12(a).

1.35   The significance of the categorisation of work as contentious is taken to be that the rules concerning CFAs only apply where the agreement relates to contentious business. It seems to be accepted that work preliminary to what could become contentious business, where the case settles before the issue of proceedings, is not itself contentious business. Work done for cases heard by the Employment Tribunal is also regarded as not being contentious business. The CLSA 1990, s 58(5) follows this understanding by excluding non-contentious business agreements from the effect of s 58(1) of rendering agreements unenforceable unless they comply with s 58.

The 1990 Act does not use the phrase 'contentious business' when defining a CFA. It uses the phrase 'advocacy or litigation services' a phrase defined in s 119 as follows—

'"advocacy services" means any services which it would be reasonable to expect a person who is exercising, or contemplating exercising, a right of audience in relation to any proceedings, or contemplated proceedings, to provide;

"litigation services" means any services which it would be reasonable to expect a person who is exercising, or contemplating exercising, a right to conduct litigation in relation to any proceedings, or contemplated proceedings, to provide.'

Work preliminary to the issue of proceedings and all work done in and for Employment Tribunal proceedings will not be done in the exercise of a right to do so and hence does not fall within these provisions.

The meaning of 'proceedings' has been altered by the Access to Justice Act 1999 (AJA 1999), s 27 which inserts s 58A into the 1990 Act.

Section 58A(4) provides—

'In section 58 and this section (and in the definitions of "advocacy services" and "litigation services" as they apply for their purposes) "proceedings" includes any sort of proceedings for resolving disputes (and not just proceedings in court), whether commenced or contemplated.'

The former definition of 'proceedings' was confined to proceedings in court.

THE INDEMNITY PRINCIPLE

1.36 The English assumption as to costs in litigation is that the losing party will pay the costs of the successful party[1]. The indemnity principle states that the costs so ordered cannot exceed the costs for which the successful party has a liability. The case most often cited in support of the principle is *Gundry v Sainsbury*[2]. Here in evidence the client said that he could pay no costs and that he had verbally arranged with his solicitor that he would not pay the costs of the action. The client's case was successful and an application for costs was made. The judge reserved consideration of that application and only at the time when he was to give his decision was an application made for the solicitor to give evidence. The judge in the exercise of his discretion refused that application. On the costs point the judge made no order for costs against the unsuccessful party. On appeal it was said that the matter of costs was governed by statute but that the common law had been clear for 50 years[3] in holding that an award of costs is intended to be no more than an indemnity. Given the facts therefore the judge was right to make no order for costs.

1   CPR, r 44.3(2)(a).
2   [1910] 1 KB 645
3   *Harold v Smith* (1860) 5 H & N 381. Bramwell B stated at 385—
    'Costs as between party and party are given by the law as an indemnity to the person entitled to them; they are not imposed as a punishment on the party who pays them, not given as a bonus to the party who receives them. Therefore, if the extent of the damnification can be found out, the extent to which costs ought to be allowed is also ascertained.'
    See also *Harrison v Watt* (1847) 16 M & W 316 where at pp 321–322, Alderson B had said that a plaintiff was entitled to 'so much costs as have been incurred'.

1.37 The application of the indemnity principle has, however, given rise to difficulty. This is especially the case where third parties have been involved in the funding of litigation and in cases where solicitors have acted for impecunious litigants. The principle has also been prayed in use where a funding arrangement has been found unlawful on grounds of maintenance and champerty.

1.38 In *Hunt v R M Douglas (Roofing) Ltd*[1] the Court of Appeal referred to earlier authority[2] establishing that a plaintiff whose litigation was in fact conducted by or under the instructions of a Trade Union on his behalf was nevertheless entitled to costs on the basis that although the solicitor was instructed by the union those instructions were given on behalf of the plaintiff who remained liable for their costs, however unlikely it was that he would ever have to pay them. The vital requirement is that the client must be primarily liable for the payment of costs. This is made clear in the more recent authority of *Joyce v Kammac*[3] where Morland J said—

> 'The general principle is that a party in whose favour the order for costs was made, the receiving party, is entitled to be indemnified in respect of such costs that he was primarily and potentially legally obliged to pay his solicitors. It matters not whether the receiving party was able or not to discharge that legal obligation, so long as the primary potential legal obligation to his solicitors existed. It matters not whether the receiving party was able to discharge that obligation from funds of his own or funds provided by friends, family, trade union, employer, insurer or otherwise, so long as the obligation was primarily his.[4]'

1 (1987) 132 Sol Jo 935.
2 *Adams v London Improved Motorcoach Builders Ltd* [1921] 1 KB 495.
3 [1996] 1 All ER 923.
4 Ibid at 928.

1.39 Impecunious clients must, therefore, have an arrangement which makes them legally liable for costs. In *British Waterways v Norman* the Divisional Court[1] took the view that there must have been an understanding between the solicitor and the client that the solicitor would not seek costs from the client if the case lost. The outcome of such an agreement is that even where the case succeeds there will be no costs recovered either from the client or from the losing opponent. There are then difficult questions of fact and fine distinctions to be drawn as a result of this application of the indemnity principle. The view, given some approval in *Thai Trading Co v Taylor*[2], that an agreement to pay in the event of a win but not a loss did not offend the indemnity principle in the event that the case wins, is difficult to support since it requires the agreement to be looked at as two agreements rather than one agreement as a whole. In *Leeds City Council v Carr; Coles v Barnsley Metropolitan Borough Council*[3] two appeals were heard together. In the Leeds case the client was in receipt of income support. Solicitors representing the client had given her letters indicating that she would be liable for costs. The council alleged that any such agreement was a sham on the basis that the solicitors knew that the client would be unable to pay their costs and that they never expected her to do so. Kennedy LJ held that the finding of fact by the magistrate that there was a legally binding agreement under which the client was liable to pay the costs was conclusive. It was a matter for the solicitors as to whether they sought to enforce that liability. In the Barnsley case the clients were again given letters making it clear that they had a liability for costs. The clients were on income support. The magistrate found as a fact that the firm of solicitors had never sought to enforce a costs liability against a client of this type. Kennedy LJ held that a finding that the solicitors did not intend to pursue their clients for costs was not determinative of the matter. There was not sufficient basis for concluding that there was an agreement to receive a contingency fee.

1 (1993) 26 HLR 232. This and other cases are dealt with under maintenance and champerty above.
2 [1998] 3 All ER 65—see maintenance and champerty above.
3 (1999) Times, 12 November.

1.40 It seems clear that an agreement that a client will pay costs only to the extent that there is an award of costs in their favour will be a breach of the indemnity principle. In *Bridgewater v Griffiths*[1] solicitors had acted after the expiry of a legal aid certificate. It was held that there was insufficient evidence to imply an agreement to pay costs if the client succeeded in recovering costs from the other side, but such an agreement would in any event offend the indemnity principle.

1   [2000] 1 WLR 524.

1.41   The Government has announced[1] that it intends to abolish the indemnity principle. By commencing the AJA 1999, s 31, the CPR are to be amended to provide that the indemnity principle will not apply when assessing costs.

Section 31 provides—

'In section 51 of the Supreme Court Act 1981 (costs), in subsection (2) (rules regulating matters relating to costs), insert at the end "or for securing that the amount awarded to the party in respect of the costs to be paid by him to such representatives is not limited to what would have been payable by him to them if he had not been awarded costs".'

1   The Government's conclusions following consultation on: *Collective Conditional Fees—* September 2000, para 29. See Chapter 9. Consultation occurred through a paper in May 1999 *Controlling Costs and the Future of the Indemnity Principle* and the consultation paper on *Collective Conditional Fees* in June 2000.

Chapter 2

The Professional Rules

THE SOLICITORS' PRACTICE RULES

2.1　The Law Society has made Rules regulating the practices of solicitors. The Rules relevant to litigation and in particular to conditional fee agreements were made under the Solicitors Act 1974, s 31[1]. The Rules are made by the Council of the Law Society with the concurrence of the Master of the Rolls. The Law Society has also issued Guidance on conduct[2].

1　The status of Law Society Rules is dealt with in Chapter 1 where the decision of the House of Lords in *Swain v Law Society* [1982] 2 All ER 827 is discussed. The full text of the Rules is given in *The Guide to the Professional Conduct of Solicitors* (1999) 8th edn, Law Society Publications (*The Guide*).
2　The Guidance on conduct is treated as authoritative by the Law Society, the Solicitors Disciplinary Tribunal and the Court and consists of 'principles and other guidance'—see *The Guide* at pp 3 and 4.

Basic principles

Practice Rule 1

2.2

'A solicitor shall not do anything in the course of practising as a solicitor, or permit another person to do anything on his or her behalf, which compromises or impairs or is likely to compromise or impair any of the following:

(a)　the solicitor's independence or integrity
(b)　a person's freedom to instruct a solicitor of his or her choice
(c)　the solicitor's duty to act in the best interests of the client
(d)　the good repute of the solicitor or of the solicitors' profession
(e)　the solicitor's proper standard of work
(f)　the solicitor's duty to the court.'

2.3　The additional guidance to Rule 1 is as follows—

'Practice Rule 1 sums up the basic principles of conduct governing the professional practice of solicitors. These principles stem from the ethical duties imposed on solicitors by the common law and it is arguable that no further rules or guidance are required. However, to assist both the public and the profession, further practice rules have been made by the Council ... .[1]'

1   Additional guidance can be found in *The Guide* at p 2, para 4.

2.4   Rule 1 will inevitably produce its own situations of conflict. Acting in the best interests of the client may conflict with any duty to the court. The additional guidance notes give the example of the client's best interests coming into conflict with the freedom of choice of solicitor. The guidance suggests that the public interest must prevail, meaning that those parts of Rule 1 representing a wider interest will prevail, such as freedom of choice and duty to the court. Stating such an ideal and achieving it are of course not the same thing.

Publicity

Practice Rule 2

2.5

'Solicitors may at their discretion publicise their practices, or permit other persons to do so, or publicise the business or activities of other persons, provided there is no breach of these rules and provided there is compliance with a Solicitors' Publicity Code promulgated from time to time by the Council of the Law Society with the concurrence of the Master of the Rolls.'

The Solicitors Publicity Code 1990[1] (as amended) makes detailed provision for publicity. Particular care is needed with regard to publicising fees. The Code requires all publicity as to charges or bases of charging to be 'clearly expressed' and for the services that will be provided for those charges to also be stated. The circumstances in which the charges may be increased must be given and it must be clear whether disbursements and VAT are included[2]. There is no guidance on the well known phrase 'no win no fee' save that if a service is stated to be free of charge there must be no condition as to commission or the provision of other services[3].

1   See *The Guide*, pp 229–237.
2   Ibid, para 5(a).
3   Ibid, para 5(c).

Introductions

Practice Rule 3

2.6

'Solicitors may accept introductions and referrals of business from other persons and may make introductions and refer business to other persons, provided there is no breach of these rules and provided there is compliance with a Solicitor's Introduction and Referral Code promulgated form time to time by the Council of the Law Society with the concurrence of the Master of the Rolls.'

The Solicitors' Introduction and Referral Code 1990[1] (as amended) makes detailed provision for the introduction of clients by and to solicitors. It has no application to referrals between solicitors nor between solicitors and counsel or lawyers from other jurisdictions[2]. Specific reference is made to the principles of Practice Rule 1[3] and Practice Rule 9[4]. The Code specifies that a solicitor must not 'reward' introducers by the payment of a 'commission or otherwise'[5]. This provision causes difficulty given the number of schemes now in existence which advertise to the public and refer cases to a solicitor who has joined the scheme, usually upon the making of a renewable joining fee and a payment for each case. Payments per case might not be seen as a commission but the use of the word 'otherwise' calls into question the basis of such payments. Further guidance from the Law Society in respect of the Code and the use of such schemes is appropriate. Section 3 of the Code deals with payments by a third party for work done by a solicitor for the third party's customer. The Collective Conditional Fee Agreements Regulations[6] provide for a bulk purchaser of legal services to make a CFA with a legal representative under which the latter acts for clients referred by the bulk purchaser. Examples of likely users of these provisions are Trade Unions and motoring organisations. In the case of Trade Unions it could be argued that members are not 'customers' for the purposes of the Code, but it is difficult to argue that subscribing members of a motoring organisation are not 'customers'. The Code requires that the solicitor should ensure that the agreement between the funder and the customer contains terms dealing with the independence of the legal representative, control and confidentiality. The main thrust of the Code is the preservation of independence such that the client shall receive advice on the same basis as a client who has not been referred in this way.

1 See *The Guide*, pp 238–243.
2 *The Guide*, Introduction paras 1 and 2.
3 See above para **2.2**.
4 See below para **2.9**.
5 *The Guide*, p 239.
6 SI 2000/2988.

Fee sharing

Practice Rule 7

2.7

'(1) A solicitor shall not share or agree to share his or her professional fees with any person except:

(a) a practising solicitor
(b) a practising foreign lawyer … .
(c) the solicitor's *bona fide* employee, … or
(d) a retired partner or predecessor of the solicitor … .'

In the context of conditional fee agreements there need be no particular concern over this Rule unless an agreement is made with a referrer of potential clients under which a share of the fees earned will be paid to the referrer[1].

1 See for example *Mohammed v Alaga & Co* [1999] 3 All ER 699. See also Chapter 1.

Contingency fees

Practice Rule 8

2.8

'(1) A solicitor who is retained or employed to prosecute or defend any
action, suit or other contentious proceeding shall not enter into any
arrangement to receive a contingency fee in respect of that proceeding,
save one permitted under statute or by the common law.

(2) Paragraph (1) of this rule shall not apply to an arrangement in respect
of an action, suit or other contentious proceeding in any country other than
England and Wales to the extent that a local lawyer would be permitted to
receive a contingency fee in respect of that proceeding.'

'"Contingency fee" means any sum (whether fixed , or calculated either
as a percentage of the proceeds or otherwise howsoever) payable only in
the event of success in the prosecution or defence of any action, suit or
other contentious proceeding.[1]'

Rule 8 is the main rule concerning CFAs and has featured in case law[2]. The
wording has been amended[3] from time to time to reflect changes either in
legislation or case law. The wording given above was agreed following the
decision of the Court of Appeal in *Thai Trading Co v Taylor*[4] and seeks to
permit whatever the common law permits. If the reasoning in *Awwad v
Geraghty*[5] is correct, the Rule is subordinate legislation which fits ill with the
decision of the Council of the Law Society to amend the rule in order to
accommodate the decision of the Court.

1 Rule 18(2)(c).
2 See Chapter 1 above.
3 Rule 8 was amended following the Courts and Legal Services Act 1990 (CLSA 1990). This
   Act introduced CFAs which would have breached Rule 8 as worded in 1990. The current
   wording in the text came into force on 7 January 1999.
4 [1998] 3 All ER 65 and see Chapter 1 above.
5 [2000] 1 All ER 608 and Chapter 1 above.

Claims assessors

Practice Rule 9

2.9

'A solicitor shall not, in respect of any claim or claims arising as a result of
death or personal injury, either enter into an arrangement for the
introduction of clients with or act in association with any person (not being
a solicitor) whose business or any part of whose business is to make,
support or prosecute (whether by action or otherwise, and whether by a
solicitor or agent or otherwise) claims arising as a result of death or
personal injury and who in the course of such business solicits or receives
contingency fees in respect of such claims.'

The referral schemes which do not rely upon a CFA will not offend this Rule
simply because they do not solicit or receive a 'contingency fee'[1]. Schemes
which introduce clients on the basis that a solicitor will enter into a CFA do
not infringe this Rule if the contingency fee is due only to the solicitor to

whom the client is referred. A difficult point arises however where a scheme is paid if the case wins but refunds the payment if the case loses. In such circumstances it can be argued that the referring party does do business on a contingency fee basis[2].

1   See Rule 18(2)(c) and para **2.8** above.
2   It must always be borne in mind that if *Geraghty v Awwad* (see note 5 at para **2.8** above) is correct, any arrangement in breach of Rule 9 will be unenforceable as being contrary to public policy because it is in breach of subordinate legislation.

Receipt of commissions from third parties

Practice Rule 10

2.10

'(1) Solicitors shall account to their clients for any commission received of more than £20 unless, having disclosed to the client in writing the amount or basis of calculation of the commission or (if the precise amount or basis cannot be ascertained) an approximation thereof, they have the client's agreement to retain it'.

Where a solicitor introduces a client to an insurer to arrange for 'after the event insurance', and the solicitor receives a commission, this must be disclosed to the client and there must be an account to the client unless there is consent to retain this sum. Unsurprisingly, *commission* is not defined in the Rules[1]. Thus if the solicitor is paid a fee for assessing the case, it may be argued that this payment is not a commission and therefore it can be retained without disclosure to the client.

1   The Law Society has issue Guidance on this subject—see *The Guide*, pp 308–332 and 277–278.

Costs information and client care

Practice Rule 15

2.11

'Solicitors shall:

(a)   give information about costs and other matters, and
(b)   operate a complaints handling procedure,

in accordance with a Solicitors' Costs Information and Client Care Code made from time to time by the Council of the Law Society with the concurrence of the Master of the Rolls … .'

The Client Care Code[1]

2.12   The essential aim of the Code is to ensure that clients are provided with the information they need to understand the legal costs not only at the outset of a case but also as it progresses. The giving of accurate costs estimates is notoriously difficult[2]. The Code provides that information must be given clearly and in a manner which is appropriate to the client[3]. There is a specific reference in the Code to CFA cases dealing with the client's ability to pay and the need to address alternative forms of funding the litigation[4].

1   See *The Guide*, pp 265–275. The Code came into force on 3 September 1999. See also Chapter 6.
2   See Goriely *Working Group on the Comparative Study of Legal Professions: Peyresq* (July 2000), Institute of Advanced Legal Studies. The research based on legal aid records showed that there were considerable problems in predicting costs in non-personal injury cases. See also *Testing the Code: Final Report* (October 1999), Legal Aid Board Research Unit: Pleasance, which found that a good proportion of estimates turned out to be wrong.
3   Research by Yarrow and Abrams found that explanations of costs and CFAs were very often not understood by clients—*Nothing to Lose? Client's Experiences of Using Conditional Fees* (1999), University of Westminster.
4   Paragraph 4(j)(iii) of the Code refers to legal aid, insurance both before and after the event and to trade union or employer provision.

Obtaining instructions

2.13   Principle 11.01[1] deals with a solicitor's independence and the client's freedom of choice and states—

'It is fundamental to the relationship which exists between solicitor and client that a solicitor should be able to give impartial and frank advice to the client, free from any external or adverse pressures or interests which would destroy or weaken the solicitor's professional independence, the fiduciary relationship with the client or the client's freedom of choice.'

It is at least arguable that, notwithstanding Practice Rule 3[2] (referrals), where a client is referred to a solicitor by a third party with whom the solicitor has some commercial arrangement, care needs to be exercised in advising the client as to the possible means of funding the litigation in order to adhere to the principle of independence. Where the client has already entered into a funding agreement with the third party before the referral occurs the giving of advice as to funding provides some difficulty given the contractual arrangement which the client has already made. In such cases the relevance of advice as to funding may be different than in cases where the client has no prior contractual arrangement but the solicitor has an arrangement with the third party. Where there is an existing contractual relationship between the client and the third party advice must take account of any liability which the client would incur under that contract and care must be taken as to inducement to breach of contract.

1   See *The Guide*, p 222.
2   See above para **2.6**.

2.14   Principle 12.09 deals further with these duties under the heading of 'not taking advantage of client'—

'A solicitor must not abuse the solicitor/client fiduciary relationship by taking advantage of the client'.

Professional fees

2.15   Chapter 14 of *The Guide* gives additional guidance on conditional fee agreements[1]. No CFA can be entered into if the client has LSC funding. If legal aid is granted during the existence of a CFA the agreement cannot apply to costs incurred whilst the client is in receipt of legal aid. Annex 14F advises that when considering whether a CFA is appropriate in a particular case, the solicitor should take care to ensure that his or her own financial interests are not placed above the general interests of the client. Clearly running a CFA case load puts a firm in a position of financial risk, and the financial interests of the firm must be a factor particularly where a refusal to act on a CFA is being considered. The risk to the client in taking out a CFA in many cases will be limited to the insurance premium to the extent that it may not be fully recovered and this may well make the CFA option one likely in many cases to be in the client's interest even if it is also in the financial interests of the firm. The alternative of insuring both own costs and adverse costs and dispensing with a CFA may prove to be a viable alternative, and in the interests of the firm, depending upon the agreements to funding whilst the case is in progress. In the current funding climate it is not realistic to suggest that the financial interests of the firm will not to some extent dictate the options which the firm can offer. The advice can of course include reference to the fact that a different firm might offer a different funding solution.

1   See *The Guide*, p 279 and Annex 14F at pp 303–307 which summarises the main practice rules of importance to CFAs.

Applying a cap

2.16   Annex 14F provides further guidance in respect of the application of a cap on the success fee so as to limit it with regard to its percentage of the damages awarded[1]. The Law Society Model CFA for personal injury no longer contains such a restriction on the success fee[2]. It has been argued[3] that there is a continuing need for a cap notwithstanding that the success fee is recoverable form the opponent. If it is thought in a particular case that it is appropriate to apply a cap there is currently a major obstacle in the form of the indemnity principle. A term of the CFA applying a cap is one which will limit the contractual liability of the client to pay the solicitor. The indemnity principle would prevent recovery of any success fee in excess of that limit. There is also the danger that by using a cap the agreement will be treated as if it were a contingency fee agreement and the ethical problems which that would cause in terms of settlement and the amount of work done would arise. The problem of not having a cap arises where the opponent has been ordered to pay the success fee but fails to do so. In those cases where this is a risk (in most cases it is not a real risk because the defendant will be insured), it may be appropriate for the client's own solicitor to carefully consider not enforcing the client's liability beyond what would have been set as a cap had one been set. This avoids the difficulties of the indemnity principle but has the disadvantage that there can be no agreement with the client (formal or informal) to that effect. Greater difficulty arises, however, with the shortfall on the success fee which can arise because of the differential between own client base costs and between the parties base costs. The opponent will be responsible for the success fee applied to the base costs ordered. To this shortfall in the success fee must be added any part of the success fee relating to waiting for payment. It is possible, therefore, that the client's contribution to the success fee will be a significant percentage of the damages awarded. The cap formerly advised was set at 25%. The recommendation of the cap was not carried forward to the current position where the success fee is recoverable from the opponent.

1 See *The Guide*, p 306 at para 6.
2 The Model is reproduced in Appendix 2. Note that reg 2(1)(d) of the Conditional Fee Agreements Regulations 2000, SI 2000/692 requires that the CFA states whether or not the success fee is limited by reference to damages.
3 *The Ethics of Conditional Fee Agreements* (January 2001), The Society for Advanced Legal Studies at pp 49–53.

Settlement

2.17 Annex 14F provides the following guidance on settlements in cases funded by a CFA—

'Solicitors should always consider their overriding duty to act in the best interests of the client in achieving a suitable settlement *for the client* irrespective of the solicitor's own interest in receiving early payment of costs in accordance with the agreement.[1]'

The danger in a CFA as regards settlement is that there may be a temptation to settle at too low a figure and as early as possible in order that the two main risks to the solicitor are removed, namely the risk of not being paid at all and the risk of having to wait for payment. Under CPR, Part 36 the claimant can make an offer of settlement at any time, thus the claimant's solicitor is in a position to influence the level of settlement at an early stage. Although there is a potential liability for negligent advice on settlement, this is unlikely to be a significant controlling factor.

1 See *The Guide*, Annex 14F, para 18.

THE BAR COUNCIL CODE OF CONDUCT

2.18 The Code of Conduct (the Code) has many provisions of relevance to the funding of litigation and set out here are those of major significance. In addition to the Code, the Bar Council Conditional Fee Agreements Panel has issue a lengthy guide to CFAs[1]. That Guide states—

'… conditional fees … have significant potential pitfalls for the bar, whose risk profile is different to that of solicitors.[2]'

The Guide also stresses the need for any member of the Bar considering entering into a CFA to be fully conversant with the relevant statutory materials. To that may be added that familiarity with the content of the Guide itself is indispensable.

1 *Conditional Fee Guidance* (February 2001), General Council of the Bar.
2 See *Conditional Fee Guidance*, General Introduction, above.

Independence

2.19 Paragraph 303 of the Code of Conduct provides that a barrister—

'(a) must promote and protect fearlessly and by all proper and lawful means the lay client's best interests and do so without regard to his own interests or to any consequences to himself or to any other person (including any professional client or other intermediary or another barrister);

(b) owes his primary duty as between the lay client and any professional client or other intermediary to the lay client and must not permit the intermediary to limit his discretion as to how the interests of the lay client can best be served;'.

This places a clear ethical burden on the barrister not only with regard to the relationship with a professional client under a CFA but also towards the lay client and any conflict of interest arising between the lay client and the professional client. The Report of the Society for Advanced Legal Studies observed that—

'… entry into a CFA puts a barrister in a position vis a vis the lay client in which there is an inherent and unavoidable potential conflict between the barrister's interests and those of the lay client.

However strong the professional ethical Code of Conduct, it is clear that the introduction of this "direct financial interest in the outcome" through CFAs carries the risks of lower standards.[1]'

1   *Report of the Society for Advanced Legal Studies,* at para 4.11. See note 3 para **2.16**.

Charges

2.20   Paragraph 405 of the Code provides—

'Subject to paragraph 307[1] a barrister in independent practice may charge for any work undertaken by him (whether or not it involves an appearance in Court) on any basis or by any method he thinks fit provided that such basis or method:

(a) is permitted by law;
(b) does not involve the payment of a wage or salary.'

This wording was first used by way of amendment to the Code made on 4 July 1998 following the decisions in *Thai Trading Co v Taylor*[2] and *Bevan Ashford v Yeandle*[3] which at the time extended the common law permitting CFAs outside of the statutory regime. The guidance[4] issued at the time of that amendment drew attention to the lack of clarity in the case law and emphasised that the wording of the amendment did not permit 'contingency fee' arrangements whereby counsel would take a percentage of the monies recovered by the client if the case won.

1   Paragraph 307 deals with independence, commissions and the handling of money.
2   [1998] 3 All ER 65. See Chapter 1 above.
3   [1998] 3 All ER 238. See Chapter 1 above.
4   Contained in a letter from the Head of the Professional Standards and Legal Services Department of the Bar Council, 6 July 1998.

The cab rank rule

2.21   Paragraphs 601 and 602 of the Bar Council Code of Conduct set out the cab rank rule—

'601. A barrister who supplies advocacy services must not withhold those services:

(a) on the ground that the nature of the case is objectionable to him or to any section of the public;

(b) on the ground that the conduct opinions or beliefs of the prospective client are unacceptable to him or to any section of the public;

(c) on any ground relating to the source of any financial support which may properly be given to the prospective client for the proceedings in question (for example, on the ground that such support will be available as part of the Community Legal Service or Criminal Defence Service).

602. A barrister in independent practice must comply with the "Cab-rank rule" and accordingly except only as otherwise provided in paragraphs 603 604 605 and 606 he must in any field in which he professes to practise in relation to work appropriate to his experience and seniority and irrespective of whether his client is paying privately or is publicly funded:

(a) accept any brief to appear before a Court in which he professes to practise;

(b) accept any instructions;

(c) act for any person on whose behalf he is instructed;

and do so irrespective of (i) the party on whose behalf he is instructed (ii) the nature of the case and (iii) any belief or opinion which he may have formed as to the character reputation cause conduct guilt or innocence of that person.'

The exceptions to the cab rank rule are set out in paragraphs 603 to 606, and in particular reference should be made to the following—

'603. A barrister must not accept any instructions if to do so would cause him to be professionally embarrassed and for this purpose a barrister will be professionally embarrassed:

(g) if he is a barrister in independent practice in a privately funded matter where the instructions are delivered by a solicitor or firm of solicitors in respect of whom a Withdrawal of Credit Direction has been issued by the Chairman of the Bar pursuant to the Terms of Work on which Barristers Offer their Services to Solicitors and the Withdrawal of Credit Scheme 1988 (reproduced in Annex G) unless the instructions are accompanied by payment of an agreed fee or the barrister agrees in advance to accept no fee for such work or has obtained the consent of the Chairman of the Bar.

604. Subject to paragraph 601 a barrister in independent practice is not obliged to accept instructions:

(c) to do any work under a conditional fee agreement;

(d) save in a matter funded by the Legal Services Commission as part of the Community Legal Service or the Criminal Defence Service:

   (i) unless and until his fees are agreed;

   (ii) if having required his fees to be paid before he accepts the instructions those fees are not paid;

(e) in a BarDIRECT matter or in a matter where the lay client is also the professional client.'

Clearly, accepting instructions on a CFA basis means that fees will not be paid before the acceptance of instructions. If a Notified[1] solicitor seeks to instruct on a CFA basis the barrister must obtain the consent of the Chairman of the Bar.

1 Annex G of the Bar Council Code of Conduct provides—
   '8. Save in the case of legal aid work or in the case of a Notified Solicitor a barrister and solicitor may (subject to any rules regarding contingent fees) make such agreement or arrangement between them as to the time or times whether at the time of delivery of the brief or instructions or subsequently thereto or otherwise at which the barrister's fees shall be paid as they may think fit and the barrister's fees shall be paid by the solicitor accordingly PROVIDED that every such agreement or arrangement shall be recorded in writing.
   9. Save in the case of legal aid work or in the case of work the fees for which are to be paid out of a fund but cannot be so paid without an order of the court a barrister may and in the case of fees payable by a Notified Solicitor a barrister (unless and except as otherwise previously authorised in writing by the Chairman) must require his fees to be agreed and paid before he accepts the brief or instructions to which the fees relate.'
   A 'Notified solicitor' means any person or firm whose name is for the time being included in the list referred to in paragraphs 17 and 18 hereof and any person who or firm which is or has at any time since the direction was issued been a connected person. See Annex G to the Bar Council Code of Conduct, para 21(vi).

THE CCBE CODE OF CONDUCT FOR LAWYERS IN THE EUROPEAN COMMUNITY

2.22   The Code was adopted by the Law Society on 28 October 1998. In relation to CFAs there are rules headed 'relations with clients' which are of direct importance—

'3.3 Pactum de Quota Litis
   3.3.1 A lawyer shall not be entitled to make a pactum de quota litis.
   3.3.2 By "pactum de quota litis" is meant an agreement between a lawyer and his client entered into prior to the final conclusion of a matter to which the client is a party, by virtue of which the client undertakes to pay the lawyer a share of the result regardless of whether this is represented by a sum of money or by any other benefit achieved by the client upon the conclusion of the matter.
   3.3.3 The pactum de quota litis does not include an agreement that fees be charged in proportion to the value of a matter handled by the lawyer if this is in accordance with an officially approved fee scale or under the control of the competent authority having jurisdiction over the lawyer.'

2.23   The Guide to the Professional Conduct of Solicitors provides the following commentary to the above rules—

'These provisions reflect the common position in all member states that an unregulated agreement for contingency fees (pactum de quota litis) is contrary to the proper administration of justice because it encourages speculative litigation and is liable to be abused. The provisions are not, however, intended to prevent the maintenance or introduction of arrangements under which lawyers are paid according to results or only if the action or matter is successful, provided that these arrangements are under sufficient regulation and control for the protection of the client and the proper administration of justice.[1]'

1 See *The Guide*, p 214.

Chapter 3

The Modern Statutory Regime

THE COURTS AND LEGAL SERVICES ACT 1990

3.1 The legislative changes to the law of maintenance and champerty brought about by the Criminal Law Act 1967[1] were limited to removing criminal and tortious liability for agreements offending these doctrines[2]. The consequences of maintenance and champerty in the law of contract remained in place[3]. The Law Commission had expressed the view that more time was needed before any proposals could be made to authorise the use of contingency fee agreements[4]. Further consideration was given to the question of lawyers using champertous agreements by the Royal Commission on Legal Services which reported in 1979[5]. The conclusion reached then was that to give a lawyer a financial interest in the outcome of a case would endanger the independence of the legal profession. It was not until 1988 that any change in attitude was to occur and it did so in that year when both the Marre Committee[6] and the Civil Justice Review[7] recommended that further consideration be given to the use of contingency fees.

1 See Chapter 1 above.
2 Criminal Law Act 1967, ss 13 and 14(1).
3 Ibid, s 14(2).
4 Law Com no 7 (1966).
5 The Benson Report (Cmnd 7648).
6 *A Time for Change—Report of the Committee on the Future of the Legal Profession* presented to the General Council of the Bar and the Council of the Law Society, July 1988.
7 Report of the Review Body on Civil Justice 1988 (Cm 394).

3.2 The major step towards the system of conditional fees which exists in 2001 was taken, in response to the Civil Justice Review, in the publication of a Green Paper in 1989 and in particular a consultation paper issued by the Lord Chancellor's Department[1]. The phrase 'contingency fee' was used there to mean an arrangement whereby the lawyer received no payment if the case lost, but some percentage or share of the award made if it won. This was therefore a consideration of agreements of a different type to the 'speculative' basis of funding which had long been permitted in Scotland[2]. The consultation paper summarised the reasons why contingency fees had been resisted in England and Wales—

'(a) they may result in a conflict of interest between lawyer and client. The lawyer will have a direct financial interest in the outcome of the case and will be unable to give the client impartial advice. This may lead to;

(i)   the lawyer being tempted to encourage the client to settle early to avoid the effort involved in fighting the case;

(ii) the lawyer concentrating on cases with a high nuisance value where the defendant is more likely to be forced into making an offer to settle; and

(iii) the lawyer being tempted to try to enhance his client's chances of success, perhaps by coaching witnesses or withholding inconvenient evidence; and

(b)   experience in the USA suggests that contingency fees:

(i)   encourage juries to award excessively high damages; and

(ii) encourage litigants to proceed with cases with very little merit, leading to an explosion of litigation.'

The paper then set out the arguments in favour of the introduction of contingency fees—

'(a) they would give individuals and organisations who do not qualify for legal aid, but who cannot support expensive litigation, the opportunity of bringing their claims to court;

(b)   they would encourage a greater level of commitment on the part of the lawyer;

(c)   they would encourage competition between lawyers, as clients would be able to shop around between solicitors to seek the most advantageous agreement.'

1 Contingency Fees (Cm 571).
2 In Scotland a speculative action is taken on the basis that the lawyer will receive a normal fee if the case wins and no fee if it loses. There is no share in damages and there is no enhancement of fees to reflect the financial risks being taken by the lawyer. The Royal Commission on Legal Services in Scotland 1980 (Cmnd 7846) concluded that contingency fees should not be introduced into Scotland.

3.3   The Civil Justice Review's main recommendation was the consideration of using regulation of the provision of legal services through contingency fees rather than the continuation of a simple ban. Accordingly the consultation paper[1] sought responses to the issues arising if such a regulatory approach were to be taken. Thus it was argued that to assume that the financial interest introduced by a contingency fee would override the standards of conduct of the profession was to assume an unreasonably low standard of conduct[2]. There was, however, a need to restrict the use of contingency fees and the terms of such agreements. A number of possible means of operating a contingency fee system were explored[3]. The normal fee in the event of a win with no fee for losing and the variation of permitting a limited uplift in the event of a win were thus first proposed in this paper. The distinction was also drawn between limiting the uplift by reference to damages and limiting it by it being an uplift on normal fees, the latter being seen as meaning that the lawyer did not have a direct interest in the level of damages. The paper also raised the prospect of the client being able to challenge the reasonableness of a contingency fee, although this was dealt with in the context of agreements for a share of the damages[4]. Much in the consultation paper of 1988 can be seen in the eventual statutory regime introduced in 1990[5] and still the basis for the use of conditional fee agreements after the Access to Justice Act 1999 (AJA 1999)[6].

1 Contingency Fees (Cm 571).
2 Ibid at para 3.3.
3 At paras 4.1–4.9.
4 At para 4.8.
5 Courts and Legal Services Act 1990 (CLSA 1990).
6 AJA 1999, s 27 inserts a new s 58 into the 1990 Act and inserts new ss 58A and 58B.

3.4 An option conspicuously omitted from the Green Paper but which had been canvassed since 1966 is the Contingency Legal Aid Fund (CLAF). This was first proposed by Justice and formed part of its evidence to the Royal Commission in 1977[1]. Both the Bar Council and the Law Society produced versions and variations of a CLAF and the Consumers' Association recommended it as late as 1997[2]. The essence of CLAF is that it is run on a national basis, provides funding at normal fee rates for claimants outside of the legal aid scheme, possibly covers opponent's costs (or requires insurance for that risk) and takes a proportion of damages into the fund to cover the costs of the unsuccessful cases. The Middleton Report[3] recommended that the establishment of a CLAF be explored, particularly for very expensive cases. Nonetheless, the idea of a CLAF has been rejected throughout the development process both on grounds of the cost for setting up such a fund (albeit likely to be recouped over a period of years) and on grounds of it being difficult to operate along side other means of funding.

1 See note 5 at para **3.1** above. Justice produced a report in 1978, *CLAF—Proposals for a Contingency Legal Aid Fund*. It also made the case again in response to the 1989 Green Paper.
2 Policy Paper November 1997.
3 Sir Peter Middleton, *Review of Civil Justice and Legal Aid:Report to the Lord Chancellor*, (September 1997).

3.5 The Government White Paper in July 1989[1] used the phrase 'contingent and conditional fees' following on from the responses to the consultation paper. The responses rejected the introduction of a true contingency fee system where the lawyer takes a share of damages. There was 'little objection' to the Scottish model of normal fee in a win and no fee in a lost case[2]. The White Paper formed the basis of the 1990 legislation—

'14.3. "The Government accordingly proposes to remove the existing prohibitions to enable clients to agree with any or all of their lawyers payment of a conditional fee on the speculative basis already permitted in Scotland." 14.4. "The Government also accepts that it would be reasonable for a lawyer who represents a client on this basis to balance the risk of losing that case and ending up with no costs by charging a higher rate than would have been appropriate but for the conditional factor. It therefore proposes that power be given to the Lord Chancellor to prescribe by subordinate legislation, after consultation with the profession, the maximum amount by which a lawyer's cost can be increased when he is working for a conditional fee. That increase will be expressed as a moderate percentage of normal costs. The legislation will recognise that different levels of increase may be appropriate for different classes of case. The lawyer and his client will be free to agree any lower percentage. The ability to agree this increased fee will not affect the amount to be paid by the losing opponent. There will be no change in the existing rule that costs should follow the event. The Lord Chancellor intends to consult further on the level of the prescribed percentage".[3]'

The CLSA 1990 received the Royal Assent on 1 November 1990. Section 58 of the Act provided[4]—

'(1) In this section "a conditional fee agreement" means an agreement in writing between a person providing advocacy or litigation services and his client which—

(a)   does not relate to proceedings of a kind mentioned in subsection (10);
(b)   provides for that persons fees and expenses, or any part of them, to be payable only in specified circumstances;
(c)   complies with such requirements (if any) as may be prescribed by the Lord Chancellor; and
(d)   is not a contentious business agreement (as defined by section 59 of the Solicitors Act 1974).

(2) Where a conditional fee agreement provides for the amount of any fees to which it applies to be increased, in specified circumstances, above the amount which would be payable if it were not a conditional fee agreement, it shall specify the percentage by which that amount is to be increased.

(3) Subject to subsection (6), a conditional fee agreement which relates to specified proceedings shall not be unenforceable by reason only of its being a conditional fee agreement.

(4) In this section "specified proceedings" means proceedings of a description specified by order made by the Lord Chancellor for the purposes of subsection (3).

(5) Any such order shall prescribe the maximum permitted percentage for each description of specified proceedings.

(6) An agreement which falls within subsection (2) shall be unenforceable if, at the time when it is entered into, the percentage specified in the agreement exceeds the prescribed maximum permitted percentage for the description of proceedings to which it relates.[5]'

1   *Legal Services: A Framework for the Future* (Cm 740).
2   Ibid at para 14.2. The Society of Conservative Lawyers in its response to the consultation paper emphasised that only 1% of the case load of the Faculty of Advocates in Scotland were run on a speculative basis. The membership of the Society narrowly rejected the introduction of even this form of contingency fee arrangement. However, if such a scheme were to be introduced, the Society favoured the provision of an uplift on normal fees for winning cases, to be controlled by a code of conduct.
3   See note 1, paras 14.3 and 14.4.
4   Section 58 as originally worded is given here. This wording was wholly replaced by AJA 1999, s 27. The substituted wording for s 58 is given below at Chapter 4. See also Appendix 1.
5   Subsections 7–10 are omitted here. For the full text of s 58 see Appendix 1.

3.6   CLSA 1990, s 58[1] was commenced in July 1993[2] but was not available until the relevant order was made describing the 'specified proceedings' which could be the subject of a CFA and the maximum percentage uplift which could be applied. The relevant order was passed in 1995[3] restricting the specified proceedings to personal injury, certain insolvency proceedings[4] and proceedings before the European Court of Human Rights. The maximum uplift permitted for all specified proceedings is stated as 100%[5].

1   See Appendix 1.
2   Courts and Legal Services Act 1990 (Commencement No 9) Order 1993, SI 1993/2132.
3   The Conditional Fee Agreements Order 1995, SI 1995/1674.
4   Proceedings in England and Wales by a company which is being wound up in England, Wales or Scotland. Proceedings by a company in respect of which an administration order

made under Pt II of the Insolvency Act 1986 is in force. Proceedings in England and Wales by a person acting in the capacity of liquidator or trustee in bankruptcy. Proceedings by a person acting in the capacity of an administrator appointed pursuant to the provisions of Pt II of the Insolvency Act 1986.

5   The moderate uplift referred to in the Government White Paper in 1989, above at para **3.5** had become controversial—

'We were told initially that only 5 per cent could be added to the cost of the solicitor. Later on it was increased to 10 per cent; then to 20 per cent; and then, with great hostility from the Lord Chancellor's own advisory committee, it went up to 100 per cent.' (Lord Ackner, House of Lords, Hansard (HL), 9 March 1998 col 85).

Lord Irvine of Lairg had, as Shadow Lord Chancellor, said in 1995—

'a 10 per cent, or at most a 20 per cent uplift was sufficient incentive. He should have adhered to that.'Hansard (HL), 12 June 1995, col 1153).

THE MIDDLETON REPORT

3.7   In 1997 there was a change of Government. In September of that year, Sir Peter Middleton delivered his report[1]. Lord Irvine of Lairg, The Lord Chancellor, in his keynote address to the Solicitor's annual conference in October 1997, announced that the availability of CFAs was to be greatly extended and to have an effect on the availability of legal aid[2]—

'My Department will be consulting over the next few months on the maximum possible extension of conditional fee agreements to all civil proceedings, other than family cases, from April 1998. Conditional fee agreements mean that the risk of bringing a case is shared between the litigant[3] and his lawyer. They therefore provide an incentive for lawyers to take more care in their advice, their assessment of prospects, and the steps they decide to take in litigation.

Some of you will, I expect, be less enthusiastic about my next proposition. The extension of conditional fee agreements to a wide range of cases must prompt the question: "should legal aid also be offered in cases where other arrangements already exist to support litigants?" I think not. Subject to consultations, I expect to exclude most claims for money or damages from legal aid. Legal aid will continue to be available for all civil cases not claiming damages or other money: for example, care of children; judicial review; and the threat of homelessness, not to mention the whole of criminal legal aid.'

1   Sir Peter Middleton, *Review of Civil Justice and Legal Aid: Report to the Lord Chancellor*, (September 1997). At para 5.46, he states that the value of conditional fee agreements has now been sufficiently well established and that their scope should therefore be widened to embrace all civil proceedings. The Report also expresses the view that contingency fees should be looked at again and that there is no essential difference between contingency and conditional fees.

2   When the Courts and Legal Services Bill (leading to the Act of 1990) was being debated, this link to the availability of legal aid was expressly prevented. Subsection (4A) was inserted into s 15 of the Legal Aid Act 1988 providing—

'A person may not be refused representation for the purposes of any proceedings on the ground (however expressed) that it would be more appropriate for him and a legal representative of his to enter into a conditional fee agreement (as defined by section 58 of the Courts and Legal Services Act 1990).'

See CLSA 1990, s 125 and Sch 17. Section 15 in its entirety was repealed by AJA 1999, s 106.

3   It can be argued that with the provision of insurance to cover opponent's costs and own disbursements, where the premium is either funded, or only payable in the event that the case wins, that there no longer is a share of risk in this way.

THE ACCESS TO JUSTICE ACT 1999

3.8 The legislative process leading to the passing of the Access to Justice Act 1999 was thus begun[1]. The consultation process was not inconsiderable and it revealed a great deal about the various views held both within the legal profession and the insurance industry.

1   The Bill was introduced as a House of Lords Bill on 2 December 1998. The Bill was introduced in the House of Commons on 17 March 1999. Royal Assent was granted on 26 July 1999.

3.9 The consultation process began in March 1998[1] dealing with the extension of CFAs and the removal of legal aid. The basis of the extension of CFAs to all civil claims (other than family) was that the barrier of legal costs which dissuades many from bringing or continuing claims could be removed by the use of CFAs. Responses were sought on whether there were any types of proceedings for which CFAs were unsuitable. It was this consultation paper which raised for the first time the prospect of recovering, from a losing opponent, the success fee and any insurance premium. It was said that to permit this would allow the claimant to retain all of the damages awarded. A summary of the responses to this paper was published in July 1998[2]. There was a generally favourable response to the proposal to extend the use of CFAs to all civil proceedings. There was less agreement on the recoverability of the success fee and insurance premium. It was argued for example that the stronger the defendant's case the higher the claimant's solicitor's uplift would be, that recoverability would lead to satellite litigation and to increases in insurance costs generally. The recoverability of the insurance premium was supported by just over half of the respondents from the finance industry. The only step taken by the Government at this stage was to extend the use of CFAs to all civil claims other than family proceedings[3]. The Access to Justice Bill was then introduced into Parliament and included provisions for the recoverability of the success fee and the insurance premium. The passage of these provisions through the House of Lords produced a great deal of opposition and many attempts to introduce amendments. Ultimately the provisions were passed in their original form. A concession was made in respect of proceedings under the Environmental Protection Act 1990 (EPA 1990) , s 82 which are technically criminal proceedings. CFAs were to be permitted in these proceedings but without a success fee.

1   *Access to Justice with Conditional Fees—A Consultation Paper*, Lord Chancellor's Department.
2   *Conditional Fees Consultation—Summary of Responses.*
3   The Conditional Fee Agreements Order 1998, SI 1998/1860 came into force on 30 July 1998. 'Specified proceedings' for the purposes of CLSA 1990, s 58(3) (see above para **3.5**) were now defined as 'All proceedings' (para 3(1)). Family proceedings continued to be excluded by s 58(10) of the CLSA 1990.

3.10 The 1999 Act effected the legislative changes by substituting CLSA 1990, s 58, with wholly new wordings and by the insertion of ss 58A and 58B[1]. The recoverability of the insurance premium is effected by s 29 of the 1999 Act[2]. The major changes brought about by the 1999 Act were—the recoverable success fee[3] and insurance premium[4]; the removal of CFAs from the common law[5]; extending CFAs to all proceedings for resolving disputes (and not just court proceedings)[6]; facilitating different forms of CFA with different conditions[7]; litigation funding agreements[8]; the recoverability of costs by membership organisations[9]; and facilitating the abolition of the

indemnity principle[10]. Some of these provisions have been implemented from
1 April 2000[11] (litigation funding agreements and changes to the indemnity
principle have not been commenced).

1 The full text of ss 58, 58A and 58B are given in Appendix 1. Section 58B is not yet in force.
2 See Appendix 1.
3 CLSA 1990, s 58A(6) as inserted by AJA 1999, s 27.
4 AJA 1999, s 29.
5 CLSA 1990, s 58(1) as substituted by AJA 1999, s 27.
6 CLSA 1990, s 58A(4) inserted by AJA 1999, s 27.
7 CLSA 1990, s 58A(3)(b) inserted by AJA 1999, s 27 (for example Collective CFAs).
8 CLSA 1990, s 58B inserted by AJA 1999, s 28.
9 AJA 1999, s 30.
10 AJA 1999, s 31. (Not in force as at 1 April 2001).
11 Access to Justice Act 1999 (Commencement No 3, Transitional Provisions and Savings) Order
2000, SI 2000/774. The Conditional Fee Agreements Order 2000, SI 2000/823 also came into
force on 1 April 2000 and limits the success fee to 100% except for proceedings under EPA
1990, s 82, where there can be no success fee.

THE SUBORDINATE LEGISLATION AND CPR

3.11   The new statutory provisions although brought into force on 1 April
2000 required a new set of Regulations and changes to the CPR. A further
consultation paper was produced in September 1999 by the Lord Chancellor's
Department[1]. The Conditional Fee Agreements Regulations 2000[2] came into
force on 1 April 2000 having been laid before Parliament on 10 March. Many
practitioners took the view that until the Regulations and CPR changes were
available it was not advisable for clients to enter into a CFA. Although the
Regulations were available on 1 April there had been little opportunity to
prepare and in any event the CPR changes were still being drafted. Drafts of
the new rules were made available via the web and Master Hurst invited
constructive comments. The final version of the rules and the Practice
Direction about Costs (CPD) came into force on 3 July 2000. To deal with the
position between 1 April and 3 July 2000 the CPR and CPD contain
transitional provisions[3].

1 *Conditional Fees: Sharing the Risks of Litigation*, Lord Chancellor's Department (September
1999). This sought responses on, amongst other points, the recovery of the success fee and
insurance premium. A Conclusions Paper was published in January 2000.
2 SI 2000/692. See Appendix 1.
3 CPR, rr 57.8 and 57.9 and the Civil Procedure (Amendment No 3) Rules 2000, SI 2000/1317,
r 39. See Part 4, Chapter 11.

3.12   The new regulations made significant changes to the required content
of a CFA[1]. In relation to the recoverability of the success fee the CFA must
now contain a brief statement of the reasons for setting the success fee at the
stated percentage level. Previously, although the solicitor's own client would
be paying the success fee, no such written or indeed any reasons were
required. The new CFA must also state what, if any, percentage of the success
fee relates to the postponement of the payment of fees and expenses. This
element is not recoverable from the opponent on the standard basis that the
opponent does not have a responsibility for the funding needs of the other
party. The regulations introduce for the first time also the disclosure of the
level of success fee to the other side at the conclusion of the case. The CFA
itself must contain a term giving the client's consent to disclosure should the

court require it. This seems to address the legal professional privilege which would otherwise prevent the legal representative from disclosing the terms of an agreement with the client. A further corollary to the recovery of the success fee from the opponent is that the CFA must contain a term providing that any reduction on assessment cannot be recouped from the client unless that is sanctioned by the court. Equally if there is a settlement which agrees a reduction of the success fee, the shortfall cannot be recovered by the solicitor from their own client unless the court allows. Once the regulations were in place the next requirement was for the production of the CPR and Practice Direction dealing with the assessment of costs by a court. The amendments to the CPR and the new CPD were not available until July 2000, coming into force on 3 July 2000[2].

1   The Regulations are fully explained in Chapters 5 and 6. The text of the regulations is contained in Appendix 1.
2   See Chapters 8 and 11.

45

Part 2

Conditional Fee Agreements made after 1 April 2000

Chapter 4

The Statutory Regime

INTRODUCTION

4.1   Major changes in the law relating to Conditional Fee Agreements (CFAs) were made by the Access to Justice Act 1999 (AJA 1999) and came into force on 1 April 2000[1]. These changes do not have retrospective effect[2]. Accordingly it is necessary to deal separately with agreements made after 1 April 2000 and those made before that date. Part 2 deals with the full statutory regime, including the amendments to the CPR and the Practice Direction about Costs (CPD), all of which were available from 3 July 2000. The pre-April 2000 position is dealt with in Part 3. Transitional Provisions were made governing CFAs entered into between 1 April 2000 and 3 July 2000 because only the Act and the Regulations were available at that time. This position is dealt with in Part 4.

1   Access to Justice Act 1999 (Commencement No 3, Transitional Provisions and Savings) Order 2000, SI 2000/774.
2   Access to Justice Act 1999 (Transitional Provisions) Order 2000, SI 2000/900. See Appendix 1.

4.2   There are no advantages to be had in terminating a CFA made in one of these periods and replacing it with a CFA made in a later period[1]. So whenever the CFA was made it will continue to be governed by the regime of rules which applied at the date it was made. If a new CFA is made after 1 April 2000, either in addition to or replacing a CFA made in an earlier period, the new CFA must comply with the requirements of the post 1 April 2000 rules. However, the new CFA does not obtain the advantages of a recoverable success fee.

1   SI 2000/900, see note 2 above.

STATUTORY DEFINITION

4.3   The AJA 1999, s 27 is intended to provide a comprehensive definition of a conditional fee agreement. It is also intended that the enforceability of an agreement which comes within that definition will depend upon compliance with the statute and any regulations made under it. The modern statutory regime, which began in 1990 with the passage of the Courts and Legal Services Act 1990 (CLSA 1990) was brought into force in July 1995[1]. The decisions of the courts following the implementation of the Act led to serious conflict within the developing case law[2]. The opportunity to remove doubt was provided by the 1999 Act which from its implementation means that the validity and enforceability of a conditional fee agreement can no longer be determined by the common law[3].

1 CLSA 1990, s 58 was brought into force on 23 July 1993 (Courts and Legal Services Act 1990 (Commencement No 9) Order 1993, SI 1993/2132) but no Regulations or Order were brought into force until 5 July 1995. See Appendix 1.
2 See Chapter 1 above.
3 CLSA 1990, s 58(1) as substituted by AJA 1999, s 27 (in force 1 April 2000). See para **4.4**.

4.4 The governing statutory provision for CFAs remains the CLSA 1990, s 58 but the AJA 1999, s 27 substitutes a newly worded s 58 into the 1990 Act—

'a conditional fee agreement is an agreement with a person providing advocacy or litigation services which provides for his fees and expenses, or any part of them, to be payable only in specified circumstances.[1]'

It must not be assumed that only agreements providing for a success fee fall within this definition. Any agreement under which different fees or expenses will be due in different circumstances will constitute a CFA. This can be posed as a question: Will the same expenses and fees be payable in all circumstances? If that question cannot be answered 'Yes', then the agreement is a CFA.

Examples—

Ordinary fee if the case wins—no fee if it loses

Ordinary fee if the case wins—half ordinary fee if it loses

Ordinary fee plus success fee if it wins—no fee if it loses

Ordinary fee plus success fee if it wins—half ordinary fee if it loses

In each of the above examples different fees will be payable in the different specified circumstances of winning or losing. Each of these agreements is a CFA within the meaning of s 58(2)(a). The consequence then is that the whole of the statutory regime[2] must be complied with.

1 CLSA 1990, s 58(2)(a) as inserted by AJA 1999, s 27.
2 See para **4.5f** below. See also Chapter 13.

UNENFORCEABILITY

4.5 A major significance of an agreement falling into the statutory definition of a CFA is provided for in CLSA 1990 s 58(1) as inserted by AJA 1999, s 27 which provides—

'A conditional fee agreement which satisfies all of the conditions applicable to it by virtue of this section shall not be unenforceable by reason only of its being a conditional fee agreement; but (subject to subsection (5)) any other conditional fee agreement shall be unenforceable.[1]'

Subsection (5) refers to the Solicitors Act 1974, s 57 dealing with non-contentious business agreements—such an agreement which is also a CFA is not made unenforceable by s 58(1). A contentious business agreement under s 59 of the 1974 Act, which is also a CFA must comply with s 58 of the 1990 Act[2].

1   CLSA 1990, s 58(1) as inserted by AJA 1999, s 27.
2   See Chapter 13 below.

4.6   It must first be noted that it is this provision which has the effect of bringing all agreements which fall within the broad definition of a CFA, as provided in s 58(2)(a), into the statutory regime and of dispensing with any possibility of such an agreement being found to be enforceable at common law. Section 58 as originally drafted did not seek to render unenforceable, agreements which did not comply with the statue.

It is then necessary to consider the 'conditions' which must be satisfied if such an agreement is to enforceable. Some of those conditions are contained in further sub-sections of s 58 itself but others are prescribed by the Lord Chancellor under the authority of s 58(3)(c). All of these conditions are dealt with below.

MEANING OF PROCEEDINGS

4.7   Section 58(2)(a) refers to the provision of advocacy and litigation services, terms defined in CLSA 1990, s 119—

> '"advocacy services" means any services which it would be reasonable to expect a person who is exercising, or contemplating exercising, a right of audience in relation to any proceedings, or contemplated proceedings, to provide;
>
> "litigation services" means any service which it would be reasonable to expect a person who is exercising, or contemplating exercising, a right to conduct litigation in relation to any proceedings or contemplated proceedings, to provide;'[1].

The meaning given to 'proceedings' in s 119 must now be read together with CLSA 1990, s 58A(4) as inserted by AJA 1999, s 27—

> 'In section 58 and this section (and in the definitions of "advocacy services" and "litigation services" as they apply for their purposes) "proceedings" includes any sort of proceedings for resolving disputes (and not just proceedings in court), whether commenced or contemplated.[2]'

The combined effect of these provisions is that any fee agreement which constitutes a CFA made for the provision of such services for such purposes must comply with the statutory regime if it is to be enforceable. It is this collection of statutory words which must be carefully considered in treading the narrow line between contentious and non-contentious business. These definitions also have the effect of bringing the statutory regime into arbitration proceedings. The definition of 'proceedings' in the 1990 Act as drafted is confined to court proceedings and was held in *Bevan Ashford (a firm) v Geoff Yeandle*[3] not to encompass arbitration.

1   CLSA 1990, s 119.
2   Ibid, s 58A(4).
3   [1998] 3 All ER 238 and see Chapter 1 above.

4.8 The reference in the 1999 Act to 'any sort of proceedings' is somewhat opaque when considering mediation. Mediation, although formal and supported by enforcement in the courts, does not readily fit the word proceedings. Where the mediation is taking place before the issue of a letter of claim then the references to advocacy and litigation services suggest that the matter is not governed by s 58 and the statutory regime. Where, however, mediation occurs after issue, whether or not as a result of a court intervention, it is submitted that the references to advocacy and litigation services in s 58 do have the effect that the mediation is included in the statutory regime, at least where the services are being provided by the same legal representative as is providing the services in respect of the court proceedings. A fee agreement for mediation in these circumstances must, if it fits the definition in s 58(2)(a) of a CFA, comply with the statutory regime[1].

The alternative argument is that representing a client during mediation does not involve the exercise of any right to conduct litigation, nor is it the exercise of a right of audience, and that the fact that proceedings have been issued does not alter that position. Accordingly a CFA to provide representation in a mediation after proceedings have been issued is arguably not a CFA within the meaning of s 58(2)(a).

SPECIFIED PROCEEDINGS

4.9 When Parliament approved the concept of conditional fees in passing the 1990 Act, it did so with a reservation to the Lord Chancellor as to the proceedings to which such agreements could relate. These were to be the 'specified proceedings' to be contained in Statutory Instruments. The 1990 Act although in force from July 1993 was only effective for CFA purposes once the relevant SIs were in force on 5 July 1995.The first list of specified proceedings was contained in SI 1995/1674[1]. Included were damages claims for personal injury, certain corporate and private insolvency claims and proceedings under the European Convention of Human Rights. By 1998, and after consultation by the Lord Chancellor, SI 1998/1860[2] simply provided that all proceedings were to be 'specified proceedings'.

1 The Conditional Fee Agreements Order 1995, SI 1995/1674. See Appendix 1.
2 The Conditional Fee Agreements Order 1998, SI 1998/1860. See Appendix 1.

4.10 However, CLSA 1990, s 58 as originally drafted, itself precluded certain proceedings from the CFA regime and subsequent amendments still have the effect of excluding certain types of proceedings. The original list was replaced by the AJA 1999 which replaced CLSA 1990, s 58 with a newly worded s 58 and inserted s 58A.

Section 58A(1) provides that the following proceedings cannot be the subject of an enforceable conditional fee agreement—

(a) Criminal proceedings other than under s 82 Environmental Protection Act 1990
(b) Family proceedings

Family proceedings are defined in s 58A(2) as follows—

(a) Matrimonial Causes Act 1973
(b) Adoption Act 1976

(c)   Domestic Proceedings and Magistrates' Courts Act 1978
(d)   Part III Matrimonial and Family Proceedings Act 1984
(e)   Parts I, II and IV Children Act 1989
(f)   Part IV Family Act 1996
(g)   The inherent jurisdiction of the High Court in relation to children.

The exception within criminal proceedings allowing for Environmental Protection Act 1990 (EPA 1990), s 82[1] cases to be taken under a CFA was the subject of considerable debate, both within and outside Parliament, before it was finally permitted on the basis that no success fee could be charged.

1   See *British Waterways Board v Norman* (1993) 26 HLR 232 and *Hughes v Kingston upon Hull City Council* [1999] 2 All ER 49 at Chapter 1 above.

SUCCESS FEES

4.11   The rationale for permitting a success fee to be charged over and above the basic fees is that the legal representative is taking a risk that no fees will be paid for the work if the case loses. Accordingly, the success fee in cases which win, is intended to enable the cost of the losing cases to be carried by the legal representative. The calculation of the success fee is dealt with fully in Chapter 8. Set out here are the statutory provisions relating to the success fee.
CLSA 1990, s 58(2)(b) provides—

'A conditional fee agreement provides for a success fee if it provides for the amount of any fees to which it applies to be increased, in specified circumstances, above the amount which would be payable if it were not payable only in specified circumstances.[1]'

Not perhaps the clearest of statements as to what is intended. It is taken to mean that a success fee is an increase on the fees which would have been charged had there been no conditional fee agreement. This assumes of course that what would have been charged can be readily ascertained. The CPD[2] refers in various places to 'base costs'. A summary assessment of base costs can separately identify solicitor's charges, counsel's fees and other disbursements and any VAT. It is essentially a matter for the CFA itself to define the charges to which the success fee is to be applied. The Law Society Model CFA[3] for use in Personal Injury cases refers to 'basic charges', meaning the charge for the time worked by the firm on the case, and applies the success fee to those charges. VAT is added to the total once the basic charges are added to the success fee.

1   CLSA 1990, s 58(2)(b).
2   See Appendix 1. The CPD is referred to extensively in the following paragraphs of this section.
3   See Appendix 2 and Chapter 7 below.

4.12   When the success fee was a matter for the client, ie before it became recoverable from the opponent[1], the success fee would be applied to the whole of the basic charges, subject to own client assessment. Thus although the client would not recover the whole of own basic charges, the success fee would apply to the whole of those charges.

1   The success fee became recoverable from the losing opponent by virtue of CLSA 1990, s 58A(6) which came into force on 1 April 2000. See Chapter 8 below.

4.13 Since 1 April 2000 the success fee is to be recovered from the opponent. The basic charges will be subject to the usual reductions as between the parties. The success fee will be applied only to the recovered part of the basic charges. To do otherwise would mean that the opponent would be paying a success fee on costs which they have not been ordered to pay. The statutory regime, Rules and Practice Direction do not directly address this aspect of the success fee. CPD, s 14.7 does however give some support for the view expressed in this paragraph—

> 'Where the court makes a summary assessment of an additional liability at the conclusion of proceedings, that assessment must relate to the whole of the proceedings; this will include any additional liability relating to base costs allowed by the court when making a summary assessment on a previous application or hearing.[1]'

The reference to 'base costs allowed by the court' means that the success fee will only be applied, as against the opponent, to the base costs allowed by the assessment. The success fee as calculated by the solicitor at the time the CFA is made is likely to be based upon the assumption that the percentage will be applied to costs billable to the client. This seems to be the assumption in the Law Society Model. An attempt to take account of this shortfall by increasing the percentage set as the success fee would fail at an assessment since it would clearly be bringing in by the back door that which has been refused at the front. The result, however, is that the value of the success fees after 1 April 2000 will be less than it was before that date, unless the shortfall is to be recovered from the client, an option some litigators will not wish to adopt, effectively being reduced by the same percentage of basic costs not allowed on an assessment. This is typically in the order of 15% to 20%.

1 See Appendix 1.

ILLUSTRATION

4.14

Pre 1 April 2000

Basic charges	£1400
Success fee 50%	£700
Total to firm	£2100

Post April 2000

Basic charges	£1400
Basic ordered against opponent	£1190
Success fee 50%	£595
Total to firm	£1995*

* This also assumes that the client will pay the basic charges not ordered against the opponent. If that shortfall is not to be paid by the client then the total would be £1790. The Law Society Model provides that the client is responsible for basic costs not recovered from the opponent.

Discounted fee agreements present an interesting question with regard to success fees. It is submitted that where the agreement specifies for normal fees for a win and 50% less if the case loses, then the basic costs are nonetheless the normal fee and there is no success fee involved. To regard the normal fee as being the discounted rate would be to misrepresent the real position since clearly that discount would not be the rate charged had there been no conditional fee agreement.

THE STATUTORY CONDITIONS

4.15   CLSA 1900, s 58(3) provides—

'The following conditions are applicable to every conditional fee agreement—

(a)   it must be in writing;
(b)   it must not relate to proceedings which cannot be the subject of an enforceable conditional fee agreement
(c)   it must comply with such requirements (if any) as may be prescribed by the Lord Chancellor.[1]'

The Lord Chancellor has by the Conditional Fee Agreements Regulations 2000[2] laid down further requirements which must be complied with. These are dealt with in Chapter 5.

1   CLSA 1990, s 58(3).
2   SI 2000/692. See Appendix 1.

CONDITIONS APPLYING ONLY TO SUCCESS FEES

4.16   CLSA 1990, s 58(4) provides—

'The following further conditions are applicable to a conditional fee agreement which provides for a success fee—

(a)   it must relate to proceedings of a description specified by order made by the Lord Chancellor;
(b)   it must state the percentage by which the amount of the fees which would be payable if it were not a conditional fee agreement is to be increased; and
(c)   that percentage must not exceed the percentage specified in relation to the description of proceedings to which the agreement relates by order made by the Lord Chancellor.[1]'

1   CLSA 1990, s 58(4).

4.17   The Conditional Fee Agreements Order 2000[1] provides for the purposes of CLSA 1990, s 58(4)(a) and (c)—

'3   All proceedings which, under S58 of the Act, can be the subject of an enforceable conditional fee agreement, except proceedings under section 82 of the Environmental Protection Act 1990, are proceedings specified for the purposes of section 58 (4)(a) of the Act.

4   In relation to all proceedings specified in article 3, the percentage specified for the purposes of section 58(4)(c) of the Act shall be 100%.[2]'

The effect of art 3 together with CLSA 1990, ss 58(3)(b) and 58A(1) is that there can be a success fee in any case other than one brought under EPA 1990, s 82. The effect of art 4 is that the success fee cannot exceed 100%.

1   SI 2000/823.
2   Ibid, arts 3 and 4.

4.18   The Government's Conclusions Paper of February 2000 following its Consultation Paper *Sharing the Risks of Litigation* proposed that the maximum success fee should remain at 100% except in the Commercial Court, Admiralty and the Technology and Construction Court. This proposal was not, however, incorporated into the CFA Regulations 2000[1].

1   The reasoning in the Conclusions paper was that the users of these courts were sophisticated litigants and that there was no need to provide a limit on the success fees. It was also recognised that the attractiveness of England and Wales as a forum for court disputes would be enhanced by the removal of a limit thus encouraging legal representatives to provide CFAs. In the House of Lords it was simply announced that the Lord Chancellor would keep this matter under review and that for the present the fee would be restricted to 100%.

Chapter 5

The Agreement

THE LEGAL REQUIREMENTS

5.1 The validity of a CFA entered into after 1 April 2000[1] is governed by the Courts and Legal Services Act 1990 (CLSA 1990), s 58(1) and (3)(c) which have the combined effect of requiring compliance not only with the statute but also with the Regulations[2] made under it. Failure to comply with the Act or the Regulations will render the CFA unenforceable[3]. The requirements of the Act itself are dealt with in Chapter 4.

1 For agreements entered into between 1 April 2000 and 3 July 2000, see Part 4, Chapter 11.
2 Conditional Fee Agreements Regulations 2000, SI 2000/692. See Appendix 1.
3 CLSA 1990, s 58(1). See Chapter 4 above.

5.2 All CFAs (whether providing for a success fee or not) must comply with the following requirements of the Act and the Regulations—

(i) must be in writing[1];
(ii) must specify[2]:

the proceedings or part of them to which it relates;
the circumstances in which the legal representative's fees and expenses or part of them are payable;
what payment, if any, is due if the circumstances only partly occur;
what payment, if any, is due irrespective of whether those circumstances occur;
what payment, if any, is due when the agreement ends for any reason;
the amount payable in the specified circumstances or the method of calculation; and
whether the amount payable is limited by reference to damages;

(iii) must state[3]:

that before making the agreement the matters required by Regulation 4 to be explained verbally and in writing were so explained; and

(iv) must be signed by the client and the legal representative[4].

1 CLSA 1990, s 58(3)(a).
2 SI 2000/692, reg 2(1).
3 Ibid, reg 2(2).
4 Ibid, reg 5(1).

5.3 A CFA which provides for a success fee must in addition to the above—

(i) briefly specify the reasons for setting the percentage increase[1]; and

(ii) specify the percentage increase (if any) which relates to waiting for payment[2].

1 SI 2000/692, reg 3(1)(a). The percentage increase is limited to 100% in all cases except under Environmental Protection Act 1990 (EPA 1990), s 82 where there can be no success fee—Conditional Fee Agreements Order 2000, SI 2000/823. For methods of risk assessment to support a success fee see Chapters 21 and 22.

2 Ibid, reg 3(1)(b). This part of the success fee is not recoverable from the losing opponent. See CPR, r 44.3B and Chapter 8 below.

5.4 Where the CFA relates to court proceedings there are still further requirements and the CFA must—

(i) provide that where costs are assessed, the legal representative may, if required by the court, disclose to the court or any other person the reasons for setting the percentage increase[1];

(ii) provide that if on assessment the percentage increase is reduced as being unreasonable, the amount disallowed ceases to be payable unless the court permits it to remain payable[2]; and

(iii) provide that where there is no assessment but the legal representative agrees with any person liable to pay the success fee that the percentage will be reduced, the amount due under the CFA will be reduced by that amount and cease to be payable unless the court is satisfied that the full amount should be payable[3].

1 SI 2000/692, reg 3(2)(a). The court's powers to require disclosure only arise at the assessment stage. See Practice Direction about Costs (CPD), s 14.9 (summary assessment) and ss 32.5 and 32.7 (detailed assessment). See also Chapter 8 below.

2 Ibid, reg 3(2)(b).

3 Ibid, reg 3(2)(c).

5.5 All of the above requirements must be incorporated as terms of the CFA. It is likely that although the language is not appropriate for the lay client, a CFA will incorporate the wordings of the regulations themselves in order that there can be no question that the regulations have been complied with. The above summary does not use the words of the Regulations[1].

1 For drafting purposes, therefore, reference should be made to the text of the Regulations which is given at Appendix 1, and to the Law Society Personal Injury Model CFA at Appendix 2.

THE PROCEEDINGS

5.6 The CFA must specify the proceedings or parts of them to which it relates including whether it relates to any appeal, counterclaim or proceedings to enforce a judgment or order[1]. It is common to exclude counterclaims and appeals by the client, but to include an appeal by the opposing party. This term is likely to particularise the nature of the legal claim which is to be the subject of the proceedings. Essentially this term of the agreement can be as broad or narrow as seems suitable. It is entirely possible that in appropriate circumstances the agreement will be limited to a specific stage of proceedings. The matter of enforcement proceedings is important since the recovery of moneys from a losing opponent has obvious implications for the legal representative as well as the client. It is common for enforcement proceedings to be excluded from the CFA.

1   SI 2000/692, reg 2(1)(a).

CIRCUMSTANCES WHEN FEES ARE TO BE PAID

5.7   A CFA by definition is an agreement providing for the payment of certain fees in some circumstances and not in others. Typically (though by no means exclusively) this will mean payment in the event that the case wins and not if it loses. The agreement must state the circumstances in which fees and expenses (or part of them) are to be paid[1]. This is a requirement irrespective of whether there is to be a success fee. Given that there will be a connection between success and the payment terms a cross-reference will usually be made here to the definition of 'success'.

1   SI 2000/692, reg 2(1)(b).

5.8   It will also be necessary to deal with the consequences of Part 36 payments and offers in the event that although the definition of success has been fulfilled there is an adverse costs order made against the client. The position may be seen to be different here, dependent upon whether the legal representative has advised acceptance of a Part 36 payment or offer where the advice has not been taken. In this circumstance it is not uncommon for the CFA to provide that the legal representative will be entitled to payment of all fees and expenses including any success fee. Variations of course can extend as far as excluding the success fee altogether or restricting it in some way such as making an allowance for the amount of the costs ordered to be paid to the other side.

It is essential that the agreement provides that the client shall be responsible for paying the success fee. CLSA 1990, s 58A(6) provides for a costs order to include the payment of a success fee but the indemnity principle[1] would present difficulties were the CFA not to provide that the client is liable to pay the success fee. Where an insurance policy is to be used in conjunction with the CFA a clause of the CFA can address the indemnity principle by providing for the client's liability to pay the insurance premium[2].

1   See above Chapter 1.
2   AJA 1999, s 29 provides for a costs order to include an insurance premium but this provision does not of itself avoid the indemnity principle. See Chapter 17 below.

5.9   SI 2000/692, reg 2(1)(b) refers not only to fees but to the legal representative's expenses. Accordingly, the client's liability to meet disbursements must be included in the terms of the CFA. As with other items, even though ultimately the client's liability may not be enforced[1] (for example if the case loses and is uninsured) it is vital that the primary liability remains with the client. If no such liability exists then an application of the indemnity principle will mean that a losing opponent will not have to pay the disbursements.

1   See Chapter 1 above and *Awwad v Geraghty* [2000] 1 All ER 608 and *Leeds City Council v Carr* (1999) Times, 12 November.

PAYMENT WHERE THERE IS PARTIAL SUCCESS

5.10 SI 2000/692, reg 2(1)(c)(i) requires the CFA to state what payment, if any, is due if the circumstances in which the CFA provides for payment of fees and expenses only 'partly occur'. This appears to be a provision anticipating a CFA where there is more than one element to the definition of success. In such a case it is necessary to provide for the combinations of outcomes. Where the desired outcome of the proceedings is a non-monetary order or settlement, the reference to partial success becomes difficult as does drafting a definition of success. The statutory scheme applicable to all CFAs has been written with the standard personal injury claim in damages as its paradigm example and it becomes in places difficult to apply outside of such a claim.

PAYMENT IRRESPECTIVE OF THE CIRCUMSTANCES

5.11 Regulation 2(1)(c) refers to payments due 'irrespective' of whether the circumstances have occurred (success) in which payment of fees and expenses is due. Thus if there is to be a payment of any kind in *all* circumstances the CFA must state this. It is common for the CFA to provide for payment of disbursements and VAT irrespective of the circumstance of success.

PAYMENT ON THE TERMINATION OF THE AGREEMENT FOR ANY REASON

5.12 The regulations are concerned only with payments and do not address the rights of termination themselves. It may be convenient and clearer if the rights to terminate and the payment consequences of the exercise of those rights are dealt with in the same paragraphs of the CFA. It is likely that there will be given rights of termination on both sides. Whichever side actually terminates the CFA, it is likely that in many instances the proceedings will still continue, either with a different legal representative or with none. To provide upon termination for the payment of basic fees and disbursements up to the date of termination, but to leave the matter of a success fee to depend upon the ultimate result in the case in terms of the definition of success, is a standard approach to this issue.

The circumstances in which there are to be rights to terminate the agreement may include: failure by the client to accept the advice of the legal representative in terms of settlement; the failure to pay disbursements when due; the failure of the client to co-operate with the legal representative in the furtherance of the case.

METHOD OF CALCULATING THE AMOUNT PAYABLE

5.13 The CFA needs to show how basic fees are to be calculated, how any success fee will be calculated and the charges for Value Added Tax. Regulation 2(1)(d) also requires there to be a statement as to whether the amounts payable are limited by reference to damages which may be recovered on behalf of the client. Basic fees will usually be dealt with by providing the scale of charges used by the firm for the various professional levels of persons engaged on the matter. Regulation 3(1)(a) requires brief written reasons to be given for setting the percentage increase. This may be conveniently given as a schedule to the CFA[1]. Regulation 3(1)(b) requires that any part of the success fee relating to the cost to the firm of waiting for payment, shall be separately identified[2].

1 See Part 9 below for methods of risk assessment and proforma which can be used for the purposes of such a schedule.
2 This part of the success fee is not recoverable from a losing opponent and thus will always be the responsibility of the client. CPR, r 44.3B.

5.14   The relationship of fees to the recovered damages must be stated even where there is no such relationship. When CFAs were first introduced in 1995, the Law Society recommended that there should be a 'cap' on the percentage of damages which could be taken in a success fee. The cap was recommended at 25%. The cap was voluntary and the recommendation referred only to personal injury. That recommendation is not now included in the Law Society Model[1], presumably because it is thought that the success fee will only be paid by the opponent and will not be taken out of damages at all. However, the client may be asked to pay that part of the success fee relating to waiting for payment and, more importantly, the difference between the success fee as applied to between the parties costs and the success fee as applied to own costs[2].

1 See Appendix 2.
2 See Chapter 4 above at para **4.13**. The report of The Society for Advanced Legal Studies—*The Ethics of Conditional Fee Arrangements* (January 2001), not only recommends that a cap should be compulsory but that it should apply to all costs sought from the client and be related to the damages recovered and not damages as awarded.

DECLARATION OF THE GIVING OF INFORMATION TO THE CLIENT

5.15   The CFA must state that before it was made the information required to be given to the client under reg 4 has been given. The CFA will be signed by the client and this is a useful mechanism for confirming that the requirements of reg 4[1] have been met. If requests for further explanation were made it is appropriate for that fact to be stated and that the requests were met.

1 See Chapter 6 below for the contents of SI 2000/692, reg 4.

AMENDMENTS TO THE CFA

5.16   Where the CFA is amended so as to cover either further proceedings or further parts of the same proceedings, it is necessary to comply separately with the above requirements as to proceedings, payment, statement of reg 4, reasons for the success fee, and reg 4 itself, as well as the legal requirements for a CFA[1].

1 SI 2000/692, reg 6. The effect seems to be that it is for practical purposes necessary to enter into a new CFA as the means of amending an existing agreement.

DEFINITION OF 'SUCCESS'

5.17   The paradigm example of a CFA which has dominated the drafting of the statutory scheme is of a personal injury claim for damages where no fees or expenses will be paid unless the claim wins. The liability to pay fees, expenses and success fees in this example depends upon winning—ie upon 'success'. Before a costs order could include a success fee there was no difficulty with the definition of success. Now that it is for an opponent to pay the success fee, the definition of success is crucial since the liability to pay the success fee only arises if the definition of success has been fulfilled and an opponent will have a keen interest in challenging that fact. It is likely that general expressions such as 'your claim for damages' will be used in order to avoid disputes as to the definition. Whilst the indemnity principle must still be applied it is not possible to define success to include reference to a costs order being made in favour of the client[1]. Success can therefore be defined in whatever way is thought appropriate. The Law Society Model[1] defines a 'win' by reference to an award of damages (not their recovery) where either an appeal has failed or is out of time.

[1]   The indemnity principle provides a difficulty in defining success as a favourable costs order, simply because that begs the question as to what costs order would then be appropriate. If there were no costs order the definition of success would not be satisfied and hence no success fee would be recoverable from the opponent. The removal of the indemnity principle from CFA and CCFA cases would enable the terms of the fee agreement to state that the success fee will be limited to that ordered against an opponent. It is submitted that until the indemnity principle is to that extent removed, a CFA or CCFA cannot define success in terms of an award of costs.

[2]   See Chapter 7 and Appendix 2, below.

Chapter 6

Giving Information to the Client

RULE 15 LAW SOCIETY RULES OF PROFESSIONAL CONDUCT

6.1 Rule 15 requires the giving of costs information in accordance with the Solicitors' Costs Information and Client Care Code. The current Code came into force on 3 September 1999. Breaches of the Code may if serious or material and persistent amount to a breach of Rule 15 itself. Other material breaches of the Code will not constitute a breach of Rule 15. All material breaches, however, may be evidence of inadequate professional services within the meaning of Solicitors Act 1974, s 37A[1]. It should be noted that the Code applies in all cases and is not restricted to cases where there is or intended to be a CFA.

1 See *The Guide to the Professional Conduct of Solicitors* (1999) 8th edn, Law Society Publications (*The Guide*).

6.2 Paragraph 4 of the Code requires the giving of the best information[1] possible about the likely overall costs, including a breakdown of fees, VAT and disbursements. The same paragraph at (j) requires the following in respect of the client's ability to pay—

'The solicitor should discuss with the client how and when any costs are to be met, and consider—

(i)   whether the client may be eligible and should apply for legal aid (including advice and assistance);

(ii) whether the client's liability for their own costs may be covered by insurance;

(iii) whether the client's liability for another party's costs may be covered by pre-purchased insurance and, if not, whether it would be advisable for the client's liability for another party's costs to be covered by after the event insurance (including in every case where a conditional fee or contingency fee arrangement is proposed); and

(iv) whether the client's liability for costs (including the costs of another party) may be paid by another person e.g. an employer or trade union.[2]'

1 'Best information' includes (para 4(c)) (i) a fixed fee; (ii) a realistic estimate; (iii) a forecast of a range of costs; (iv) an explanation of why (i) to (iii) cannot be given plus the best information possible about the next stage of the matter.
2 *The Guide*, para 4(j).

THE CONDITIONAL FEE AGREEMENT REGULATIONS 2000

Information

6.3
Regulation 4 of the CFA Regulations 2000 provides a list of information to be given, before a CFA, with or without a success fee, is made and specifies the form in which it has to be given. The information must be given to the client by the legal representative[1] defined as 'the person providing the advocacy or litigation services to which the conditional fee agreement relates.[2]'

1   SI 2000/692, reg 4(1).
2   Ibid, reg 1(3). The reference to 'person' is perhaps surprising given that in many cases these services will be provided by a firm. Further difficulty would arise where the information is given by an appointed agent.

6.4   The information to be given is as follows[1]—

1   When will the client have to pay their own costs.
2   When and how the client can seek assessment of those costs.
3   Whether the solicitor thinks the client is already insured against any costs liability likely to arise.
4   How else those costs might be financed in this case.
5   Whether the solicitor thinks a particular method(s) of financing costs is appropriate.
6   The reasons for recommending insurance or a particular insurance as a method.
7   Any interest the solicitor has in recommending insurance.

1   The above numbering is not that used in SI 2000/692, reg 4. For the full text see Appendix 1.

Form in which this information must be given

6.5   All of the information above must be given orally[1] (whether or not also given in writing). The information in 5, 6 and 7 must be given in writing as well as orally.

In addition to the above, the 'effect' of a CFA must be explained both orally and in writing before the CFA is made[2]. The Regulations give no definition of 'effect'. The Law Society Solicitor's Costs Information and Client Care Code 1999 together with Annex 14F[3] provides a means of complying with reg 4(3). A client care letter is a further means of ensuring that the effect of a CFA is explained in writing. The Law Society leaflet 'Conditional Fees Explained' is to be re-drafted. The Law Society has advised that old leaflets should no longer be used[4]. If the client requires any further explanation, advice or other information, further explanation, advice or other information as the client may reasonably require, is to be provided[5].

1   'Orally' is not defined. It would be surprising were this not to include a telephone communication. There is seemingly no recognition of the provision of advice to those with a hearing disability.
2   SI 2000/692, reg 4(3).
3   See *The Guide to the Professional Conduct of Solicitors* (1999) 8th edn, Law Society Publications.
4   *Law Society Gazette* 97/27— 6 July 2000 at p 42.
5   SI 2000/692, reg 4(1)(b).

TABLE OF INFORMATION TO BE GIVEN AND FORM IN WHICH TO BE GIVEN

6.6

Information to be given	*Method*	*Regulation*
When client must pay their own costs	Oral	4(2)(a)
When and how client can seek assessment of costs	Oral	4(2)(b)
Whether solicitor thinks client already insured against costs liability	Oral	4(2)(c)
How else costs might be financed	Oral	4(2)(d)
Whether the solicitor thinks a particular method(s) of funding costs is appropriate	Oral and written	4(2)(e)
The reasons for recommending insurance or a particular contract of insurance	Oral and written	4(2)(e)(i)
Any interest the solicitor has in recommending insurance	Oral and written	4(2)(e)(ii)

COMMENTARY

6.7 Research[1] has shown that clients do not understand how CFAs work. The requirements of both the Client Care Code and the CFA Regulations must proceed on the basis that the giving of this information is in the interests of the client. An oral explanation of all of the matters referred to above will, depending upon the nature of the client, be a time consuming exercise with no guarantee at the end of it that the client has understood anything nor even listened to it. The Law Society checklist[2] for solicitors entering into CFAs provides some guidance to ensure that important information is not omitted but the task of communicating a complex system will, it seems always fall to the legal representative.

1   Yarrow and Abrams *Nothing to Lose?—Client's experiences of using Conditional Fees,* University of Westminster, (1999).
2   See Appendix 2.

6.8 The research highlighted a great deal about how clients approached litigation in personal injury actions. Most of the findings are likely to be applicable to private clients whatever legal action is being contemplated.

Clients generally had no previous knowledge of CFAs nor of what was involved in litigation, nor indeed how they could or should choose a solicitor. Thus in the great majority of cases the explanations required to be given are being communicated to a person with little if any knowledge or experience of the subject matter. The physical and psychological effects of the accident made it difficult in some cases for the client to absorb the information and make any considered decision. This is not likely to be confined to personal injury cases since private clients will often be emotionally involved with the facts and may be under considerable financial pressure as a result of the facts complained of.

As to costs, some had not been aware that under a CFA there may still be costs to pay before the conclusion of the case. In particular the insurance premium and other disbursements were not anticipated. Although the insurance market has, since the research, provided a good many funded products, there will remain cases and clients where for whatever reason these are not used. Understanding of what a success fee was, and how it was calculated, was found to be seriously lacking. With some clients there was no awareness that their own solicitor would not be paid should the case lose. Reasons given for this lack of understanding related not only to the intrinsic complexity of CFAs but to the use of what they saw as being 'legal language' used not only in documents but in the oral explanations given. It seems unlikely that a legal representative will seek to move far away from a careful explanation in words of legal significance given that any misunderstandings arising will be the responsibility of the person giving the explanation.

Clients being represented under a CFA did to some extent feel that they were not concerned with costs and that they need not worry about them. This can have an effect in both directions. A client may seriously underestimate their potential liability for costs having assumed that a CFA meant that there was never any liability. It could also mean that decisions are made without the thought that would be given had the costs implications been understood. A client who already believes that there will be no costs liability may perhaps find explanations which appear to be to the contrary very hard to grasp.

Clearly the provision of information, in whatever format, does not and cannot mean that the client understands. It is likely that legal aid clients did not understand the rules and that privately funding clients could not give an accurate explanation of their costs liabilities. Research which shows that one form of funding arrangement is not understood cannot be taken of course to mean that the arrangements are fundamentally flawed but they can be taken to indicate where the difficulties lie and there may be a basis for changes to the protections given by the law and the professional rules.

Chapter 7

The Law Society Model CFA for Personal Injury Cases

7.1   The Law Society produced in 1995 a model agreement for use only in personal injury cases not including clinical negligence. The Model[1] has been redrafted to comply with the requirements of the CFA Regulations 2000. Users who intend to change the content of the Model will need to ensure that what remains fully complies with the 1990 Act and the CFA Regulations 2000.

1   The full text of the Model current as at 30 April 2001 is reproduced with kind permission of the Law Society in Appendix 2.

THE CLAUSES

The proceedings

7.2   The agreement must state[1] the proceedings or part of proceedings to which it applies. The phrase used to describe the proceedings is 'your claim against […] for damages for personal injury suffered on […]' and is taken to include all interim applications since clearly these will be necessary for bringing the proceedings. Appeals brought by the opponent are included[2]. The Model excludes counterclaims brought against the client and own client appeals against final judgment. Appeals against interim orders made during the proceedings are included. Enforcement of judgment is dealt with in the Law Society Conditions annexed to the CFA. Condition 4 gives the solicitor power to take enforcement proceedings in the name of the client and makes the costs of such proceedings part of the basic charges under the CFA.

1   Conditional Fee Agreements Regulations 2000, SI 2000/692, reg 2(1)(a). See Chapter 5.
2   Ibid, reg 3(1), requires brief written reasons for the success fee. An appeal by the opponent will arise where the client has already been successful—it is difficult to see how a risk assessment can be made at any time before the appeal is launched since the issues involved at appeal and the basis upon which an appeal court can interfere with a judgment could not be known until then. The difficulty arises because the Model has as its definition of 'win' that the claim for damages is 'finally' decided in the favour of the client. 'Finally' is defined in terms of the opponent not being allowed to appeal or being out of time to appeal or having lost an appeal. Were the Model to not include these provisions it could be argued that a definition of win confined to a first instance decision irrespective of the fate of an appeal would be wholly unacceptable.

The fees

7.3   Regulation 2(1)(c)[1] is complied with by detailing the liability of the client to pay fees and disbursements in a number of situations falling short of success as well as in the event of success. Thus it provides that in the event of a win the client pays basic charges, disbursements and the success fee[2]. This part of the Model also states that the success fee is not limited by reference to damages[3]. The ordinary rules on proportionality contained in CPR, r 44.5 apply to the success fee but there is no requirement that the success fee be limited by reference to damages, although if it were so limited that would provide evidence of proportionality[4].

1   Conditional Fee Agreements Regulations 2000, SI 2000/692. See Appendix 1.
2   Thus ensuring compliance with the indemnity principle (see Chapter 1) even though it is expected that the success fee will be paid by the opponent. This clause also enables recovery from the client where there is a shortfall because the basic costs recovered from the opponent are lower than own costs on assessment and the success fee recovered from the opponent has been applied to the reduced basic costs. See also Chapters 5 and 8. This provision also leaves with the client the primary liability to pay an insurance premium even though it is expected that the premium will be recovered from the opponent. See Chapter 17.
3   Earlier editions of the Model had included a provision known as 'the cap' whereby the success fee (which at the time was not recoverable from the opponent) could not exceed 25% of the damages awarded. The cap was a recommended term of the Model. The current Model does not include a cap provision. See further Chapter 5 above at para **5.14**.
4   See Chapter 8.

7.4   CPR Part 36 is dealt with here in terms of a rejection of an offer or payment where with the advice of the legal representative the proceedings continue and the damages awarded are less than the offer. In these circumstances the Model applies the success fee to the basic costs relating to work done up until receipt of the notice of the Part 36 offer or payment. An alternative of course would be to disapply the success fee entirely on the basis that the advice given in respect of settlement has proved to be wrong. The serious position with regard to recovery of the success fee from the opponent in these circumstances might indicate that a full waiver of the success fee would be more reasonable than the provision contained in the Model.

Where the client receives interim damages the Model provides for the payment of disbursements already incurred and a payment of a reasonable sum to meet future disbursements. In the event that provisional damages are awarded it is provided that not only are basic charges and disbursements immediately payable but that the success fee is also. It may be thought, especially with regard to interim damages, that the need of the client for those damages outweighs any reason for the payments to the legal representative. Given that the success fee is expected to be claimed from the opponent[1], that on an assessment it may be reduced[2], and that the shortfall cannot be claimed from the client without the approval of the court[3], it could be argued that this provision, with respect to the success fee, is premature in its effect.

1   CLSA 1990, s 58A(6). See generally Chapter 8.
2   CPR, r 44.16 and CPD, s 20.
3   SI 2000/692, reg 3(2)(b).

7.5   The terms which apply where the agreement is terminated before the end of the case are mainly contained in Condition 7 to the Model. The basic term (not contained in the conditions section) is that where the client terminates the agreement they are to pay basic charges irrespective of the outcome of the case and to pay the success fee if the case wins. Either party to the CFA may wish to terminate the agreement, the main issue then arising is the amount payable and particularly the position of the success fee. Where the client terminates the agreement, Condition 7 contradicts the main term of the agreement. Condition 7 provides the solicitor with a choice of seeking payment of basic charges and disbursements at any time irrespective of the outcome of the case, or to wait for the outcome of the case when a success fee will also be payable in the event that the case ultimately succeeds. This choice is not referred to in the main clause of the Model. In particular the effect of Condition 7 will be that the client will not know what their liability for the success fee will be.

Where it is the solicitor who terminates the agreement the reasons for termination will affect the question of payment. Where termination is for failure to take advice on settlement it may be seen as legitimate to seek a success fee, at least where the case wins little or no more than the advised settlement. If termination is because the client has misled the solicitor, payment of the success fee irrespective of the outcome of the case may be appropriate. It is important that these provisions which lead to the client being liable for paying the success fee in circumstances where it may not be recovered from the opponent are carefully explained.

Regulation 2(1)(d) is complied with by providing for an hourly rate at various scales according to the experience of the person doing the work.

The success fee

7.6   The reasons for setting the level of the success fee are set out in the Model in a separate schedule to the agreement in compliance with reg 3(1)(a). That schedule requires brief reasons of the assessment of the risk of the individual case failing. The schedule sets out the parts of the success fee relating to waiting for payment, arrangements about disbursements and the risk of the individual case[1]. Regulation 3(1)(b) is complied with by setting out in the same schedule the percentage of the success fee which relates to waiting for payment of fees and disbursements. That part of the success fee cannot be recovered from the opponent and remains the responsibility of the client[2]. If the success fee does not incorporate such a calculation the agreement should state that no part of the success fee relates to waiting for payment[3].

1   See Chapter 22 for the calculation of the success fee.
2   CPR, r 44.3B.
3   SI 2000/692, reg 3(1)(b).

7.7   Condition 4 complies with the requirements of reg (2)(a) and (b) relating to the assessment of the success fee. The same Condition provides that the client will not instruct the solicitor to accept an offer of a lower success fee than that contained in the CFA. Condition 4 also states that the client will normally be entitled to recover part or all of the basic charges, disbursements and success fee from the opponent. The possibility of there being a shortfall[1] in the success fee because the basic charges, as between the parties, are assessed as being lower than own party costs, is a difficult matter but it ought to be explained as part of the overall explanation given before the client enters into the CFA.

1   See note 2 above at para **7.3**.

Value Added Tax

7.8   The Model applies VAT to the total basic charges and the success fee.

Giving of information

7.9   The Model conforms to the requirements of reg 2(2) to incorporate a statement that the information to be given to the client under reg 4 has been given.

The insurance policy

7.10   The Model enables compliance with reg 4(2)(e) which requires reasons to be given for recommending insurance or a specific contract of insurance.

An additional wording is provided at the end of the Conditions to comply with the requirements of the Accident Line insurance scheme. Similar wording may be required to comply with the requirements of other insurers.

Chapter 8

Recoverability of the Success Fee

DATE OF THE CFA

8.1 Section 58A(6) of the Courts and Legal Services Act 1990 Act provides for a costs order to include a success fee—

'A costs order made in any proceedings may, subject in the case of court proceedings to rules of court, include provision requiring the payment of any fees payable under a conditional fee agreement which provides for a success fee.'

This section applies only where the first CFA in respect of the proceedings or cause of action was made after 1 April 2000[1]. This was the method adopted to avoid any retrospective effects of the bringing into force of the Access to Justice Act 1999[2]. It is clear that the cancellation of a CFA made before 1 April 2000 and the making of a new agreement will not mean that the new agreement will attract the recoverability provisions. Where an action has involved legal advice before 1 April 2000 it will be important to determine upon what funding basis that advice was given. It should be noted that it is the date of the first CFA which governs the applicability of the recoverability provisions and not the date of the incident giving rise to the cause of action, nor the date on which legal advice was first given. Section 58A(6) recognises that the award of costs is always in the discretion of the court. The CPR and Practice Direction about Costs (CPD) make detailed provision as to the recoverability of the success fee within the general discretion of the court[3].

1 Access to Justice Act 1999 (Transitional Provisions and Saving) Order 2000, art 2(1). See Appendix 1.
2 The Lord Chancellor's Department received a variety of views from its consultation process—see *Conditional Fees: Sharing the Risks of Litigation*, September 1999. The Government's conclusions paper was published in February 2000.
3 CPR, Pt 44 and the CPD are dealt with in the following paragraphs of this chapter. Relevant extracts are given in Appendix 1.

MEANING OF SUCCESS FEE

8.2 Section 58(2)(b) CLSA 1990 defines a success fee as an increase, in specified circumstances, above the amount which would be payable if it were not payable only in specified circumstances. This is taken to mean that a success fee is an increase in fees in the specified circumstances (success) over the fees which would have been charged had there not been a CFA at all. This assumes that there is a recognisable 'normal' charging rate for the work done. The use of differential or discounted fees, whilst being a CFA, does not involve a fee increase over the fee which would have been charged had the same fee be charged in all circumstances. To regard the fee which would have been charged had no CFA been made as the discounted rate, with an uplift to the normal charging rate in the event of a win, and hence as including a success fee, would not give true effect to the agreement nor, it is submitted, to the words of the Act. The Practice Direction about Costs uses the term 'base costs', a term not used in CPR, Pt 44 dealing with costs[1]. The CPR uses the phrase 'percentage increase'[2] to refer to the 'percentage by which the amount of a legal representative's fee can be increased in accordance with a conditional fee agreement which provides for a success fee'[3]. It is clear that the success fee is applied to the 'fee' not to the 'base costs'.

1   CPD, s 2.2 defines 'base costs' as costs other than the amount of any additional liability. 'Additional liability' is defined in CPR, r 43.2(1) as the percentage increase, the insurance premium, or the additional amount in respect of provision made by a membership organisation.
2   See for example CPR, r 44.3B(1).
3   CPR, r 43.2(1).

RECOVERY WHERE THE CFA WAS MADE AFTER 1 APRIL 2000 AND BEFORE 3 JULY 2000

8.3   The success fee is only recoverable in respect of things done and costs incurred from the date the CFA was made[1]. This appears to mean that although the CFA may cover work done before it was made, a not unusual position, the opponent is not at risk of paying a success fee in respect of that period. If it is intended by the CFA that the client should remain liable for that part of the success fee this should be carefully explained. Apportioning the work on a date basis ought to provide no difficulty and it should be clear from that as to what base fees the success fee to be paid by the opponent shall apply.

1   CPD, s 57.9(3). This provision itself recognises that by the law of contract a solicitor could agree that a CFA should cover all the work done before it was made.

RECOVERY WHERE THE CFA IS MADE AFTER 2 JULY 2000

8.4   There is no provision limiting the period of work to be covered by the recoverable success fee. An opponent is at risk of having to pay a success fee in respect of work done before a CFA is made since the CFA, when made will usually relate to all work done in respect of the cause of action. On ordinary principles of contract such an agreement with the client would be valid. If this is correct, then the steps taken to prevent any retrospective effect of the changes to the 1990 Act have not prevented some retrospective effect. A CFA made after 2 July, where there was no CFA before that date, and which covers work done even before 1 April 2000 would appear to fall within the post 2 July regime. The success fee would then be recoverable from the opponent on fees for work done before the change to the law putting the burden of success fees onto the opponent. Such an arrangement would fail, however, if the fee arrangement in place before the CFA was made would breach the indemnity principle.

STATUTORY LIMIT TO THE SUCCESS FEE

8.5   The success fee cannot exceed 100% of the basic fee[1]. Proposals[2] to remove this limit from the Commercial Court, Construction and Technology Court and Admiralty matters have not been implemented.

1   Conditional Fees Agreement Order 2000, SI 2000/823. In cases brought under EPA 1990, s 82 this order prohibits any success fee. For full text of the Order see Appendix 1.
2   See the Lord Chancellor's Department Consultation Paper *Conditional Fees: Sharing the Risks of Litigation* (September 1999). See Chapter 3 above.

THE RECOVERABLE ELEMENT

8.6   Rule 44.3B(1)[1] precludes recovery of any part of a success fee which relates to waiting for payment of fees and expenses. This element remains payable by the client. The same rule prohibits recovery of any additional liability for a period during which there was a failure to provide information about a funding arrangement in accordance with a rule, practice direction or court order. Any percentage increase where a party has failed to comply with a requirement in the costs practice direction or a court order, to disclose in any assessment proceedings the reasons for setting the percentage increase, will not be recovered from the opponent[2].

1   See the Civil Procedure (Amendment No 3) Rules 2000, SI 2000/1317.
2   Rule 44.3B(2) provides that r 43B(1) does not apply 'in an assessment under r 48.9 (assessment of a solicitor's bill to his client)'.

DISCLOSURE OF INFORMATION TO OPPONENTS AND THE COURT

8.7   The requirements for disclosure are contained in r 44.15 and s 19 of the Practice Direction About Costs[1]. There are no requirements relating to pre-issue disclosure but such is recommended in the CPD[2] and the Personal Injury Protocol. The CPD uses the phrase 'funding arrangement' which refers both to a CFA with success fee and to an insurance policy[3]. Where more than one such arrangement has been made in respect of a case a single notice can provide the information relating to each arrangement[4].

1   In force 3 July 2000. For CFAs entered into between 1 April and 3 July 2000, see Part 4, Chapter 11.
2   CPD, s 19.2(5).
3   CPR, r 43.2—
    ' "funding arrangement" means an arrangement where a person has—entered into a conditional fee agreement which provides for a success fee within the meaning of s 58(2) of the Courts and Legal Services Act 1990; taken out an insurance policy to which s 29 of the Access to Justice Act 1999 (recovery of insurance premiums by way of costs) applies; or made an agreement with a membership organisation to meet his legal costs.'
4   CPD, s 19.4(5).

73

Claimant funding arrangement in place before issue

8.8   Notice of the funding arrangement must be given to the court when issuing the claim form[1]. Form N251[2] sets out the details required. Sufficient copies of Form N251 must be provided to the court for service on all other parties. If the claimant is serving the claim form in person then Form N251 must be served at the same time.

1   'Claim form' includes petition and application notice. CPD, s 19.2(1).
2   A copy of N251 is contained in Appendix 3.

Defendant funding arrangements in place before filing a document

8.9   Notice to the court must be given when filing the first document[1]. Sufficient copies of the notice should be provided to the court for service on all other parties. If the defendant serves the first document in person then notice of the funding arrangement must be served at the same time.

1   First document includes an acknowledgement of service, a defence, application to set aside default judgment or any other document. CPD, s 19.2(3)(a).

Funding arrangements made after issue

8.10   A party must file and serve notice to the court and to all other parties within seven days of making the funding arrangement[1].

1   CPD, s 19.2(4).

The information which must be disclosed

8.11   The information required to be disclosed is set out in CPD, s 19.4. No information need be given of a CFA which does not provide for a success fee. Where the CFA does provide for a success fee then the notice must state that such a CFA has been entered into, the date of the CFA and identity of the claim or claims to which it relates (including Part 20 claims if any)[1]. This provides very little information to the other side and in particular the level of the success fee does not have to be disclosed in order that the perceived strength of the case is not revealed.

1   CPD, s 19.4(1) and (2).

Estimates of Costs

8.12   A party intending to seek to recover from another party an additional liability is not required to reveal the amount of that additional liability when giving an estimate of costs[1]. This provision is needed to preserve the confidentiality given in the rules concerning disclosure.

1   CPD, s 6.2(2).

ASSESSMENT OF AN ADDITIONAL LIABILITY

Stage at which assessment to be made

8.13   CPR, r 44.3A[1]—

'The court will not assess any additional liability until the conclusion of the proceedings[2], or the part of the proceedings, to which the funding arrangement relates.'

1   Inserted by the Civil Procedure (Amendment No 3) Rules 2000, SI 2000/1317.
2   CPD, s 2.4 provides that proceedings are concluded when the court has finally determined the matters in issue in the claim, whether or not there is an appeal. The making of an award of provisional damages (Pt 41) is also treated as a final determination of the matters in issue. CPD, s 2.5 provides that proceedings are to be treated as concluded, although they are continuing, where the court so orders or the parties in writing so agree.

8.14   Again this rule is needed to protect the confidentiality of the advice to the client as to the strength of the case. This has the result that the assessment powers of the court before the conclusion of the case differ from the powers once the case has finished.

Assessment powers

At the conclusion of the case

8.15   CPR, r 44.3A(2)—

'At the conclusion of the proceedings, or the part of the proceedings, to which the funding arrangement relates the court may

(a)   make a summary assessment of all the costs, including any additional liability[1];
(b)   make an order for detailed assessment of the additional liability but make a summary assessment of the other costs[2]; or
(c)   make an order for detailed assessment of all the costs[3].'

1   The court may assess base costs alone or both base costs and the additional liability—CPD, s 3.1. Where the summary assessment includes an additional liability the assessment must be of the additional liability for the whole of the proceedings—CPD, s 14.7.
2   If such a summary assessment does not identify separately the amounts allowed for solicitor's charges, counsel's fees and other disbursements, a court which later makes an assessment of an additional liability may apportion the base costs previously ordered—CPD, s 9.2(2).
3   Unless base costs have already been assessed, the court will, on a detailed assessment, assess both the base costs and the additional liability—CPD, s 3.4.

8.16   Where, however, there have been separate trials of different issues, there will not normally be an assessment of the additional liability until all issues have been tried[1]. Where the parties do not agree the additional liability, the court may make a summary assessment or order detailed assessment of that liability[2].

1   CPD, s 14.5—
    'Where there has been a trial of one or more issues separately from other issues, the court will not normally order detailed assessment of the additional liability until all issues have been tried unless the parties agree.'

2   CPD, s 14.8—
  'Paragraph 13.13 [no court approval of disproportionate costs where agreed] applies where
  the parties are agreed about the total amount to be paid by way of costs, or are agreed
  about the amount of the base costs that will be paid. Where they disagree about the
  additional liability the court may summarily assess that liability or make an order for a
  detailed assessment.'

Before conclusion of the case

8.17   The court should make a summary assessment of base costs at any
hearing or application unless there is good reason not to do so[1]. The existence
of a funding arrangement is not sufficient reason to not carry out a summary
assessment[2]. The court has power to summarily assess costs other than an
additional liability[3]. Rule 44.3A prevents a court from making a summary
assessment of an additional liability before the conclusion of the proceedings
or part of the proceedings to which the funding arrangement relates[4].

1   CPD, s 13.12(1)—
  'Attention is drawn to rule 44.3A which prevents the court from making a summary
  assessment of an additional liability before the conclusion of the proceedings or the part of
  the proceeding to which the funding arrangement relates. Where this applies, the court
  should nonetheless make a summary assessment of the base costs of the hearing or
  application unless there is a good reason not to do so.'
  CPD, s 13.12(2)—
  'Where the court makes a summary assessment of the base costs all statements of costs and
  costs estimates put before the judge will be retained on the court file.'
  For r 44.3A see para **8.13**.
2   CPD, s 14.1—
  'The existence of a conditional fee agreement or other funding arrangement within the
  meaning of rule 43.2 is not by itself a sufficient reason for not crying out a summary
  assessment.'
3   CPD, s 14.2—
  'where a legal representative acting for the receiving party has entered into a conditional fee
  agreement the court may summarily assess all the costs (other than any additional liability).'
4   See above para **8.13**.

8.18   Where there has been a summary assessment before the conclusion of
the case, no order for payment will be made unless the court is satisfied that
the receiving party is at the time liable to pay the legal representative[1]. The
court has power to order costs to be paid into court and to make orders to
postpone the receiving party's right to payment[2].

1   CPD, s 14.3—
  'Where costs have been summarily assessed an order for payment will not be made unless
  the court has been satisfied that in respect of the costs claimed, the receiving party is at the
  time liable to pay his legal representative an amount equal to or greater than the costs claimed.
  A statement in the form of the certificate appended at the end of Form N260 may be sufficient
  proof of liability. The giving of information under rule 44.15 (where that rule applies)' is not
  sufficient.
  Form N260 is reproduced at Appendix 1.
2   CPD, s 14.4—
  'The court may direct that any costs, for which the receiving party may not in the event be
  liable, shall be paid into court to await the outcome of the case, or shall not be enforceable
  until further order, or it may postpone the receiving party's right to receive payment in
  some other way.'

Preparation for summary assessment at conclusion of the case

8.19   The party seeking an additional liability must prepare and have
available for the court a bundle including all notices of funding

arrangements (N251), estimates and statements of costs filed and a copy of the risk assessment prepared at the time any funding arrangement was made[1]. In compliance with the CFA Regulations 2000, reg 3, the CFA will contain brief written reasons for the success fee. Those reasons form part of communications between lawyer and client and as such are privileged. The CFA must contain a term enabling the solicitor and client to comply with any requirement of the court to disclose, to the court or any other person, the reasons stated in the CFA for setting the percentage success fee if the additional liability is to be assessed. CPD, s 14.9 anticipates the court requiring such disclosure. The CFA thus gives a contractual waiver of the privilege only in respect of assessment of the additional liability.

1   CPD, s 14.9—

'In order to facilitate the court in making a summary assessment of any additional liability at the conclusion of the proceedings the party seeking such costs must prepare and have available for the court a bundle of documents which must include—

(1)   a copy of every notice of funding arrangement (Form N251) which has been filed by him;

(2)   a copy of every estimate and statement of costs filed by him;

(3)   a copy of the risk assessment prepared at the time any relevant funding arrangement was entered into and on the basis of which the amount of the additional liability was fixed.'

Detailed assessment hearing

Summary

8.20   The time limits applicable to this procedure are contained in CPR, rr 47.7 and 47.8. Notice of commencement (CPR, r 47.6) must be given to the paying party and to all 'relevant persons' (defined in CPD, s 32.10). In addition to the notice of commencement there must be given 'relevant details' (CPD, ss 32.5 and 32.7) of the additional liability. The paying party and any other party has 21 days from the serving of notice in which to serve 'points of dispute', to be served on the receiving party and 'relevant persons', identifying the item disputed, the grounds of dispute and proposing an alternative amount (CPR, Pt 18 and CPD, s 35).

COMMENCEMENT OF DETAILED ASSESSMENT PROCEEDINGS

8.21   CPR, r 47.6—

'(1) Detailed assessment proceedings are commenced by the receiving party serving on the paying party—

(a)   notice of commencement in the relevant practice form; and

(b)   a copy of the bill of costs.

(Rule 47.7 sets out the period for commencing detailed assessment proceedings)

(2) The receiving party must also serve a copy of the notice of commencement and the bill on any other relevant persons[1] specified in the costs practice direction.

(3) A person on whom a copy of the notice of commencement is served under paragraph (2) is a party to the detailed assessment proceedings (in addition to the paying party and the receiving party).

(The costs practice direction deals with—

other documents which the party must file when he requests detailed
assessment;
the court's powers where it considers that a hearing may be
necessary;
the form of a bill; and
the length of notice which will be given if a hearing date is fixed).'

1   CPD, s 32.10 see para **8.28** below.

8.22   CPD, s 32—

'32.1   Precedents A, B, C and D in the Schedule of Costs Precedents annexed
to this Practice Direction are model forms of bills of costs for detailed
assessment. Further information about bills of costs is set out in Section 4.

32.2   A detailed assessment may be in respect of:

(1)   base costs, where a claim for additional liability has not been made or
has been agreed;
(2)   a claim for additional liability only, base costs having been summarily
assessed or agreed; or
(3)   both base costs and additional liability.'

ADDITIONAL LIABILITY ONLY

8.23   CPD, s 32.4   'If the detailed assessment is in respect of an additional
liability only, the receiving party must serve on the paying party and all other
relevant persons the following documents:

(a)   a notice of commencement;
(b)   a copy of the bill of costs;
(c)   the relevant details of the additional liability;
(d)   a statement giving the name and address of any person upon
whom the receiving party intends to serve the notice of
commencement.'

MEANING OF RELEVANT DETAILS

8.24   CPD, s 32.5   'The relevant details of an additional liability are as
follows:

(1)   In the case of a conditional fee agreement with a success fee:

(a)   a statement showing the amount of costs which have been
summarily assessed or agreed, and the percentage increase
which has been claimed in respect of those costs;
(b)   a statement of the reasons for the percentage increase given in
accordance with Regulation 3 of the Conditional Fee
Agreement Regulations 2000.'

[32.5(2) deals with insurance policies[1]; 32.5(3) deals with Access to Justice Act
1999, s 30 amounts[2]].

1   See Chapter 17.
2   See Chapter 9.

ASSESSMENT OF BOTH BASE COSTS AND ADDITIONAL LIABILITY

8.25 CPD, s 32.7 'If a detailed assessment is in respect of both base costs and an additional liability, the receiving party must serve on the paying party and all other relevant persons the documents listed in paragraph 32.3 and the documents giving relevant details of an additional liability listed in paragraph 32.5.'

FORM OF THE NOTICE OF COMMENCEMENT

8.26 CPD, s 32.8—

'(1) The Notice of Commencement should be in Form N252[1].
(2) Before it is served, it must be completed to show as separate items:

    (a) the total amount of the costs claimed in the bill;
    (b) the extra sum which will be payable by way of fixed costs and court fees if a default costs certificate is obtained.'

1 See Appendix 3.

SERVICE OUT OF ENGLAND AND WALES

8.27 CPD, s 32.9—

'(1) This paragraph applies where the notice of commencement is to be served outside England and Wales.
(2) The date to be inserted in the notice of commencement for the paying party to send points of dispute is a date (not less than 21 days from the date of service of the notice) which must be calculated by reference to Part 6 Section III as if the notice were a claim form and as if the date to be inserted was the date for the filing of a defence.'

MEANING OF 'RELEVANT PERSON'

8.28 CPD, s 32.10—

'(1) For the purposes of rule 47.6(2) a 'relevant person' means:

    (a) any person who has taken part in the proceedings which gave rise to the assessment and who is directly liable under an order for costs made against him;
    (b) any person who has given to the receiving party notice in writing that he has a financial interest in the outcome of the assessment and wishes to be a party accordingly;
    (c) any other person whom the court orders to be treated as such.

(2) Where a party is unsure whether a person is or is not a relevant person, that party may apply to the appropriate office for directions.
(3) The court will generally not make an order that the person in respect of whom the application is made will be treated as a relevant person, unless within a specified time he applies to the court to be joined as a party to the assessment proceedings in accordance with Part 19 (Parties and Group Litigation).'

COMPUTER DISK COPIES

8.29 CPD, s 32.11—

'(1) This paragraph applies in cases in which the bill of costs is capable of being copied onto a computer disk.

(2) If, before the detailed assessment hearing, a paying party requests a disk copy of a bill to which this paragraph applies, the receiving party must supply him with a copy free of charge not more than 7 days after the date on which he received the request.'

PERIOD FOR COMMENCING DETAILED ASSESSMENT PROCEEDINGS

8.30 CPR, r 47.7—

'The following table shows the period for commencing detailed assessment proceedings—

SOURCE OF RIGHT TO DETAILED ASSESSMENT	TIME BY WHICH DETAILED ASSESSMENT PROCEEDINGS MUST BE COMMENCED
Judgment, direction, order, award or other determination	3 months after the date of the judgment etc. Where detailed assessment is stayed pending an appeal, 3 months after the date of the order lifting the stay.
Discontinuance under Part 38	3 months after the date of service of notice of discontinuance under rule 38.3; or 3 months after the date of the dismissal of application to set the notice of discontinuance aside under rule 38.4
Acceptance of an offer to settle or a payment into court under Part 36	3 months after the date when the right to costs arose.'

8.31 CPD, s 33—

'33.1 The parties may agree under rule 2.11 (Time limits may be varied by parties) to extend or shorten the time specified by rule 47.7 for commencing the detailed assessment proceedings.

33.2 A party may apply to the appropriate office for an order under rule 3.1(2)(a) to extend or shorten that time.

33.3 Attention is drawn to rule 47.6(1). The detailed assessment proceedings are commenced by service of the documents referred to.

33.4 Permission to commence assessment proceedings out of time is not required.'

SANCTION FOR DELAY IN COMMENCING DETAILED ASSESSMENT PROCEEDINGS

8.32 CPR, r 47.8—

'(1) Where the receiving party fails to commence detailed assessment proceedings within the period specified—

(a)   in rule 47.7; or

(b)   by any direction of the court,

the paying party may apply for an order requiring the receiving party to commence detailed assessment proceedings within such time as the court may specify.

(2)   On an application under paragraph (1), the court may direct that, unless the receiving party commences detailed assessment proceedings within the time specified by the court, all or part of the costs to which the receiving party would otherwise be entitled will be disallowed.

(3)   If—

(a)   the paying party has not made an application in accordance with paragraph (1); and

(b)   the receiving party commences the proceedings later than the period specified in rule 47.7,

the court may disallow all or part of the interest otherwise payable to the receiving party under—

(i)   section 17 of the Judgments Act 1838; or

(ii)   section 74 of the County Courts Act 1984,

but must not impose any other sanction except in accordance with rule 44.14 (powers in relation to misconduct).

(4)   Where the costs to be assessed in a detailed assessment are payable out of the Community Legal Service Fund, this rule applies as if the receiving party were the solicitor to whom the costs are payable and the paying party were the Legal Services Commission.'

8.33   CPD, s 34—

'34.1—

(1)   An application for an order under rule 47.8 must be made in writing and be issued in the appropriate office.

(2)   The application notice must be served at least 7 days before the hearing.'

POINTS OF DISPUTE

8.34   CPR, r 47.9—

'(1)   The paying party and any other party to the detailed assessment proceedings may dispute any item in the bill of costs by serving points of dispute on—

(a)   the receiving party; and

(b)   every other party to the detailed assessment proceedings.

(2)   The period for serving points of dispute is 21 days after the date of service of the notice of commencement.

(3)   If a party serves points of dispute after the period set out in paragraph (2), he may not be heard further in the detailed assessment proceedings unless the court gives permission.

(The costs practice direction sets out requirements about the form of points of dispute)

(4)   The receiving party may file a request for a default costs certificate if—

   (a)   the period set out in rule 47.9 (2) for serving points of dispute has expired; and
   (b)   he has not been served with any points of dispute.

(5)   If any party (including the paying party) serves points of dispute before the issue of a default costs certificate the court may not issue the default costs certificate.

(Section IV of this Part sets out the procedure to be followed after points of dispute have been filed)′

FORM OF POINTS OF DISPUTE

8.35   CPD, s 35—

′35.1   The parties may agree under rule 2.11 (Time limits may be varied by parties) to extend or shorten the time specified by rule 47.9 for service of points of dispute. A party may apply to the appropriate office for an order under rule 3.1(2)(a) to extend or shorten that time.

35.2   Points of dispute should be short and to the point and should follow as closely as possible Precedent G of the Schedule of Costs Precedents annexed to this Practice Direction.

35.3   Points of dispute must—

(1)   identify each item in the bill of costs which is disputed,
(2)   in each case, state concisely the nature and grounds of dispute,
(3)   where practicable suggest a figure to be allowed for each item in respect of which a reduction is sought, and
(4)   be signed by the party serving them or his solicitor.

35.4—

(1)   The normal period for serving points of dispute is 21 days after the date of service of the notice of commencement.
(2)   Where a notice of commencement is served on a party outside England and Wales the period within which that party should serve points of dispute is to be calculated by reference to Part 6 Section III as if the notice of commencement was a claim form and as if the period for serving points of dispute were the period for filing a defence.

35.5   A party who serves points of dispute on the receiving party must at the same time serve a copy on every other party to the detailed assessment proceedings, whose name and address for service appears on the statement served by the receiving party in accordance with paragraph 32.3 or 32.4 above.

35.6—

(1)   This paragraph applies in cases in which Points of Dispute are capable of being copied onto a computer disk.

(2)   If, within 14 days of the receipt of the Points of Dispute, the receiving party requests a disk copy of them, the paying party must supply him with a copy free of charge not more than 7 days after the date on which he received the request.

35.7—

(1)   Where the receiving party claims an additional liability, a party who serves points of dispute on the receiving party may include a request for information about other methods of financing costs which were available to the receiving party.
(2)   Part 18 (further information) and the Practice Direction Supplementing that part apply to such a request.'

Procedure where points of dispute are served

SERVING A REPLY

8.36   CPR, r 47.13—

'(1)   Where any party to the detailed assessment proceedings serves points of dispute, the receiving party may serve a reply on the other parties to the assessment proceedings.
(2)   He may do so within 21 days after service on him of the points of dispute to which his reply relates.

(The costs practice direction sets out the meaning of reply)'

MEANING OF REPLY

8.37   CPD, s 39—

'39.1—

(1)   Where the receiving party wishes to serve a reply, he must also serve a copy on every other party to the detailed assessment proceedings. The time for doing so is within 21 days after service of the points of dispute.
(2)   A reply means—

(i)   a separate document prepared by the receiving party; or
(ii)   his written comments added to the points of dispute.

(3)   A reply must be signed by the party serving it or his solicitor.'

REQUEST FOR DETAILED ASSESSMENT AFTER POINTS OF DISPUTE ARE SERVED

8.38   CPR, r 47.14—

'(1)   Where points of dispute are served in accordance with this Part, the receiving party must file a request for a detailed assessment hearing.
(2)   He must file the request within 3 months of the expiry of the period for commencing detailed assessment proceedings as specified—

(a)   in rule 47.7; or
(b)   by any direction of the court.

(3)   Where the receiving party fails to file a request in accordance with paragraph (2), the paying party may apply for an order requiring the receiving party to file the request within such time as the court may specify.

(4)   On an application under paragraph (3), the court may direct that, time specified by the court, all or part of the costs to which the receiving party would otherwise be entitled will be disallowed.

(5)   If—

  (a)   the paying party has not made an application in accordance with paragraph (3); and

  (b)   the receiving party files a request for a detailed assessment hearing later than the period specified in paragraph (2),

the court may disallow all or part of the interest otherwise payable to the receiving party under—

  (i)   section 17 of the Judgments Act 1838[73]; or

  (ii)   section 74 of the County Courts Act 1984[74],

but must not impose any other sanction except in accordance with rule 44.14 (powers in relation to misconduct).

(6)   No person other than—

  (a)   the receiving party;

  (b)   the paying party; and

  (c)   any party who has served points of dispute under rule 47.9,

may be heard at the detailed assessment hearing unless the court gives permission.

(7)   Only items specified in the points of dispute may be raised at the hearing, unless the court gives permission.

(The costs practice direction specifies other documents which must be filed with the request for hearing and the length of notice which the court will give when it fixes a hearing date.)'

THE PRACTICE DIRECTION WHERE POINTS OF DISPUTE ARE SERVED:

8.39

Counsel's fees

CPD, s 20—

CPD, s 20.4—

'(1)   Where detailed assessment proceedings have been commenced, and the paying party serves points of dispute (as to which see Section 34 of this Practice Direction), which show that he is seeking a reduction in any percentage increase charged by counsel on his fees, the solicitor acting for the receiving party must within 3 days of service deliver to counsel a copy of the relevant points of dispute and the bill of costs or the relevant parts of the bill.

(2)   Counsel must within 10 days thereafter inform the solicitor in writing whether or not he will accept the reduction sought or some other

reduction. Counsel may state any points he wishes to have made in a reply to the points of dispute, and the solicitor must serve them on the paying party as or as part of a reply.

(3) Counsel who fails to inform the solicitor within the time limits set out above will be taken to accept the reduction unless the court otherwise orders.'

[CPD, s 20.5 is dealt with below—see Disallowance of Success Fee—para **8.46**].

CERTIFICATE OF RECEIVING PARTY'S SOLICITOR

8.40

CPD, s 20.6—

'Where the solicitor acting for a receiving party files a request for a detailed assessment hearing it must if appropriate, be accompanied by a certificate signed by him stating:

(1) that the amount of the percentage increase in respect of counsel's fees or solicitor's charges is disputed;

(2) whether an application will be made for an order that any amount of that increase which is disallowed should continue to be payable by his client;

(3) that he has given his client an explanation in accordance with paragraph 20.5; and,

(4) whether his client wishes to attend court when the amount of any relevant percentage increase may be decided.'

NOTIFICATION TO THE CLIENT AND COUNSEL

8.41   CPD, s 20.7—

'(1) The solicitor acting for the receiving party must within 7 days of receiving from the court notice of the date of the assessment hearing, notify his client, and if appropriate, counsel in writing of the date, time and place of the hearing.

(2) Counsel may attend or be represented at the detailed assessment hearing and may make oral or written submissions.'

POWER TO DECIDE OR ADJOURN

8.42   CPD, s 20.8—

'(1) At the detailed assessment hearing, the court will deal with the assessment of the costs payable by one party to another, including the amount of the percentage increase, and give a certificate accordingly.

(2) The court may decide the issue whether the disallowed amount should continue to be payable under the relevant conditional fee agreement without an adjournment if:

   (a) the receiving party and all parties to the relevant agreement consent to the court deciding the issue without an adjournment,

   (b) the receiving party (or, if corporate, an officer or employee who has authority to consent on behalf of the receiving party) is present in court, and

(c) the court is satisfied that the issue can be fairly decided without an adjournment.

(3) In any other case the court will give directions and fix a date for the hearing of the application.'

DISALLOWANCE OF ANY PART OF THE SUCCESS FEE

8.43 The Access to Justice Act 1999, s 27 provides for the recovery of the success fee from the losing party by inserting s 58A(6) into the Courts and Legal Services Act 1990. Section 58A(6) is expressed to be subject to rules of court. At no time during the passage of this provision through Parliament was there any doubt that the paying party would be permitted to challenge the success fee. The detailed provisions below set out the procedure for such disputes and the criteria which a court may use in an assessment. The rules enable a court to disallow all or part of the success fee. If a court does disallow the success fee in whole or in part there is then a provision enabling the client's solicitor to apply to the court for a direction that the disallowed part should remain payable by the client. A CFA will provide for the client to be legally responsible for the whole of any agreed success fee but that contractual provision cannot be relied upon in the absence of a court's direction.

8.44 CPR, r 44.16—

'Where–

(a) the court disallows any amount of a legal representative's percentage increase in summary or detailed assessment proceedings; and

(b) the legal representative applies for an order that the disallowed amount should continue to be payable by his client,

the court may adjourn the hearing to allow the legally represented party to be notified of the order sought.

The Practice Direction provides detailed rules concerning the procedure where the legal representative seeks to recover from the client the disallowed part of the success fee. Those rules differ according to whether there is a summary assessment or detailed assessment of costs.'

PROCEDURE FOLLOWING SUMMARY ASSESSMENT

8.45 CPD, s 20.3—

'(1) If the court disallows any amount of a legal representative's percentage increase, the court will, unless sub-paragraph (2) applies, give directions to enable an application to be made by the legal representative for the disallowed amount to be payable by his client, including, if appropriate, a direction that the application will be determined by a costs judge or district judge of the court dealing with the case.

(2) The court that has made the summary assessment may then and there decide the issue whether the disallowed amount should continue to be payable, if:

(a)   the receiving party and all parties to the relevant agreement consent to the court doing so;

(b)   the receiving party (or, if corporate, an officer) is present in court; and

(c)   the court is satisfied that the issue can be fairly decided then and there.'

If either the client is not present, or, where relevant, counsel is not present and has not consented to a summary assessment, the court must give directions to enable an application to be made for the disallowed part of the success fee to be payable by the client. It is unclear from the CPR and PD what procedure is to be followed once such directions have been given although it may be assumed that the directions given can include a direction that the additional liability by assessed summarily or by detailed assessment.

Procedure following Detailed Assessment

RECOVERY FROM CLIENT OF DISALLOWED SUCCESS FEE

8.46   CPD, s 20.5—

'Where the paying party serves points of dispute seeking a reduction in any percentage increase charged by a legal representative acting for the receiving party, and that legal representative intends, if necessary, to apply for an order that any amount of the percentage disallowed as against the paying party shall continue to be payable by his client, the solicitor acting for the receiving party must, within 14 days of service of the points of dispute, give to his client a clear written explanation of the nature of the relevant point of dispute and the effect it will have if it is upheld in whole or in part by the court, and of the client's right to attend any subsequent hearings at court when the matter is raised.'

CHALLENGE TO THE SUCCESS FEE BY THE CLIENT

8.47   The client will be a party to any challenge to the success fee on the basis that the result of a challenge by a paying party could lead to an application by the solicitor that any disallowed amount should be payable by the client. But it is not only this disallowed part of a success fee for which a client may be liable. A success fee may include a charge for waiting for payment—an element expressly excluded from the provisions as to recovery from the losing party. The question arises as to how a client may challenge the percentage of a success fee referable to waiting for payment. Before the change to the statutory provisions made by the Access to Justice Act 1999, only the client was concerned with the success fee. It was clear that such a client was able to challenge the level of that fee[1].

1   CPR, r 48.9, as it was until January 2001. See Chapter 10.

The current position

8.48   CPR, r 48.8(3)[1] applies to all CFAs whenever made. The position is also governed by the Solicitors Act 1974, s 70 under which the client may make an application to the court for the costs to be assessed. Part 8 is applicable unless there are existing proceedings in which case Pt 23 applies. There is no special procedure for the assessment of the success fee on the application of the client. The court can take into account the fact that the client has agreed the success fee, but that does not preclude a finding that the fee is unreasonable. Any other relevant factors can also be taken into account and the criteria applicable where an opponent makes the challenge may be relevant[2].

1   CPR 22nd Amendment 12 March 2001. Previously the position was governed separately for pre-April 2000 CFAs. This distinction has now been removed from the CPR and will be removed from the CPD.
2   See para **8.52**.

Procedure

8.49   CPR, r 48.9—

'(1)   This rule sets out the procedure to be followed where the court has made an order under Part III of the Solicitors Act 1974 for the assessment of costs payable to a solicitor by his client.

(2)   The solicitor must serve a breakdown of costs within 28 days of the order for costs to be assessed.

(3)   The client must serve points of dispute within 14 days after service on him of the breakdown of costs.

(4)   If the solicitor wishes to serve a reply, he must do so within 14 days of service on him of the points of dispute.

(5)   Either party may file a request for a hearing date—

(a)   after points of dispute have been served; but

(b)   no later than 3 months after the date of the order for the costs to be assessed.

(6)   This procedure applies subject to any contrary order made by the court.'

Recovery from the client of a shortfall following recovery from the opponent

8.50   Whatever the position with regard to that part of the success fee relating to waiting for payment, there is also the question of any shortfall in the recovery of a success fee. The CPR and CPD deal expressly with any part of the success fee which is disallowed. This does not seem to refer to the application of the success fee to that part of the base costs not allowed between the parties but which are allowed on an own client basis. It is doubtful that the wording of CPD, s 20 is intended to cover the situation where the percentage increase is not disallowed but the level of base costs to which that percentage is applies is reduced. Whilst it may be the case that most solicitors will not seek to recover this sum, it is important to address the recoverability. This assumes that the terms of the CFA are such that the client could, as a matter of contract, be liable for such a shortfall. The Law Society Model refers only to the success fee and does not refer to this situation. Given that it is common practice for own costs to exceed between the parties costs, this is an unwelcome omission. The requirement to explain the costs liability of a client will also need to take account of the potential liability for a success fee applying to this shortfall. Whether the clause of the Law Society Model referring to the fact that the client will 'usually' recover the success fee from the loser is sufficient to satisfy the requirement of the Practice Rules to give the best costs information must therefore remain in doubt.

FACTORS TAKEN INTO ACCOUNT IN AN ASSESSMENT OF THE SUCCESS FEE

8.51 The court will consider the amount of the success fee separately from considering the base costs[1]. The proportionality rule applies then to the success fee and the factors set out in r 44.5 apply in the usual manner[2] but a success fee is not to be reduced simply because when added to the base costs the total appears disproportionate[3]. The assessment is made on the basis of the circumstances as they reasonably appeared to the solicitor at the time the funding arrangement was made or varied[4]. However, in costs only proceedings, the costs judge or district judge should have regard to the time when and the extent to which the claim has been settled and to the fact that the claim has been settled without the need to commence proceedings[5].

1   CPD, s 11.5. In deciding whether the costs claimed are reasonable and (on a standard basis assessment) proportionate, the court will consider the amount of any additional liability separately from the base costs.
2   CPR, r 44.5—
    '(1) The court is to have regard to all the circumstances in deciding whether costs were—
        (a) if it is assessing costs on the standard basis—
            (i)   proportionately and reasonably incurred; or
            (ii) were proportionate and reasonable in amount, or
        (b) if it is assessing costs on the indemnity basis—
            (i)   unreasonably incurred; or
            (ii) unreasonable in amount.
    (2)   In particular the court must give effect to any orders which have already been made.
    (3)   The court must also have regard to—
        (a) the conduct of all the parties, including in particular—
            (i)   conduct before, as well as during, the proceedings; and
            (ii) the efforts made, if any, before and during the proceedings in order to try to resolve the dispute;
        (b) the amount or value of any money or property involved;
        (c) the importance of the matter to all the parties;
        (d) the particular complexity of the matter or the difficulty or novelty of the questions raised;
        (e) the skill, effort, specialised knowledge and responsibility involved;
        (f) the time spent on the case; and
        (g) the place where and the circumstances in which work or any part of it was done.'
    (Rule 35.4(4) gives the court power to limit the amount that a party may recover with regard to the fees and expenses of an expert)
3   CPD, s 11.9—
    'A percentage increase will not be reduced simply on the ground that, when added to bases costs which are reasonable and (where relevant) proportionate, the total appears disproportionate.'
4   CPD, s 11.7—
    'Subject to paragraph 17.8(2), when the court is considering the factors to be taken into account in assessing an additional liability, it will have regard to the facts and circumstances as they reasonably appeared to the solicitor or counsel when the funding arrangement was entered into and at the time of any variation of the arrangement.'
5   See CPD, s 17.8(2) at para **8.55** below.

8.52 As to the factors which may be taken into account on an assessment of the success fee these were the subject of some change during the process of drafting the Practice Direction about Costs. The final version lists three factors which may be included as relevant: the risk that the case may lose (with the effect that no fees will be payable); the legal representative's liability for disbursements; what other methods of funding the costs were available to the receiving party—

CPD, s 11.8—

'(1) In deciding whether a percentage increase is reasonable relevant factors to be taken into account may include—

    (a) the risk that the circumstances in which the costs, fees or expenses would be payable might or might not occur[1];

    (b) the legal representative's liability for any disbursements;

    (c) what other methods of financing the costs were available to the receiving party.

(2) The court has the power, when considering whether a percentage increase is reasonable, to allow different percentages for different items of costs or for different periods during which costs were incurred.[2]'

1 Here the risk assessment which was made at the time that the success fee was set will be relevant in determining the reasonableness of the success fee. This must be included in the bundle of documents prepared for the assessment. The CFA itself must contain a term giving the client's consent to the disclosure of the risk assessment—SI 2000/692, reg 3(2)(a).

2 It is difficult to reconcile this provision with the general principle of CPD, s 11.7 (above para **8.51** n 4) that hindsight must be avoided. Where the success fee has not been re-negotiated during the currency of the CFA the exercise of the power in CPD, s 11.8(2) would seem to be an application of hindsight in that it would be imposing a view as to risk which could not have been held at the time the CFA was made. Having to review success fees throughout the case and to carry out the necessary advice and negotiation with the client would be likely to escalate overall costs rather than produce a reduction by way of any alteration to the success fee.

8.53 The process of risk assessment is dealt with in Part 9. The calculation of the success fee and the factors affecting it are fully considered in Chapter 22.

The wording of the CPD suggests that other factors may be relevant. In an earlier draft of the CPD the disadvantages of waiting for payment were included. This element is not recoverable from the losing party but can be recovered from the client.

THE POSITION OF COUNSEL'S SUCCESS FEE

8.54 Counsel's base fee is a disbursement, the solicitor being liable to pay counsel and the lay client being liable to reimburse the solicitor. The position of counsel's success fee, which is contained in a CFA made between the solicitor and counsel (not between counsel and the lay client) is also a disbursement. That success fee is governed by the rules on the recoverability of additional liabilities. Accordingly the opponent can challenge counsel's success fee in the same way as solicitor's success fee can be challenged.

CPD, ss 20.3 and 20.4[1] clearly envisage a challenge by the opponent to the level of counsel's success fee. Those provisions set out the rights of counsel to be informed and to make representation. If counsel's success fee is reduced on an assessment there will then arise the question of recovery from the solicitor. From that will arise the recovery by the solicitor from the lay client. The rules of the CPD are not drafted to address these matters. It seems that CPD, s 20 will apply to counsel whose success fee has been reduced. This means that counsel must follow the same procedure as the solicitor and make application to the court for directions that the amount disallowed should remain payable. The lay client is not a party however to the relevant agreement which causes a difficulty with a summary assessment—CPD, s 20.3 requires only the consent of the parties to the relevant agreement. It is likely that the court would decide that the issue cannot be fairly decided summarily. On a detailed assessment, CPD, s 20.5[2] requires the receiving party's solicitor to give the client a clear written explanation of the dispute and of the client's right to attend any hearing. Alternatively, given that the lay client's responsibility for counsel's fees arise through the agreement with the solicitor, the client can seek an assessment of the disbursement of counsel's success fee in the ordinary way[3].

1 CPD, ss 20.3 and 20.4 are given at paras **8.45** and **8.39** respectively above.
2 CPD, s 20.5 is given at para **8.46** above.
3 See CPR, r 48.10 at para **8.49** above.

COSTS ONLY PROCEEDINGS

8.55 Rule 44.12A provides for a new procedure to apply where no proceedings have been started and where the parties have reached agreement on all issues, including which party is to pay costs, but have failed to agree the amount of costs. Either party may make an application under Pt 8 for an order for costs. This can therefore include an additional liability. The claim form under Pt 8 must include or be accompanied by a written agreement or written conformation of agreement as to the issues and the matter of which party is to pay costs. The court may make an order for costs or dismiss the claim. If it makes an order for costs this is treated as an order for the amount of costs to be decided by a detailed assessment under Pt 47. There can, therefore, be no summary assessment in connection with costs only proceedings. If the claim is opposed then under this Rule the claim must be dismissed. In such circumstances it is open to a party to issue a new claim, under Pt 7 or Pt 8, to enforce the agreement.

The CPR, r 44.12A, Pt 8 procedure is not confined to CFAs. However, where there is a CFA with a success fee, a costs judge or district judge should take into account the time at which the claim was settled and that it was settled without the issue of proceedings[1]. Where a success fee has been properly set in accordance with a risk assessment process, the usual test of the reasonableness of that success fee, in the circumstances reasonably known to the legal representative at that time, seemingly does not apply and the fact that the case settles pre-issue is a factor affecting the decision of the court[2]. CPD, s 17.8(2) does not contradict CPD, s 11.7 since the latter was amended to recognise the former. There are no provisions in the statutory scheme to require that the success fee be reviewed periodically or in response to a change or perceived change in the chances of success. The legal representative takes a risk, therefore, whenever a success fee is set, that the recovery of that fee will be affected by early settlement, yet another risk factor which needs to be recognised and which could, ironically, justify an increase in the success fee. The introduction of the pre-issue procedure was designed to encourage settlement. It was also to address the discouraging effect on settling which an inability to compel the inclusion of the success fee in any settlement offer tended to have[3].

1 CPR 16th Update, July 2000, Consequential Changes adding s 17.8(2) to CPD, s 17. See also *Callery v Gray* (29 January 2001, unreported) at para **8.63** below.
2 CPD, s 11.7.
3 See Lord Chancellor's Department Consultation Paper, *Sharing the Risks of Litigation—Conclusions*, (February 2000) at paras 50–54.

8.56 CPR, r 44.12A—

'(1) This rule sets out a procedure which may be followed where—

(a) the parties to a dispute have reached an agreement on all issues (including which party is to pay the costs) which is made or confirmed in writing; but

(b) they have failed to agree the amount of those costs; and

(c) no proceedings have been started.

(2) Either party to the agreement may start proceedings under this rule by issuing a claim form in accordance with Part 8.

(3) The claim form must contain or be accompanied by the agreement or confirmation.

(4) In proceedings to which this rule applies the court—

(a) may

(i) make an order for costs; or
(ii) dismiss the claim; and

(b) must dismiss the claim if it is opposed.

(5) Rule 48.3 (amount of costs where costs are payable pursuant to a contract) does not apply to claims started under the procedure in this rule. (Rule 7.2 provides that proceedings are started when the court issues a claim form at the request of the claimant.)

(Rule 8.1(6) provides that a practice direction may modify the Part 8 procedure.)'

COURT FOR ISSUE

8.57 CPD, s 17—

'17.1 A claim form under this rule should be issued in the court which would have been the appropriate office in accordance with rule 47.4 had proceedings been brought in relation to the substantive claim. A claim form under this rule should not be issued in the High Court unless the dispute to which the agreement relates was of such a value or type that had proceedings been begun they would have been commenced in the High Court.

17.2 A claim form which is to be issued in the High Court at the Royal Courts of Justice will be issued in the Supreme Court Costs Office.'

8.58

'17.3   Attention is drawn to rule 8.2 (in particular to paragraph (b)(ii)) and to rule 44.12A(3). The claim form must:

(1)   identify the claim or dispute to which the agreement to pay costs relates;
(2)   state the date and terms of the agreement on which the claimant relies;
(3)   set out or have attached to it a draft of the order which the claimant seeks;
(4)   state the amount of the costs claimed; and,
(5)   state whether the costs are claimed on the standard or indemnity basis. If no basis is specified the costs will be treated as being claimed on the standard basis.

17.4   The evidence to be filed and served with the claim form under Rule 8.5 must include copies of the documents on which the claimant relies to prove the defendant's agreement to pay costs.'

JURISDICTION AND ORDERS

8.59

'17.5   A costs judge or a district judge has jurisdiction to hear and decide any issue which may arise in a claim issued under this rule irrespective of the amount of the costs claimed or of the value of the claim to which the agreement to pay costs relates. A court officer may make an order by consent under paragraph 17.7, or an order dismissing a claim under paragraph 17.9 below.

17.6   When the time for filing the defendant's acknowledgement of service has expired, the claimant may by letter request the court to make an order in the terms of his claim, unless the defendant has filed an acknowledgement of service stating that he intends to contest the claim or to seek a different order.

17.7   Rule 40.6 applies where an order is to be made by consent. An order may be made by consent in terms which differ from those set out in the claim form.

17.8—

(1)   An order for costs made under this rule will be treated as an order for the amount of costs to be decided by a detailed assessment to which Part 47 and the practice directions relating to it apply. Rule 44.4(4) (determination of basis of assessment) also applies to the order.
(2)   In cases in which an additional liability is claimed, the costs judge or district judge should have regard to the time when and the extent to which the claim has been settled and to the fact that the claim has been settled without the need to commence proceedings.'

OPPOSED PART 8

8.60

'17.9   A claim will be treated as opposed for the purposes of rule 44.12A(4)(b) if the defendant files an acknowledgement of service stating that he intends to contest the proceedings or to seek a different remedy.' An order dismissing it will be made as soon as such an acknowledgement is filed. The dismissal of a claim under rule 44.12A(4) does not prevent the claimant from issuing another claim form under Part 7 or Part 8 based on the agreement or alleged agreement to which the proceedings under this rule related.'

NO TRACK ALLOCATION

8.61

CPD, s 17.10—

'(1)   Rule 8.9 (which provides that claims issued under Part 8 shall be treated as allocated to the multi-track) shall not apply to claims issued under this rule. A claim issued under this rule may be dealt with without being allocated to a track.

(2)   Rule 8.1(3) and Part 24 do not apply to proceedings brought under rule 44.12A.'

SUING ON A SETTLEMENT AGREEMENT

8.62

CPD, s 17.11

'Nothing in this rule prevents a person from issuing a claim form under Part 7 or Part 8 to sue on an agreement made in settlement of a dispute where that agreement makes provision for costs, nor from claiming in that case an order for costs or a specified sum in respect of costs.'

RECOVERY OF THE SUCCESS FEE PRE-ISSUE

8.63   The costs only procedure has been introduced to facilitate settlement including settlement of the success fee. The procedure expressly recognises that an assessment under Pt 8 will include the assessment of a success fee. Agreeing and seeking to recover a success fee pre-issue is therefore within the Pt 8 procedure. The question which then arises is the extent (if any) to which the fact that a case has settled pre-issue can affect the decision on a challenge to the level of the success fee. It can also be argued that to set a success fee before providing an opportunity to a defendant to respond to a prospective claim is itself unreasonable. CPD, s 17.8(2) provides that regard should be had to the time when a claim has been settled and the extent to which it has been settled. It is likely that in may cases the client is seeking a CFA at the outset and based only upon what they have provided to the solicitor, either directly or via a third party such as a claims handler. The test to be applied (subject to CPD, s 17.8(2) on a cost only procedure) is concerned with the level of the success fee (in the light of what was reasonably known) and not the decision to offer a CFA at a particular time. CPD, s 17.8(2) encourages the application of hindsight and suggests that the decision to enter into a CFA at a particular time can be second guessed.

These issues arose in what is believed to be the first appeal from a decision of a district judge in the unreported decision of His Honour Judge Edwards in *Callery v Gray*[1] where the district judge, having reduced the base costs by nearly 50%, allowed a success fee of 40%, a decision upheld on appeal to the Chester county court. This was a road traffic claim by a passenger. The success fee was set before any letter was sent to the defendant. There appears in the judgment to be some application of hindsight in that reference is frequently made to the fact that thereafter a letter was sent by the defendant admitting liability as to 'negligence but not to causation'. Whilst with hindsight this can be seen as a validation of a decision made before the letter was received, it is respectfully submitted that this is not a factor which ought to be taken into account since it cannot have affected the decision as to the level of the success fee. No reference is made to CPD, s 17.8(2). The decision on appeal causes, with respect, grave concern. His Honour states his own view as to the prospects of success, which is neither an application of the standard basis of the circumstances as they reasonably appeared to the solicitor at the time the success fee was set, nor is it an application of CPD, s 17.8(2). If a solicitor's view of the prospects of success, with the reasons stated in the CFA itself, are to be second guessed, that ought to occur with no knowledge of what actually transpired, and certainly without reference to what actually transpired. It is submitted that the basis of disallowing a part of a success fee (or in theory the whole success fee) is that when set the fee level was unreasonable, a wholly different test to whether a judge on an appeal would have reached the same, or even a similar conclusion. The decision does illustrate that cases which might sometimes be considered certain, are subject to risk. In this case the county court judge took the view that there was no certainty in liability and that the approach of the insurers for the defendant was such as to leave liability open on the basis of causation. It will be seen in Part 9 of this work that the basis of risk assessment is not the identification of actual problems but the realisation of the risk or possibility of such problems. The *Callery* case is a prime example of the prediction of risk and, as it happens, the realisation of such a risk. The crucial point is that when the decision to offer a CFA is taken it may only be possible to predict risk and not to know what problems actually exist in the case.

1   (29 January 2001, unreported), Case No. MC002977—Chester County Court—(Associated Verbatim Reporters).

GUIDANCE BY THE SENIOR COSTS JUDGE—NOVEMBER 2000/JANUARY 2001

8.64   A revised Guide to all Designated Civil Judges to include guidance in relation to funding arrangements was published in January 2001, earlier guidance having been published in November 2000. The January Guidance does not address costs only proceedings.

The November Guidance deals with Costs only proceedings and states that the 'procedure appears to be being misused by both claimants and defendants in breach of the overriding objective'. There is a view that in principle a success fee ought not to be recovered pre-issue and that the insurance premium ought not to be recovered pre-issue and it seems that a threat to use Pt 8 having agreed liability and quantum has been used as a matter of course by claimants. Defendants have made offers which state that consent is not given to a Pt 8 procedure. The Guidance warns that if a claimant is forced to use Pt 7, rather than costs only, defendants are exposed to the costs of the Pt 7 proceedings (including on the indemnity basis where the defendant has acted unreasonably in compelling Pt 7.)

As to the procedure for a costs only hearing, the November Guidance states that for bills of modest size, detailed assessment may be unnecessarily cumbersome. Consideration is being given to a disposal procedure or a short form of bill.

Chapter 9

Collective Conditional Fee Agreements

DEFINITION AND SCOPE OF COLLECTIVE CONDITIONAL FEE AGREEMENTS

9.1 Collective Conditional Fee Agreements (CCFAs) are a response to concerns expressed during the passage of the Access to Justice Act 1999 (AJA 1999) that the individual CFA regime was not administratively suitable for the bulk purchase of legal services. In particular, commercial organisations and membership organisations such as motoring associations and trade unions were not able to use the existing CFA provisions because of the practical and physical difficulties of administering the rules on an individual basis. A new consultation process was launched in June 2000[1] and the CCFA Regulations[2] were published in November 2000. Those Regulations and the use of CCFAs are however dependent upon either the amendment of the indemnity principle[3] or its abolition. Amendments to the CPR to remove the indemnity principle are being drafted by the Rules Committee at the time of writing. The statutory authority for the abrogation of the indemnity principle is AJA 1999, s 31[4]. That provision has not been commenced as at 30 April 2001. Thus, although the CCFA Regulations came into force on 30 November 2000, a CCFA made before the indemnity principle has been abolished must raise the question as to the effect of that abolition on any funding agreements entered before the commencement of s 31 of the 1999 Act. It may be argued that a reversal of case law by statute cannot be retrospective. However, the implementation of that reversal will be through the CPR which are applied at the time of a costs assessment. On this basis any lawful CCFA made after 30 November 2000 would not be cut down at an assessment hearing which takes place after the reversal of the indemnity principle[5]. It remains to be seen whether the wording of the CPR will shed any light on the retrospective effect.

---

1 Lord Chancellor's Department Consultation Paper 12, *Collective Conditional Fees* (June 2000). The Government's conclusions paper was published in September 2000.
2 SI 2000/2988 in force 30 November 2000. See Appendix 1.
3 See Chapter 1 above.
4 See Appendix 1.
5 Compliance with the CCFA Regulations 2000 ensures the legality of the funding arrangement where the client is not also the funder, for example in Trade Union schemes. That is not the same as saying however that the costs will be recoverable. Once AJA 1999, s 31 is commenced a court can include in a costs order costs for which the party was not liable. It remains to be seen whether the amendments to the CPR will permit such an order in respect of work done before s 31 was commenced. It is important to note that neither s 31 nor the CCFA

Regulations envisage the funder being a receiving party where they are not also the client. Any argument that the member was to be liable to pay the costs would of course be met with the questions of the basis upon which that liability existed and whether there was also an individual CFA between each member and the solicitor.

9.2   A CCFA is defined in the CCFA Regulations 2000—

'3.—(1)   Subject to paragraph (2) of this regulation, a collective conditional fee agreement is an agreement which—

(a)   disregarding section 58(3)(c)[1] of the Courts and Legal Services Act 1990, would be a conditional fee agreement; and

(b)   does not refer to specific proceedings, but provides for fees to be payable on a common basis in relation to a class[2] of proceedings, or, if it refers to more than one class of proceedings, on a common basis in relation to each class.

(2)   An agreement may be a collective conditional fee agreement whether or not—

(a)   the funder is a client; or

(b)   any clients are named in the agreement.[3]'

1   CLSA 1990, s 58(3) provides—
  'The following conditions are applicable to every conditional fee agreement—
  (c) it must comply with such requirements (if any) as may be prescribed by the Lord Chancellor.'
  Regulation 3(1)(a) of the CCFA Regulations is necessary in order to disapply the individual CFA Regulations. Regulation 7 of the CCFA Regulations further provides that, by the insertion of reg 8 into the CFA Regulations 2000, the CFA Regulations shall not apply to Collective Conditional Fee Agreements.
2   'Class' is not defined.
3   SI 2000/2988, reg 3.

9.3   In essence a CCFA differs from an individual CFA in that it does not specify the proceedings to which it relates but instead refers to a class or classes of proceedings. The CCFA will in general be made prospectively, that is before the individual proceedings to which it applies are contemplated. There is nothing in the regulations to prevent a CCFA covering proceedings which have already begun at the time the CCFA is made. In these circumstances the CCFA need only describe the class of proceedings into which the existing proceedings falls. This application of the CCFA regime raises no more of a question about the retrospective effect which a fee agreement can have than is raised by the individual CFA regime. On the ordinary principles of the law of contract a CCFA can be retrospective in effect, in being an agreement entered into in consideration of giving up any rights arising out of the contract which it replaces. The Regulations provide that an agreement must be made on or after 30 November 2000[1], but no provision stipulates that a CCFA made after that date cannot relate to work done before that date. Without the relevant amendments to the Civil Procedure Rules (CPR) (with or without amendments also to the Practice Direction about Costs (CPD)) it cannot be said whether a CCFA can be retrospective to a date prior to 30 November 2000. It is unlikely that the CPR will provide that CCFAs entered into on or after that date cannot relate to work done before the agreement is made but they may preclude work prior to 30 November 2000.

1 CCFA Regulations 2000, reg 2 provides—
   'These Regulations shall apply to agreements entered into on or after 30th November 2000,
   and agreements entered into before that date shall be treated as if these Regulations had
   not come into force.'

9.4 The CCFA Regulations 2000[1] make provision for all CCFAs irrespective
of the context in which they are to be used. From the consultation papers[2] it is
clear that the Regulations apply to bulk purchasers of legal services, such as
the legal department of a multi-national company, and to bulk providers of
legal services such as the legal representatives retained by a trade union to act
for its members. There is a crucial difference between these two categories in
that the bulk purchaser is also the client, whereas the bulk provider situation
will involve numerous clients who are not funding the litigation. Regulation
3(2) provides that an agreement may be a CCFA whether or not the funder is
a client and whether any clients are named in the agreement. During the
consultation period concerns were raised as to the consumer protection
requirements for funding agreements. Where the funder is also the client, with
bulk requirements, it is seen as desirable to dispense with the administration
that would be needed if the individual CFA regime applied, there being no
need for a new CFA to be entered into in respect of each new matter. Where,
however, the CCFA is to be used in respect of bulk supply where individuals
are to be the beneficiaries of the legal services but not the funders of those
services, the need for consumer protection and additional client care arises.
The Regulations reflect this difference in the requirements laid down for the
CCFA but do so by seemingly applying consumer protection provisions to all
CCFAs, including those where the client is also the funder. The intended
saving in terms of the administration are thus not as great as they might have
been. The Regulations are not set out so as to have provisions applying
according to whether the CCFA is for a bulk purchaser or not.

1 SI 2000/2988.
2 See note 1 at para **9.1** above.

Definitions of 'client' and 'funder'

9.5 Regulation 1(2) defines 'client' as a person who will receive advocacy
or litigation services to which the agreement relates[1]. 'Funder' is defined as
the party who under the CCFA will pay the legal representative's fees. The
client may or may not therefore also be the funder. This will call for the
application of Rule 15 of the Law Society Rules of Professional Conduct[2] to
the person fitting the description of 'client' under the Regulations, whether or
not that person is also the funder. Where the funder is not a person fitting
the definition of 'client' for the purposes of the Regulations, that person will
still be the subject of Rule 15.

1 SI 2000/2988.
2 See Chapter 2 above.

CONTENTS OF A CCFA

Specified circumstances in which fees to be paid

9.6 Regulation 4(1) requires the CCFA to specify the circumstances in which
the legal representative's fees and expenses, or part of them, are payable[1].

The definition of a CCFA[2] in effect requires reference to the individual CFA provisions of the CLSA 1990, s 58 and the definition therein of a CFA, and of a CFA which provides for a success fee. The CCFA Regulations are then applied to those definitions. Hence 'specified circumstances' pre-supposes that there is an agreement that some or all of the fees and expenses will be payable only in specified circumstances. The CCFA then must set out what those circumstances are.

1   SI 2000/2988.
2   See para **9.2** above.

Information and advice in the specific proceedings

9.7   Regulation 4(2)[1] requires the CCFA to contain a term as to the giving of information to the client concerned in the specific proceedings. These requirements apply to a client whether or not he is also the funder. The CCFA must contain a term that when accepting instructions in relation to any specific proceedings, the legal representative must inform the client as to the circumstances in which the client may be liable to pay the costs of the legal representative. There must be a term that further explanation, advice or information about the costs liability, as may be reasonably required by the client must also be given. There must be a term that the legal representative must also confirm in writing his acceptance of the instructions in respect of the specific proceedings. All of these requirements are designed with 'consumer protection' in mind. The opportunity to recognise that these requirements are irrelevant where the funder and the client are the same legal person was ignored, with the result that this administrative requirement applies to all CCFAs. These provisions differ from the individual CFA Regulations. Where the individual regulations apply there is an actual requirement that costs information is given and a further requirement that there must be a term of the CFA stating that immediately before the CFA is signed the costs information was given. That method of ensuring that the consumer has the information necessary to understand their liability has been omitted from the CCFA Regulations, albeit it may be assumed that the contractual term required by the Regulations will also be performed. Under the CCFA there is no regulation as to the giving of costs information but only as to the terms of the agreement itself. The requirements as to costs information do not apply to a CCFA between a legal representative and an additional legal representative.

1   SI 2000/2988.

9.8   Regulation 4 provides—

'(2) A collective conditional fee agreement must provide that, when accepting instructions in relation to any specific proceedings the legal representative must—

(a)   inform the client as to the circumstances in which the client may be liable to pay the costs of the legal representative; and

(b)   if the client requires any further explanation, advice or other information about the matter referred to in sub-paragraph (a), provide such further explanation, advice or other information about it as the client may reasonably require.

(3) Paragraph (2) does not apply in the case of an agreement between a legal representative and an additional legal representative.

(4) A collective conditional fee agreement must provide that, after accepting instructions in relation to any specific proceedings, the legal representative must confirm his acceptance of instructions in writing to the client.[1]'

During the consultation period it became clear that there was concern that where the CCFA was to be used to fund the litigation of an individual who was not a party to the CCFA, that individual should be informed that the case was being conducted under a funding arrangement[2]. Regulation 4 appears to address that concern, but of course applies to all CCFAs. In the case of a CCFA relating to an individual who is not a party to the CCFA, the Rules of Professional Conduct[3] will in any event impose a requirement for the giving of advice to the client.

1   SI 2000/2988, reg 4.
2   Lord Chancellor's Department Consultation Paper 12, *Collective Conditional Fees* (June 2000), para 252.
3   See Chapter 2 above. In particular Rule 15 and the Client Care Code must be applied.

Further requirements where there is a success fee

9.9   Regulation 5(1) provides—

'Where a collective conditional fee agreement provides for a success fee the agreement must provide that, when accepting instructions in relation to any specific proceedings the legal representative must prepare and retain a written statement containing—

(a)   his assessment of the probability of the circumstances arising in which the percentage increase will become payable in relation to those proceedings ("the risk assessment")[1];

(b)   his assessment of the amount of the percentage increase in relation to those proceedings, having regard to the risk assessment; and

(c)   the reasons, by reference to the risk assessment, for setting the percentage increase at that level.[2]'

The legal representative is thus to prepare and retain a statement containing the following—

(a)   an assessment of the probability of winning—the 'risk assessment';
(b)   an assessment of the percentage increase having regard to (a);
(c)   the reasons, by reference to the risk assessment, for setting the percentage increase.

1   Risk assessment is dealt with fully in Part 9.
2   SI 2000/2988, reg 5.

9.10   The above requirements are more detailed requirements than those applicable to an individual CFA. Each of the three requirements requires consideration.

(A)   RISK ASSESSMENT

9.11   This is an expression of the level of confidence in winning. Many practitioners are familiar with the use of percentages to indicate a level of confidence[1]. Practitioners who use a risk assessment method based upon a weighted list of factors which produces a score expressed as a number will convert that number into a percentage of the maximum number which could have been scored and from that into a percentage increase. For example a score of 12 out of a possible 20 represents a 60% confidence level which is then converted into a percentage increase.

1   The expression of levels of confidence as a percentage figure is dealt with in Chapter 22. See also Chapter 23 on probability.

(B)   PERCENTAGE INCREASE

9.12   The assumption here is that the expression of the chances of success can be and needs to be converted into a success fee. That can be satisfied by the explanation of any conversion method which is being used, such as the ready reckoner contained in the Law Society publication *Conditional Fees—A Survival Guide*[1], and the methods described in Chapter 21 below. (b) does not appear to ask for any percentage increase relating to waiting for payment nor for disbursement liability.

1   Napier and Bawdon *Conditional Fees—A Survival Guide* Law Society Publications (1995). See Part 9 for a detailed explanation of conversion methods.

(C)   THE REASONS FOR THE LEVEL OF THE SUCCESS FEE

9.13   This calls for a reasoned explanation of (a) and its link to (b). Any additional factors affecting the success fee seem not to be referred to any part of this regulation but should nonetheless be included in (b). Thus there will need to be a written explanation as to the level of confidence in winning and then an explanation of how that figure was translated into a success fee. Formal methods of risk assessment are dealt with in Chapter 21 where templates are provided which will comply with this requirement. The conversion to a success fee is dealt with in Chapter 22 where explanation of the method of conversion is provided. The success fee may also include an element for waiting for payment and for a liability for disbursements. If these are included in the figure at (b) then that needs to be explained at (c) albeit this is not strictly a reference to 'the risk assessment' as defined in (a).

Example—
   (a)   75%
   (b)   50%
   (c)   The risk assessment—here attach completed template from Part 10. Attach the conversion chart from Chapter 22 indicating the assumed costs ratio of costs in won cases to lost cases. [The figure in (b) in this example assumes a ratio of 1.5. The figure is 33% if the assumed ratio is 1] Add percentage for waiting for payment and or disbursement liability if applicable, Chapter 22 (eg 5% waiting plus 1.5% liability). The waiting for payment element cannot be recovered from an opponent—CPR, r 44.3B(1)(a).

Other factors affecting the success fee

9.14   The CCFA Regulations make no reference to other factors which under an individual CFA would be included in the success fee. In particular there is no reference to an amount reflecting a liability for disbursements and no reference to a percentage increase representing the cost of the postponement of the fees. This latter element cannot be recovered from an opponent and in an individual CFA must be stated separately, or, where no such figure is included in the success fee, it should be stated that there is no such inclusion. It is recommended that the same approach be adopted for CCFAs.

Information to be given where the client is also the funder

9.15 Here it is envisaged that a bulk purchaser of legal services must be informed[1] as to costs liability[2] each time new specific proceedings are included under the CCFA and each time the legal representative must confirm in writing an acceptance of instructions[3]. It is likely that these requirements will be combined in one note making reference to the proceedings and to the terms of the CCFA and to an acceptance of instructions. If there is a success fee there must be retained a written risk assessment statement[4]. The Regulations do not, therefore, make the risk assessment a term of the CCFA although it is likely that a CCFA with a success fee will, when defining the success fee, refer to this risk assessment and incorporate it into the contract. The CCFA will contain a provision that the client will permit disclosure of the reasons for setting the success fee to the court or other person at the direction of the court. If the CCFA itself incorporates the risk assessment it would be better were it also to provide that the party to the CCFA gives permission for such disclosure.

1 SI 2000/2988, reg 4(2)(a) uses the word 'inform' but does not specify that this must be in writing.
2 Ibid, reg 4(2)(a).
3 Ibid, reg 4(4).
4 Ibid, reg 5(1).

Information to be given where the client is not the funder

9.16 Where a CCFA is being used to fund an individual's litigation, for example, of a member by a Trade Union, the CCFA must state that the legal representative will inform the individual of the circumstances in which he or she will be liable to pay the costs of the legal representative. This is rather less than the advice and information which Practice Rule 15 requires, particularly given there is no reference to adverse costs liability. The legal representative must confirm to the individual in writing the acceptance of instructions for the specific proceedings. Where there is a success fee the CCFA (to which the individual client is not a party) must state that if the legal representative or the client is required to disclose the reasons for the success fee to the court or any other person, the legal representative may do so. There is no provision in the Regulations entitling the client as client to a copy of the reasons for the success fee nor even a provision that the client is to be provided with a copy if they so request.

TABLE OF THE INFORMATION TO BE GIVEN TO THE CLIENT UNDER A CCFA

9.17

Information	To Client	Regulation
Circumstances in which client liable for legal representative's costs	Yes	4(2)(a)
Further explanation, advice or information reasonably required by the client	Yes	4(2)(b)
Written confirmation of the acceptance of instructions	Yes	4(4)
Written risk assessment	No	5(1)

CCFAs providing for a success fee in the case of court proceedings

9.18   Following the regime of the individual CFA the CCFA must contain terms concerning disclosure of the reasons for a success fee and the recoupment of disallowed amounts of the success fee.
Regulation 5(2) provides—

'(2) If the agreement relates to court proceedings it must provide that where the success fee becomes payable as a result of those proceedings, then—

[Disclosure]

(a)   if—

   (i)   any fees subject to the increase are assessed, and
   (ii)   the legal representative or the client is required by the court to disclose to the court or any other person the reasons for setting the percentage increase at the level assessed by the legal representative,

he may do so,

[Disallowed amounts]

(b)   if—

   (i)   any such fees are assessed by the court, and
   (ii)   any amount in respect of the percentage increase is disallowed on the assessment on the ground that the level at which the increase was set was unreasonable in view of facts which were or should have been known to the legal representative at the time it was set

that amount ceases to be payable under the agreement, unless the court is satisfied that it should continue to be so payable, and

[Lower amounts on settlement]

(c)   if—

    (i)   sub-paragraph (b does not apply, and

    (ii) the legal representative agrees with any person liable as a result of the proceedings to pay fees subject to the percentage increase that a lower amount than the amount payable in accordance with the conditional fee agreement is to be paid instead,

the amount payable under the collective conditional fee agreement in respect of those fees shall be reduced accordingly, unless the court is satisfied that the full amount should continue to be payable under it.[1]'

The above provisions are identical to those applying to individual CFAs. There are some complications for CCFAs arising from the fact that the party seeking a costs order may not be a party to the CCFA and may not have received a copy of the risk assessment supporting the level of the success fee.

1   SI 2000/2988, reg 5(2).

Disclosure

9.19   A CCFA is governed in the same way as an individual CFA in terms of the disclosure requirements of the CPR and Practice Direction about Costs. The CCFA Regulations define a CCFA as a CFA but for s 58(3)(c) and it is assumed that for the purposes of the CPR and CPD a CFA includes a CCFA. A CCFA is therefore a 'funding arrangement' within the meaning of CPR, r 43.2(1)[1]. It follows that the rules concerning the disclosure of funding arrangements apply to CCFAs in the same way as for individual CFAs[2]. The Practice Direction about Costs requires disclosure of the existence of a CCFA but not its terms[3]. Notice must be given at the time of issue of a claim form, if the CCFA is already in place[4]. Where a CCFA is made after the issue of proceedings notice must be given within seven days of the making of the agreement[5]. There is no requirement for pre-issue disclosure[6]. The Personal Injury protocol does provide for pre-issue disclosure. Where the CCFA relates to a defendant, notice of it must be given when filing the first document[7]. CCFAs made after the serving of the first document must be notified within seven days of the making of the agreement[8]. All of these provisions are identical to those applying to individual CFAs[9]. Form N251 may be used for the giving of this information[10].

1   CPR, r 43.2 (1) provides—
    'In Parts 44 to 48, unless the context otherwise requires "funding arrangement" means an arrangement where a person has—(i) entered into a conditional fee agreement which provides for a success fee within the meaning of section 58(2) of the Courts and Legal Services Act 1990.'
2   CPR, r 44.15(1) provides–
    'A party who seeks to recover an additional liability must provide information about the funding arrangement to the court and to other parties as required by a rule, practice direction or court order.'
3   CPD, s 19.1(1).
4   Ibid, s 19.2(2)(a).
5   Ibid, s 19.2(4).
6   Ibid, s 19. 2(5) which does not require but does recommend pre-issue disclosure.
7   Ibid, s 19.2(3).
8   Ibid, s 19.2(4).
9   See Chapter 8 above.
10   See Appendix 3 below.

Shortfalls

9.20   Where the funder and the client are the same legal entity the recovery of a shortfall in the success fee following an assessment or agreement raises no difficult questions. The CCFA will provide that the funder-client is liable for the success fee. The provisions relating to the disallowance by a court and the acceptance of a lower sum by any settlement are dealt with above. A shortfall will arise outside of those circumstances. The success fee will be paid by the losing party as a multiplier of the assessed base costs which will in most, if not all cases be a lower sum than the own party bases costs. If it is intended that that shortfall should be recoverable by the legal representative the terms of the CCFA must make that clear. Where the funder and client are the same legal entity there is no difficulty. Where, however, the client is not the same legal entity as the funder, the CCFA will only be able to provide for recovery from the funder. Any circumstances in which the client is to be liable for any costs cannot be dealt with by the CCFA because the client here is not a party to the CCFA. There must therefore be a separate funding agreement between the legal representative and the individual for any circumstances in which the individual is to be liable for costs. Work done outside of the terms of a CCFA but without there being an agreement with the individual is likely to prove to be a difficult issue if costs are sought from the individual.

MEMBERSHIP ORGANISATIONS

9.21   The Lord Chancellor's Department issued a Consultation Paper in 1998[1] which encompassed the provision of legal services by membership organisations, such as Trade Unions, to their members as a benefit of membership. The maintenance of legal actions by a trade union has long been recognised as being in the public interest[2]. Such organisations not only funded the action by the member but also indemnified the member against adverse costs. This was recognised as a service which contributed to access to justice but which at the same time was a financial burden on the organisation concerned. It was also recognised that such organisations did not use commercially available insurance products but effectively 'self insured'. With the introduction of recoverable insurance premiums, the question addressed was whether some equivalent recoupment could be established for such organisations. By AJA 1999, s 30 and the Access to Justice (Membership Organisations) Regulations 2000[3] provision is made for the recoupment of a sum no greater than the equivalent of the cost to a member of taking out a personal insurance policy covering adverse costs only. This still leaves to the organisation the administration of the litigation and ensuring that an agreement exists with the member which can give rise to the recoupment of the costs. Trade Unions and other organisations are likely to consider CCFAs rather than the Membership Organisations provisions. A CCFA would mean that the organisation could avoid the costs of administering its own scheme. The organisation would not then be left trying to recoup costs—it could instead transfer that risk to its lawyers who could approach the matter of costs in the usual manner under a CCFA where a success fee can be charged and recovered from the losing opponent. Whether any Membership Organisations will seek to make use of CCFAs rather than s 30 will however depend upon the interpretation which is given to AJA 1999, s 29 dealing with the recovery of insurance premiums, and to the amendments to the CPR to abolish the indemnity principle. A statutory regime which permitted a Membership Organisation to use a CCFA with insurance for adverse costs and own disbursements in the case of failed proceedings, would need to overcome the wording of s 29[4]. The indemnity principle provides further difficulty because the individual member in whose favour a costs order can be made is not a party to the CCFA and will generally be intended to not have a personal liability for any costs.

1   Access to Justice with conditional fees. See also *Conditional Fees: Sharing the Risks of Litigation* (1999) CP7/99.
2   See *Hill v Archbold* [1967] 3 All ER 110 at 112, CA.
3   SI 2000/693. See Appendix 1.
4   See para **9.29** below and Appendix 1.

The statutory requirements

9.22   The Regulations are based upon the individual CFA Regulations. The basis of the recovery of the amount representing the 'self insurance cost' to the organisation is a provision which enables the member to recover such an amount. The Regulations make no requirement that the member be under any liability to account to the organisation for such an amount. Provisions are made for the giving of a written statement to the member of the circumstances in which the member may be liable for costs, but the recovery of the sum intended to reflect the cost to the organisation is a recovery by the member. As to the costs actually incurred by the organisation in 'self insuring', the relevant figure appears to be that at which an individual could have obtained insurance. Had the organisation itself purchased an insurance policy to cover its entire litigation activities on behalf of its members it is likely that the cost would be substantially lower than the cost to an individual member obtaining insurance for his or her own case alone.

9.23   AJA 1999, s 30 provides—

'30—

(1) This section applies where a body of a prescribed description undertakes to meet (in accordance with arrangements satisfying prescribed conditions) liabilities which members of the body or other persons who are parties to proceedings may incur to pay the costs of other parties to the proceedings.
(2) If in any of the proceedings a costs order is made in favour of any of the members or other persons, the costs payable to him may, subject to subsection (3) and (in the case of court proceedings) to rules of court, include an additional amount in respect of any provision made by or on behalf of the body in connection with the proceedings against the risk of having to meet such liabilities.
(3) But the additional amount shall not exceed a sum determined in a prescribed manner; and there may, in particular, be prescribed as a manner of determination one which takes into account the likely cost to the member or other person of the premium of an insurance policy against the risk of incurring a liability to pay the costs of other parties to the proceedings.

(4) In this section "prescribed" means prescribed by regulations made by the Lord Chancellor by statutory instrument; and a statutory instrument containing such regulations shall be subject to annulment in pursuance of a resolution of either House of Parliament.

(5) Regulations under subsection (1) may, in particular, prescribe as a description of body one which is for the time being approved by the Lord Chancellor or by a prescribed person.[1']

Subsection (1) makes it clear that the provision which can lead to the recovery of an additional amount is a provision to meet a member's liability for his opponent's costs, not his own costs[2]. The 'provision' made by the organisation is thus an 'additional liability' which can be claimed by the individual and may be included in a costs order. Section 30(2) can be taken to mean that there has to be evidence of the making of such a provision. The assumption will be made that where a body such as a trade union or motoring organisation is providing an indemnity to its membership for own and opponent's costs (ie costs liability should the case lose), there is a clear provision in the accounts to enable such indemnity to be financed. By subsection (3) the amount claimed cannot exceed the 'likely' cost to an individual in purchasing an insurance policy to provide cover only for opponent's costs. That is more restrictive than the provisions of s 29[3] which permit the recovery by an individual of a premium paid in respect not only of opponent's costs but own disbursements and costs.

1   AJA 1999, s 30.
2   Section 30 refers to 'the costs of other parties'. In the LCD Conclusions paper *Conditional Fees: Sharing the Risks of Litigation* (February 2000), at para 98, it is assumed that AJA 1999, s 30 covers own disbursements. However it seems difficult to read the words of the section to mean this.
3   See Appendix 1.

The Regulations[1]

Body of a prescribed description

9.24   The Regulations make reference to an approval by the Lord Chancellor of the bodies to which s 30 may apply[2]. All Trade Unions listed by the Certification Office for Trade Unions and Employers Organisations[3] are approved together with the following bodies—

The Automobile Association
The Defence Police Federation
The Engineering Employer's federation
The Police Federation of England and Wales
RAC Motoring Services

1   The Access to Justice (Membership Organisations) Regulations 2000 SI 2000/693. See Appendix 1.
2   The Lord Chancellor's Department has issued guidance relating to applications for approval and this provides as follows—
    'In deciding whether an organisation should be approved, the Lord Chancellor would take account of any relevant representations in its application for approval, but would consider, so far as it is relevant, whether the organisation in question:
    • exists to protect, defend, represent and promote the interest of its members;
    • has an exclusive range of benefits for members;

- offers litigation funding as one of those benefits and on a discretionary basis, at no additional charge;
- publishes annual accounts;
- invests its membership payment within the organisation for the benefit of the members and the organisation; and
- covers all those deemed eligible by the organisation (not only members).'

The guidance was published in April 2001.

3   The maintenance of a list of Trade Unions is a power conferred by the Trade Union and Labour Relations (Consolidation) Act 1992.

Requirements for arrangements to meet costs liabilities

9.25   The Regulations lay down requirements concerning the 'arrangements' between the body and the individual, under which the body agrees to meet the individual's liabilities. The arrangements must be in writing and must contain a statement specifying the individual's liability for costs. A copy of that statement must be provided to the individual. The Regulations specify the details in terms similar to the requirements for a CFA.

Regulation 3 provides—

'3 (1)   Section 30(1) of the Access to Justice Act 1999 applies to arrangements which satisfy the following conditions.
(2)   The arrangements must be in writing.
(3)   The arrangements must contain a statement specifying—

  (a)   the circumstances in which the member or other party may be liable to pay costs of the proceedings,
  (b)   whether such a liability arises—

    (i)   if those circumstances only partly occur,
    (ii)   irrespective of whether those circumstances occur, and
    (iii)   on the termination of the arrangements for any reason,

  (c)   the basis on which the amount of the liability is calculated, and
  (d)   the procedure for seeking assessment of costs.

(4)   A copy of the part of the arrangements containing the statement must be given to the member or other party to the proceedings whose liabilities the body is undertaking to meet as soon as possible after the undertaking is given.[1]'

Trade Unions and similar bodies commonly provide, as a benefit to members, legal representation with no liability for costs unless there is fraud or if the member ceases to be a member but continues to receive the legal services. The above provisions suggest that the member has a liability to pay costs on a CFA basis and if that were to be the case the provisions of reg 3 need to be complied with in addition to the CFA Regulations[2]. Where there is no liability on a member to pay costs on a CFA basis, reg 3 must still be complied with. This arrangement therefore is as administratively cumbersome as would be the application of an individual CFA for each case. The advantages of using a CCFA will be lost if it is intended that the prescribed body's provision for a costs liability is to be claimed by the individual. A CCFA is intended to be administratively much simpler than an individual CFA albeit requiring an individual risk assessment to be produced in each case. The requirements for prescribed bodies are not modified by the CCFA Regulations.

1   SI 2000/693, reg 3.
2   See Chapter 8 above.

COMPLYING WITH REGULATION 3

9.26   Until CCFAs are fully operational with the removal of the indemnity principle, it is highly likely that Membership Organisations will continue to provide legal services to members by the use of an indemnity agreement under which the member is indemnified for own and opponents costs and the member's appointed legal representative will not be acting under a CFA. In these circumstances compliance with reg 3 is required but presents problems. The difficulty arises because the wording of reg 3 has been transferred directly from the individual CFA Regulations. Accordingly there is a reference to the circumstances in which fees will be payable and a further reference to the failure in part of those circumstances. Such wording is relevant and meaningful where there is a CFA because there will be circumstances in which fees will be payable and others when fees will not be payable. In most Membership Organisation cases this will not be the case but to obtain an arrangement satisfying s 30 and leading to a recoupment of the provision made for meeting this liability, that arrangement must comply with reg 3. Section 30 and the indemnity principle require that the member has a primary legal liability to pay fees, albeit that there is an arrangement whereby that liability is to be indemnified by the organisation. The arrangement must accordingly make this primary liability clear. It must also make reference to the terms of the indemnity, in particular when the indemnity will not be given, such as for any period in which membership has lapsed. An arrangement which referred only to the primary liability and omitted explanation of the indemnity would be unlikely to satisfy reg 3. It should be borne in mind that Practice Rule 15 and the Client Care Code will require this information to be given in any event. It could be argued that these requirements are unnecessarily cumbersome and of no real benefit to the member who in nearly all circumstances will be indemnified against all costs. However, there will always be circumstances in which such an indemnity will not apply and those circumstances need to be explained.

SUGGESTED WORDINGS TO COMPLY WITH REGULATION 3

9.27

   (i)   You [the member] are ultimately responsible for paying the fees and disbursements of your legal representative, whether you win your case or not. If you win you are entitled to seek recovery of your costs from your opponent. Your legal representative's own costs are calculated as follows: [insert charging rate(s) of the legal representative who will act for the member].

   (ii)   If you lose you are ultimately responsible for paying the fees and disbursements of your opponent, in addition to your own costs.

(iii)   The [Name of membership organisation] has agreed to indemnify you for the liability for costs mentioned in (i) and (ii) above.

(iv)   This arrangement between you and [name of membership organisation] may be ended by [set out any terms in the Membership organisation's rules under which it or the member can terminate the indemnity arrangement].

(v)   If this arrangement is ended you will be ultimately liable for all the costs referred to in (i) and (ii) above but you will not be entitled to an indemnity for that liability from the [name of membership organisation].

(vi)   You are entitled to apply to the court for a detailed assessment of the costs of your legal representative which means that the court will check the bill. There are strict time limits for doing this. If you apply to the court within one month of receiving the bill the court will order that the bill be assessed. If you apply after that time but within 12 months of receiving the bill the court may, but does not have to, order an assessment. If 12 months have passed since you received the bill, or you have paid the bill and 12 months have not passed since you paid it, you will have to show special circumstances to the court if it is to order an assessment. If 12 months have passed since you have paid the bill you cannot obtain an assessment. An application for an assessment and the assessment itself can be an expensive process if you lose.

There has here been no attempt to incorporate the language of the regulation. The wording of the Regulation is inappropriate for a non-CFA funded case, particularly reg 3(3)(b)(ii) and (iii)—clearly the member's primary liability will not differ according to circumstances in a non CFA funded case.

9.28   Recovery of additional amount for insurance costs. Regulation 4 provides—

'4 (1) Where an additional amount is included in costs by virtue of section 30(2) of the Access to Justice Act 1999 (costs payable to a member of a body or other person party to the proceedings to include an additional amount in respect of provision made by the body against the risk of having to meet the member's or other person's liabilities to pay other parties' costs), that additional amount must not exceed the following sum.

(2)   That sum is the likely cost to the member of the body or, as the case may be, the other person who is a party to the proceedings in which the costs order is made of the premium of an insurance policy against the risk of incurring a liability to pay the costs of other parties to the proceedings.[1]'

This is to operate as an upper limit and no guidance is provided as to how the actual sum is to be calculated. Given the considerable variety of policies available in the commercial insurance market and the variation in premiums, the use of this hypothetical as a measure of the recoverable sum is unlikely to be helpful[2].

1   SI 2000/693, reg 4.

2 In the LCD Consultation Paper *Conditional Fees: Sharing the Risks of Litigation* (September 1999), concern was expressed that the paying party should not be faced with a liability to pay a sum greater than the costs of a commercial insurance policy. It was suggested that indeed the recoverable sum should be less than such a premium since the latter includes a profit element not taken by a membership organisation. The final wording does not provide for such a deduction which in any event would have been a meaningless provision given no benchmark premium can be established.

Application of section 29 of the Access to Justice Act to Membership Organisations

9.29 Section 29[1] provides for a costs order to include the premium of an insurance policy but it refers only to such a policy taken out by a 'party'. A Membership Organisation which uses a CCFA will not be a party in whose favour a costs order can be made. Such an organisation can only recover the costs of insurance by the indirect method of the Membership Organisation Regulations discussed above. Alternatively, the Membership Organisation can fund the individual member to purchase an insurance policy and then the member can seek to recover that cost under s 29. Given that the basis of the CCFA is that the membership organisation is the funder of the litigation and as such has a direct liability for adverse costs, the body will be seeking to insure its liability as well as any potential liability of the individual. Whether such a policy would be recognised as being within s 29 is unclear[2]. The administrative costs of operating such a method may well also be unattractive. It is difficult to argue that once s 31 is commenced the cost of a policy providing cover for the Membership Organisation and the member can be recovered in costs without the need for s 29. Section 29 clearly is the provision enabling an insurance premium to be included in a costs order. Section 31 would enable the recovery of a premium even though the party was not liable to pay it but that cannot address the problem that the premium recoverable under s 29 does not seemingly extend to a policy covering a Membership Organisation's liability.

1 Section 29 is reproduced at Appendix 1.
2 See further Part 7, in particular, Chapter 17.

Illustration of a typical membership organisation arrangement using a CCFA

9.30

In the illustration below it has been assumed that the policy of insurance (however funded) provides cover for both the individual (who as a party to the proceedings has a costs liability) and the union (which as a funder has a costs liability). That policy may cover own disbursements as well as adverse costs. Section 29 permits the member to claim the cost of the policy against the risk of incurring a liability, wording which does not fit well with a policy giving cover to a non-party.

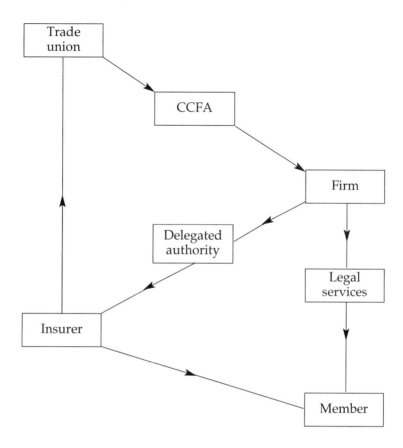

Disclosure of the existence of a section 30 arrangement

9.31   A s 30 arrangement is a 'funding arrangement' within the meaning of CPR, r 43.2(1)[1]. It follows that the rules concerning the disclosure of funding arrangements apply to s 30 arrangements[2]. The Practice Direction about Costs requires disclosure of the existence of a s 30 agreement but not its terms[3]. Notice must be given at the time of issue of a claim form if the s 30 agreement is already in place[4]. Where a s 30 agreement is made after the issue of proceedings notice must be given within seven days of the making of the agreement[5]. There is no requirement for pre-issue disclosure[6]. The Personal Injury Protocol does provide for pre-issue disclosure. Where the s 30 agreement relates to a defendant, notice of it must be given when filing the first document[7]. Section 30 agreements made after the serving of the first document must be notified within seven days of the making of the agreement[8]. All of these provisions are identical to those applying to individual CFAs[9]. Form N251 may be used for the giving of this information[10].

1   CPR, r 43.2(1) provides—
     'In Parts 44 to 48, unless the context otherwise requires "funding arrangement" means an arrangement where a person has—(iii) made an agreement with a membership organisation to meet his legal costs;'.
2   CPR, r 44.15(1) provides—
     'A party who seeks to recover an additional liability must provide information about the funding arrangement to the court and to other parties as required by a rule, practice direction or court order.'
3   CPD, s 19.1(1).
4   Ibid, s 19.2(2)(a).
5   Ibid, s 19.2(4).
6   Ibid, s 19. 2(5) which does not require but does recommend pre-issue disclosure.
7   Ibid, s 19.2(3).
8   Ibid, s 19.2(4).
9   See Chapter 8 above.
10 See Appendix 3.

LITIGATION FUNDING AGREEMENTS

9.32   AJA 1999, s 28 makes detailed provision for such agreements which are intended to enable greater access to justice along lines similar to those provided by membership organisations and similar to proposals by Justice, the Law Society and the Bar for a CLAF[1]. This section has not been commenced. Essentially the section provides for a funder to pay for legal services provided by someone other than the funder, to an individual. That individual, if their case is successful, would pay their recovered costs to the funder together with a success fee which would also be recovered form the losing opponent. The intention here is that such payments will produce a fund from which other cases can be funded.

1   Contingency Legal Aid Fund—this is dealt with in Chapter 3.

Part 3

Conditional Fee Agreements made before
1 April 2000

Chapter 10

The Statutory Regime

INTRODUCTION

10.1 Conditional Fee Agreements (CFAs) were introduced to the English legal system, as a recognised and lawful method of funding litigation, by the Courts and Legal Services Act 1990 (CLSA 1990). Informal (or even formal) agreements before then, under which the client understood that (usually for reasons of impecuniosity) they would not pay their lawyer unless the case succeeded, were unlawful maintenance[1]. The 1990 Act was brought into force in 1993[2] but the necessary Regulations and Order were not brought into effect until 1995[3]. The 1995 Order was replaced by the 1998 Order[4]. This chapter deals with the statutory provisions from 1995 to 1 April 2000 when major changes to the rules were made[5]. Any CFA made between 1995 and 1 April 2000 must comply with the statutory regime as it applied when the CFA was made. If the CFA was altered during that period then the statutory regime applicable at the date of amendment will apply. If the CFA is amended after 1 April 2000, the statutory regime applicable is covered in Chapter 8 but it must be noted that such an amendment will not attract the benefits of that statutory regime[6]. Similarly, if a pre-1 April 2000 CFA is wholly replaced with a post 31 March 2000 CFA, the benefits of the statutory regime applicable from 1 April 2000 cannot be gained[6].

1 See Chapter 1.
2 Courts and Legal Services Act 1990 (Commencement No 9) Order 1993, SI 1993/2132.
3 The Conditional Fee Agreements Regulations 1995, SI 1995/1675 and the Conditional Fee Agreements Order 1995, SI 1995/1674 both came into force on 5 July 1995.
4 Conditional Fee Agreements Order 1998, SI 1998/1860 which came into force on 30 July 1998.
5 See Chapter 8.
6 The Access to Justice Act 1999 (Transitional Provisions) Order 2000, SI 2000/900 which came into force 1 April 2000. See Appendix 2. The Practice Direction about Costs (CPD) reiterates the position at s 57.8(2)—
   'The Access to Justice Act 1999 (Transitional Provisions) Order 2000 provides that no conditional fee agreement or other arrangement about costs entered into before 1 April 2000 can be a funding arrangement, as defined in rule 43.2 The order also has the effect that where an conditional fee agreement or other funding arrangement has been entered into before 1 April 2000 and a second or subsequent funding arrangement is entered into on or after 1 April 2000, the second or subsequent funding arrangement does not give rise to an additional liability which is recoverable from a paying party.'

STATUTORY DEFINITION

10.2 CLSA 1990, s 58 (as originally enacted) provides—

'(1) In this section "a conditional fee agreement" means an agreement in writing between a person providing advocacy and litigation services and his client which—

(a) does not relate to proceedings of a kind mentioned in subsection (10)[1];
(b) provides for that person's fees and expenses, or any part of them, to be payable only in specified circumstances;
(c) complies with such requirements (if any) as may be prescribed by the Lord Chancellor[2]; and
(d) is not a contentious business agreement (as defined by section 59 of the Solicitors Act 1974).[3]'

In essence, therefore, a CFA was an agreement under which the fees would be paid in some circumstances (typically described as a success) and not in others. A CFA could provide that only part of the fees were dependent upon circumstances. The statute went on to provide that a CFA complying with the statute was not unenforceable by reason only of its being a CFA[4]. The detail for the contents of a statutory CFA were to be provided in Regulations[5]. The 'specified proceedings' to which a CFA could lawfully relate under the statute were to be defined in an Order[6].

1 Criminal proceedings and family proceedings under the Matrimonial Causes Act 1973; Domestic Violence and Matrimonial Proceedings Act 1976; Adoption Act 1976 and Domestic Proceedings and Magistrates' Courts Act 1978.
2 The Conditional Fee Agreements Regulations 1995, SI 1995/1675.
3 The 1990 Act did not seek to provide an exclusive regime for CFAs. A contentious business agreement which was also a CFA (ie it provided for payment of fees only in certain circumstances) and which satisfied the provisions of the Solicitor's Act 1974, s 59, was a lawful agreement without complying with s 58.
4 CLSA 1990, s 58(3).
5 Conditional Fee Agreements Regulations 1995, SI 1995/1675. See Appendix 2.
6 Conditional Fee Agreements Order 1995, SI 1995/1674. See Appendix 2.

RELATIONSHIP OF STATUTE WITH THE COMMON LAW

10.3 A CFA authorised by the statute was a statutory exception to the common law doctrine of Maintenance and Champerty[1]. The statute was effectively in force when the Regulations detailing the contents of a CFA and the Order detailing the proceedings to which it could relate, were brought into force in 1995[2]. The Court of Appeal was very soon faced with a CFA which not only failed to comply with the requirements as to form and content but also related to proceedings of a type not included in the 1995 Order[3]. The decision in *Thai Trading v Taylor* was, however, doubted by the High Court[4] and then by a differently constituted Court of Appeal[5]. Agreements or 'understandings' made on the basis of *Thai Trading* are at best questionable and at worst wholly unenforceable.

1 See Chapter 1 above.
2 Conditional Fee Agreements Regulations 1995, SI 1995/1675 and the Conditional Fee Agreements Order 1995, SI 1995/1674.
3 *Thai Trading Co v Taylor* [1998] 3 All ER 65—see above Chapter 1.
4 *Hughes v Kingston upon Hull City Council* [1999] 2 All ER 49.
5 *Awwad v Geraghty* [2000] 1 All ER 608.

LAW SOCIETY PRACTICE RULE 8

10.4 [From 5 July 1995—ie when the CFA Order came into force].

'(1) A solicitor who is retained or employed to prosecute or defend any action, suit or other contentious proceeding shall not enter into any arrangement to receive a contingency fee[1] in respect of that proceeding.

(1A) Paragraph (1) of this rule shall not apply to a conditional fee agreement relating to specified proceedings as defined in s 58 of the Courts and Legal Services Act 1990, provided the agreement complies with all the requirements of that section and any order made thereunder.'

[From 7 January 1999]

'(1) A solicitor who is retained or employed to prosecute or defend any action, suit or other contentious proceeding shall not enter into any arrangement to receive a contingency fee[1] in respect of that proceeding, save one permitted under statute or by the common law.[2]'

1 'Contingency fee' is defined in rule 18(2)(c) as 'any sum (whether fixed, or calculated either as a percentage of the proceeds or otherwise howsoever) payable only in the event of success in the prosecution or defence of any action, suit or other contentious proceeding'.
2 This amendment was in response to the Court of Appeal's decision in *Thai Trading Co v Taylor* [1998] 3 All ER 65 which has since been doubted—see Chapter 1.

MEANING OF PROCEEDINGS

10.5 CLSA 1990, s 58(3) provides—

'(3) Subject to subsection (6)[1], a conditional fee agreement which relates to specified proceedings[2] shall not be unenforceable by reason only of its being a conditional fee agreement'.

The statute permitted CFAs which related to the type of proceedings defined in the 1995 Order and which therefore related to 'proceedings'. CLSA 1990, s 119 defines 'proceedings' as 'proceedings in any court'. It was held in *Bevan Ashford (a firm) v Geoff Yeandle*[3] that arbitration proceedings constituted litigation but were clearly not within the statutory definition of proceedings. A fee agreement in arbitration proceedings, where payment of the fees or expenses or part of them depended on certain circumstances, was held to be lawful notwithstanding that the 1990 Act did not validate them[4].

1 CLSA 1990, s 58(6) renders unlawful any CFA where the success fee exceeds the maximum permitted percentage. That maximum was set at 100% by the CFA Order 1995, SI 1995/1674, art 3.
2 See below para **10.6**.
3 [1998] 3 All ER 238.
4 See Chapter 1. The decision in *Bevan Ashford v Geoff Yeandle* (see above), has not been doubted although it purported to rely on *Thai Trading Co v Taylor* [1998] 3 All ER 65, which has since been doubted. The decision in *Bevan Ashford* proceeds on the basis that it would be absurd for an agreement which complied with the requirements of the 1990 Act and would thus be valid in court proceedings were held to be invalid in arbitration proceedings. To reach that conclusion however, the court relied upon *Thai Trading* as authority for the validity of any CFA outside the statute. To this extent therefore, *Bevan Ashford* is doubtful authority itself.

SPECIFIED PROCEEDINGS

10.6 Section 58(3) (above) permits CFAs which relate to 'specified proceedings'. The 1995 Order[1] specified the proceedings for this purpose as being personal injury cases, certain insolvency proceedings and proceedings under the European Convention on Human Rights. Those categories could not constitute specified proceedings if the client had legal aid[2]. The Order came into force on 5 July 1995. A CFA relating to any other proceedings was not validated by s 58[3]. Proceedings remained specified for these purposes notwithstanding that they were concluded without the commencement of court proceedings[4].

1 SI 1995/1674. See Appendix 2.
2 Ibid, art 2(1). If legal aid was granted after the making of a CFA the proceedings ceased to be 'specified proceedings' from the date of the grant—art 4.
3 *Thai Trading v Taylor*, supra. In *Bevan Ashford v Geoff Yeandle*, supra, the arbitration proceedings fell into the insolvency provisions of the 1995 Order but not into the statutory definition of 'proceedings'.
4 SI 1995/1674, art 2(2).

10.7 The Conditional Fee Agreements Order 1998[1] came into force on 30 July 1998 and extended the definition of specified proceedings for the purposes of CLSA 1990, s 58(3). From this date all proceedings were specified proceedings. This provision must however be read in conjunction with s 58(10) which excludes all criminal proceedings and family proceedings from the statutory scheme without reference to the Order. The maximum permitted percentage increase (success fee) remained at 100%[2].

1 SI 1998/1860. See Appendix 2.
2 Ibid, art 4.

SUCCESS FEES

10.8 CLSA 1990, s 58[1] does not use the phrase 'success fee' but does refer to a 'percentage increase'. Section 58(2) requires a CFA which provides for the amount of fees to be increased, in specified circumstances, above the amount which would be payable if it were not a CFA, to specify the percentage by which that amount is to be increased. This percentage increase became known as the success fee. By the 1995 Order that percentage increase cannot exceed 100%[2]. The Law Society Model CFA for use in Personal Injury (non-clinical negligence) cases incorporated a 'cap' whereby the success fee could not exceed 25% of the damages[3].

1 As originally worded. The phrase 'success fee' was introduced in the substituted wording to s 58 which applies from 1 April 2000. See Chapter 8.
2 SI 1995/1674, art 3.
3 Research by the Policy Studies Institute (Yarrow *The Price of Success* (1997)) found that the Model was used almost universally as was the cap. Nonetheless, the cap was a voluntary contractual term and could be omitted altogether or be applied at a different percentage.

THE REGULATIONS

10.9 The 1995 Regulations[1] lay down the conditions which must be satisfied if a CFA is to be within the statutory scheme[2]. The CFA must be in writing and must (if it is a CFA between a client and a legal representative) be signed by the client and the legal representative[3]. The requirements of an agreement are set out in reg 3—

3 'An agreement shall state—

(a) the particular proceedings or parts of them to which it relates (including whether it relates to any counterclaim, appeal or proceedings to enforce a judgment or order);

(b) the circumstances in which the legal representative's fees and expenses or part of them are payable;

(c) what, if any, payment is due—

(i) upon partial failure of the specified circumstances to occur;
(ii) irrespective of the specified circumstances occurring; and
(iii) upon termination of the agreement for any reason

(d) the amount payable in accordance with sub-paragraphs (b) or (c) above or the method to be used to calculate the amount payable; and in particular whether or not the amount payable is limited by reference to the amount of any damages which may be recovered on behalf of the client.'

Sub-paragraph (c)(i) assumes that although, in accordance with sub-paragraph (b), the CFA states the circumstances in which specific fees are due (eg that a success fee is payable if damages are awarded), there is a need to state what happens if those circumstances occur in part only. The Law Society Model does not make specific provision for such partial failure.

1 SI 1995/1675.
2 Ibid, reg 2 provides that unless an agreement complies with the regulations it is not a CFA.
3 Ibid, reg 6.

10.10 Additional requirements are laid down as to the giving of information to the client in reg 4—

4 '(1) The agreement shall also state that, immediately before it was entered into, the legal representative drew the client's attention to the matters specified in paragraph (2).

(2) The matters are—

(a) whether the client might be entitled to legal aid in respect of the proceedings to which the agreement relates, the conditions upon which legal aid is available and the application of those conditions to the client in respect of the proceedings;

(b) the circumstances in which the client may be liable to pay the fees and expenses of the legal representative in accordance with the agreement;

(c) the circumstances in which the client may be liable to pay the costs of any other party to the proceedings; and

(d) the circumstances in which the client may seek taxation of the fees and expenses of the legal representative and the procedure for so doing.'

These additional requirements are not applicable to a CFA made between one legal representative and an additional legal representative[1]. If a CFA is extended to cover further proceedings or parts of them then the requirements of regs 3 to 6 apply to the CFA as extended[2].

1   SI 1995/1675, reg 5.
2   Ibid, reg 7.

THE CLIENT'S RIGHT TO CHALLENGE THE SUCCESS FEE

10.11   Civil Procedure Rules 1998 (CPR), r 48.9 was amended by the Civil Procedure (Amendment No 3) Rules 2000[1] with effect from 3 July 2000, and governed the assessment of a success fee in a CFA which was entered into before 1 April 2000. That rule has now been removed and an amendment made to CPR, r 48.8 which now governs the assessment of success fees in all cases whenever the CFA was made.

1   SI 2000/1317.

10.12   CPR, r 48.8—

'(3)   Where the court is considering a percentage increase, whether on the application of the legal representative under rule 44.16 [application by solicitor where success fee disallowed] or on the application of the client, the court will have regard to all the relevant factors as they reasonably appeared to the solicitor or counsel when the conditional fee agreement was entered into or varied.'

The client can therefore challenge the success fee by an assessment under this rule. As to the factors which the court may take into account, the CPD reproduces the list originally contained in the RSC[1], which is not intended to be an exhaustive list of the factors. The CPD is to be amended to reflect the new CPR, r 48.8[2]. The rule refers to the test as being based upon the factors as they reasonably appeared to the solicitor or counsel when the CFA was entered into[3] (no reference is here made to any amendment to the success fee at a later date).

1   RSC Ord 62, r 15A which also applied to the County Court by virtue of CCR Ord 38, r 21(4A).
2   The CPD was not amended at the same time that CPR, r 48.9 was removed. For the factors listed in CPD, s 55.3 see para **10.13** below. CPD, s 55.2 requires the client to state the reasons for reducing the percentage increase and to state what the percentage increase should be. CPD, s 55.1 referring to CPR, r 48.9 in its July 2000 form, refers to CPR, r 48.8(2) in relation to a client's application to have base costs assessed.
CPD, s 55.1—
  '(1) Attention is drawn to rule 48.9(1) as amended by the Civil Procedure (Amendment No 3) Rules 2000 (SI 2000/1317) with effect from 3 July 2000. Rule 48.9 applies only where the solicitor and the client have entered into a conditional fee agreement as defined in section 58 of the Courts and Legal Services Act 1990 as it was in force before 1 April 2000. A client who has entered into a conditional fee agreement with a solicitor may apply for assessment of the base costs (which is carried out in accordance with rule 48.8(2) as if there were no conditional fee agreement) or for assessment of the percentage increase (success fee) or both.
  (2) Where the court is to assess the percentage increase the court will have regard to all the relevant factors as they appeared to the solicitor or counsel when the conditional fee agreement was entered into.'
3   CPD, ss 55.1(2) and 55.4 reiterate that requirement.

The Practice Direction

10.13 Client's application—

CPD, s 55.2—

'Where the client applies to the court to reduce the percentage increase which the solicitor has charged the client under the conditional fee agreement, the client must set out in his application notice:

(a) the reasons why the percentage increase should be reduced; and

(b) what the percentage increase should be.'

Relevant factors—

CPD, s 55.3—

'The factors relevant to assessing the percentage increase include—

(a) the risk that the circumstances in which the fees or expenses would be payable might not occur;

(b) the disadvantages relating to the absence of payment on account;

(c) whether the amount which might be payable under the conditional fee agreement is limited to a certain proportion of any damages recovered by the client;

(d) whether there is a conditional fee agreement between the solicitor and counsel;

(e) the solicitor's liability for any disbursements.'

It may be that some CFAs have been entered into between 1995 and 1 April 2000 without a written risk assessment to address the risk of not being paid. It is also possible that some CFAs applied a blanket 100% success fee (with or without also applying a cap). An assessment will have to take account of these factors at the same time avoiding the use of hindsight.

Part 4

Conditional Fee Agreements made between 1 April and 3 July 2000

Chapter 11

The Transitional Provisions

THE STATUTORY PROVISIONS

11.1 The relevant sections of the Access to Justice Act 1999 (AJA 1999) relating to CFAs and to after the event insurance were brought into force on 1 April 2000[1]. There was at that time considerable concern that in the absence of the accompanying amendments to the Civil Procedure Rules 1998 (CPR) and a new Practice Direction about Costs (CPD), it was unwise to enter into a CFA or advise that a client purchase an after the event insurance policy, although the statute was now in force[2]. Where, however, it became necessary, usually because of limitation periods, to issue proceedings between 1 April and 3 July 2000, it is likely that advice to clients was couched in terms that there was an expectation that success fees and insurance premiums would be recovered from a losing opponent but that the law was as yet unclear.

1   Access to Justice Act 1999 (Commencement No 3, Transitional Provisions and Savings) Order 2000, SI 2000/774 bringing into force AJA 1999, ss 27 and 29. The text of ss 27 and 29 is given at Appendix 1.
2   The Law Society produced a 'running repair' version of its model CFA for use in personal injury cases from 1 April 2000.

11.2 Section 27 of the Access to Justice Act 1999 inserts a new s 58[1] into the Courts and Legal Services Act 1990 (CLSA 1990) from 1 April 2000. Any CFA made on or after that date must comply with the substituted s 58. A major significance of an agreement falling into the statutory definition of a CFA is provided for in CLSA 1990, s 58(1) as substituted by AJA 1999, s 27—

> 'A conditional fee agreement which satisfies all of the conditions applicable to it by virtue of this section shall not be unenforceable by reason only of its being a conditional fee agreement; but (subject to subsection (5))[2] any other conditional fee agreement shall be unenforceable.[3]'

Any funding arrangement made on or after 1 April 2000, which falls into the statutory definition of a conditional fee agreement[4] is unenforceable unless it complies with the statutory scheme. Thus whatever the standing of the case law on the legality of such agreements at common law[5], from 1 April 2000 the only permissible CFA is one which is made in accordance with the statutory scheme.

1   See Appendix 1.
2   Subsection (5) refers to the Solicitors Act 1974, s 57 dealing with non-contentious business agreements. Such an agreement which is also a CFA is not made unenforceable by s 58(1). A

contentious business agreement under s 59 of the 1974 Act, which is also a CFA must comply with s 58 of the CLSA 1990.
3   CLSA 1990, s 58(1).
4   See Chapter 13 below.
5   *Thai Trading Co v Taylor* [1998] 3 All ER 65 was doubted in *Awwad v Geraghty & Co* [2000] 1 All ER 608—see Chapter 1.

11.3   The changes brought about by AJA 1999 include the recoverability of the success fee and insurance premium from a losing opponent. Section 27 inserts s 58A into the CLSA 1990 and makes provision with respect to the recoverability of the success fee by providing for the making of a costs order to include the success fee—

'A costs order made in any proceedings may, subject in the case of court proceedings to rules of court, include provision requiring the payment of any fees payable under a conditional fee agreement which provides for a success fee'[1].

1   CLSA 1990, s 58A(6).

11.4   Section 29 of the AJA 1999 provides for the recoverability of an insurance premium. That section does not use the mechanism of inserting a provision into the CLSA 1990.

'Where in any proceedings a costs order is made in favour of any party who has taken out an insurance policy against the risk of incurring a liability in those proceedings, the costs payable to him may, subject in the case of court proceedings to rules of court, include costs in respect of the premium of the policy.'[1]

1   AJA 1999, s 29.

11.5   The transitional position for the application of ss 27 and 29 of the AJA 1999 are dealt with by the Access to Justice Act 1999 (Transitional Provisions) Order 2000.

11.6   The Order preserves the validity of CFAs made before 1 April 2000 by the following provision—

'(2) The coming into force of section 27 (Conditional fee agreements) shall not affect the validity of any conditional fee agreement entered into before 1st April 2000, and any such agreement shall continue to have effect after that date as if section 27 had not come into force.'[1]

1   SI 2000/900, art 2(2).

11.7   Although the substituted statutory regime must be complied with when a CFA is made after 1 April 2000, the provisions relating to the recovery of success fees from an opponent do not, by virtue of art 2 of the Order, apply where there was a CFA in place before 1 April—

'(1) Section 58A(6) and (7) of the Courts and Legal Services Act 1990 shall not apply, as regards a party to proceedings, to:

(a) any proceedings in relation to which that party entered into a conditional fee agreement before 1st April 2000; or

(b)   any proceedings arising out of the same cause of action as any proceedings to which sub-paragraph (a) refers.[1]'

1   SI 2000/900, art 2(1).

11.8   Thus terminating a pre-April CFA and replacing it with a post-April CFA would mean that the requirements of the substituted statute had to be complied with but the benefits of it would not apply.

11.9   A similar result applies to an insurance policy taken out after 1 April 2000 where there was already in place a policy taken out before April—

'Section 29 (Recovery of insurance premiums by way of costs) shall not apply, as regards a party to proceedings, to:

(a)   any proceedings in relation to which that party took out an insurance policy of the sort referred to in section 29 before 1st April 2000; or
(b)   any proceedings arising out of the same cause of action as any proceedings to which sub-paragraph (a) refers.[1]'

1   SI 2000/900, art 3.

THE CPR AND THE PRACTICE DIRECTION ABOUT COSTS

11.10   The recovery of a success fee and an insurance premium is subject to the Rules of Court. The CPR were amended by Statutory Instrument, and a Practice Direction about Costs was issued in July 2000. For the transitional period of 1 April to 3 July 2000, there are complex provisions which seek to restrict the applicability of the new statutory regime. The changes to the CPR came into effect on 3 July 2000 with provisions applying to the period from 1 April to 3 July 2000.

Civil Procedure (Amendment No 3) Rules 2000[1]

11.11

'r 39(1) This rule applies where a person has—

(a)   entered into a funding arrangement, and
(b)   started proceedings in respect of a claim the subject of that funding arrangement, before the date on which these Rules come into force.[2]'

The transitional provisions of r 39 seemingly apply only where proceedings have been issued before 3 July 2000. Sub-paragraph (b) seems to have the effect of applying r 39 only to claimants since a defendant cannot be a person who has started proceedings. There is no obvious reason why a defendant who has entered into a funding arrangement between 31 March and 3 July 2000 should be in a different position to a claimant but that appears to be the effect of r 39. It is clear that if a person has entered into a funding arrangement before 3 July but has not issued proceedings before that date then r 39 does not apply.

11.11 *Part 4   CFAs made between 1 April and 3 July 2000*

1   SI 2000/1317, made 12 May 2000. Laid before Parliament 15 May 2000. Coming into force
    3 July 2000.
2   SI 2000/1317, r 39(1).

11.12

'(2) Any requirement imposed—

(a) by any provision of the Civil Procedure Rules 1998 amended by these
     Rules, or
(b) by a practice direction

in respect of that funding arrangement may be complied with within
28 days of the coming into force of these Rules, and that compliance
shall be treated as compliance with the relevant rule or practice
direction'[1].

The time limits applicable to the provisions of the CPR relating to the giving
of notice are disapplied and replaced with a period of 28 days from 3 July, ie
31 July 2000. The requirements for disclosure are contained in CPR, r 44.15
and CPD, s 19[2]. There are no requirements relating to pre-issue disclosure
but such is recommended in the CPD[3] and the Personal Injury Protocol. The
CPD uses the phrase 'funding arrangement' which refers both to a CFA with
success fee and to an insurance policy[4]. Where more than one such
arrangement has been made in respect of a case a single notice can provide
the information relating to each arrangement[5].

1   SI 2000/1317, r 39(2).
2   In force, 3 July 2000.
3   CPD, s 19.2(5).
4   CPR , r 43.2(k)—

    '"funding arrangement" means an arrangement where a person has—

        (i)   entered into a conditional fee agreement or a collective conditional fee agreement
              which provides for a success fee within the meaning of section 58(2) of the Courts
              and Legal Services Act 1990;
        (ii) taken out an insurance policy to which section 29 of the Access to Justice Act 1999
              (recovery of insurance premiums by way of costs) applies; or
        (iii) made an agreement with a membership organisation to meet his legal
              costs;'.

5   CPD, s 19.4(5).

Notice requirement where a Claimant's funding arrangement is in place before issue

11.13 Notice of the funding arrangement was to be given to the court
when issuing the claim form[1]. Form N251[2] sets out the details required.
Sufficient copies of Form N251 were to be provided to the court for service
on all other parties. If the claimant served the claim form in person then
Form N251 was to be served at the same time. Thus a funding arrangement
entered into after 31 March and before 3 July 2000 had to be disclosed by
31 July if proceedings were issued before 3 July. For proceedings issued
after 3 July 2000 notice of the funding arrangement must be given at the
time of issuing proceedings.

1   'Claim form' includes petition and application notice. CPD, s 19.2(1).

130

2   A copy of N251 is contained in Appendix 3.

Notice requirement where a Defendant's funding arrangement is in place before filing a document

11.14   Here the wording of SI 2000/1317, r 39 means that the normal rules on the giving of notice will apply. Thus notice to the court must be given when filing the first document[1]. Sufficient copies of the notice were to be provided to the court for service on all other parties. If the defendant served the first document in person then notice of the funding arrangement was to be served at the same time. The 28 days provided to claimants does not apply.

1   CPD, s 19.2(3). First document includes an acknowledgement of service, a defence, application to set aside default judgment or any other document. See CPD, s 19.2(3)(a).

Notice where a Claimant's funding arrangement is made after issue

11.15   Where both the making of the funding arrangement and the issue of proceedings occurred before 3 July 2000, notice of the funding arrangement had to be given by 31 July[1].

1   CPD, s 19.2(4) subject to SI 2000/1317, r 39.

Notice where the Defendant's funding arrangement is made after filing first document

11.16   Notice of the funding arrangement made before 3 July 2000 had to be given within seven days[1].

1   CPD, s 19.2(4).

The information which must be disclosed

11.17   The information required to be disclosed is set out in CPD, s 19.4. No information need be given of a CFA which does not provide for a success fee. Where the CFA does provide for a success fee then the notice must state that such a CFA has been entered into, the date of the CFA and the identity of the claim or claims to which it relates (including Part 20 claims if any). This provides very little information to the other side and in particular the level of the success fee does not have to be disclosed thus ensuring that the perceived strength of the case is not revealed. As to insurance policies, notice must be given of the name of the insurer, the date of the policy and the identity of the claim or claims to which it relates (including Part 20 claims if any).

Retrospective funding arrangements

11.18   The Practice Direction about Costs makes a special provision in the Transitional Arrangements which restricts costs orders to costs in relation to things done and costs incurred after the funding arrangement was made—

'(3)   Nothing in the legislation referred to above makes provision for a party who has entered into a funding arrangement to recover from another party any amount of an additional liability which relates to anything done or any costs incurred before the arrangement was entered into.[1]'

The legislation referred to includes ss 28 to 31 of the AJA 1999 which are the provisions dealing with the recovery of success fees and insurance premiums. The result of this transitional provision is that the success fee to be recovered from the losing party can only apply to costs relating to the period after the CFA was made in cases where the CFA itself provides for its application to work done before it was made. The resulting shortfall is recoverable from the client subject to challenge on assessment. It is submitted that the provisions relating to disallowed additional liabilities do not apply to this situation since it is not a disallowance by a court on assessment which is being sought to be recovered from the client[2]. CPD, s 57.9(3) also applies to an insurance policy and would seem to require an apportionment to be made in terms of the premium relating to that part of the costs incurred before the policy was purchased. The simplest method for this is to deduct pre-policy costs as a percentage of total costs and to allow the remaining percentage of the premium to be recovered. The rationale appears to be that there should be no retrospective liability in the transitional period. If, however, proceedings were not issued until after 3 July 2000, this prevention of retrospective liability does not apply.

1 CPD, s 57.9(3).
2 The relevant provisions are contained in CPD, s 20 and clearly envisage a power to disallow an amount of the percentage increase. In the case of the transitional provision in CPD, s 57.9(3) the court has no power to order the losing party to pay that part of the success fee relating to work done or costs incurred before the CFA was made and no question arises as to it being 'disallowed'.

THE RELEVANT EXTRACTS FROM THE CPR AND PRACTICE DIRECTION

11.19 CPR, r 44.15—

'(1) A party who seeks to recover an additional liability must provide information about the funding arrangement to the court and to other parties as required by a rule, practice direction or court order.

(2) Where the funding arrangement has changed, and the information a party has previously provided in accordance with paragraph (1) is no longer accurate, that party must file notice of the change and serve it on all other parties within 7 days.

(3) Where paragraph (2) applies, and a party has already filed—(a) an allocation questionnaire; or (b) a listing questionnaire,

he must file and serve a new estimate of costs with the notice.

(The costs practice direction sets out—

— the information to be provided when a party issues or responds to a claim form, files an allocation questionnaire, a listing questionnaire, and a claim for costs;
— the meaning of estimate of costs and the information required in it) (Rule 44.3B sets out situations where a party will not recover a sum representing any additional liability).'

11.20 CPD, s 57—

(Transitional Provisions)

'57.8—

(1) Sections 28 to 31 of the Access to Justice Act 1999, the Conditional Fee Agreements Regulations 2000, the Access to Justice (Membership Organisations) Regulations 2000, and the Access to Justice Act 1999 (Transitional Provisions) Order 2000 came into force on 1 April 2000. The Civil Procedure (Amendment No 3) Rules come into force on 3 July 2000.

(2) The Access to Justice Act 1999 (Transitional Provisions) Order 2000 provides that no conditional fee agreement or other arrangement about costs entered into before 1 April 2000 can be a funding arrangement, as defined in rule 43.2 The order also has the effect that where an conditional fee agreement or other funding arrangement has been entered into before 1 April 2000 and a second or subsequent funding arrangement is entered into on or after 1 April 2000, the second or subsequent funding arrangement does not give rise to an additional liability which is recoverable from a paying party.

57.9—

(1) Rule 39 of the Civil Procedure (Amendment No 3) Rules 2000 applies where between 1 April and 2 July 2000 (including both dates)—

a funding arrangement is entered into, and

proceedings are started in respect of a claim which is the subject of that agreement.

(2) Attention is drawn to the need to act promptly so as to comply with the requirements of the Rules and the Practice Directions by 31 July 2000 (ie within the28 days from 3 July 2000 permitted by Rule 39) if that compliance is to be treated as compliance with the relevant provision. Attention is drawn in particular to Rule 44.15 (Providing Information about Funding Arrangements) and Section 19 of this Practice Direction.'

11.21 CPD, s 19—

Providing information

'19.1—

(1) A party who wishes to claim an additional liability in respect of a funding arrangement must give any other party information about that claim if he is to recover the additional liability. There is no requirement to specify the amount of the additional liability separately nor to state how it is calculated until it falls to be assessed. That principle is reflected in rules 44.3A and 44.15, in the following paragraphs and in Sections 6, 13, 14 and 31 of this Practice Direction. Section 6 deals with estimates of costs, Sections 13 and 14 deal with summary assessment and Section 31 deals with detailed assessment.

(2) In the following paragraphs a party who has entered into a funding arrangement is treated as a person who intends to recover a sum representing an additional liability by way of costs.

(3) Attention is drawn to paragraph 57.9 of this Practice Direction which sets out time limits for the provision of information where a funding arrangement is entered into between 31 March and 2 July 2000 and proceedings relevant to that arrangement are commenced before 3 July 2000.'

Method of giving information

'19.2—

(1) In this paragraph, "claim form" includes petition and application notice, and the notice of funding to be filed or served is a notice containing the information set out in Form N251.

(2)

(a)   A claimant who has entered into a funding arrangement before starting the proceedings to which it relates must provide information to the court by filing the notice when he issues the claim form.
(b)   He must provide information to every other party by serving the notice. If he serves the claim form himself he must serve the notice with the claim form. If the court is to serve the claim form, the court will also serve the notice if the claimant provides it with sufficient copies for service.

(3) A defendant who has entered into a funding arrangement before filing any document

(a)   must provide information to the court by filing notice with his first document. A "first document" may be an acknowledgement of service, a defence, or any other document, such as an application to set aside a default judgment.
(b)   must provide information to every party by serving notice. If he serves his first document himself he must serve the notice with that document. If the court is to serve his first document the court will also serve the notice if the defendant provides it with sufficient copies for service.

(4) In all other circumstances a party must file and serve notice within 7 days of entering into the funding arrangement concerned.

(5) There is no requirement in this Practice Direction for the provision of information about funding arrangements before the commencement of proceedings. Such provision is however recommended and may be required by a pre-action protocol.'

Notice of change of information

'19.3—

(1) Rule 44.15 imposes a duty on a party to give notice of change if the information he has previously provided is no longer accurate. To comply he must file and serve notice containing the information set out in Form N251. Rule 44.15(3) may impose other duties in relation to new estimates of costs.

(2) Further notification need not be provided where a party has already given notice:

(a) that he has entered into a conditional fee agreement with a legal representative and during the currency of that agreement either of them enters into another such agreement with an additional legal representative; or

(b) of some insurance cover, unless that cover is cancelled or unless new cover is taken out with a different insurer.

(3) Part 6 applies to the service of notices.

(4) The notice must be signed by the party or by his legal representative.'

Information which must be provided

19.4—

(1) Unless the court otherwise orders, a party who is required to supply information about a funding arrangement must state whether he has—

entered into a conditional fee agreement which provides for a success fee within the meaning of section 58(2) of the Courts and Legal Services Act 1990;

taken out an insurance policy to which section 29 of the Access to Justice Act 1999 applies;

made an arrangement with a body which is prescribed for the purpose of section 30 of that Act;

or more than one of these.

(2) Where the funding arrangement is a conditional fee agreement, the party must state the date of the agreement and identify the claim or claims to which it relates (including Part 20 claims if any).

(3) Where the funding arrangement is an insurance policy the party must state the name of the insurer, the date of the policy and must identify the claim or claims to which it relates (including Part 20 claims if any).

(4) Where the funding arrangement is by way of an arrangement with a relevant body the party must state the name of the body and set out the date and terms of the undertaking it has given and must identify the claim or claims to which it relates (including Part 20 claims if any).

(5) Where a party has entered into more than one funding arrangement in respect of a claim, for example a conditional fee agreement and an insurance policy, a single notice containing the information set out in Form N251 may contain the required information about both or all of them

19.5—

Where the court makes a Group Litigation Order, the court may give directions as to the extent to which individual parties should provide information in accordance with rule 44.15. (Part 19 deals with Group Litigation Orders.)'

Part 5

Conditional Fee Agreements between Solicitors and the Bar

Chapter 12

Model Agreements

12.1 Neither the Bar Council nor the Law Society currently produce a model agreement for use between solicitors and barristers. Attempts since 1995 to produce a model which was acceptable to both bodies proved unsuccessful. There are however, model CFAs produced by specialist Bar associations such as the Chancery Bar Association and there is a Model Agreement produced by the Association of Personal Injury Lawyers and the Personal Injury Bar Association—the APIL/PIBA agreement. Both the Chancery Bar Association and APIL/PIBA models are approved by the Bar Mutual Indemnity Fund (BMIF). A CFA between a solicitor and a barrister is an agreement between a legal representative and an additional legal representative. By reg 4 of the Conditional Fee Agreements Regulations 2000[1] the requirements of that regulation concerning the giving of information do not apply. By reg 5 there is no requirement for the client to sign the CFA between solicitor and barrister.

1 SI 2000/692, reproduced at Appendix 1.

APIL/PIBA 5[1]

12.2 This model is designed only for personal injury and clinical negligence cases and only where counsel's CFA is with a claimant's solicitor. Adaptations to the model in order to provide a CFA outside these narrow parameters will require approval from the BIMF[2].

1 The full text is given in Appendix 2.
2 BMIF, rule 10.1.1. BMIF shall indemnify the insured against claims by a solicitor of payment of all or part of the solicitor's fees under a conditional fee agreement between the insured barrister and that solicitor, only if and to the extent that the conditional fee agreement entered into by the barrister and the solicitor is in a form previously approved in writing by the Directors.

THE PROCEEDINGS

12.3 Clause 3 of APIL/PIBA 5 sets out a list of the issues covered by the agreement, including jurisdiction, breach of duty, causation, limitation and damages. It also sets out the stages of legal proceedings covered, including appeals by the client if advised by counsel. It is intended that the list offered as clause 3 will be adapted by the deletion of any matters which are not intended to be included. Where the solicitor has an existing CFA with his client it is likely that its terms will suggest the appropriate extent of clause 3.

Information to be provided to the barrister

12.4 Clause 5 requires that a copy of the solicitor/client CFA be provided. Also required is written confirmation that 'after the event' insurance is in place or reasons why it is not. Where more than one defendant is being sued clause 5 requires copies of correspondence from the after the event insurer clarifying whether and when defendant costs are covered in the event that the claimant does not succeed against all defendants. The concern that the lay client is to some extent uninsured relates both to the duty of the barrister to that client and to the possibility of the barrister being made the subject of a third party costs order. Clause 5 further requires that any advice and risk assessment provided to the client by experts, other barristers and solicitors be given to the barrister as well as any offers of settlement made by and to the client.

Lay client's consent

12.5 By clause 6 the solicitor confirms that the lay client (or Litigation Friend) consents to the terms of the CFA between counsel and the solicitor. There is no provision in the Model Agreement under which the lay client gives consent for the terms of the CFA between counsel and the solicitor to be disclosed, for example where a court orders such disclosure. The lay client is not a party to the CFA although by clause 6 the solicitor is confirming the lay client's consent to all terms. Clause 30 gives permission to disclose the reasons for the success fee if the court so orders but it may be preferable that the CFA between the solicitor and his client contains such consent and that the CFA with counsel confirms the existence of such a term.

Other funding methods

12.6 Clause 6 addresses the availability of methods of funding the litigation other than a CFA. The solicitor confirms by that clause that either there are no other methods of funding available or that although there are other methods, the client reasonably decided to use a CFA. The other method(s) available must be specified. Regulation 4(2) of the Conditional Fee Agreements Regulations 2000[1] requires the solicitor to inform the client of other funding methods which may be available, the purpose of clause 6 being to obtain confirmation that this has occurred and the result of it.

1 SI 2000/692.

Obligations of the solicitor

12.7 Clause 10 sets out the obligations which deal with the running of the case in terms of providing counsel with the necessary support. It also deals with the summary assessment of costs in counsel's absence and provides an obligation to inform counsel within two days of any reduction in counsel's fees on summary assessment in counsel's absence. The solicitor is to write to the after the event insurer where there is more than one defendant to seek clarification as to whether and when costs will be paid should the client win against only some of the defendants.

Counsel's right to terminate and the effect on fees

12.8 Under clause 11 counsel's right to terminate is based upon the failure of the solicitor to carry out his responsibilities under clause 10 of the agreement. Upon such termination counsel can elect from two options as to his fees—

'Option A' to receive payment of normal fees but not a success fee within three months of termination.

'Option B' to await the outcome of the case and receive payment of both normal fees and the success fee if it ends in success.

Termination is also permitted if the solicitor, client or Litigation Friend rejects counsel's advice as to—

(a) making, accepting or rejecting a Part 36 or other offer
(b) accepting or rejecting a Part 36 payment
(c) incurring/not incurring expenditure in obtaining evidence
(d) instructing leading counsel
(e) the case being likely to be lost (here counsel has no entitlement to any fees at all)
(f) it being unreasonable or uneconomic to proceed (here only Option B can be elected).

If a set-off or counterclaim materially affects the likelihood of success or the financial recovery, counsel may terminate the agreement and elect between Option A and B. This provision must be related to the definition of success which by clause 19 takes the same meaning as 'win' in the CFA between the solicitor and client. The other provisions of clause 11 relate to falsehood and to the provisions of the Code of Conduct of the Bar requiring counsel to cease to act, to which the election between Option A and B does apply. Under clause 15 if counsel takes silk the agreement may be terminated by counsel or the solicitor whereupon Option B automatically applies.

Automatic termination and its effect on counsel's fees

12.9 Clause 13 provides for automatic termination in a number of circumstances. The granting of public funding by the Legal Services Commission, death of the client, the making of a Group Litigation Order, terminate the agreement under this clause and automatically apply Option B. Option B automatically applies where the agreement is automatically terminated because counsel accepts a full-time judicial appointment or retires.

12.10 Where the agreement between solicitor and client is terminated before the conclusion of the case then clause 13 provides for the automatic termination of the agreement between solicitor and counsel. In these circumstances the election between Option A and B applies except where the client's CFA has been terminated for a reason connected with the prospects of success or the making of a settlement. If the client agreement has been terminated because the solicitor considers the case will lose but counsel considers it will win, the solicitor must pay counsels' normal and success fee if the case goes on to win—effectively Option B. If the client agreement has been terminated because the advice of the solicitor or counsel to settle has been rejected then counsel's normal fee is payable in any event and the success fee is payable if the case wins, irrespective of whether damages are awarded in excess of the advised settlement figure.

Solicitor's right to terminate and its effect on counsel's fees

12.11   Clause 12 provides 'The solicitor may terminate the agreement at any time on the instructions of the client or any Litigation Friend'. The nature of the relationship between solicitor and client and between solicitor and counsel is such that there must be such a right of termination. Counsel can here elect between Option A and Option B.

Counsel's fees where Part 36 is involved

12.12   Clause 20 provides for the situation where the amount of damages and interest awarded by a court is less than a Part 36 payment or effective offer. If counsel advised rejection the agreement states that normal and success fees are payable up to the date of the receipt of notice of the Part 36, with normal fees thereafter. This mirrors the provision in the Law Society Model Client/Solicitor Agreement. There is a potential therefore for the lay client to be faced with paying own unrecovered costs. Where counsel advised acceptance of the Part 36 then normal and success fees are payable for all work done.

Errors and indemnity for fees

12.13   Clause 22 deals with breach of duty to the client by the solicitor and by the barrister which has the result of dismissing or striking out the claim. If the solicitor is in breach he shall indemnify counsel as to counsel's normal fees. If the barrister is in breach he shall indemnify the solicitor for basic costs. These indemnities shall not exceed £25,000. Clause 22(3) deals with particular breaches by the solicitor of clause 10 relating to the requirements of the Civil Procedure Rules, Practice Direction about Costs, pre-action protocols and court orders with regard to CFAs and insurance premiums. It also deals with breaches of clause 10 concerned with assessment of costs. Where, as a result of any of the breaches listed, counsel's success fee is not payable by the opponent or by the client, then the solicitor shall pay the success fee. The purpose of this clause is to reinforce the duties in clause 10 as to matters which must be dealt with by the solicitor but which can have an adverse effect on counsel's fees if not done. Oddly the clause does not relate to part of the success fee being not payable by the opponent or client. Clause 22(3) is of no application if counsel has terminated the agreement for a breach of clause 10.

Solicitor's liability to pay counsel

12.14   Clause 27 provides that the solicitor shall pay counsel's fees and expenses whether or not the solicitor will be paid by the client[1]. This clause also states that counsel's fees are not limited by the amount of damages recovered. Clause 31 provides that any part of the success fee disallowed on assessment ceases to be payable under the agreement unless the court permits it to remain payable. Clause 32 deals with offers form the opponent to pay fees at a rate lower than that provided in the agreement. The solicitor must calculate a pro rata reduction and obtain counsel's consent to accept such an offer.

1   For the recovery of counsel's success fee see below at para **12.27**.

Return of work

12.15   Clause 25 deals with counsel's return of a brief in accordance with the Bar's Code of Conduct. Under the agreement counsel is to use his best endeavours to secure an appropriate alternative barrister to act on the same terms. As to the costs involved if no such can be found, the model provides an option for an obligation on the barrister to defray the additional costs. Work done before the return attracts a success fee if the case succeeds. This clause also addresses the position where the advice of the replacement barrister as to Part 36 and the running of the case is rejected (as in para **12.12** regarding counsel's right to terminate) and provides in effect that Option A or Option B is available to counsel under clause 23. Clause 25 is unclear whether the agreement is thus terminated by counsel.

THE CHANCERY BAR ASSOCIATION

Terms of engagement for preliminary work in contemplation of a CFA

12.16   The Chancery Bar Association proceeds on the basis that an agreement for work preliminary to entering into a CFA will itself be a CFA unless it provides that fees will be payable irrespective of outcome or that they are not payable in any event. The Association has produced terms of engagement for preliminary work[1] in terms of investigation and advice. The terms provide for fees to be paid if no CFA is entered into between counsel and the solicitor, irrespective of whether the solicitor is paid by the client. If counsel does enter into a CFA the terms upon which counsel is to be paid for preliminary work range from no payment to payment irrespective of outcome and to payment where the definition of success is satisfied. The Association's advice is that the cost of the preliminary work incurred for the purpose of enabling the barrister to decide whether to accept instructions on a CFA basis may not be recoverable from an opponent at assessment. The Model CFA has a clause incorporating preliminary work as attracting fees under it (paragraph 18). That clause is to be amended or deleted depending upon the terms of the preliminary agreement.

1   Version 2 September 2000. See Appendix 2.

THE MODEL CFA

Interlocutory hearings

12.17 In common with APIL/PIBA 5, the model provides that counsel will not appear at any interlocutory hearing where counsel of lesser experience and seniority would ordinarily be instructed or the court would conclude that counsel was not warranted. Counsel agrees to use best endeavours to ensure other counsel is willing to represent the client at such a hearing.

Returned briefs

12.18 Counsel will endeavour to obtain alternative counsel where a brief is returned in accordance with the Bar's Code of Conduct. There is no obligation to defray any additional expenses. If the case ultimately succeeds then counsel is entitled to the success fee. This is a less generous provision than that contained in the APIL/PIBA model.

Solicitor's obligations

12.19 Paragraphs 6 and 7 provide in detail these obligations. This includes the usual obligations to keep counsel informed of material developments in the case. It also includes obligations with regard to the assessment of fees.

Counsel's fees at base rate and reduced rate

12.20 The model provides for agreement that counsel will be paid fees, irrespective of the outcome of the case, at a reduced rate below normal rate (paragraph 22). This is an optional provision. Where this option for a reduced rate is included it has effect upon termination of the agreement as well as where the agreement is not terminated but the case fails[1].

1 See below para **12.22**.

Counsel's right to terminate

12.21 There are no circumstances giving rise to automatic termination. Under paragraphs 11 and 12 of the agreement counsel may terminate if the Code of Conduct requires him to cease to act or the client dies or is made bankrupt (including corporate insolvency). There is also a right to terminate if the solicitor fails to comply with the obligations under the agreement or advice as to Part 36 is rejected or there is a set-off or counterclaim materially affecting the likelihood of success. If funding is provided by the Community Legal Service or the client/solicitor CFA is terminated, or counsel retires or takes up a full time judicial appointment then the agreement must be terminated. There is no apparent reason why the agreement does not provide that in these latter circumstances the agreement is automatically ended, but on the wording which has been used, notice seemingly will need to be given in order to terminate the agreement.

Solicitor's right to terminate

12.22 By paragraph 8 the solicitor is given the right to terminate the agreement without cause and by paragraph 9(2) to terminate if he has good reason to believe that the relationship of trust has broken down. In each of these circumstances the solicitor must pay base rate fees. If the case goes on to succeed then the success fee must also be paid (paragraph 26). If counsel becomes unavailable for trial the solicitor may terminate the agreement (paragraph 9(1)). Payment of fees in this circumstance depends upon the terms of the agreement as to payment in the event of failure and success. The position is governed by paragraph 27. If the agreement provides for a reduced rate in the event of failure then upon termination under this paragraph the solicitor must pay that rate up to the time of termination. If the case succeeds then the solicitor must pay the difference between the reduced rate and the success fee rate. If the agreement provides for no payment in the event of failure then on termination under this paragraph no fees are payable. If the case succeeds then fees at the success rate are payable for the work done up to termination. By paragraph 9(3) the solicitor also has the right to terminate if he has good reason to believe that counsel has been incompetent to a degree justifying termination. In this case paragraph 28 governs the payment of fees in the same manner as paragraph 27 making the same distinction according to the terms of the agreement in the event of failure and success.

Counsel's option to terminate

12.23 Paragraph 11 provides in detail for termination at the option of counsel. The grounds include breakdown of trust and failure by the solicitor to comply with obligations under the agreement. A rejection of counsel's advice as to Part 36 and the existence of a counter-claim or set-off are included. As with the APIL/PIBA Model, counsel may, if required by the Code of Conduct of the Bar, cease to act. The death or insolvency of the client gives rise to the option to terminate as does the insolvency of a corporate client. In all circumstances where counsel terminates under paragraph 11 the solicitor must immediately pay counsel's fees at the base rate or reduced rate if that applies. If the case goes on to succeed the success fee becomes payable (paragraph 29).

Where counsel must terminate

12.24 Paragraph 12 provides for the same circumstances as the APIL/PIBA Model—ie public funding, termination of client/solicitor CFA, acceptance of full-time judicial appointment and retirement. In the case of appointment or retirement counsel must endeavour to arrange a suitable replacement. Upon such termination counsel's fees are payable according to the terms of the agreement depending on failure and success. Thus where the agreement provides for payment of fees in the event of failure such fees are payable upon termination with the success fee payable if the case goes on to win. Where under the agreement no payment of fees is due if the case fails then on termination no fees are due unless the case goes on to win in which case the fees at the success fee rate become payable (paragraph 30).

Interim payments

12.25 Paragraph 34 provides for the payment of counsel's base rate or reduced rate fees where the client has been awarded an interim payment by the court or by agreement of the opponent. This clause has a similar effect to a clause in the Law Society solicitor/client model which provides for such interim payments to be used to fund disbursements. That clause has been criticised as being an inappropriate use of such funds which are usually awarded because of a pressing need of the client[1].

1   *The Ethics of Conditional Fee Arrangements*, The Society for Advanced Legal Studies (January 2001).

Indemnity

12.26 Paragraph 24 provides that where, due to breach of duty by counsel, the case is dismissed or ends in failure, counsel shall pay the solicitor's basic costs as would have been recoverable from the client, subject to such breach being one which would give rise to a claim in damages. The maximum sum payable is £25,000.

RECOVERY OF THE BARRISTER'S SUCCESS FEE

12.27 The recovery of success fees, including counsel's success fee, is dealt with in Chapter 8. Counsel's fees are a matter between counsel and the solicitor, there being no direct relationship between counsel and the lay client. Section 20 of the Practice Direction about Costs[1] clearly reflects this relationship and provides for the solicitor to keep counsel informed. It also provides for counsel to attend or be represented at an assessment hearing. Counsel's success fee, whilst regarded as a disbursement, is an additional liability for the purposes of CPR, r 44.15. It seems clear that a party is claiming an additional liability where the client is seeking payment of counsel's success fee. The client has a liability to the solicitor for the solicitor's disbursements which will include counsel's success fee. The indemnity principle[2] is not offended therefore by a costs order which includes counsel's success fee as an additional liability.

1   See Chapter 8, para **8.39**.
2   See Chapter 1, para **1.36**.

Part 6

Other Funding Agreements

Chapter 13

Is it a Conditional Fee Agreement?

13.1 Consideration needs to be given to whether a funding agreement—

(a) constitutes a CFA for the purposes of the Courts and Legal Services Act 1990;
(b) complies with the Solicitors' Practice Rules; and
(c) changes its nature if proceedings are issued.

13.2 Section 58(1) of the Courts and Legal Services Act 1990 (CLSA 1990) as substituted by s 27 of the Access to Justice Act 1999 (AJA 1999) contains the all important provision that any funding arrangement, fitting the definition of a conditional fee agreement, must comply with the statutory regime if it is to be enforceable. It is essential therefore to consider funding arrangements which will constitute a CFA and not to attach a label to them which erroneously gives the impression that they are not CFAs and are not therefore governed by the statute.

13.3 CLSA 1990, s 58(1)—

'A conditional fee agreement which satisfies all of the conditions applicable to it by virtue of this section[1] shall not be unenforceable by reason only of its being a conditional fee agreement; but (subject to subsection (5))[2] any other conditional fee agreement shall be unenforceable.'

---

1 See Chapter 4.
2 Subsection (5) takes non-contentious business agreements out of the scope of s 58(1).

Conditional Fee Agreement defined

13.4 CLSA 1990, s 58(2)—

'For the purposes of this section and section 58A—

(a) a conditional fee agreement is an agreement with a person providing advocacy or litigation services which provides for his fees and expenses or any part of them, to be payable only in specified circumstances;'.

The provision of 'advocacy or litigation' occurs when a person provides a service which it would be reasonable to expect a person who is exercising, or contemplating exercising, a right of audience or a right to conduct litigation to provide[1]. A right of audience means the right to exercise the functions of appearing before and addressing a court; a right to conduct litigation means a right to exercise the function of issuing proceedings and ancillary functions such as entering an appearance[2]. The Act does not use the phrase 'contentious business' but seemingly the definitions amount to a description of contentious business. A funding agreement not relating to such work will not come within the 1990 Act. It is odd that s 58(5) should need expressly to exempt non-contentious business agreements since such, would by their own definition, not involve the provision of advocacy or litigation services.

1   CLSA 1990, s 119.
2   Ibid.

Work done pre-issue

13.5   Work done before the issue of proceedings can be seen to fall outside of the definitions in s 119 of the CLSA 1990 since there can be no question of the exercise of a right. Thus the fact that this work is being done by a person who could exercise the rights referred to in s 119 does not mean that the work is within those definitions. Therefore many personal injury matters are settled without the need for an exercise of a right of audience or a right to conduct litigation. *Re Simpkin Marshall Ltd*[1] seems to support the commonly held view that this work is non-contentious unless proceedings are issued. In considering the giving of advice to a liquidator as to whether proceedings should be brought, Wynn-Parry J said—

> 'The advice was obtained for the purpose of deciding whether or not to begin substantive legal proceedings and is therefore, referable to those legal proceedings. If, therefore, legal proceedings are begun, the business involved in giving or procuring the advice must be treated as contentious business; but if legal proceedings are not begun, then the advice must be treated as having been obtained in the course of the proceedings ... and must, therefore, be treated as non-contentious business.[2]'

1   [1958] 3 All ER 611.
2   Ibid at 616h–616j.

13.6   Those who can exercise rights of audience and to conduct litigation are in a more difficult position than those who are not. A solicitor for example will not know at the beginning of a case whether rights of the kind referred to in s 119 will be needed. The position appears to be that where proceedings are issued, the work prior to issue, if conducted on a basis that fees will be paid in some circumstances but not in others, is work done under an agreement which will become an agreement as to contentious business. This must give rise to difficulties in that when the work was done there was a fee agreement which at the time was not a CFA for the purposes of the 1990 Act and at the time did not need to comply with the Act. Once proceedings are issued, the question arises as to the enforceability of an agreement which provides for fees to be paid in some but not all circumstances. The *Simpkin* decision was directly concerned with the basis of the assessment of costs and clearly decides that pre-issue work will be assessed as contentious if proceedings are issued. The question then arises as to whether this means that the work done pre-issue can be governed still by a fee agreement which does not comply with s 58. Had proceedings not been issued s 58 would not apply provided the work did not amount to the provision of advocacy or litigation services. That pre-issue work has been regarded as contentious business does not answer the question as to whether the services provided fall within the definitions of advocacy or litigation services[1]. If it is accepted that the governing question is whether the pre-issue funding agreement is governed by the 1990 Act then it is submitted that the work done, not being the provision of advocacy or litigation services, can continue to be governed by the pre-issue agreement. It is further submitted that such agreement cannot offend the doctrine of Maintenance and Champerty since it is not relating to litigation.

1 *Re Solicitor, Re Taxation of Costs* [1955] 2 All ER 283 held that work was contentious business according to the tasks done not the time when they were done. The issue of proceedings was not to be regarded as the determining factor. The definition of contentious business in the Solicitors Act 1974, s 87(1) however, refers now to work done in contemplation of proceedings issued. The issues raised by the 1990 Act are however different to those raised in *Re Solicitor*.

The difficulty illustrated

13.7

Time scale	Work done	Costs agreement	
January		Contingency—30% of recovered sum	Status of agreement Jan–Dec governed by fact of issue of proceedings
	Preparation Advice Letters Negotiation Mediation	Not Advocacy or Litigation services Lawful contingency fee	Simpkin Marshall: Contentious If Advocacy or Litigation services Contingency unlawful
December		Settled pre-issue	Issue of proceedings
July			s 58 compliant CFA only— Need to cover pre-issue work?

Put simply, the agreement in January is lawful when made. Does the fact that proceedings are issued render it unlawful? If proceedings had not been issued the agreement would have remained lawful. The January agreement needs to contain a provision as to the effect of an issue of proceedings but as argued above, provided it cannot be read as applying to the provision of advocacy or litigation services, it is not governed by s 58 of the 1990 Act. The Chancery Bar Association1 agreement relating to preliminary work concerning whether to offer a CFA, contains an option to provide that where a CFA is subsequently entered into, no fees are payable for the preliminary work under the preliminary agreement. The CFA can then provide, when subsequently made, that the preliminary work be paid under its terms. A similar arrangement can be made for all work done pre-issue by a solicitor. A further alternative is to enter into a new agreement on commencement of proceedings which covers all work done to date.

1   This is an agreement between solicitor and counsel but the same problems arise. See below para **13.9**.

Solicitors' Practice Rule 8

13.8   Rule 8 governs an agreement to receive a fee only in the event of success where the agreement relates to the prosecution or defence of any action, suit or other contentious proceedings within the meaning of Solicitors Act 1974, s 87(1). The question arises therefore as to whether a fee agreement for work done pre-issue of proceedings is governed by Rule 8. If it is not so governed then it is submitted that the fact that proceedings are issued does not serve to apply Rule 8 where that pre-issue agreement remains separate from the post issue agreement.

Pre-CFA agreements—preliminary work agreements

13.9   Depending upon the complexity of the matter involved there may be a need for substantial work to be undertaken by a solicitor before a decision can be made as to whether a CFA should be offered. Counsel will, in most cases, be instructed when considerably more information has been obtained and again substantial work will be involved before counsel can decide to offer a CFA. If it is desired to enter into a funding agreement for this preliminary work the question arises as to whether it will constitute a CFA, whether intended to or not. The Chancery Bar Association has produced model terms of engagement for preliminary work to a CFA. These anticipate in some cases that a CFA will be entered into after the preliminary work has been done and that this CFA will govern the preliminary work as well. In other cases the model provides for payment for the preliminary work irrespective of whether it leads to a CFA. If a preliminary agreement provides that fees for that work will be payable in some circumstances, but not all, then the question arises as to whether that will be a CFA and thus be governed by the 1990 Act. This must depend upon whether the work done constitutes the provision of advocacy or litigation services. It has been argued above that where proceedings are issued then all of the preliminary work will be assessed as contentious work[1] but that there remains the question of the applicability of CLSA 1990, s 58.

1   A letter from the Vice-Chairman of the Chancery Bar Association dated July 2000 refers to the risk that unless the preliminary agreement provides that the fees for preliminary work are

payable in any event or are not payable in any event the agreement will itself constitute a CFA. Nonetheless, the model preliminary agreement has a capacity for a provision that fees will be payable in some circumstances and not others. In so doing, where proceedings are issued, there is clearly a need for the preliminary agreement to comply with s 58, not only in terms of success fees but also in terms of complying with the CFA Regulations 2000, SI 2000/692. The Association Model CFA itself also has an optional provision whereby preliminary work is retrospectively covered by the CFA. This provides then a form of agreement post issue which will include all pre-issue work and which will constitute a CFA which must comply with the 1990 Act. If proceedings are not issued then different provisions of the pre-issue agreement will apply.

CONTINGENT FEE AGREEMENTS

13.10   To a great extent the development of fee arrangements in the 1990s led to a confusion in terminology. The phrase 'contingent fee' appears to have been adopted to refer to an agreement where no fee was payable if the case lost and an ordinary, un-enhanced, fee was payable if the case succeeded. The facts of *Thai Trading Co v Taylor*[1] provide an example. The payment of normal fees was said to be contingent upon success, however defined. The essence nonetheless of such an agreement is that there are circumstances in which no fee is due and other circumstances in which fees are due. Such an agreement, after the coming into force of s 58 of the CLSA 1990 as substituted by s 27 of the AJA 1999, is a CFA and is enforceable only if it complies with the statutory scheme. It is recommended that such agreements be labelled 'CFAs without a success fee' and the phrase 'contingent fee agreement' be consigned to history.

1   [1998] 3 All ER 65. See Chapter 1, para **1.12**. In *Awwad v Geraghty & Co* [2000] 1 All ER 608, Schiemann LJ dealt with the differences in nomenclature as follows—

'There are three categories of reward for success: (1) where the lawyer will recover some of the client's winnings; (2) where the lawyer will recover his normal fees plus a success uplift; (3) where the lawyer will only recover his normal fees. They used all to be described as contingent fees but, in what Judge Cook in his book on *Costs* (3rd edn, 1998) refers to a triumph of semantics, situations (2) and (3) have in recent years been given the name conditional fees whereas situation (1) is still described as a contingent fee.' At 610h–610j.

CONTINGENCY FEE AGREEMENTS

13.11   The phrase 'contingency fee'[1] seems to be reserved for an agreement whereby the fees are defined as a percentage share of the damages either awarded or recovered—a 'share of the spoils'. Frequent reference is made to certain US jurisdictions where such arrangements are the norm. It should be remembered that in those states, the legal system is significantly different to the English legal system. A contingency fee agreement is not lawful in England and Wales. It would constitute a conditional fee agreement because it provides for fees to be payable only in specified circumstances. But s 58[2] of the 1990 Act restricts such agreements to those complying with the statutory scheme. In particular a contingency fee agreement would not comply with the CFA Order 2000[3] in respect of the success fee. A success fee, being an increase in the fees which would have been charged had there not been a CFA, can only be calculated as a percentage, not exceeding 100%, of the normal fees[3]. Fee agreements which calculate fees by reference to damages cannot satisfy the statutory scheme because they cannot refer to a percentage increase in fees. A contingency fee agreement is also contrary to Rule 8 of the Law Society Rules of Professional Conduct[4].

1   *Thai Trading Co v Taylor* supra: Millet LJ here uses the phrase to refer to agreements for a fee
    in the event of success.
2   See Appendix 1.
3   Section 58(2)(b) of the 1990 Act as substituted (see Appendix 1) and the Conditional Fee
    Agreements Order 2000, SI 2000/823 art 4 (see Appendix 2).
4   See Chapter 2 and Appendix 3.

DIFFERENTIAL FEE AGREEMENTS

13.12   The fee arrangement made in *Aratra Potato Co Ltd v Taylor Joynson Garrett*[1] provided for a reduced fee for unsuccessful cases and a normal fee for successful case. Such an arrangement is sometimes known as a 'discounted fee' agreement. An agreement of this kind does provide for the payment of part of the fees only in specified circumstances and accordingly it does constitute a CFA for the purposes of s 58. It follows that such an agreement is a CFA and will only be enforceable if it complies with the statutory regime[2].

1   [1995] 4 All ER 695.
2   The statutory regime is dealt with in Chapter 4.

13.13   The question whether such an agreement contains a success fee requires a consideration of s 58(2)(b) of the 1990 Act—

> 'a conditional fee agreement provides for a success fee if it provides for the amount of any fees to which it applies to be increased, in specified circumstances, above the amount which would be payable if it were not payable only in specified circumstances.'

A differential fee agreement may or may not provide for such an increase. If the agreement provides for a differential below the normal fees which would be charged for the work then it is submitted that there is no success fee. Thus in an agreement to charge normal fees in a win and 50% of the normal fee if the case loses there is no success fee. Where the agreement provides in some circumstances for fees above the normal rate then there is a success fee. Thus an agreement that if the case wins the fee payable is the normal fee plus 30% and in the event of a loss the fee is 70% of the normal fee, does contain a success fee. The s 58(2)(b) definition pre-supposes that there is a normal fee, ie that it can be determined what would have been charged had there not been a conditional fee arrangement. This pre-supposes either that there is a known normal fee for the firm for doing the work of the kind covered or that there is at least such a figure with regard to the particular client.

CONTENTIOUS BUSINESS AGREEMENTS

13.14   Solicitors Act 1974, s 59—

> '(1) Subject to subsection (2), a solicitor may make an agreement in writing with his client as to his remuneration in respect of any contentious business done, or to be done, by him (in this Act referred to as a "contentious business agreement") providing that he shall be remunerated by a gross sum [or by reference to an hourly rate], or by a salary, or otherwise, and whether at a higher or lower rate than that at which he would otherwise have been entitled to be remunerated.

(2) Nothing in this section or in sections 60 to 63 shall give validity to—

(a) any purchase by a **solicitor** of the interest, or any part of the interest, of his client in any action, suit or other contentious proceeding; or

(b) any agreement by which a **solicitor** retained or employed to prosecute any action, suit or other contentious proceeding, stipulates for payment only in the event of success in that action, suit or proceeding; or

(c) any disposition, contract, settlement, conveyance, delivery, dealing or transfer which under the law relating to bankruptcy is invalid against a trustee or creditor in any bankruptcy or composition.[1']

---

1   Words in square brackets added by CLSA 1990, s 98(5).

13.15 Contentious business is defined in s 87(1) of the Solicitors Act 1974 as—

'"contentious business" means business done, whether as solicitor or advocate, in or for the purposes of proceedings begun before a court or before an arbitrator … , not being business which falls within the definition of non-contentious or common form probate business contained in section 128 of the Supreme Court Act 1981;'.

A Contentious Business Agreement is a particular form of fee agreement under which the usual rights to assessment at the insistence of the client do not apply. In the context of agreements which provide for the payment of fees in some but not all circumstances, a Contentious Business Agreement , because it relates to the provision of advocacy or litigation services within the meaning of the 1990 Act, must also comply with s 58 of the 1990 Act. It has been argued above that the classification of work as contentious rather than non-contentious is not the same question as whether the agreement must comply with the 1990 Act, but in the case of a Contentious Business Agreement advocacy or litigation services are being provided. It is clearly not possible to avoid the provisions of the 1990 Act by entering into a Contentious Business Agreement under s 59 of the 1974 Act.

TEST OF WHETHER A FUNDING AGREEMENT IS A CFA

13.16 The most important question in all funding agreements relating to the provision of advocacy or litigation services is whether the CLSA 1990 definition of a CFA means that the particular agreement is a CFA and must comply with the complex set of rules contained in the statutory scheme. In order to answer that question it is necessary to answer the following question:

Will the same fees and expenses be payable in all circumstances?

If the answer to that question is 'no' then assuming the agreement does relate to the provision of advocacy or litigation services, the agreement is a CFA within the meaning of CLSA 1990, s 58(2)(a).

The following questions and answers should be considered—

1   Will the same fees and expenses be payable in all circumstances?
2   Does the agreement relate to the provision of advocacy or litigation services?

13.16 *Part 6   Other Funding Agreements*

The table below provides typical examples of funding agreements—

Type of agreement	Question 1	Question 2	Must s 58 be complied with?
Pre-issue work	No	No	No
Pre-CFA agreements	No	No	No
Contingent fees	No	Yes	Yes
Contingency fees	No	Yes	Yes[1]
Differential fees	No	Yes	Yes
Contentious Business Agreements	No[2]	Yes	Yes

1   An agreement to receive a contingency fee meaning a share of damages could not satisfy s 58 but it would be a CFA for the purposes of s 58(1) and would therefore be unenforceable.

2   A Contentious Business Agreement to which this answer is 'yes' would not need to comply with s 58.

Part 7

Insurance and Funding

Chapter 14

Legal Expenses Insurance

DEFINITION

14.1　The major distinction to be drawn in the insurance products available to provide cover for the costs of litigation is between policies sold where the event which gives rise to the legal claim has not occurred and those sold where that event has already occurred. The phrases 'before the event' and 'after the event' are used to refer to this distinction. The generic term used is Legal Expenses Insurance (LEI). Before the event LEI is sold in two forms. Either as an add-on to other insurance products or, more rarely, as a stand-alone policy. Many household and motor insurance policies have an add-on benefit of cover for legal expenses. In some cases there is no charge for this addition, in others the policyholder will have paid a sum in the region of £15. The limits of indemnity in these policies will vary but generally start from £10,000. Before the event LEI is also available to businesses in respect of commercial activities. LEI is Class 17 of general business defined in the Insurance Companies Act 1982, Sch 2 as 'effecting and carrying out contracts of insurance against risks of loss to the persons insured attributable to their incurring legal expenses (including costs of litigation)'. Before a CFA is signed the client must be informed as to whether the legal representative considers that the client's costs liability is insured under an existing policy[1]. Whether the litigation is to be funded by a CFA or not, the client must be informed of costs including the question of whether the costs are or can be insured[2].

1　CFA Regulations 2000, SI 2000/692, reg 4(2)(c) and see Chapter 16.
2　Law Society Practice Rule 15 and Solicitors' Costs Information and Client Care Code para 4 (j). See Chapter 16.

THE UNITED KINGDOM MARKET FOR LEI

14.2
TABLE 77: LEGAL EXPENSES INSURANCE

	GROSS EARNED PREMIUMS £000	CLAIMS INCURRED £000	NUMBER OF CLAIMS NOTIFIED
77a TOTAL			
1990	50,228	41,936	339,715
1991	52,513	60,605	352,578
1992	74,332	70,941	367,167
1993	83,667	63,229	452,792
1994	85,688	46,662	353,650
1995	89,948	43,297	370,940
1996	90,675	41,068	318,417
1997	99,128	39,476	336,740
1998	102,916	42,900	375,134
77b MOTOR			
1990	27,571	21,959	320,068
1991	30,083	27,575	331,999
1992	41,675	33,153	337,853
1993	44,450	31,572	433,420
1994	47,227	22,714	336,965
1995	48,730	20,788	353,360
1996	47,488	18,830	301,041
1997	56,177	16,771	318,540
1998	58,342	16,580	354,443
77c NON-MOTOR PERSONAL			
1990	9,109	7,006	6,321
1991	10,407	14,145	7,579
1992	16,701	14,696	11,782
1993	17,617	11,871	9,652
1994	19,936	10,648	10,420
1995	23,193	12,009	11,583
1996	24,118	13,376	11,444
1997	21,827	11,503	11,619
1998	21,098	11,623	12,286
77d NON-MOTOR COMMERCIAL			
1990	13,548	12,971	13,326
1991	12,023	18,885	13,000
1992	15,956	23,092	17,532
1993	21,600	19,786	9,720
1994	18,525	13,300	6,265
1995	18,025	10,500	5,997
1996	19,069	8,862	5,932
1997	21,124	11,202	6,581
1998	23,476	14,697	8,405

Source: Association of British Insurers
Coverage: Companies writing Legal Expenses Insurance.
Gross Earned Premiums are defined as being gross of both reinsurance and commission, ie the total gross premium paid by the policy holder, but exclusive of Insurance Premium Tax.

THE INSURANCE COMPANIES (LEGAL EXPENSES INSURANCE) REGULATIONS 1990[1]

14.3 The Regulations are mainly concerned with the organisation of insurance companies in circumstances where the same insurer might be providing LEI in a dispute over a liability which it was also insuring. The potential for a conflict of interest is addressed by a requirement to put in place one of three mechanisms for ensuring that a conflict of interest cannot occur[2].

1 SI 1990/1159—in force 1 July 1990 implementing The Legal Expenses Insurance Directive (Dir/87/334/EEC).
2 Ibid, reg 5(1). The three options are contained in reg 5(2)–(4). Ensuring no staff handling LEI also handle any other class of general insurance business; using a separate company to handle LEI claims; permitting the insured to appoint a lawyer of their choice.

Freedom of choice of lawyer

14.4 Regulation 6 provides—

'(1) Where under a legal expenses insurance contract recourse is had to a lawyer (or other person having such qualifications as may be necessary) to defend, represent or serve the interests of the insured in any inquiry or proceedings, the insured shall be free to choose that lawyer (or other person).
(2) The insured shall also be free to choose a lawyer (or other person having such qualifications as may be necessary) to serve his interests whenever a conflict of interest arises.
(3) The above rights shall be expressly recognised in the policy.[1]'

1 SI 1990/1159, reg 6 does not apply to LEI concerned with contracts for assistance in the event of accident or breakdown involving a road vehicle if certain requirements are fulfilled, see reg 7. Regulation 3 makes further exemption from the application of the regulations, including a civil liability insurer who acts in defending or representing its own interests.

14.5 The importance of reg 6(1) is in the distinction between the position before and after the commencement of proceedings. Before commencement of proceedings there is no entitlement to a free choice of lawyer (although it may have been given by the insurer under reg 5) unless there is a conflict of interest[1]. Once proceedings are commenced reg 6 applies to provide a right to choose a lawyer without there being a need for a conflict of interest to have arisen. There is no provision in the Regulations giving the insurer any control over this choice even where it is unreasonably expensive or generally unsuitable.

1 The Insurance Ombudsman ruled in 1993 to this effect. IOB Annual Report 1993, paras 6.56–6.65. In the ruling reference is made to the need to emphasise in brochures or summaries of cover, that the choice of lawyer only arises once proceedings have begun.

14.6 Complaints to the Ombudsman about this class of insurance have mainly concerned the view taken by the insurer of the prospects of success. The context for the 1990 Regulations is whether a disagreement between the policyholder and the insurer as to the prospects of success can amount to a conflict of interest and, if so, what consequences follow with regard to choice of lawyer. The Regulations do not make clear what manner of conflict of interest is required for there to be a right to choose a lawyer to be funded under the insurance. If a disagreement over prospects of success did constitute a conflict for the purposes of the Regulations it could be argued that there is a tangible conflict beyond that which will exist in all cases, that is, the interests of the insurer that the case is not pursued, thereby obviating a risk of a claim on the policy, and the interest of the policyholder in bringing the claim. To regard the latter as sufficient for the purposes of the Regulations would seem to mean that the freedom of choice would apply in all cases— clearly a result not intended by the Regulations.

The Directive[1] which the Regulations implement also uses the phrase 'conflict of interest'. Recitals to the Directive refer to conflicts arising because the insurer is also providing other classes of insurance to the same insured and because the insurer is providing cover for another party to the dispute. Where the provider of legal expenses insurance belongs to a group which includes a liability insurer conflict may also be seen to arise. These conflicts arise out of the nature of the business generally conducted by the insurer and appear to be of a different nature to a disagreement over prospects of success which is a case specific matter. Clearly a conflict of interest can arise on a case specific basis, the most obvious example being where the claim is directly against the insurer. While such conflicts are not the purpose behind the Directive they would clearly be governed by it and by the Regulations. Little assistance is gained therefore from an examination of the main purpose of these measures and it is still an unresolved question as to whether a rejection of cover on the grounds of prospects of success brings the insurer into a conflict of interest with the insured. Assuming however that this is sufficient to constitute a conflict of interest for the purposes of the Regulations, the consequences flowing would ultimately be that the insured who was represented by a lawyer of their own choice would have a claim against the policy at least where the case succeeded. It is more difficult to see the consequences where the case has failed. If the case had been pursued with cover having been granted the insurer would have been informed of progress and would have been in a position to withdraw cover if the prospects deteriorated sufficiently. This process will not have occurred however, where the insured has proceeded with their own choice of lawyer, cover having been refused. A more likely approach in the case of a disagreement on prospects is a complaint to the Ombudsman leading to a ruling as to choice of lawyer.

1   87/344/EEC.

TYPICAL COVER UNDER A LEGAL EXPENSES POLICY

14.7   Cover will depend upon which sections of a policy have been purchased but typically might include employment, personal injury, contract and motoring claims brought by or against the insured. The policy may include cover for family members as well as the insured. It is essential to ascertain that the client is within the class of persons covered and that the class of claim is within the sections of the policy which have been purchased. Cover will be for irrecoverable legal costs of the insured and the opponent. The limit of indemnity is likely to be on a standard term basis, typically £25,000 or £50,000. It has to be borne in mind that this limit will need to accommodate the costs and disbursements of both sides. The policy may contain a compulsory excess clause. The policy will require the insured to persuade the insurer that the case should be pursued, ie that the prospects of success are sufficient to justify the action. Once action has been given cover there will be reporting conditions to ensure that the insured's lawyer keeps the insurer informed.

Motoring, personal and commercial policies

14.8   Policies are typically classified as relating to motoring, personal or commercial risks and cover will therefore be provided as relevant to the classification. A motor related policy is likely to provide cover for uninsured motor loss recovery (ULR) which essentially covers the bringing of an action to recover loss for which the policyholder is himself not insured. Thus in a typical motor accident, if the policyholder's car insurance does not give 'comprehensive' cover, the damage to property of the policyholder will be uninsured. The major element in ULR is often cover for personal injury claims arising out of an event covered by the policy. A 'personal' policy, not related to motoring, typically purchased as part of a house contents policy, is likely to provide cover in respect of employment matters (both tribunal and court based disputes), disputes arising from the purchase or hire of goods and services and for personal injury suffered by the insured. Commercial policies are available to cover a vast range of matters including intellectual property disputes and taxation investigations as well as employment dispute defence and health and safety interventions. In the commercial field the range of cover available is considerable and reference needs to be made to the individual policy in order to determine the exact extent of cover.

Date of event leading to the dispute

14.9   Cover for legal expenses under some policies relates only to disputes relating to events which have themselves occurred during the period of insurance. To some extent a policy written on this basis is seeking to ensure that a purchaser is not able to insure in respect of pre-existing events which are likely to give rise to a dispute. In a complaint to the Insurance Ombudsman[1] relating to asbestos damage to health the policy referred to the 'date of occurrence' which had to be within the period of insurance. It was ruled that this was clear in meaning and was a reference to the events causing the loss and could not be understood to mean the date when the loss was diagnosed. A policy of legal expenses insurance written on the basis of the date that a dispute arises would in this instance have provided cover even though the physical events giving rise to the claim, as will often be the case, occurred decades before that date.

1   IOB Bulletin 16.4 (1998), p 5.

TYPICAL CONDITIONS

Notifying the insurer of a potential claim

14.10   All policies will require notification that circumstances have arisen which have the potential to result in a claim on the policy, ie that legal advice and representation will be required. The exact requirements will vary from policy to policy but the Association of British Insurers Statement of General Insurance Practice provides as follows—

'(a) Under the conditions regarding notification of a claim, the policyholder shall not be asked to do more than report a claim and subsequent developments as soon as reasonably possible except in the case of legal processes and claims which a third party requires the policyholder to notify within a fixed time where immediate advice may be required.[1]'

1   January 1986—reprinted August 1997.

Prospects of success

14.11   The purchase of legal expenses insurance does not mean that the decision to take or defend legal action rests with the policyholder. The policy will provide that support will be given where there are reasonable prospects of success. Continuation of cover throughout the dispute will depend upon such prospects also continuing. A typical wording is that the insured shall have 'both a reasonable case and a reasonable chance of a worthwhile outcome'. The latter reference is similar to the Ombudsman's indication[1] that an application of the Legal Aid Board's merits test would be an appropriate method of determining reasonable prospects. Insurers will require a prospective outcome justifying the potential costs. The 'merits test' has been replaced by the Funding Code[2] of the Community Legal Service which also relates prospects of success to the benefits to be obtained and the costs involved in obtaining them. The Funding Code includes as a criteria for the refusal of support the suitability of the case for alternative funding, such as through insurance. The criteria for providing Full Representation includes the matter of the suitability of the case for a CFA[3]. If the case is suitable for a CFA support will be refused. It is unlikely that a before the event LEI provider will adopt this later aspect of the Code given the competition between such providers and the providers of after the event insurance. The Code's cost-benefit criteria make a link between the likely costs and the percentage prospects of success[4]. For the purposes of the Code costs means own side's only, whereas under LEI the insurer is providing cover for costs on both sides. A further criteria applied by the Code and insurers is the test of what the reasonable privately paying client would do. If such a client would not fund the case themselves this is an indication that the insurer will not provide support.

1   Insurance Ombudsman Bureau Annual Report 1993, p 31.
2   Community Legal Service Funding Code (in force 1 April 2000), section 4 lays down Standard Criteria. Section 5 lays down the criteria for different levels of support.
3   Section 5.7.1 of the Funding Code.
4   Section 5.7.3 of the Funding Code. Thus if prospects are between 60% and 80% the likely damages must exceed likely costs by a ratio of 2:1.

Choice of legal representative[1]

14.12   The policy is likely to include a condition that the insurer will appoint a legal representative. This may then be from a panel of approved solicitors or may be its own in-house staff. The 1990 Regulations have the effect that the insured cannot insist that their choice of legal representative be accepted unless proceedings have begun. Before the issue of proceedings the matter may be handled without the need of a lawyer and the insurer may thus handle the matter without appointing a legal representative. The policy will be worded in such terms that the obligation upon underwriters is to provide representation, it will not state that such representation will necessarily be through a legal representative.

1 Freedom of choice of lawyer within the Insurance Companies (Legal Expenses Insurance) Regulations 1990, SI 1990/1159 is dealt with above at para **14.4**.

Conduct and control

14.13 The insurer will require the insured's co-operation in running the case, whether run in-house or through an appointed representative. A failure to co-operate is likely to lead not only to withdrawal of cover but to the insured being liable for all costs incurred. Co-operation will extend not only to meeting any instructions given to the insured but to the insured not acting in any way detrimental to the prospects of the case and to not settle the claim without reference to the insurer. All of these requirements are essential to protect the insurer's interest in recovering costs through a successful outcome, either through settlement or the court process. Co-operation will also be required in recovering costs from an opponent, including the instigation of proceedings to recover such costs.

Application of costs recovered

14.14 The policy is likely to prescribe the order of priority in the application of any costs recovered from an opponent. The likely order will be firstly the legal expenses incurred by the insurer in the case, claims handling expenses and finally any excess in the policy for which the insured would be responsible.

INSOLVENCY OF THE INSURED

14.15 Many LEI policies, both before and after the event, provide a right in the insurer to terminate the policy in the event of the insured's insolvency. The assumption behind such a condition is that the insured will receive no benefit from the proceedings and the insurer has not provided cover with the purpose of benefiting third party creditors. If the policy provides for automatic termination there can be no question of the insurer being persuaded that the insured will in fact benefit from continuing the proceedings.

A further consequence of the insolvency of an insured is the position of legal representatives as against the insurer. The Third Parties (Rights Against Insurers) Act 1930 provides to a third party who has a right against the insured a right of subrogation in the event of the insured's insolvency. The third party thus has direct access to the insurer—

> 'Where, under any contract of insurance, a person (hereinafter referred to as the insured) is insured against liabilities to third parties which he may incur, then—

(a) in the event of the insured becoming bankrupt or making a composition or arrangement with his creditors; or

(b) in the case of the insured being a company, in the event of a winding-up order being made … ;

if, either before or after that event, any such liability as aforesaid is incurred by the insured, his rights against the insurer under the contract in respect of the liability shall, notwithstanding anything in any Act or rule of law to the contrary, be transferred to and vest in the third party to whom the liability was so incurred.[1']

1 The Third Parties (Rights Against Insurers) Act 1930, s 1.

14.16 The position of a legal representative whose client becomes insolvent was addressed in the recent decision in *Tarbuck v Avon Insurance plc*[1] where Toulson J posed the following question—

'Is the [1930 Act] capable of applying to the right of a litigant, under a policy of legal expenses insurance ("LEI"), to payment by the insurer of costs owed by the insured litigant to her solicitor, so as to cause the insured's right to be transferred to the solicitor in the event of the insured's bankruptcy?'[2].

The insurer argued that a legal expenses policy was not a liability insurance and accordingly that the Act did not apply. It was further argued that liability insurance meant cover for a potential liability for damage caused to another person and not the insured's own pecuniary loss. In any event with regard to own legal costs insured under the policy this could not come within the Act because there was no third party involved, only the insured's own voluntarily incurred debt.

Toulson J expressed himself as troubled by the unfairness of the result if the insurer was right but also troubled by the claimant's argument on the construction of the Act—

'This case may, on its facts, seem out of the ordinary in that the insurers were happy to have paid the claimant with Miss Nicholson's consent, knowing of her bankruptcy, and they only refrained from doing so because of her objection. But if their argument is right, counsel for the insurer accepts and indeed submits that they would have had no business to pay the claimant, even with her consent, after she became bankrupt, because the proceeds of the policy ought to have gone to her trustee for the benefit of her general creditors. Once that is recognised, the potential seriousness of the matter for solicitors acting for clients with LEI is obvious. If they are to guard against the insolvency risk, they need to ensure that they have adequate money on account or are otherwise secured for their fees, possibly by assignment in advance of the benefits of the policy. They cannot regard the client's LEI as available to cover their fees in the event of insolvency, however honourable the intentions of the client may be and however good their relationship with the client.

So the construction contended for by the insurers produces a result with which I am frankly not happy on the facts of this case, and has implications for all concerned in this class of work which they are likely to find disturbing. But there are difficulties to my mind, both historic and substantive, in construing "liabilities to third parties which he may incur" as including a simple contract debt voluntarily incurred. As a matter of legislative history, it is improbable that the draftsman of the Act intended such a broad meaning.[3]

It was held that the claimant had no right to costs by an application of the Act. Reference is made in the judgment to the Law Commission's[4] consideration of the 1930 Act and its apparent recognition that LEI is not covered by it. A final report is expected in 2001 but there has been no indication that this issue will have been addressed. Toulson J raised other issues of concern, in particular the order of priority under an LEI policy for the payment of own costs and opponent's costs. This is certainly of importance if a policy is to be used as security for costs. It is likely that unless the policy includes a loss payee clause specifying the opponent as the payee that security for costs will not be satisfied without the assignment of the policy to the opponent.

1   [2001] 1 All ER (Comm) 422, QBD.
2   Ibid at p 423.
3   Ibid at p 427.
4   LCCP No 152 (January 1998).

Chapter 15

After the Event Insurance

DEFINITION

15.1   Legal Expenses Insurance (LEI) has traditionally been provided as a before the event policy, that is, the insurance is taken out at a time before the event which gives rise to the legal dispute has arisen. The introduction of CFAs in 1995 led the insurance industry to develop products which could be purchased to give cover for legal expenses after the event giving rise to the dispute has occurred. Such products existed before 1995 but were by no means commonplace. This form of insurance is known as after the event legal expenses insurance or ATE. The essential difference therefore is that the insurer knows at the time of granting cover that there has been an event which has the potential to lead to legal proceedings. The insurer in these circumstances will take the view that the risk of legal proceedings occurring is far greater in this particular case than it would be with a purchaser of before the event insurance. If proceedings have already been issued then clearly the ATE insurer has to assess the risks in actual rather than contemplated proceedings. With before the event insurance there will be no cover for a pre-existing event giving rise to litigation. Consequently the entire pool of insured persons can be treated as having an equal (and low) risk of an event leading to legal proceedings. With ATE insurance the pool of purchasers is far smaller and each of them has already been involved in an event which has a potential to give rise to litigation or has already led to the issue of proceedings. The premiums needed to provide a viable market in this field will consequently be significantly higher than premiums for before the event insurance. The premiums for this type of LEI are capable of being included in an order for costs made against a losing party[1].

1   See Chapter 17.

CONDITIONAL FEE AGREEMENT POLICIES

15.2   After the event insurance products are relatively new in that they effectively came about to support the availability of CFAs which became lawful in England and Wales in July 1995. The number of providers of such policies has grown considerably since 1995[1] and the variations in cover are accordingly many and complex. AEI policies are available to support litigation funded by a CFA and funded without a CFA. In addition to the many policies available to insure the liability which a client has in costs, there are policies available also to the solicitor to enable the firm to insure on a stop-loss basis and to insure its work in progress.

1   By November 2000 there were at least 17 providers of ATE insurance—see *Litigation Funding* Issue 10 (November 2000) Law Society Publications.

15.3   A client with a CFA is at risk of being liable for the costs of the opponent. The client may also be liable for own disbursements including counsel's fees depending upon the terms of the CFA and whether own counsel is acting on a CFA or not. All of these liabilities can be insured on an after the event basis. Although this client liability is equally applicable to defendants, not all of the policies offered are available to defendants.

Typical cover

15.4   The commercially available ATE market has grown to the extent that even with personal injury cases there is a significant diversity in cover and conditions as well as premium levels. Once litigation outside of personal injury is considered, particularly commercial litigation, the availability and variety of insurance cover becomes far more complex. Add to that the infinite variety of variable factors involved in non-personal injury cases and the question of when, if and with which provider to insure reaches a new level of sophistication. In that context it is not possible to describe typical cover other then to set out the variable features which need to be considered.

Adverse costs

15.5   The major liability of a client who is a party to a CFA is that arising out of an order for adverse costs. All policies in this field provide cover for such liability, dependent upon the Limit of Indemnity LOI—ie the level of cover purchased. The trigger for a claim against the policy will usually be a court order that costs be paid. Cover may also be given for a post issue settlement or abandonment of a claim where the insurer has consented to the settlement or withdrawal. Under the Civil Procedure Rules 1998 (CPR) it is possible that there will be costs orders in both directions and it is possible that there will be an award of damages in favour of a claimant but an adverse costs order at the same time. In these circumstances, although there has been an adverse costs award, the policy is likely to provide cover only on the basis of a deficiency in net result. Thus to the extent that the adverse costs award (or any net balance due if there have been mutual costs awards) can be met from the damages award, the insurer will not provide cover. It will only be net adverse costs after exhaustion of damages which will be covered. The insurance market is beginning to introduce products which at least protect a certain level of damages in these circumstances and it may be that products will emerge which do not take account of damages at all. Clearly it is vital to be clear as to the basis of the cover in this respect. However, many policies at present reflect the terms of standard CFAs in respect of CPR, Pt 36 and provide no cover for opponent's costs after a rejection of an offer/payment which the insurer considers reasonable. Where there has been more than one defendant with adverse costs orders in respect of some but not all, cover is likely to be again on a net effect basis and only where damages are first exhausted. Not all policies will cover opponent's success fees and not all extend to counterclaims.

Interim costs awards

15.6 The variation in policies with regard to an interim adverse costs award is between policies which will provide the funds to meet such orders within the usual 14 day deadline and those which do not. Where funds are provided there will be a claw back at the end of the proceedings in accordance with the net effect of all costs orders made, with cover being provided where there is a deficit and the damages have been exhausted. Where no funds are provided at the time of an interim order, cover will be not given until and unless at the end of the case there is a net deficit and damages have been exhausted. There are signs that products may evolve to ring fence at least part of the damages awarded in these circumstances.

Retrospective cover for adverse costs

15.7 It is also important to be clear as to whether the cover for adverse costs applies to opponent's costs incurred before the insurance policy was purchased. Not all policies provide retrospective cover. Where a policy does provide retrospective cover for opponent's costs incurred pre-policy, this will be reflected in the premium. A policy which does not provide retrospective cover will accordingly provide less cover the nearer the matter is to trial when the policy incepts. Conversely, if cover is being sought after a trial date has been set and retrospective cover is sought, the premium will be at a higher percentage rate than it would have been had cover been sought at an earlier time. Some providers will not provide cover at all within a certain period of a trial date, others specify that cover must be sought within three months of the first consultation with the client if standard premium rates are to apply. Where it is possible that security for costs will need to be given, a policy which does not provide retrospective cover is less likely to be accepted as security for costs. In such cases therefore it is vital to clarify the retrospective cover.

Own disbursements

15.8 Under a CFA the client has a liability for own disbursements such as expert reports, medical records and such like. Unless the solicitor is to take responsibility for those disbursements in the event that the case fails, there is a costs risk to the client which can be insured. The CFA related policies do provide such cover as standard. Variations occur, however, as to whether disbursements already incurred at the time the policy incepts are covered, with some policies excluding this. A further variation relates to discontinued cases pre-issue of proceedings. Some policies do not provide cover for own disbursements where the case is discontinued or abandoned without the issue of proceedings. Cover for own disbursements will not include a failure of an opponent to meet a costs order to pay those disbursements (although it is sometimes possible to insure the risk of the opponent's insolvency).

Own counsel's fees

15.9   Some policies relating to CFAs assume that where counsel is instructed the instructions will be accepted on a CFA basis. Accordingly no cover is offered in respect of own counsel's fees even where counsel is not acting on a CFA. Own counsel's fees will be excluded in these policies in the definition of disbursements. There are, however, a good number of policies which do provide cover for counsel's fees as a standard cover in a CFA related policy.

Own costs

15.10   The standard assumption often made is that a CFA will provide that there will be no liability for own costs except in the event of a win. Accordingly most products do not provide cover, even as an option, for own costs in the event that the case fails. Products are beginning to emerge, however, where a part of the solicitor's own costs can be covered. Some of these products are linked to funding options but there are products available which do not depend upon funding of work in progress. The essence of such a product is that the solicitor is transferring to an insurer part of the risk of not being paid. It is arguable that where such insurance is taken out the success fee in the CFA ought to reflect the fact that although the client will not be paying any fees in the event that the case loses, the solicitor is not taking all of that risk. Whether the cost of insuring that part of own costs can be included in a recoverable success fee is a difficult question but the better approach is to leave the premium as a whole premium with the potential to recover that from a losing opponent[1].

1   See further Chapter 17 below on recovery of insurance premiums.

Failure of opponent to pay costs including through insolvency of opponent

15.11   The obtaining of a costs order against an unsuccessful opponent will usually mean that there can be no question of a claim on the policy. There will have been a successful outcome in terms of the policy wording. There are circumstances, including but not confined to the insolvency of the opponent after judgment, in which the order for costs does not lead to a full or indeed any recovery of costs. There may or may not have been a recovery of some damages. This is a risk of all litigation but is generally not one for which insurance cover is provided. Some policies do provide optional cover for insolvency though actually obtaining an offer of such cover will depend upon the risk and the amount of knowledge as to credit-worthiness which can be provided.

'Deficiency of damages'

15.12   This is a commonly used phrase which tends to convey an unintended meaning. The cover under such a clause does not deal with a failure to recover from an opponent the full amount of damages as awarded by a court or agreed in a settlement. It is a reference to a net deficit of adverse costs after allowance for any favourable costs awards and the award of damages. Only where the insured after exhausting damages has a net liability to the opponent to pay costs will this clause of cover provide an indemnity.

The 'deficiency' referred to therefore is a deficiency in the capacity of damages to satisfy an adverse costs award.

Unrecovered premiums

15.13 With the introduction of recoverable insurance premiums subject to the CPR which permits a challenge to the level of premium and disallowance at an assessment of some and ultimately all of the premium, there is yet another risk which can be insured. The provision of cover for the disallowed part of a premium is a feature which may emerge once there is some experience and case history upon which to base an assessment of the risk. Provision at the present is rare. It is likely that there will be a requirement in the case of such cover that there should be a vigorous defence of the premium and a willingness to consider an appeal, possibly with the co-operation of the insurer. Currently the risk in respect of this factor is being placed on the client (or in some delegated authority schemes on the solicitor).

Typical conditions

Withdrawal

15.14 It is usual for the policy to provide that withdrawal from the case without the consent of the insurer will mean that no indemnity is provided. Clearly the insurer has no means of limiting its liability once the case has been abandoned and its only means of protection is to deny all cover.

Excluded proceedings

15.15 Many policies exclude defamation, tobacco related, matrimonial and pharmaceutical claims. Other providers will cover these types of risk on a case by case basis. The risks in these areas of litigation are considered to be exceptionally high and where cover is available the premium levels will reflect that perceived level of risk.

Co-operation in the running of the case

15.16 A failure to co-operate is likely to lead not only to withdrawal of cover but to the insured being liable for all costs incurred. Co-operation will extend not only to meeting any instructions given to the insured but to the insured not acting in any way detrimental to the prospects of the case and to not settle the claim without reference to the insurer. All of these requirements are essential to protect the insurer's interest in recovering costs through a successful outcome, either through settlement or the court process. This will be applicable to CFA policies as well as both sides' policies, since as a minimum there is likely to be cover for own disbursements.

Privileged documents

15.17 Policies will usually provide that the insured will give access to all relevant materials and that the insurer's access takes precedence over any legal privilege or rights of confidentiality. To refuse access in these circumstances will again give rise to a withdrawal of cover leaving the insured with an uninsured risk.

Prospects of success[1]

15.18   The policy will provide that support will be given where there are reasonable prospects of success. Continuation of cover throughout the dispute will depend upon such prospects also continuing. There will be a reporting requirement in respect of significant changes in the case, and in particular notification of a change in the prospects. A typical wording is that the insured shall have 'both a reasonable case and a reasonable chance of a worthwhile outcome'. Given that with after the event insurance the insurer will at the time of granting cover have taken the view that the prospects of success are sufficient to warrant the granting of cover it is the reporting requirement which is of greater importance. If a case fails but there has been no reporting of material changes which could have led to a decision to withdraw cover from a particular stage it is likely that the insurer will rely on that failure when a claim is made.

1   Further consideration of 'prospects of success' is given in Chapter 14, para **14.11**.

Reporting requirements

15.19   It is standard for policies to require the insured to inform the insurer of all material developments and to require prompt reporting. In particular the contents of any defence and any evidence disclosed by an opponent must be communicated, but the obligation is a general one and is designed to ensure that the insurer is in a position to limit their liability where the merits of the case are no longer seen as favourable. Any settlement offer received will be a material development.

Delegated authority

15.20   A delegated authority means that the decision to offer insurance cover, and thereby to bind the underwriter, is delegated by the underwriter to the firm of solicitors with whom the arrangement exists. In personal injury there are a great many such schemes, some of which are 'off the peg' schemes for which application is invited and others are bespoke schemes which have been written with the firm concerned. A requirement of such schemes which is frequently made is of exclusivity, by which the firm agrees, contractually, to insure all eligible cases and to do so exclusively with that insurer. The premium levels for such schemes reflect the expectation that such an agreement is honoured which may call for difficult judgments in some cases where it may be thought unnecessary to take out an insurance policy at all, or certainly at the time at which the delegated authority agreement requires. It is notable that the providers of insurance longest in the field have recently revised their schemes and increased premiums even in the relatively high volume personal injury field[1]. For a firm to obtain a delegated authority it will be necessary for it to meet the assessment criteria of the insurer in terms of the throughput in volume and the success rate as well as the average cost of claims. In essence the insurer has assessed the firm and is prepared to delegate authority on the basis of the track record and risk assessment processes of the firm and on the assumption that the volume of cases and the success rate are high enough to support the premium levels.

1   The Law Society endorsed scheme, Accident Line Protect, was relaunched in 2000 with a considerably reduced number of firms taken onto its panel and an increase in premiums.

Premium levels[1]

15.21   The variation in the terms of cover available in the commercial market are such that comparisons between products solely on the basis of the premium level will be misleading. Nonetheless the provisions relating to recovery of premium have inevitably focused attention on premiums. The range is itself difficult to determine. Insurers provide guide figures in promotional materials and a comparison based upon such information will produce a wide range of figures. A more important comparison would be between the average premium actually charged for a policy in a particular category over a given period of time. Such information is not made available. There are a good number of products available in the personal injury field where the premium is fixed according to certain criteria so that it is possible to make a more accurate comparison, provided the criteria are sufficiently similar. Where the product does not have a fixed tariff the usual method of arriving at a premium is by the application of a percentage figure to the Limit of Indemnity being given. One alternative is to link the premium, payable at the conclusion of the case, to the level of base costs actually incurred by the insured's own solicitor. The percentage figure to be applied to the LOI will be arrived at on the basis of the perceived risk of an adverse costs order being made as a reflection of the legal risk involved. A major factor affecting this risk is the stage in proceedings at which the insurance is sought. Lower premiums are charged the earlier in the dispute it is when cover is sought. Once proceedings have been issued the risk is considered to be much higher and thus premiums are higher. Once a trial date has been set then premiums will be still higher and at this point not all providers will offer insurance at all. It is likely also that the prospects of success in a case which has reached a setting of a trial date have deteriorated significantly from the prospects at an early stage and again cover may be difficult if not impossible to obtain.

1   Funding and deferring the premium, and insuring it are dealt with in Chapter 18.

Assessment fees

15.22   Outside of delegated authority schemes there may be an assessment fee payable when a proposal for insurance is submitted. This is less common in personal injury cases than other fields. Some providers use external assessors for some categories of case which usually means a fee is required. For both sides' policies it is more usual for an assessment fee to be charged. Where cover is then purchased it is common but not universal that any assessment fee is incorporated as part of the quoted premium.

INSURANCE IN NON-CFA CASES—INSURING BOTH SIDES' COSTS

15.23   Many but not all providers of ATE insurance have policies to cover costs in cases where there is no CFA and there is at least one provider that only provides policies not connected to a CFA. Typically therefore, cover is for both sides' costs and disbursements. Not all policies will provide retrospective cover for own costs but most do provide retrospective cover for adverse costs. Given that both sides' costs are to be covered, the limit of indemnity which the client will need will be higher than that needed under a CFA simply because the costs of both sides, rather than one, are to be insured. The premium percentage rate will also be higher than for a CFA case on the basis that there is no sharing of the risk with the solicitor, unlike in a CFA case where the solicitor takes the risk of not being paid fees should the case fail. In many policies cover for adverse costs will be retrospective from the date of the policy but own costs will be covered only from the date of the policy. The variations in policy conditions are as wide as for CFA policies and generally the same points arise. The premium paid for a both sides policy is recoverable to the same extent as a premium for a policy in support of a CFA[1].

1   See Access to Justice Act 1999, s 29. See also Chapter 17 and Appendix 1.

Own costs partly insured and partly covered by a CFA

15.24   Some providers offer policies which cover adverse costs and a percentage of own costs in a case where there is a CFA. In such a case there is a question of whether the success fee for the CFA should be lower than it would have been had the solicitor taken the risk of receiving no costs at all. To apply the success fee to the whole of the costs without reducing the success fee in proportion to the costs insured would give a distorted result. The alternative here would be for the CFA to provide that the success fee will be applied only to the proportion of costs uninsured which is a truer reflection of the risk being taken by the solicitor and enables the success fee to reflect the risk assessment which will have been done. To reduce the percentage figure of the success fee to try to reflect the part of the fees not being risked is an unnecessary complication. It is likely that the insurance premium rate will be higher than for a traditional CFA policy since the solicitor is not sharing in the risk to the same extent.

THE LIMIT OF INDEMNITY

15.25   Irrespective of whether the policy is to support a CFA the crucial factor in the insurance cover provided for a client is the limit of indemnity (LOI). The estimation of own costs is not without difficulty and any proposal for insurance must be considered in the light of the uncertainties which affect the accuracy of such estimates. It is, however, important where there is a policy of insurance to keep actual costs under review. With opponent's costs reliance upon any formal estimates is likely to be possible only after a policy has been purchased, but they will provide significant information as to the risk of exceeding the LOI and of thus exposing the client to an uninsured liability[1]. Insurers are likely to consider an application for an increase in cover to meet an underestimate of costs with some concern given that such an application may be taken as an indication that the prospects of success are not high and the potential value of a claim is rising. There is, conversely, a danger in over estimating the necessary LOI in that the premium may be challenged by a losing opponent on the basis that the level of cover purchased was unreasonable[2]. This tension and the likelihood that additional premiums for increasing the LOI late in the case will be at higher rates, if available at all, requires a careful consideration of the estimate of costs and the provision of accurate estimates by the other side. In the event that the case fails and the LOI is insufficient, whether that be a both sides policy or a CFA policy, the shortfall will mean that the client has an uninsured liability. The ATE policy is not likely to contain a priority clause but will meet a claim made by the insured within the LOI, leaving distribution to the decision of the client. With both sides' cover the client will be left with a liability either to the opponent or their own solicitor. Given the former will have a court order for costs it is likely that that liability will be chosen by the client as being the recipient of the proceeds of the claim in priority to their own solicitor's costs. This situation clearly underlines the need for the review of costs estimates throughout the litigation with appropriate advice being given where there is reason to believe that the client may be underinsured.

1 See the litigation between members of Newcastle United Football Club and the Club—where the clients in a group action were potentially liable for a significant uninsured amount of opponent's costs having paid a not insignificant sum for ATE insurance—*Litigation Funding* Issue 10 (November 2000).
2 See Chapter 17.

INVOLVEMENT OF INSURER IN SETTLEMENT AND THE RUNNING OF THE CASE

15.26   The variation in the terms of policies are also considerable when it comes to the involvement of the insurer in settlement and in some cases in the running of the case. An insurer may for example provide its own settlement figure at the time of proposal requiring the client's figure to be lower if cover is to be provided. Others will require a figure at proposal stage and require a request for approval for continued cover should an offer at or above that figure be rejected by the insured. In such cases the insurer may terminate cover. The reporting requirements of a typical policy will mean that offers of settlement, received or to be made, must be communicated to the insurer. Policy wordings differ on the operation of CPR, Pt 36 and the relationship of costs to damages. As discussed above, policies may provide cover only where there is a net deficit between damages paid to the insured and costs paid by the insured. Other control requirements may include the use of experts from the insurer's own approved list (or the gaining of prior approval to use an non-list expert), the obtaining of counsel's advice before the issue of proceedings or where a change is sought to a pre-agreed settlement figure.

INSOLVENCY OF THE INSURED

15.27
Difficult issues arise where the policyholder becomes insolvent. These are fully dealt with in Chapter 14 above at para **14.15**.

Chapter 16

Informing Clients

THE LAW SOCIETY RULES OF PROFESSIONAL CONDUCT

16.1   Practice Rule 15[1] and the Solicitors' Costs Information and Client Care Code which that Rule applies, require information to be given to a client with respect to the funding of litigation, including information as to insurance.

Paragraph 4(j) of the Code[2] provides—

'The solicitor should discuss with the client how and when any costs are to be met, and consider:

(ii)   whether the client's liability for their own costs may be covered by insurance;

(iii)   whether the client's liability for another party's costs may be covered by pre-purchased insurance and, if not, whether it would be advisable for the client's liability for another party's costs to be covered by after the event insurance (including in every case where a conditional fee or contingency fee arrangement is proposed);'.

1   The *Guide to the Professional Conduct of Solicitors*, 8th edn, (1999), p 265.
2   Ibid at p 268.

16.2   The requirement to consider insurance is a general one and not confined to cases where a CFA is being considered. The Code means that insurance must be discussed but at what length is not clear. It is also unclear whether a solicitor can 'consider' whether the client is already insured without first taking steps to discover, presumably from the client, whether such insurance may exist. If such pre-existing insurance does exist, there then arises the question as to the extent of the cover, whether the terms of the insurance policy as to notifying the insurer can still be complied with and whether in all other respects, including the choice of lawyer[1], the policy is suitable for the client's needs. Early attacks on the recoverability of after the event insurance premiums have focussed on the availability of pre-purchased insurance, it being argued that where insurance already exists, it is unreasonable to purchase an after the event policy[2]. The advice to a client should therefore include consideration of the recoverability of the premium and the responsibility of the client for the premium if not recovered.

1   See Chapter 14.
2   See Chapter 17.

Additional guidance

16.3

> 'Other methods of funding the matter should be explored with the client. The client may have insurance that will cover the matter. In respect of covering another party's costs, the solicitor should find out if the client has pre-purchased insurance, or whether it is advisable for the client to purchase after-the-event insurance. These possibilities should be explored in all cases, as well as when a conditional fee or contingency fee arrangement is proposed.[1]'

The requirement described in the additional guidance is to find out if there is pre-purchased cover. The assumption is that if there is such insurance it will cover both sides' costs. If there is no pre-purchased cover, consideration should be given to purchasing after the event cover, albeit only in respect of adverse costs. This appears to assume that a CFA will be offered, obviating a need for own side's insurance, other than for own disbursements (which may need to include counsel's fees). The Code itself seems to make the same assumption and distinguishes 'own' from adverse costs in the insurance to be considered. It seems inappropriate to make this distinction if it is to mean that consideration is not to be given to after the event both sides' cover as an alternative to a CFA where no pre-purchased insurance exists.

1 *The Guide to the Professional Conduct of Solicitors*, 8th edn (1999), p 273.

'Best advice'

16.4 A phrase often used in reference to the advice which the Code requires is that the solicitor is under a duty to give 'best advice'. This seems to mean that the solicitor is required to survey the market for insurance and warrant that the product recommended is the most suitable to the client's needs. There is clearly no such requirement in the Code. What is required is a discussion of the methods of funding the litigation available and consideration of insurance as a method. If a solicitor wishes to recommend a particular product the question then arises, although not as a matter of interpretation of the Code, as to the potential liability of the solicitor for that recommendation. It is advisable in these circumstances, and has become standard practice, for the solicitor to state in writing that although the product recommended is believed to be suitable for the client's needs, the solicitor is not an insurance broker and cannot give advice as to the full range of products available. The client can be directed to an insurance broker for further advice should that be seen to be appropriate. The after the event insurance market has expanded considerably since 1995 with a vast range of providers each with variations on the terms of the policies offered and it seems improbable that there will be an expectation in each case for the market to be surveyed and a consideration of each policy potentially available to be made[1].

1 The Law Society advice is that solicitors do not need to act as insurance brokers in order to comply with the obligations as to the giving of advice—see *Law Society Gazette* (16 June 2000). Choice of policy is dealt with below at para **16.14**.

CONFLICTS OF INTEREST

16.5   Practice Rule 10

'(1) Solicitors shall account to their clients for any commission received of more than £20 unless, having disclosed to the client in writing the amount or basis of calculation of the commission or (if the precise amount or basis cannot be ascertained) an approximation thereof, they have the client's agreement to retain it.'

Where a solicitor introduces a client to an insurer to arrange for after the event insurance, and the solicitor receives a commission, this must be disclosed to the client and there must be an account to the client unless there is consent to retain this sum. 'Commission' is not defined in the rules[1]. Thus if the solicitor is paid a fee for assessing the case, it may be argued that this payment is not a commission and therefore it can be retained without disclosure to the client. The solicitor's fiduciary relationship however, may require disclosure in any event.

1   The Law Society has issued Guidance on this subject—see *The Guide to the Professional Conduct of Solicitors*, 8th edn, (1999), pp 277–8 and pp 308–32.

16.6   Principle 11.01 of The Guide[1]—

'It is fundamental to the relationship which exists between solicitor and client that a solicitor should be able to give impartial and frank advice to the client, free from any external or adverse pressures or interests which would destroy or weaken the solicitor's professional independence, the fiduciary relationship with the client or the client's freedom of choice'.

It can be seen that any pre-existing relationship between a solicitor and an insurer has the potential to lead to a conflict of interest at least to the extent that that relationship may militate against introducing the client to a different insurer or recommending that no insurance be taken at all[2].

1   See *The Guide to the Professional Conduct of Solicitors*, 8th edn, (1999), p 222.
2   See further below—ethical perspectives on the use of insurance para **16.9**.

THE CONDITIONAL FEE AGREEMENTS REGULATIONS 2000[1]

16.7   Where a CFA is entered into on or after 1 April 2000, reg 4 of the CFA Regulations 2000 provides—

'(1) Before a conditional fee agreement is made the legal representative must—

(a)   inform the client about the following matters, and
(b)   if the client requires any further explanation, advice or other information about any of those matters, provide such further explanation, advice or other information about them as the client may reasonably require.

(2) Those matters are—

(a)   the circumstances in which the client may be liable to pay the costs of the legal representative in accordance with the agreement,

    (b)   the circumstances in which the client may seek assessment of the fees and expenses of the legal representative and the procedure for doing so,

    (c)   whether the legal representative considers that the client's risk of incurring liability for costs in respect of the proceedings to which agreement relates is insured against under an existing contract of insurance,

    (d)   whether other methods of financing those costs are available, and, if so, how they apply to the client and the proceedings in question,

    (e)   whether the legal representative considers that any particular method or methods of financing any or all of those costs is appropriate and, if he considers that a contract of insurance is appropriate or recommends a particular such contract—

        (i)   his reasons for doing so, and

        (ii)   whether he has an interest in doing so.'

The information required in reg 4(2)(c) above must be given orally, whether or not also given in writing. The information required in reg 4(2)(e) must be given both orally and in writing.

The Regulations must be fully complied with for the CFA to be enforceable[2]. Regulation 4 has the effect of requiring certain information to be given to the client before the CFA is made. Failure to give that information will mean that the CFA itself is unenforceable. With regard to the information relating to insurance, although the Regulation itself does not require all of the information to be in writing, it is recommended that a written note, signed by the client, be kept of the giving of oral advice. The advice required by reg 4(2)(c) is the same as that required by the Law Society Client Care Code and must mean a reference to before the event insurance which could have been used had a CFA not been chosen as the method of funding the case. It is unlikely that a pre-purchased policy will enable a solicitor to act for the client under a CFA, although it might enable the solicitor to act for the client with the benefit of both sides' cover. Regulation 4(2)(e) means that the solicitor must tell the client why a particular method of funding potential costs is being recommended, but it is assumed this does not mean explaining why a CFA is being used as the particular method of funding the case. It will include however, any formal funding options[3]. It further requires the solicitor to tell the client why insurance is being recommended and why any particular policy of insurance is being recommended. Given that the context here is that the client is about to enter into a CFA and potentially will be liable for the opponent's costs and their own disbursements, it is likely that in all cases the solicitor will advise (or indeed require) that the client be insured. As to any particular policy of insurance it is likely that the solicitor will be able to advise that the policy is believed to be suitable to the case and the client's particular needs[4].

1   SI 2000/692. See Chapter 6, para **6.6** for a table of the information provisions.
2   Courts and Legal Services Act 1990, s 58(1) and (3)(c) as substituted by s 27 of the Access to Justice Act 1999.
3   See Chapter 18.
4   For choice of policy, see below para **16.14**.

16.8   Where the solicitor has an 'interest' in recommending a particular policy that must be disclosed. This appears to be wider than a matter of disclosing a commission[1]. It is however, unclear as to how wide a meaning the word 'interest' is likely to be given. Where the client has been referred to the solicitor by an third party, for example an insurer, and the solicitor is contractually bound to the introducer to insure all CFA cases, it could be argued that the solicitor's contractual obligation is an 'interest' which has to be conveyed to the client. Given that the validity of the ensuing CFA itself depends upon satisfying the Regulation a solicitor must err on the side of over disclosure to be sure that the CFA is inviolable.

1 Commission is dealt with above at para **16.5**.

ETHICAL PERSPECTIVES ON THE USE OF INSURANCE

16.9   The Society for Advanced Legal Studies[1] (SALS) published a report in January 2001 entitled *The Ethics of Conditional Fee Arrangements*. In the report, the ethical issues relating to the relationship between solicitors and insurance companies and in the giving of advice to clients about insurance were given careful consideration.

1 Copies of the report can be obtained from the Society at 17 Russell Square, London. The following extracts from the report are reproduced with permission which is gratefully acknowledged.

'Ethics and Insurance Companies'

16.10   Delegated authority schemes where the insurer has assessed the solicitor's firm rather than the individual case and has delegated to the solicitor the authority to bind the insurer in an individual case without reference to the insurer received particular attention in the report—

> 'In a delegated authority scheme, participating firms are in an ongoing contractual arrangement with the insurer. A key term of the contract is that all the CFA and speculative fee cases done by the member firms must be covered by the relevant insurer. This is to ensure that the participating insurers are able to spread the risk among weaker and stronger cases, and they hope to avoid the risk of adverse selection of cases by participating firms.' [para 3.90]

> 'It is important to emphasise the significance of adverse selection to the insurance market. It comes about when then client group is skewed in some way towards those with less strong claims, as would happen if solicitor firms could opt just to insure what they saw as their weaker CFA cases. Adverse selection leads to greater than expected claims which in turn leads to the insurer increasing premiums to compensate for the higher payouts. The higher the premium, the greater the incentive for firms to be selective in the cases they insure, which leads to even greater adverse selection. Insurers rightly insist that once this vicious circle gains momentum, the insurance product is doomed.' [para 3.91]

Whether or not a firm is a member of a delegated authority scheme, and whether or not such schemes have a requirement that all CFA cases be insured, the claims history of a firm will build up over time and will inevitably influence premium rates and ultimately the decision to offer insurance at all. Whilst many delegated authority schemes do provide for exclusive use this is but one mechanism to try to maintain the principle of losers being paid for by winners. The reality for the insurance market of adverse selection was evident with the long running Law Society approved scheme[1] not only suspending the membership of some of its approved firms but ultimately to an entire re-launch of the product with different underwriters and far fewer firms[2]. It had discovered that the practice of running personal injury cases under non-contentious business agreements and only converting to a CFA once issue of proceedings became likely was widespread enough that it amounted to adverse selection. The available pool of cases was not therefore that which had been expected when the scheme had been devised. The costs involved in that adverse selection are being borne by subsequent policyholders whose premiums are significantly higher than those imposed in the earlier scheme.

1   Accident Line Protect (ALP). In November 1999 premiums went up by 60% for road traffic cases and by 103% for all other cases. Delegated authority was withdrawn for multi-track cases.
2   The scheme was re-launched in November 2000 with all existing members invited to re-apply for membership. Not all applications were successful. Premiums are quoted as being between £300 and £2,900. Over 80,000 policies had been sold under the old scheme. Under the new scheme all CFA cases must be insured (whether referred by ALP or not) and must be insured from the outset. See Litigation Funding November 2000.

16.11   The SALS report concluded that there was an inevitable conflict of interest in delegated authority schemes where there is a requirement that all cases be insured—

'In circumstances where it is not in the financial interest of the client to take out ATE (because the case is a "near certainty") but the firm is obliged to insure all CFA cases under their delegated authority scheme, there is a conflict between the client's interests and the insurers' contractual insistence on exclusivity vis à vis the solicitor firm.' [Para 3.93]

It is acknowledged later in the report that the recoverability of the insurance premium from the opponent will to some extent ease the problem of advising clients where there is a delegated authority scheme in place. This does still leave the question of any unrecovered part of the premium in such cases, given that the premium relates to a policy which the solicitor has introduced under a contractual obligation. The implication for advising clients once a premium for a particular product has been reduced on an assessment has yet to be faced and there is no advice as yet from the Law Society as to how to deal with such a situation.

16.12   The Report sets out certain advantages which the delegated authority schemes have, both for firms and clients (para 3.94). It is stated that cover is instant and automatic thus avoiding lengthy application procedures, and that such schemes are cheaper to administer and easier to understand. It is recognised however that premiums can be higher and indeed that the Law Society approved scheme has premiums in some instances significantly higher than comparable products on the open market. It is recognised that such schemes are attempting to provide a solution in the interests of a wider population of users than any individual client but when taken together with the size of premium the conclusion reached is that there is a major problem of conflict of interest. It is open to question as to what conclusion might have been reached had the Report been looking at the rates charged by the Law Society Scheme before November 1999, since that may have kept separate the issues about compulsory insurance and the issue of its cost.

'Obligations to give Advice on Insurance'

16.13   The Report then links these conflicts with the giving of advice and it starkly puts the point that a solicitor may be advising a client to purchase a product which in the opinion of the solicitor the client does not need on the basis that the case is so strong that there is no appreciable risk. Clearly such a view looks to the individual and the not any wider interest but it is a problem for delegated authority schemes which will not arise outside of such schemes except to the extent that a firm is concerned with its claims history. Consideration is given to a disclaimer approach whereby clients are told of the exclusivity contract and advised that other firms may offer a CFA without such a scheme. It was recognised that this would not be palatable to firms nor to insurers.

A further ethical issue raised is the ability of a firm which has a delegated authority scheme to act for clients whose cases are in a ground breaking field. This assumes that such cases would be within the delegated authority, would have to be insured under the scheme, but may distort the claims record of the firm. The ultimate result of such a dilemma may be that a firm will not be able to work for clients who would be referred under a delegated authority scheme if it wishes to continue to act for clients in ground breaking fields. Effectively it is argued, the insurer has become the gate-keeper of the civil justice system.

The report concludes with the following recommendation—

> 'We recommend that it is made clear in the Law Society's Practice Rules that a solicitor's duty to their client under Practice Rule 1 puts the solicitor in a situation of conflict with their client if the solicitor is aware that the insurance is unnecessary or unnecessarily expensive.'

CHOICE OF AFTER THE EVENT INSURANCE POLICY

16.14   The details of the range of cover available in the after the event insurance market are dealt with in Chapter 15. The following sets out as a check list the most likely factors to affect a decision as to which policy to recommend to a client.

ATE Insurance for a CFA[1]

16.15

Nature of the case covered (not all insurers will insure all types of case)	
Own counsel's fee cover needed (not all insurers will give this cover)	
Standard limit of indemnity too high	
Standard limit of indemnity too low	
Have proceedings been issued (not all insurers will provide cover after issue)	
Premium funding needed	
Deferred premium required	
Premium insured if the case loses	
Client's damages left intact if Part 36 lost	
Non-returnable application or assessment fee	
Have used this policy/insurer before	

1   It is assumed here that the CFA provides that no fees will be due if the case fails. If the CFA provides for some payment of fees in the event of a loss it should be noted that some CFA policies will not apply at all and some will not provide cover for own fees in the event of loss. If cover is sought for the percentage of own fees payable if the case loses, products to meet this 'hybrid' CFA are available either as variants of CFA products of both sides' cover products.

Premium levels

16.16   Variation in the terms of cover between the many policies in the market is met with an even greater variation in the premiums quoted in product literature and in response to media questions[1]. The premium levels quoted are difficult to compare due to the variations in cover which a premium will reflect. It is also the case that two of the providers longest in the market quote the highest premium level ranges[2] and that premium levels have been increased by many providers. Nonetheless, the recoverability[3] of the premium in full must be a consideration in recommending a policy to a client and the level of premium is the most obvious factor for an opponent to challenge.

1   See for example Litigation Funding (November 2000). It is important to note that a premium level quoted in publications does not mean that the individual case will be offered cover at that rate or even at all.
2   Abbey Legal Protection and Litigation Protection Limited as at November 2000—(*Litigation Funding* as note 1 above). Both providers have offered CFA policies since 1995.
3   Recoverability is dealt with in Chapter 17.

ATE Insurance where both sides' cover is sought

16.17

Nature of the case covered (not all insurers will insure all types of case)	
Limit on % of own side's cover	
Standard limit of indemnity too high	
Standard limit of indemnity too low	
Top up of limit of indemnity available	
Policy available if proceedings issued (not all providers will give this cover)	
Own costs retrospectively covered	
Premium funding	
Deferred premium	
Premium insured if the case loses	
Client's damages left intact if Part 36 lost	
Non-returnable application or assessment fee	
Have used this policy/insurer before	

Premium levels

16.18   As with CFA policies there will be a reflection in the premium level of the degree of cover being provided. Typically premiums are calculated as a percentage of the limit of indemnity and range from 10% to 40%. If there is a CFA with some own costs in the event of a loss the rate may be expected to reflect the degree of risk being taken by the solicitor. Where own costs are payable in full in the event of a loss the premium level is likely to be higher.

Chapter 17

Recoverability of Insurance Premiums

THE STATUTORY PROVISION

17.1   The Government first canvassed opinion concerning the proposal to make insurance premiums recoverable from a losing opponent in its consultation paper *Access to Justice with Conditional Fees* published in March 1998. In that paper the proposal regarding insurance premiums was put in the context of conditional fees and the Government's wish to widen the use of CFAs as a means of providing access to justice.

> 'The Government is, on the whole, minded to amend the present law to allow the success fee to be recoverable and, either by statute or changes to rules of court, to allow the insurance premium to be recovered as a disbursement. It is keen to learn whether theses changes would be welcomed in making conditional fees more useful and attractive.[1]'

1   *Access to Justice with Conditional Fees* (March 1998), para 2.17. Responses were specifically requested to the following question; 'Should the success fee and any insurance premium be recoverable against the losing party?'.

17.2   The responses summary[1] to that consultation paper states that two-thirds of those who commented on the recoverability of the insurance premium supported the proposal. That support was greater than that expressed for the recoverability of the success fee. There was a concern expressed that recoverability might lead to an overall increase in insurance premiums, it is assumed a reference to liability insurers' premiums having to rise to meet the cost of recoverability.

1   *Conditional Fees Consultation—Summary of Responses* (July 1998).

17.3   During the debate on the Conditional Fee Agreements Order 1998[1], Lord Hunt of Wirral raised the concerns of defendant insurers over the proposal—

> 'My third point, which I make as a member of FOIL, the Forum of Insurance Lawyers, is about his indication that he might well be minded to introduce primary legislation at a future stage to allow the success fee and insurance premium to be payable by the defendant. Surely in CFAs this removes from the plaintiff and his solicitor the risk that they are being asked to bear, which risk sharing has always underpinned the concept of CFAs. The defendant is being asked to pay for those cases he has won

through a levy on the cases he has lost. It is as simple as that. Surely access to justice requires fairness on both sides of the equation.

FOIL has made a very strong case. Surely if we are to have a system of no fault compensation for plaintiffs we ought to debate that proposal, just as we did following the Pearson Commission in the 1970s. I am troubled. Christopher Hodges was troubled in the New Law Journal when he said:

"Is it really right that virtually all risk should be removed from a plaintiff in litigation?".

The defendant stands to pay out far more than he or she does currently. I hope that the noble and learned Lord the Lord Chancellor will listen carefully to the evidence of FOIL.[2']

1   SI 1998/1860.
2   House of Lords Official Report [Session 1997–98], Volume 592 No 193, col 1108.

17.4   The Access to Justice Bill was introduced in December 1998 and contained a clause which became s 29 of the 1999 Act.
Access to Justice Act 1999 (AJA 1999), s 29—

'Where in any proceedings a costs order is made in favour of any party who has taken out an insurance policy against the risk of incurring a liability in those proceedings, the costs payable to him may, subject in the case of court proceedings to rules of court, include costs in respect of the premium of the policy.'

17.5   Amendments to that clause were proposed in the House of Lords to restrict the recoverability of the premium by reference to certain criteria. The Government's preferred method was to leave the matter of what considerations should affect recovery to the Rules of Court. It is notable, however, that during the debate on these unsuccessful amendments the matter of the applicability of what was to become s 29 to both sides' costs policies was made clear—

'Amendment Nos. 226 and 227 seem to proceed on the assumption that the provisions of Clause 28 apply only to premiums used to support conditional fee agreements. Clause 28 extends to other forms of "after the event" insurance and the premiums paid for such insurance. Consequently, it is not only concerned with the recovery of premiums in cases where a conditional fee is used.[1']

1   House of Lords Official Report [Session 1998–99], Volume 596 No 25, col 980.

CONSULTATION ON THE IMPLEMENTATION OF SECTION 29

17.6   The Government's consultation process continued with the publication of a further paper in September 1999[1] given that Rules of Court had to be drafted in order for s 29 to be fully implemented. That paper described s 29 as ensuring that the insurance premium can be claimed and that, '...the court retains the discretion whether to allow the disbursement and at what level, applying the normal tests on assessment.[2'] Responses were sought on matters such as challenges to the insurance premium and the question of notification to an opponent of the existence of an insurance policy.

1 *Conditional Fees: Sharing the Risks of Litigation* CP 7/99.
2 Ibid, para 24. At para. 26 it was stated '…the Government is concerned to ensure that the assessment of whether an insurance premium is reasonable should not be distorted by hindsight. The court will need to decide whether the level of cover was fair and reasonable when the policy was taken out.' At para 27, 'It is not proposed that solicitors are required to seek the cheapest insurance policies, since this is not a requirement when procuring other forms of disbursement, such as expert reports. However, the court will wish to consider whether the cover purchased was appropriate and proportionate to the case being assessed.'

17.7   The Government's final paper was published in February 2000. Rules of Court were to provide for notification to the opponent and to the court of the fact that insurance was in place. There were to be sanctions for failure to notify the opponent. Full disclosure of the terms of insurance was to be provided for at the time of assessment. The premium was to be recoverable only for cases of action in respect of which the first policy was purchased after 1 April 2000. All of these statements have been implemented by the Civil Procedure Rules (CPR) and the Practice Direction about Costs (CPD).

17.8   The final paper however also contained significant details as to the assessment and recovery of the premium which have not been implemented by the wordings of the CPR and the CPD. Paragraph 68 states—

'Rules of court should provide that on final assessment the losing opponent (but not the client) should be able to challenge the client's choice of insurance cover and the cost of insurance premium by demonstrating to the court that the choice was wholly unreasonable and generated excessive costs.[1]'

1   The Government's conclusions following consultation on the paper *Conditional Fees: Sharing the Risks of Litigation*.

17.9   Paragraph 70 provides an explanation of the phrase—

'By "wholly unreasonable" and "excessive costs" the Government means a choice and cost that no reasonable person would think it appropriate respectively to make or pay. The purpose of setting so tough a test is to preclude the court having to decide between insurance arrangements which are marginally different or where the advantages and disadvantages of different products may be open to debate but not such that a clear decision that choosing one was more or less reasonable than choosing the other.[1]'

The phrase 'wholly unreasonable and generated excessive costs' was not incorporated into the CPR or the Practice Direction.

1   The Government's conclusions following consultation on the paper *Conditional Fees: Sharing the Risks of Litigation*.

17.10   A lengthy list of issues which a court may wish to consider was given in para 71:

- the type of claim, for example personal injury, medical negligence, commercial;*
- the anticipated complexity of the case at the time insurance was taken out, including to which "track" it is to be allocated if it gets to court;
- the anticipated value of the claim at the time insurance was taken out;
- where the insurance cover is purchased in support of a conditional fee agreement with a success fee, the percentage of the premium compared to the level of cover;

- where the insurance cover is not purchased in support of a conditional fee agreement with a success fee how its cost compares with the likely costs of a similar case running under a success fee and supporting insurance cover;*
- the level of cover provided;
- the extent of the cover provided, for example against the other side's costs or both sides' costs;
- the availability and accessibility of alternative products to the one chosen;
- the ability of the client to pay the premium—a client without the means to pay the premium would need to use an insurance product with no requirement to pay out monies at the start or during the lifetime of the proceedings;
- the level of service provided to the client and the ease and convenience of the product from the client's perspective;
- the certainty of ultimate cost to the client;
- for higher cost insurance products, whether there is a rebate in the premium for early settlement; and
- any other relevant issues raised by the challenging party, including whether the level of the success fee and the price of the premium taken together are unreasonable and constitute excessive costs.'

The Practice Direction about Costs[1] refers to only two of these issues (marked *).

1 CPD, s 11.

Conditional fee policies and both sides' policies

17.11 The legislative history of s 29 clearly shows that insurance premiums in respect of policies purchased in support of a CFA are intended to be recoverable from an unsuccessful opponent. The wording of s 29 hints at the after the event market by referring to policies purchased against the risk of a liability in 'those proceedings', a reference which before the event insurance cannot meet since such policies cannot specify particular proceedings given they are not at the time known to exist. Section 29 includes policies which cover both sides' costs and are not allied to a CFA[1]. A both sides' cover policy is a policy which does cover the risk of incurring a liability in the particular proceedings. The relevant section of the CPD refers specifically to this form of insurance in providing the factors to be taken into account in the assessment of costs—

'where the insurance cover is not purchased in support of a conditional fee agreement with a success fee, how its cost compares with the likely cost of funding the case with a conditional fee agreement with a success fee and supporting insurance cover.[2]'

1 See para **17.5** above.
2 CPD, s 11.10(1).

Disclosure to the other side

17.12 The majority of those responding to the consultation paper supported the proposal that the opponent should be informed that insurance has been taken out. The justification was seen to be that recoverability of the premium altered the paying party's liability for costs. It was thought however that disclosure of the amount of the premium paid was not desirable as it might indicate views on the strength of the case. The eventual provision in the Practice Direction[1] implements these conclusions.

1   CPD, s 19.1.

Disclosure to the court

17.13   Although disclosure to the court of the reasons for the success fee was raised in the consultation paper, the conclusion reached relates to disclosing the existence of a CFA with a success fee but no disclosure of the level of the success fee nor any reasons for it until assessment. No explanation is given as to the purpose of disclosure to the court of the fact that a CFA with success fee is in existence. The Practice Direction about Costs[1] implements this conclusion.

1   CPD, s 19.2(a).

Who can challenge the premium?

17.14   This matter received mixed views during the consultation process—

'The consultation paper proposed that both the client and the opponent should be able to challenge the level of the insurance premium. The majority of respondents agreed that the opponent should be allowed to challenge having to pay all or part of the premium. The Law Society and the ABI believed that it would be inappropriate to make the terms of an insurance contract subject to challenge by the insured, because to do so would seriously undermine the development of the insurance market. The same bodies also believed that if the solicitor had acted negligently in recommending a policy then the remedy for the client would be a complaint or a negligence action rather than assessment of costs. In contrast, the Senior Costs Judge and the Bar felt that the client should be able to challenge the level of the premium, which could be treated as any other disbursement. Any solicitor who encouraged his client to accept an excessively high premium would be acting negligently and it was right that the client had the opportunity to challenge their responsibility for paying that premium. They also agreed, however, that a successful challenge would result in the solicitor, not the insurer, meeting the difference between the amount the client should have paid and the amount which was actually paid. The Government is of the view that allowing the insured to challenge the premium could lead to the insurers not being paid which might undermine the insurance market and in so doing deny access to justice to many thousands of people.[1]'

The Government's conclusion to permit a challenge to the premium only by the opponent was incorporated into the CPD by s 11[2] which provides the factors to be taken into account on an assessment under CPR, r 44.5 where an additional liability is claimed. No changes were made to the CPR to permit a client to challenge the insurance premium. A client's right to challenge a bill of costs under the Solicitors Act 1974 was not amended in respect of the success fee nor an insurance premium. It is clear that the success fee can be challenged under that Act[3]. An insurance premium paid by the client would not come within the Act. Where the premium has been paid by the solicitor on behalf of the client it is arguable that given s 29 was deemed necessary to enable a premium to be recovered, such a premium cannot be regarded as a disbursement for if it could be so regarded, s 29 was an unnecessary provision. If that is the correct position, it seems to mean that a solicitor can deduct the insurance premium even though held in part to be unreasonable and the client is unable to challenge that deduction other than by suing the solicitor in negligence.

1   Government Conclusions Paper (note 1 at para **17.8**) (February 2000), para 74.
2   See para **17.2** below.
3   See Chapter 8.

The make up of the premium

17.15

'It was suggested that there were elements of the cost of the insurance that it would be inappropriate to ask the losing party to meet. However, the insurance premium is calculated with regard to the insurers' business costs in the same way as solicitors' hourly costs are calculated with regard to the business costs of their firms and have to be reflected in the success fee which under a conditional fee agreement is the premium that solicitors in effect charge for bearing the risk of not recovering their own costs. Trying to tease out and disallow certain elements of business overheads, whether in respect of insurance premiums or the success fee, would be impractical and unjustifiable in the Government's view.[1]'

The Government's view was not clearly implemented through the wording of the Practice Direction nor any changes made to the CPR. The court may assess the premium in terms of reasonableness and although the factors referred to in the Practice Direction about Costs[2] do not refer to the make up of the premium, in determining the reasonableness of that premium it may be that arguments will be advanced in some cases that there are elements of it which it is unreasonable to expect an opponent to cover.

1   Government Conclusions Paper (February 2000) para 75.
2   CPD, s 11—see para **17.24** below.

Pre-action settlement

17.16   A further issue raised in the consultation period was the place of recoverable premiums in the fulfilment of the spirit of pre-action protocols and the intention of the Woolf reforms of cutting costs—

'It has also been suggested that the client should not enter into an insurance policy until all the steps under a pre action-protocol had been taken and a response received from the opponent, because this would prevent the premium being assessed at a point where the extent of the risk could be uncertain and hence over-estimated. Limiting the ability of a client to recover premiums only on insurance policies entered into at such a late stage in the proceedings would mean that in the vast majority of cases that settle early, no premium would be recoverable. That would seriously undermine the Government's policy. Without recovery it would often be uneconomic for claimants seeking smallish damages or making non-money claims and for defendants to take out insurance at the outset. That in the Government's view would impede access to justice unnecessarily.[1]'

The Government's response to this issue is to assume that policies would be taken out at the outset even though the premium would not be recovered and that in many cases this would not improve access to justice since in low damages cases the premium would take too large a proportion of damages. Indeed it was because damages were being seriously reduced both by the success fee and the premium that recovery from the opponent was considered to be the desirable change to the way CFAs were to operate. At paragraph 71 of the Report, one of the factors listed which a court may wish to consider in assessing the reasonableness of a premium was '…for higher cost insurance products, whether there is a rebate in the premium for early settlement'. Such a factor is a partial response to concerns that the pre-action protocols should continue to encourage early cost effective settlements. The Practice Direction refers to rebate of premium without any reference to that being confined to higher cost products[2].

1 Government Conclusions Paper (February 2000), para 76.
2 CPD, s 11.10(4).

THE CPR AND PRACTICE DIRECTION ABOUT COSTS

Disclosure

17.17 The disclosure of information about the existence of an insurance premium is governed by the CPR and Practice Direction about Costs—CPR, r 44.15—

'(1) A party who seeks to recover an additional liability must provide information about the funding arrangement to the court and to other parties as required by a rule, practice direction or court order.'

An 'additional liability' is defined in r 43.2 to include the insurance premium.

PRACTICE DIRECTION ABOUT COSTS, s 19

17.18 CPD, s 19.1(1)—

'A party who wishes to claim an additional liability in respect of a funding arrangement must give any other party information about that claim if he is to recover the additional liability. There is no requirement to specify the amount of the additional liability separately nor to state how it is calculated until it falls to be assessed.'

A 'funding arrangement' is defined in CPR, r 43.2 to include an insurance policy to which AJA 1999, s 29 applies. The CPD provides for the giving of notice of funding to the court and the opponent. The notice must contain the information set out in Form N251[1].

CPD, s 19.2(2)—

'(a) A claimant who has entered into a funding arrangement before starting the proceedings to which it relates must provide information to the court by filing the notice when he issues the claim form.

   (b) He must provide information to every other party by serving the notice. If he serves the claim form himself he must serve the notice with the claim form. If the court is to serve the claim form, the court will also serve the notice if the claimant provides it with sufficient copies for service.'

1 See Appendix 3.

17.19   Defendants who have purchased insurance policies where the premium will be recoverable under s 29 must similarly give notice to the opponent—
CPD, s 19.2(3)—

'A defendant who has entered into a funding arrangement before filing a document

   (a) must provide information to the court by filing notice with his first document. A "first document" may be an acknowledgement of service, a defence, or any other document, such as an application to set aside a default judgment.
   (b) must provide information to every party by serving notice. If he serves his first document himself he must serve the notice with that document. If the court is to serve his first document the court will also serve the notice if the defendant provides it with sufficient copies for service.'

Section 19.2(4) provides that where the insurance policy is taken out by a claimant after starting proceedings or by a defendant after filing his first document, notice must be given both to the court ands opponent within seven days. Section 19.2(5) recommends that information be provided before the commencement of proceedings albeit there is no requirement in the Practice Direction. A pre-action protocol may also provide for the giving of this information pre-issue.

THE DETAILS WHICH MUST BE DISCLOSED

17.20   CPD, s 19.4(3)—

'Where the funding arrangement is an insurance policy the party must state the name of the insurer, the date of the policy and must identify the claim or claims to which it relates (including Part 20 claims if any).'

Where more than one funding arrangement has been made, for example a CFA with success fee and an insurance policy, a single notice containing the information set out in form N251 may be given[1]. If the insurance is cancelled or there is a change of insurer, notice must again be given of the information set out in Form N251[2].

1 CPD, s 19.4(5).
2 CPD, s 19.3(2).

The costs assessment

17.21   The general provisions of the CPR as to costs continue to apply where an additional liability is claimed.

CPR, r 44.4(1)—

'…the court will not…allow costs which have been unreasonably incurred or are unreasonable in amount.'

CPR, r 44.4(2)—

'Where the amount of costs is to be assessed on the standard basis, the court will—

only allow costs which are proportionate to the matters in issue; and resolve any doubt which it may have as to whether costs were reasonably incurred or reasonable and proportionate in amount in favour of the paying party.'

CPR, r 44.5(3) sets out the factors which a court must take into account in deciding the amount of costs. With regard to the cost of insurance the following are of significance:

CPR, r 44.5(3)—

'…the efforts made, if any, before and during the proceedings in order to try to resolve the dispute;

the amount or value of any money or property involved;

the importance of the matter to all the parties;

the particular complexity of the matter or the difficulty or novelty of the question raised…'.

17.22 The provisions of the CPR specifically addressing the recovery of an insurance premium must be read in conjunction with the above general principles—

CPR, r 44.3A—

'(1) The court will not assess any additional liability until the conclusion of the proceedings, or part of the proceedings, to which the funding arrangement relates.

(2) At the conclusion of the proceedings, or part of the proceedings, to which the funding arrangement relates the court may—

(a) make a summary assessment of all the costs, including any additional liability;
(b) make an order for detailed assessment of the additional liability but make a summary assessment of the other costs; or
(c) make an order for detailed assessment of all the costs.'

17.23 The Practice Direction about Costs sets out the factors to be taken into account in deciding whether the cost of insurance cover is reasonable and provides that the assessment is on the basis of the facts as they reasonably appeared at the time the insurance policy was purchased.

CPD, s 11.7—

'Subject to paragraph 17.8(2)[1], when the court is considering the factors to be taken into account in assessing an additional liability, it will have regard to the facts and circumstances as they reasonably appeared to the solicitor or counsel when the funding arrangement was entered into and at the time of any variation of the arrangement.'

1   CPD, s 17.8(2) refers to costs only proceedings—see para **17.28** below.

17.24   CPD, s 11.10—

'In deciding whether the cost of insurance cover is reasonable, relevant factors to be taken into account include—

(1) where the insurance cover is not purchased in support of a conditional fee agreement with a success fee, how its cost compares with the likely cost of funding the case with a conditional fee agreement with a success fee and supporting insurance cover;

(2) the level and extent of the cover provided;

(3) the availability of any pre-existing insurance cover;

(4) whether any part of the premium would be rebated in the event of early settlement;

(5) the amount of commission payable to the receiving party or his legal representatives or other agents.'

Sub-paragraph (1) provides for a difficult task. In accordance with s 11.7 the court must assess the likely cost at the time the insurance was taken out of running the case under a CFA with success fee and insurance. This seemingly requires a consideration of the prediction of the length of time the case will take made at the time the policy was purchased. It also requires a prediction of the success fee which would have been set at that time had one been set. It is submitted that the danger of applying hindsight faced with this factor is unacceptably high and that the number of hypotheticals involved makes the application of the test impractical. Where the additional liability being claimed is for a CFA with success fee and insurance there is no requirement to compare that cost with the likely cost of running the case not under a CFA but with (presumably) both sides cover.

Meaning of premium

17.25   CPR, r 43.2 defines 'insurance premium' as—

'...a sum of money paid or payable for insurance against the risk of incurring a costs liability in the proceedings, taken out after the event that is the subject matter of the claim.'

Arguments based upon the elements which go to make up the premium charged for insurance are not best addressed to this definition[1]. The overriding principle that costs to be awarded must be reasonable is apt to encompass any such arguments. It is submitted that once an argument is accepted that some of the charge made by a provider of insurance is not made in respect of the 'risk of incurring a costs liability' there would be limitless potential for disputes as to recovery of the premium. If a premium charged is seen to be unreasonable in amount, for whatever reason, the court has ample power to recognise that fact in the amount of costs awarded.

1   See above para **17.15**.

Availability of before the event insurance

17.26 One of the factors to be taken into account in considering the reasonableness of the cost of insurance is the 'availability of any pre-existing insurance cover'[1]. An amendment to the Access to Justice Bill[2] was proposed which provided that a CFA could not be used in substitution for before the event legal expenses insurance. In rejecting that amendment it was said that it must be a matter for the individual to decide whether he will take advantage of an insurance product he has already purchased or whether for some reason he prefers to engage a solicitor and take out insurance[3]. The Practice Direction leaves the question of the reasonableness of the cost of after the event insurance where before the event insurance is in place to be decided in the circumstances of the individual case .

1   CPD, s 11.10(3).
2   Amendment 144 in the name of Lord Hunt of Wirral.
3   House of Lords Official Report [Session 1998–99], Volume 597 No 37, col 601.
4   Before the event insurance is dealt with in Chapter 14.

Settlement pre-issue and the insurable interest

17.27 An early challenge to the recoverability of both the success fee and the insurance premium has come in the form of an argument that until proceedings are issued the claimant has no insurable interest. From that it is argued that no premium should be recoverable. Difficult issues of insurance law would arise out of such an argument, not least the matter of whether a policy would thus be an illegal contract with possible recovery of the premium from the insurer. It is submitted however that this argument fails in that the insured does have an interest in a potential liability for costs in the same way that such an interest exists in respect of before the event legal expenses insurance[1]. The insured knows that circumstances may arise in the future which could give rise to a liability to a third party to pay their legal costs and there is clearly an insurable interest for which the insured seeks an indemnity. It will also be the case in virtually all policies that the insured's liability for his own disbursements will be covered which would be sufficient to give an insurable interest to support the contract of insurance.

1   See *Tarbuck v Avon Insurance plc* [2001] 1 All ER (Comm) 422, where it was recognised that such a policy may cover both a liability for an opponent's costs and the voluntarily incurred contract debt to the insured's own solicitor.

Costs only proceedings[1]

17.28 The changes to the CPR brought about in July 2000 were mainly concerned with CFAs. However, a new procedure was introduced which is not confined to CFAs and which permits a Part 8 application to be made where the only matter in dispute between the parties is costs.

CPR, r 44.12A—

(1) This rule sets out a procedure which may be followed where—

(a)   the parties to a dispute have reached an agreement on all issues (including which party is to pay the costs) which is made or confirmed in writing; but

(b)   they have failed to agree the amount of those costs; and

(c)   no proceedings have been started.

…

(4) In proceedings to which this rule applies the court—

(a)   may

>   (i)   make an order for costs; or
>   (ii)   dismiss the claim;

and

(b)   must dismiss the claim if it is opposed.

1   The costs only procedure is dealt with fully in Chapter 8 para **8.55**.

17.29   The costs which are in dispute can include an additional liability and hence an insurance premium. This costs only procedure is only applicable where proceedings in the dispute have not been started.

CPD, s 17.8—

> '(1) An order for costs made under this rule will be treated as an order for the amount of costs to be decided by a detailed assessment to which Part 47 and the practice directions relating to it apply. Rule 44.4(4) (determination of basis of assessment) also applies to the order.
>
> (2) In cases where an additional liability is claimed, the costs judge or district judge should have regard to the time when and the extent to which the claim has been settled and to the fact that the claim has been settled without the need to commence proceedings.'

These provisions put beyond doubt that an additional liability can be awarded in costs only proceedings. However, where the additional liability consists of an insurance premium recourse must first be had to AJA 1999, s 29[1]. That section refers to the making of a costs order in proceedings where the risk of incurring a liability in those proceedings has been insured. It has been held[2] that costs only proceedings under Part 8 are part and parcel of the proceedings which are the subject of the insurance. The Part 8 proceedings are to be regarded as being a part of the substantive proceedings which might have been issued. In other words the 'proceedings' in contemplation when a policy is taken out necessarily includes a prospect of Part 8 proceedings to recover costs[3]. To hold otherwise would force a party who has an insurance policy to issue proceedings solely to recover costs, a process which the new procedure was designed to avoid. Nonetheless the wording of s 29 is not helpful in this regard if it is intended to provide for recovery of a premium where no substantive proceedings have been commenced.

1   See above para **17.4**.
2   *Callery v Gray* (His Honour Judge Edwards) unreported Case No MC002977, Chester County Court.
3   That is not the same as saying that the insurance is taken out to cover a liability in Part 8 proceedings themselves.

Guidance from the Senior Costs Judge

17.30   The Senior Costs Judge issued guidance in November 2000 to the Designated Civil Judges Conference.

Costs only proceedings

17.31

'The new procedure appears to be being misused by both claimants and defendants in breach of the overriding objective. This misuse has given rise to difficulties for District Judges.

It appears that solicitors acting on behalf of claimants, having settled the amount of damages, are saying to defendants: "Our costs as £x and if this figure is not agreed/paid within 14 days costs only proceedings will be commenced".

Defendants' representatives for their part make unreasonably low offers in respect of pre-proceedings costs and in some cases accompany the offer with a statement that the offer is made for the purpose of negotiation only and that they do not agree to the matter being resolved by use of the costs only procedure.

If a claimant is forced to commence proceedings under Part 7, rather than costs only proceedings under Part 8, defendants will find themselves having to pay, not only the reasonable and proportionate costs of the claim itself, but also the costs of the Part 7 proceedings and any related assessment proceedings. If the defendant has acted unreasonably in compelling the commencement of part 7 proceedings, consideration should be given to making an order for costs on the indemnity basis.'

17.32   The Guidance sets out the steps for the CPR, r 44.12A procedure—

'(1)   The parties must have reached an agreement on all the issues including which party is to pay the costs.

(2)   That agreement must be made or confirmed in writing.

(3)   No proceedings must have been started and the parties (*after a proper attempt at agreement*)[1] must have failed to agree the amount of costs.

(4)   Either party may start costs only proceedings under rule 44.12A.

(5)   The part 8 claim form must:

(a)   identify the claim or dispute to which the agreement to pay costs relates;

(b)   state the date and terms of the agreement on which the claimant relies;

(c)   set out a draft of the order sought;

(d)   state the amount of the costs claimed; and

(e)   state whether costs are claimed on the standard or the indemnity basis.

(6)   The evidence in support of the claim must include copies of the documents on which the claimant relies to prove the defendant's agreement to pay the costs.

(7)   The matter should not be listed before the District Judge until an acknowledgement of service has been filed. If the defendant agrees that the order should be made, or a consent order is filed,

the court will make the order without the necessity of a hearing.

(8)   If the time for filing acknowledgement of service expires, the claimant may request the court by letter to make an order in the terms of the claim. If the defendant files an acknowledgement of service out of time but before the court has made an order in the terms of the claim paragraph 9) applies.

(9)   The court may (i) make an order for costs; or, (ii) dismiss the claim. The court must dismiss the claim if it is opposed. A claim is treated as opposed if the defendant states in the acknowledgement of service that it intends to contest the proceedings or to seek a different remedy. The court will then dismiss the claim without a hearing.

(10)   The court may make an order by consent in terms which differ from those set out in the claim form. The order is treated as an order for the amount of costs to be decided by detailed assessment.

In no circumstances should a District Judge or Costs Judge attempt to hear the application and then immediately embark upon a summary assessment of the costs in dispute. Arguments that the District Judge/Costs Judge should do so are incorrect, since a summary assessment is an assessment made by a Judge who has decided the substantive issue. In costs only proceedings the only issue decided by the judge is whether or not there should be an assessment of the costs.'

1   Original emphasis.

Provision in a policy of insurance for non-recovery of premium

17.33   An after the event policy may include a provision that in the event that some of the premium is not recovered in a costs order then it ceases to be payable to the insurer. Arguments based upon the indemnity principle may mean that this becomes self-defeating since under the terms of the policy in some circumstances no premium at all would be paid for the cover and thus there is no liability for which a costs order would be granted as an indemnity. Once the indemnity principle is removed such an argument would be less likely to succeed.

SHORTFALLS AND INTEREST PAYMENTS

17.34   If costs awarded include only part of the insurance premium consideration needs to be given to the liability of the client for the whole premium where its payment has been deferred until the conclusion of the case. Where the premium has already been paid there will be a shortfall in recoveries over expenditure. This risk must be recognised when the policy is taken out and should form part of the advice given. Where the policy provides that the premium due will not exceed any costs awarded as an additional liability in respect of the premium then the shortfall issue cannot arise. Where the premium has been funded by way of a loan the interest payments on the loan will not be recoverable as costs[1] and again this is a shortfall of recovered costs over expenditure which must be advised at the time of taking out the loan.

1   See *Hunt v RM Douglas (Roofing) Ltd* [1988] 3 LS Gaz R 33, CA. '...the court will not look beyond the litigant's means themselves so as to enquire how a litigant is to fund the base costs....', Purchas LJ. See note 1 at para **18.2** below.

Section 29 and Collective Conditional Fee Agreements

17.35   Section 29 provides for a costs order to include the premium of an insurance policy but it refers only to such a policy taken out by a 'party'. A Membership Organisation which uses a CCFA will not be a party in whose favour a costs order can be made. Such an organisation can only recover the costs of insurance by the indirect method of the Access to Justice (Membership Organisation) Regulations[1]. Alternatively, the Membership Organisation can fund the individual member to purchase an insurance policy and then the member can seek to recover that cost under s 29. Given that the basis of the CCFA is that the membership organisation is the funder of the litigation and as such has a direct liability for adverse costs, the body will be seeking to insure its liability as well as any potential liability of the individual. Whether such a policy would be recognised as being within s 29 is unclear.

1   SI 2000/693. See Chapter 9.

17.36   Where the CCFA is used by a funder other than a Membership Organisation the application of s 29 is clear only where the funder is also the client. In such a case the policy will have been purchased by the party to the proceedings. Where a CCFA is being used by a funder who is not also the client, the difficulty of the wording of s 29 arising in the case of Membership Organisations again arises but the solution via the Membership Organisation Regulations is not available. Whilst the abolition of the indemnity principle will overcome any argument that the policy has not been paid for by the party to the proceedings, that abolition will not address the wording of s 29. It seems that the funder must therefore ensure that the policy is in the name of the party albeit funded by the funder and albeit that the funder is also named in the policy.

Chapter 18

Funding

THE NEED FOR FUNDING

18.1 The developments in insurance products since the introduction of CFAs has led to a proliferation of financing products offered by the insurers and in some cases independently of insurers. These products address the funding needs of the solicitor and of the individual client in a wide range of facilities, some offered to clients and others only to or through solicitors. These products are not confined to cases run on a CFA although many are designed for such cases. In a CFA the solicitor is, in effect, funding the litigation by foregoing all payment until the conclusion of the case. The effect on the cash flow of the firm is likely to be marked and can be reduced by the use of funding products. For the client in a CFA there will be the question of funding the insurance premium and other disbursements. In some of these situations it is likely that any funding provided will be insured in the event that the case is unsuccessful.

RECOVERY OF THE COST OF FUNDING

18.2 Although a client may have to borrow funds in order to bring litigation it is clear that such costs are not recoverable from a losing opponent. The Court of Appeal in *Hunt v RM Douglas (Roofing) Ltd*[1] dealt with the question of funding in the context of an award of costs. Per Purchase LJ—

> '...the court will not look beyond the litigant's means themselves so as to enquire how a litigant is to fund the base costs which otherwise are established as being reasonable and proper for achieving justice... A moment's reflection demonstrates the impossibly wide spectrum of possibilities and variations upon the theme once one looks at either the cost of raising the sum of money or the opportunities lost by the payer because money available has been diverted.[2]'

1 [1988] LS Gaz R 33, CA. See note 1 at para **17.34** above.
2 Lexis transcript—Transcript Association.

18.3 The cost to the solicitor of funding the litigation under a CFA is specifically not recoverable from a losing opponent.

CPR, r 44.3B—

'(1) A party may not recover as an additional liability—

(a) any proportion of the percentage increase relating to the cost to the legal representative of the postponement of the payment of his fees and expenses;'.

Thus any charge made by the solicitor in respect of funding disbursements and his own fees can only be recovered form the client and there is no mechanism available for ensuring that this cost does not effectively reduce the damages recovered for the befit of the client where the solicitor is not bearing that cost himself.

FUNDING INSURANCE PREMIUMS

18.4   Where a client wishes to purchase an insurance policy in respect of legal costs there are many products available which will provide the funding for the premium. Such products exist in relation to CFA policies and in relation to policies which provide cover for the costs of both sides. In the personal injury field these products are widely available but many providers of insurance outside of this field also provide funding options in respect of the premium.

There are two methods by which funding in the form of a loan is provided for premiums. Either a loan is arranged for the client or funding is provided to the solicitor and then made available on an individual matter basis. Clearly if the funding is provided to the solicitor it is the primary debt of the solicitor and not the client, albeit the solicitor may recover that cost from the client. There are products which do not have any recourse to the solicitor. If the loan is to the client then the funder will be responsible for complying with the Consumer Credit Act 1974 and can be expected to provide an agreement complying with the terms of the Act as to the content of the agreement and its prescribed form as well as the provision of a cooling off period. Given that the source of the funding will be a financial institution these statutory requirements should not represent an obstacle to the solicitor or the client. The range of funding options available is large and the variations therefore preclude an exhaustive treatment of the terms upon which such loans will be made. It is common however for an option to be given for the whole loan to be repaid at the conclusion of the case. With this method there will be an insurance policy in place which provides for the repayment of the loan and interest if the case fails. The cost of the borrowing will not be recoverable form a losing opponent although the premium itself can form part of the costs awarded[1].

1   Access to Justice Act 1999 (AJA 1999), s 29. See Chapter 17.

18.5   There are alternative methods available such as an instalment plan for the payment of the premium or the deferral of payment of the premium until the conclusion of the case. Clearly each of these is a form of funding with the cost of the loan included in the repayments. With instalments there is a requirement that the client is in funds to enable this to be covered. Again the insurance policy relating to the litigation should cover the premium funding, including interest, in the event that the case fails. With deferred premium payment, again there needs to be Consumer Credit Act agreement in place to ensure enforceability[1] and the insurance policy will need to cover the premium should the case fail. A deferred premium is paid when the case wins and the premium is potentially recoverable under AJA 1999, s 29. Unless a separate charge for credit is made the cost of funding the premium is itself contained in the premium. It is not clear whether that element can be included in a costs award but in any event it could be taken into account on a costs assessment as a factor which may lead to the order not including the entire premium. If the client is intended to bear such a shortfall[2] this needs to be made clear at the time the policy is purchased.

1   See para **18.10** on the Consumer Credit Act 1974 below.
2   The insurance policy may provide that the premium payable is that which on an assessment is permitted to be recovered from the opponent. Clearly in such a case there will not be any shortfall between the amount due and the amount recovered.

FUNDING DISBURSEMENTS

18.6   The most common method of funding disbursements other than by the client doing so at the time they are incurred is for the solicitor to pay the disbursement and wait for payment. There are many funding facilities available to meet this otherwise potentially heavy drain on the firm's cash flow. Here the funding is commonly provided to the firm for it to draw down against invoiced disbursements as the case proceeds. Some schemes require approval in advance for disbursements over a certain value. It is likely that a global and an individual case limit will be placed on such a facility. Because the loan is to the firm the status of the individual client is unlikely to be a factor for the lender. There is likely to be a requirement that the disbursements themselves are covered by an insurance policy such that should the case fail the lender is assured that funds will be available for the repayment of the loan. As with premium funding, some schemes fund the client rather than the firm, with the Consumer Credit Act requirements handled by the funder. Repayment of the loan will be expected to occur either from the costs awarded in the event that the case succeeds or from the insurance policy covering disbursements if the case fails. Most such schemes provide the funder with recourse to the solicitor for repayment of the loan. Interest charged on such funding varies across the providers. In some instances an administration allowance is paid to the solicitor in respect of the work involved in arranging the loan to the client whereas others charge a fee for funding each case.

THE EFFECT OF ABANDONMENT OF THE CASE OR DEATH OF THE CLIENT

18.7   The funding of premiums and disbursements does not increase the risks involved in respect either of the discontinuance of the case or the death of the client. Where the solicitor has a liability to the funder these circumstances affect the ability to meet that liability rather than the liability for the disbursements or premium themselves. The only added risk relates therefore to the interest charges. The disbursements were the responsibility of the client. In the event of death the usual rules will apply and the solicitor's liability on the loan will be defrayed by recovery of the debt. Where the case is discontinued the position will be governed by the terms of any insurance policy or alternatively the ability and willingness of the client to reimburse the solicitor. This position is not altered by the fact that there is a loan other than by the fact that the solicitor will be liable to repay the loan whether or not the client meets their responsibility to the solicitor. Thus, these are circumstances where the insurance policy is of importance to the solicitor since the loan agreement will provide for repayment of the loan in any event.

FUNDING WORK IN PROGRESS

18.8   A main feature of a CFA is that even where the case succeeds the solicitor does not recover fees until the conclusion of the case. A firm will have work in progress which cannot be billed until the case ends. As the caseload taken on CFAs grows there will be cases outstanding with variable levels of work in progress ranging from months to years. The funding of that work in progress across the litigation department thus becomes an issue for the firm and is not an issue for the individual case. There are funding facilities available through many of the providers of insurance which provide for a percentage of the work in progress to be funded. This usually involves a loan to the firm rather than the individual client although there is at least one provider who structures the client's loan to include a work in progress provision albeit with recourse to the solicitor in the event of discontinuance, part recovery and unsuccessful claims. The main attraction of work in progress funding is in the management of the cash flow of firms which have a significant CFA caseload. The providers vary as to the value of the work in progress which can be funded. Some provide a percentage of the billable costs, typically between 30% and 40%. Others provide a fixed sum according to the track to which the case has been or is likely to be allocated. The cost in terms of interest for such funding will depend on the provider and the overall package which is being arranged. The charges can be included as the part of the success fee relating to the postponement of the payment of fees, not recoverable from the opponent. Whether the work in progress is funded in such a way or not, there will always be a cost attached to the, in some cases significant, delay in the payment of fees. As with all of these funding options introduced by insurers it is possible to obtain insurance to cover the failure to recover for the item against which the loan has been used. In the case of work in progress attached to a CFA, if that work in progress is insured in the event that the case fails then the success fee needs to reflect the fact that the solicitor is not taking the risk with regard to that percentage of the fees should the case fail[1].

1   It is submitted that the success fee itself should be a reflection in the usual way of the risks in the case but should then be applied to the percentage of own costs which the solicitor would not have received had the case failed.

INFORMATION ABOUT THE FIRM'S FINANCIAL STATUS AND ADMINISTRATIVE SYSTEMS

18.9   Many of the funding facilities are made either to or through the firm of solicitors. In order for such facilities to be obtained it will be necessary to provide the funder with financial information and details of the administrative systems used. The financial status of the firm will determine whether and if so what funding will be available. The administrative systems will be important to the funder in terms of the time taken to arrange loans with clients and the record keeping necessarily involved once a loan has been granted. Profit and loss details are likely to be required for at least the most recent two year's accounts with statements of assets and liabilities current at the date of application. Once funding facilities are granted it is usual for there to be a requirement for yearly provision of the financial materials.

THE CONSUMER CREDIT ACT 1974

18.10   The 1974 Act controls the provision of credit to the 'individual' and it is important to note the wide definition used:

Consumer Credit Act 1974, s 189—

'"individual" includes a partnership or other unincorporated body of persons not consisting entirely of bodies corporate.'

The relevance of the Act and the considerable quantity of subordinate legislation to litigation funding becomes clear form the concept of credit. Section 9(1) of the Act defines credit to include 'a cash loan, and any other form of financial accommodation.' The Court of Appeal has approved the following definition of credit—

'...credit [is] extended, whenever the contract provides for the debtor to pay, or gives him the option to pay, later than the time at which payment would otherwise have been earned under the express or implied terms of the contract.[1]'

1   *Dimond v Lovell* [1999] 3 All ER 1 at 11 citing with approval, *Goode: Consumer Credit Law and Practice*, **I[443]** (Butterworths). Lord Hoffmann referred in the House of Lords to the reliance by the defendant's insurers on Professor Goode's definition—*Dimond v Lovell* [2000] 2 All ER 897.

18.11   There will be a consumer credit agreement where the credit provided does not exceed £25,000. Where credit is being given the agreement under which it is provided will be a regulated agreement unless it comes within the definition of an exempt agreement. Thus under art 3(1)(a) of the Consumer Credit (Exempt Agreements) Order 1989[1] a consumer credit agreement where the total number of payments to be made does not exceed four and those payments are required to be made within a period of 12 months beginning with the date of the agreement is an exempt agreement. The funding options discussed above will all involve a consideration of the exempt agreements provisions but it is likely that the funder will assume that the agreement is a regulated agreement and will ensure compliance with the statutory provisions relating to such agreements and to the rules as to advertising of credit. The Law Society has a group licence[2] for the purposes of the 1974 Act.

1   SI 1989/869.
2   The need for a licence is a separate statutory requirement and does not affect the need also to comply with the Act in terms of regulated agreements.

IS A CFA A CREDIT AGREEMENT?

18.12 Whether or not a CFA, or indeed any agreement between a solicitor and client amounts to the provision of credit must depend upon the terms of the agreement, both express and implied. This much was made clear in the *Dimond v Lovell*[1] case. A CFA will not amount to the provision of credit where, as is standard, the agreement does not require payment before the entire services governed by the contract have been performed. This is usually the case even where the CFA provides for the payment of some fees in the event that the case fails. Under non-CFA funding agreements unless the agreement provides for interim final bills there will be no contractual right to payment before completion of the entire services governed by the agreement. Thus again there is no provision of credit. Thus although a client is receiving the benefit of legal services before paying for those services, this will not amount to the provision of credit for the purposes of the 1974 Act.

1   [1999] 3 All ER 1.

TABLE OF FUNDING OPTIONS

18.13

Item to be funded	Options
Insurance premium	Direct to client—no recourse to solicitor
CFA and non-CFA policies	To client but with recourse to solicitor
	Only to solicitor
	Instalment plan
	Deferred premium
	Premium only if case wins
	Premium can be insured if case fails
	Unrecoverable premium can be insured
Disbursements	Same funding routes as for premium
	Draw-down against invoices
	Can include insurance cover
	Can include counsel's fees
	Individual case and global limits
	Arrangement fee may be charged
	Admin allowance may be paid to solicitor
	Approval may be required for high value
Work in progress	Direct to solicitor—no client liability
	Added to loan to client
	WIP can be insured if case loses
	Available for CFA and non-CFA cases
	Limited sum or % of WIP

Part 8

Costs Orders against Third Parties

Chapter 19

Third Parties and Conditional Fee Agreements

19.1   Supreme Court Act 1981 (SCA 1981), s 51[1]—

'(1) Subject to the provisions of this or any other enactment and to rules of court, the costs of and incidental to all proceedings in—

(a)   the civil division of the Court of Appeal;
(b)   the High Court; and
(c)   any county court,

shall be in the discretion of the court.

(2) Without prejudice to any general power to make rules of court, such rules may make provision for regulating matters relating to the costs of those proceedings including, in particular, prescribing scales of costs to be paid to legal or other representatives [or for securing that the amount awarded to a party in respect of the costs to be paid by him to such representatives is not limited to what would have been payable by him to them if he had not been awarded costs][2].

(3) The court shall have full power to determine by whom and to what extent the costs are to be paid.

...

(6) In any proceedings mentioned in subsection (1), the court may disallow, or (as the case may be) order the legal or other representative concerned to meet, the whole of any wasted costs or such part of them as may be determined in accordance with rules of court.

(7) In subsection (6), "wasted costs" means any costs incurred by a party—

(a)   as a result of any improper, unreasonable or negligent act or omission on the part of any legal or other representative or any employee of such a representative; or
(b)   which, in the light of any such act or omission occurring after they were incurred, the court considers it is unreasonable to expect that party to pay.

...

(13) In this section "legal or other representative", in relation to a party to proceedings, means any person exercising a right of audience or right to conduct litigation on his behalf.'

1   As substituted by the Courts and Legal Services Act 1990 (CLSA 1990), s 4. An English court has jurisdiction under s 51 to determine whether a non-party should be liable to pay the costs

of proceedings, even though such a person was outside the court's territorial jurisdiction or was domiciled in another contracting state of the Brussels Convention. This was an exercise of powers in the context of substantive proceedings over which the court had jurisdiction – *National Justice Compania Naviera SA v Prudential Assurance Co Ltd (The Ikarian Reefer) (No 2)* [2000] 1 All ER 37.

2   Sub-s (2): words in square brackets inserted by the Access to Justice Act 1999 (AJA 1999), s 31. This provision is not in force at 1 April 2001.

19.2   The construction of SCA 1981, s 51 has been considered in respect of third parties by the House of Lords in *Aiden Shipping Co ltd v Interbulk Ltd (The Vimeira)*[1]. Lord Goff of Chieveley dismissed an argument that the section limited the court to ordering costs to be paid by a party to the proceedings[2]. The award of costs was held to be a matter for the discretion of the court and that although in the vast majority of cases it would be unjust to make an award of costs against a non-party, the court had the power to make such an order.

1   [1986] 2 All ER 409.
2   It was accepted that s 51(6) applied to non-parties and that costs orders could also be made against a relator in a relator action and against a next friend – see [1986] 2 All ER 409 at 415.

19.3   CPR, r 48.2—

'(1) Where the court is considering whether to exercise its power under section 51 of the Supreme Court Act 1981 (costs are in the discretion of the court) to make a costs order in favour of or against a person who is not a party to proceedings—

(a)   that person must be added as a party to the proceedings for the purposes of costs only; and

(b)   he must be given a reasonable opportunity to attend a hearing at which the court will consider the matter further.

(2) This rule does not apply—

(a)   where the court is considering whether to—

(i)   make an order against the Legal Services Commission;
(ii)   make a wasted costs order (as defined in 48.7); and

(b)   in proceedings to which rule 48.1 applies (pre-commencement disclosure and orders for disclosure against a person who is not a party).[1']

1   For the procedure where the third party is outside the jurisdiction see *The Ikarian Reefer* above para **19.1** note 1.

19.4   In *Nordsyern Allgemeine Versicherungs AG v Internav*[1] it was held that the court may make an order against a third party even though no order has been made against a party. The Court of Appeal also held that if an agreement was champertous that would be a very firm basis for exercising the jurisdiction under SCA 1981, s 51 against a non-party and that the procedure must be fair to the third party, for example by ensuring an opportunity to deal with allegations and to cross-examine witnesses.

1   [1999] 2 Lloyd's Rep 139.

EXERCISE OF DISCRETION

19.5   The leading authority is *Symphony Group plc v Hodgson*[1] where Balcombe LJ set out some principles for the exercise of the court's discretion:

'(1)   An order for the payment of costs by a non-party will always be exceptional: see per Lord Goff in *Aiden Shipping Co Ltd v Interbulk Ltd* [1986] AC 965, 980F. The judge should treat any application for such an order with considerable caution.

(2)   It will be even more exceptional for an order for the payment of costs to be made against a non-party, where the applicant has a cause of action against the non-party and could have joined him as a party to the original proceedings. Joinder as a party to the proceedings[2] gives the person concerned all the protection conferred by the rules, as to, for example, the framing of the issues by pleadings; discovery of documents and the opportunity to pay into court or to make a Calderbank offer (*Calderbank v Calderbank* [1976] Fam 93); and the knowledge of what the issues are before giving evidence.

(3)   Even if the applicant can provide a good reason for not joining the non-party against whom he has a valid cause of action, he should warn[3] the non-party at the earliest opportunity of the possibility that he may seek to apply for costs against him. At the very least this will give the non-party an opportunity to apply to be joined as a party to the action.

Principles (2) and (3) require no further justification on my part; they are an obvious application of the basic principles of natural justice.

(4)   An application for payments of costs by a non-party should normally be determined by the trial judge: see *Bahai v Rashidian* [1985] 1 WLR 1337.

(5)   The fact that the trial judge may in the course of his judgment in the action have expressed views on the conduct of the non-party constitutes neither bias nor the appearance of bias. Bias is the antithesis of the proper exercise of a judicial function: see *Bahai v Rashidian* [1985] 1 WLR 1337, 1342H, 1346F.

(6)   The procedure for the determination of costs is a summary procedure, not necessarily subject to all the rules that would apply in an action. Thus, subject to any relevant statutory exceptions, judicial findings are inadmissible as evidence of the facts upon which they were based in proceedings between one of the parties to the original proceedings and a stranger: see *Hollington v F Hewthorn & Co Ltd* [1943] KB 587; *Cross on Evidence* (7th edn 1990), pp 100–101. Yet in the summary procedure for the determination of the liability of a solicitor to pay the costs of an action to which he was not a party, the judge's findings of fact may be admissible: see *Brendon v Spiro* [1938] 1 KB 176, 192, cited with approval by this court in *Bahai v Rashidian* [1985] 1 WLR 1337 1343D, 1345H. This departure from basic principles can only be justified if the connection of the non-party with the original proceedings was so close[4] that he will not suffer any injustice by allowing this exception to the general rule.

(7)   Again, the normal rule is that witnesses in either civil or criminal proceedings enjoy immunity from any form of civil action in respect of evidence given during those proceedings. One reason for this immunity is so that witnesses may give their evidence fearlessly: see *Palmer v Durnford Ford (a firm)* [1992] QB 483, 487. In so far as the evidence of a

witness in proceedings may lead to an application for the costs of those proceedings against him or his company, it introduces yet another exception to a valuable general principle.

(8) The fact that an employee, or even a director or the managing director, of a company gives evidence in an action does not normally mean that the company is taking part in that action, in so far as that is an allegation relied upon by the party who applies for an order for costs against a non-party company: see *Gleeson v J Wippell & Co Ltd* [1977] 1 WLR 510, 513.

(9) The judge should be alert to the possibility that an application against a non-party is motivated by resentment of an inability to obtain an effective order for costs against a legally aided litigant.[5']

1 [1993] 4 All ER 143. An SCA 1981, s 51 application here was made against the new employer of the defendant to the litigation who was in breach of a restrictive covenant with the plaintiff. The defendant had been represented by the new employer's solicitors. The new employer successfully appealed against the s 51 order. The plaintiff had an action against the new employer in tort but had not pursued it nor warned of the possibility that it might seek costs. The judge's findings of fact would not have been admissible had the claim for costs been the subject of an action.

2 See now CPR, r 48.2(a) above which requires the third party to be joined for the purposes of costs only.

3 See *Shah v Karanjia* [1993] 4 All ER 792—para **19.14** below.

4 In *Wiggins v Richard Read (Transport) Ltd* (1999) Times, 14 January, CA, it was held that a close relationship between the third party and the litigant was not sufficient to justify an order, such as where the third party had encouraged the action for his own benefit. Here the 'encouragement and driving force' of a father was not sufficient to bring the case within the exceptional category justifying a third party order.

5 [1993] 4 All ER 143 at 152–154.

19.6 The Court identified six categories of cases where the courts have been prepared to order a third party to pay costs—

'(1) Where a person had some management of the action, eg a director of an insolvent company who causes the company improperly to prosecute or defend proceedings: see *Re Land and Property Trust Co plc* [1991] 3 All ER 409, [1991] 1 WLR 601, *Re Land and Property Trust Co plc (No 2)* (1993) Times, 16 February, *Re Land and Property Trust Co plc (No 3)* [1991] BCLC 856, *Taylor v Pace Developments Ltd* [1991] BCC 406, *Re a company (No 004055 of 1991), ex p Doe Sport Ltd* [1991] BCLC 865, [1991] 1 WLR 1003 and *Framework Exhibitions Ltd v Matchroom Boxing Ltd* [1992] CA Transcript 873. It is of interest to note that, while it was not suggested in any of these cases that it would never be a proper exercise of the jurisdiction to order the director to pay the costs, in none of them was it the ultimate result that the director was so ordered.

(2) Where a person has maintained or financed the action. This was undoubtedly considered to be a proper case for the exercise of the discretion by Macpherson J in *Singh v Observer Ltd* [1989] 2 All ER 751, where it was alleged that a non-party was maintaining the plaintiff's libel action. However, on appeal the evidence showed that the non-party had not been maintaining the action and the appeal was allowed without going into the legal issues raised by the judge's decision: see *Singh v Observer Ltd* [1989] 3 All ER 777.

(3) In *Gupta v Comer* [1991] 1 All ER 289, [1991] 1 QB 629 this court approached the power of the court to order a solicitor to pay costs under

Ord 62, r 11 as an example of the exercise of the jurisdiction under s 51 of the 1981 Act.

(4) Where the person has caused the action. In *Pritchard v JH Cobden Ltd* [1988] Fam 22 the plaintiff had suffered brain damage through the defendant's negligence. That resulted in a personality change which precipitated a divorce. This court held that the defendant's agreement to pay the costs of the divorce proceedings could be justified as an application of the *Aiden Shipping* principle (see [1988] Fam 22 at 51).

(5) Where the person is a party to a closely related action which has been heard at the same time but not consolidated as was the case in *Aiden Shipping* itself.

(6) Group litigation where one or two actions are selected as test actions: see *Davies (Joseph Owen) v Eli Lilly & Co* [1987] 3 All ER 94, [1987] 1 WLR 1136.[1]'

1   [1993] 4 All ER 143 at 151, per Balcombe LJ.

19.7   In *Globe Equities Ltd v Kotrie*[1] an action was brought against a commercial tenant (G) for rent and service charges arrears. G was represented by a firm of solicitors which occupied the premises. An SCA 1981, s 51 third party costs order was made against the firm. It was held that the firm could be presumed to know of the s 51 jurisdiction and there was no need to warn it. The fact that the claimant had a remedy against G did not preclude a s 51 order. The firm had not acted in the usual way but had been left to conduct the actions in its own interests knowing that G could not pay costs. The firm as licensee of G had benefited from the free occupation for over two years by staving off the actions. It was not necessary in order to exercise the jurisdiction of s 51 for the court to conclude that the firm had acted improperly. The Court of Appeal also considered whether there had to be a causal link between the exceptional factors and the costs being claimed. It was held that it would necessarily be the case that costs were to some extent caused by the non-party for s 51 to be exercised. It was not, however, necessary to show that all of the exceptional factors had caused costs to be incurred.

1   [1999] All ER (D) 226.

19.8   Morritt LJ considered the first of Balcombe LJ's principles and referred to Phillips LJ in *Chapman v Christopher*[1]—

'The test is whether they (ie the features relied on) are extraordinary in the context of the entire range of litigation that comes to the court.[2]'

1   *TGA Chapman v Chrisptopher and Sun Alliance* [1998] 2 All ER 873.
2   *Globe Equities Ltd v Kotrie* [1999] All ER (D) 226.

19.9   Morrit LJ continued–

' I would also comment that there appears to me to be a danger of treating the requirement that the circumstances are "exceptional " as being part of the statute to be applied. It is not.

Ultimately, the test is whether in all the circumstances it is just to exercise the power conferred by subsections (1) and (3) of **section 51** of the Supreme Court Act 1981 to make a non-party pay the costs of the proceedings.

Plainly, in the ordinary run of cases where the party is pursuing or defending the claim for his own benefit through solicitors acting as such there is not usually any justification for making someone else pay the costs. But there will be cases where either or both these two features are absent. In such cases, it will be a matter for judgment and the exercise by the judge of his discretion to decide whether the circumstances relied on are such as to make it just to order some non-party to pay the costs. Thus, as it seems to me, the exceptional case is one to be recognised by comparison with the ordinary run of cases, not defined in advance by reference to any further characteristic.[1]'

1   *Globe Equities Ltd v Kotrie* [1999] All ER (D) 226.

INSURERS

19.10   The issue arising in relation to insurers is whether there can be a liability in excess of any contractual limit to the indemnity of the policy of insurance. In *Murphy v Young & Co's Brewery plc*[1], having reviewed the doctrine of maintenance and considered public policy, the High Court concluded that a risk inherent in any litigation is that after its conclusion it becomes clear that the unsuccessful party has no means. It was held that the legal expenses insurer of the unsuccessful plaintiffs should not be made the subject of a costs order in excess of the policy's limit of indemnity. There was no evidence of maintenance, of management or control and there were no public policy grounds for imposing such a liability.

1   [1996] LRLR 60. Affirmed on appeal [1997] 1 All ER 518.

19.11   Liability insurers may however be found to have pursued litigation to defend their own interests and thereby may expose themselves to an SCA 1981, s 51 order. In *TGA Chapman v Christopher*[1] both the plaintiff and the defendant were insured. The plaintiff succeeded but the judgment exceeded the defendant's insurance limit of indemnity. The plaintiff obtained an order for costs under s 51 against the defendant's insurers. The Court of Appeal upheld that order, holding that in so doing they were not rewriting the policy but giving effect to a liability independent of the policy. The defendant's insurers had not been guilty of unlawful maintenance but had determined that the claim would be fought, had funded the defence, conducted the litigation and fought it exclusively to defend their own interests. The defence had failed in its entirety.

1   [1998] 2 All ER 873. In *Tharros Shipping Co Ltd v Bias Shipping Ltd (No 3)* [1997] 1 Lloyd's Rep 246, the Court of Appeal approved a decision to restrict a PI club's liability to its contractual limit. Here the club had no interest in the litigation although it had exercised some supervision of the case.

19.12   Further guidance where an insurer has an interest in the litigation is given by the Court of Appeal in *Cormack v Washbourne*[1] where it was found that the insured defendant had a continuing substantial interest in his defence. Auld LJ—

'The norm in such cases is that the insurer has control of the litigation and may act predominantly in its own interest in doing so. In most cases of professional indemnity and product liability cover – certainly up to the limit of cover provided – its interests should coincide with those of the insured, and it may not be necessary to involve him closely in the decision-making. In some cases, within or in excess of the cover limit, there may be some tension or potential for conflict between the two interests, matters which it is for the responsible insurer to balance in its conduct of the litigation.[2]'

'However, I would not exclude the possibility of a finding of exceptionality when an insurer's self-interest, though not its exclusive motivation (or effect) in its conduct of litigation, predominated over that of the insured to such an extent and in such circumstances that it strayed beyond an appropriate balance of the sort indicated by Sir Wilfrid Greene MR in *Groom v Crocker*[3]. It must always be remembered that the test of exceptionality is a servant to that of reason and justice and that both guide the exercise of a discretionary function.[4]'

1 [2000] 15 LS Gaz R 39.
2 Ibid.
3 [1939] 1 KB 194.
4 See note 1 above.

COMPANY LAW CASES

19.13   The making of SCA 1981, s 51 orders in the field of company law has particular application to directors and to liquidators and has also arisen in the context of parent and subsidiary companies. The directors of a company were held personally liable for costs arising out of an adjournment of an application for the appointment of a provisional liquidator in *Gamelstaden plc v Brackland Magazines Ltd*[1]. Chadwick J summarised the factors to be taken into account–

'The court has unlimited discretion to make such an order as to costs as it thinks the justice of the case requires; but that discretion is to be exercised judicially and in relation to the facts of the case before it. The grounds on which that discretion is exercised must be connected with the case before it; but may include any matter relating to the litigation, the parties conduct in it, or the circumstances which led to the litigation. A party who gives another party cause to have recourse to the court will normally be required to compensate that other party in costs.[2]'

1 [1993] BCC 194.
2 Ibid at 198E.

19.14   In *Shah v Karanjia*[1] an application under SCA 1981, s 51 against an individual and the companies controlled by him, failed. It was alleged that the individual had induced the plaintiffs to bring proceedings which he knew to be maliciously motivated and had also funded the proceedings. As against the individual it was held that no order should be made since he had not been a party, had not been separately represented, had not been warned and the claim was made after the proceedings had closed. The application with respect to the companies failed on the basis that it was not proved that they had funded the action. In arriving at these conclusions Vinelott J considered the relevance of maintenance and champerty to s 51—

'I am not persuaded that the old law of maintenance offers any guide to the exercise of the court's discretion under s 51. It may be that in a case where it is plain or admitted that the action is brought by a nominal plaintiff at the expense and on behalf of another with an interest in the action (as in *Hayward v Giffard*)[1] or where it is funded by a trade union on behalf of a member or by a person liable to indemnify the plaintiff, the court could properly exercise its discretion by ordering the funder to pay the costs of the successful defendant, although the court would have to bear in mind the danger in exercising a summary jurisdiction of relying on a finding which would not be admissible in proceedings against the funder, However, all these cases fell outside the scope of the old law of maintenance and, if the court is to make an order, it must be, in the words of Lord Abinger CE on the ground of justice and reason in the exercise of the jurisdiction under section 51.[2]'

1 [1993] 4 All ER 792.
2 Ibid at 810.

19.15 It was observed in *Re Freudiana Holdings Ltd*[1] that under the law of Maintenance a close connection between the maintainer and the litigation tended to render the maintenance unlawful, whereas, in the context of the discretion conferred by SCA 1981, s 51, a close connection between the funder and the litigation is in effect a necessary fact for the exercise of the discretion. In that case a dispute had arisen between W and B, the two parties to a joint venture. The dispute was litigated by each party bringing actions under s 459 of the Companies Act 1985. B, the successful party was awarded costs assessed at £2m. W, the unsuccessful party, was made bankrupt by his own petition. B then sought to recover costs from a company controlled by W, from a pension fund set up by that company and against W's wife. The company and W's wife were joined as parties to B's s 459 actions on the day that judgment was given. It was found in the s 459 actions that W's case was in effect 'trumped up and an exercise in oppression'. In acceding to each of the applications for costs under s 51 Parker J applying *Symphony*[2] and *Shah*[3] found there to be a sufficiently close connection of each respondent to the main proceedings to justify a summary procedure and an order for costs. Each respondent was held jointly and severally liable for the whole of B's costs.

1 [1994] NPC 89, Ch D before Parker J.
2 *Symphony Group plc v Hodgson* [1994] QB 179.
3 *Shah v Karanjia* [1993] 4 All ER 792.

19.16 An important decision in the context of subsidiary companies is *Stocznia v Latreefers*[1]. Latco and its subsidiary, Latmar, incorporated a third company, Latreefers, in order to enter into six contracts with Stocznia(S). S brought actions for breach of those contracts against Latco and Latreefers. Those actions succeeded. A winding up petition was presented in respect of the unpaid judgment debt. S had been and continued to be funded by a third party. Latreefers applied for the petition to be stayed on the grounds of champerty. That application was dismissed by Lloyd J who also made an SCA 1981, s 51 order against Latco as to any increase costs in the petition proceedings caused by the opposition to the petition. The Court of Appeal, applying *Globe Equities*[2], upheld the decision of Lloyd J.

Morritt LJ—

'This is an area of the law in which the truism that each case depends on its individual facts is particularly applicable, and in which satellite litigation (including, of course, appeals) is to be discouraged. Parliament has given the judiciary an unfettered discretion to make orders for costs which are just, and further judicial guidance beyond that which exists already, designed to identify what may or may not be just in different factual circumstances is, in our judgment both unnecessary and likely to expand the scope for further argument.[3]'

1   *Stocznia Gdanska SA v Latreefers Inc* [2000] All ER (D) 148.
2   *Globe Equities Ltd v Kotrie* [1999] All ER (D) 226.
3   Ibid note 1 above.

19.17   His Lordship then went on to consider the exercise of discretion by Lloyd J who had summarised his reasons in the following terms–

'My principal reasons are that this company is not and was not a trading company, that it has had no realisable assets beyond the tiny credit balance in its bank account and that it is, on any footing, insolvent; and that the effective decision to contest the petition was a decision taken by Latco to make available the funds for the conduct of that defence. In my judgment, the circumstances of this case show that, in so doing, Latco was consulting its own interests and not that of Latreefers, and that makes it appropriate to order Latco to pay those costs.[1]'

The Court of Appeal having emphasised that the order had been restricted to the increase in costs which Latco's opposition to the petition had caused went on to consider Lloyd J's treatment of the authorities including *The Kommunar (No 3)*[2] where it had been recognised that a parent company has a legitimate interest in preserving and maximising the assets of its subsidiary. Morritt LJ agreed with Lloyd J's basis for considering the circumstances of the present case to be wholly different to Kommunar—

'The Kommunar lays down no general principle. It simply decides that on the facts of that case the parent company in question had a legitimate interest in preserving and maximising the assets of its solvent subsidiary. In the instant case the question is not, as in The Kommunar. whether the parent company's funding of the litigation could be justified on the basis that the interests of the shareholders were synonymous with those of the parent company; the proper question in the instant case is whether or not persistence by Latco in the defence of the winding up petition was in the interests of Latreefers' creditors – a proposition to which there could only be one answer.[3]'

1   *Stocznia Gdanska SA v Latreefers Inc* [2000] All ER (D) 148.
2   [1997] 1 Lloyd's Rep 22.
3   Ibid note 1 above.

19.18   Thus the Court reached the conclusion that the petition had been opposed in the interests of Latco and not those either of Latreefers nor any of its creditors. It was just, therefore, to order the parent company to pay the costs incurred as a result of the opposition.

Where a company is effectively controlled by a single director it is not appropriate to hold that director liable in costs save in exceptional circumstances—

'The controlling director of a one-man company is inevitably the person who causes the costs to be incurred, in one sense, by causing the company to defend the proceedings. But it could not be right that in every case he should be made personally liable for costs, even if he knows that the company will not be able to meet the plaintiff's costs, should the company prove unsuccessful. That would be far too great an inroad on the principle of limited liability. I do not say that there may not be cases where a director may not properly be liable for costs. Thus he might be made liable if the company's defence is not bona fide, as, for example, where the company has been advised that there is no defence, and the proceedings are defended out of spite, or for the sole purpose of causing the plaintiffs to incur irrevocable costs. No doubt there will be other cases. But such cases much necessarily be rare. In the great majority of cases the directors of an insolvent company which defends proceedings brought against it should not be at personal risk of costs.[1]'

1   *Taylor v Pace Developments Ltd* [1991] BCC 406 at 409, per Lloyd LJ. See also *Re Land and Property Trust (No 4)* [1994] 1 BCLC 232, [1993] BCC 462 where the directors had the support of insolvency practitioners, solicitors and counsel and had acted in the interests of the company. It was held on appeal that an SCA 1981, s 51 order had been wrongly made and effectively had pierced the corporate veil.

19.19   Exceptional circumstances were found to exist in *Secretary of State for Trade and Industry v Backhouse*[1] where the sole director had treated the businesses of two companies as his own. The costs of resisting winding-up petitions were incurred solely in the interests of that director who was running his business in the names of the companies. The director had only been warned of a possible SCA 1981, s 51 application after judgment but in all the circumstances the Court of Appeal did not consider that to be sufficient reason to overturn the judge's order. The order extended to all costs incurred including those prior to the presentation of the petitions. The extent of the order was upheld on the ground that the director had caused the costs to be incurred by failing to co-operate with the Secretary of State's authorised representative.

In the course of his judgment Aldous LJ considered the position of directors who take a decision to resist an action knowing that the company will be unable to bear the costs unless it succeeds—

'A crucial question is whether the relevant directors (or director) hold a bona fide belief that (i) the company has an arguable defence, and (ii) it is in the interests of the company for it to advance that defence. If they do then, (in the absence of special circumstances) to make them pay costs of proceedings in which they are not a party would constitute an unlawful inroad into the principle of limited liability. It follows that directors of a company which is served with a petition would be well advised to consider with the company's, or their, legal advisers what defences the company has and, having regard thereto, whether it is in the interests of the company to defend the petition. If the bona fide decision of the directors (or director) is that it is, (in the absence of special circumstances) the directors (or director) should be able to cause the company to defend without fear of being made liable to pay any costs, unless the position should change materially during the lead up to the hearing, or at the hearing. If so, the decision would need to be reconsidered.[2]'

1   [2001] EWCA Civ 67, CA.
2   Ibid.

19.20   The position of a liquidator in bringing an action by an insolvent company has been considered by the Court of Appeal in *Metalloy Supplies Ltd v MA (UK) Ltd*[1] where a liquidator had been forced to abandon proceedings upon a successful application by the defendants that security for costs be provided. The defendants had then obtained an order that the liquidator pay the costs already incurred. The Court held that there was jurisdiction to order a liquidator to pay costs but that there had to be impropriety for that jurisdiction to be exercised. It was in the public interest that liquidators are able to perform their duties. The primary remedy of a defendant is security for costs. On the facts the order was quashed.

1   [1997] 1 All ER 418.

PROCEDURE

19.21   Vinelott J in *Shah v Karanjia*[1] addressed the question of the summary procedure applicable to s 51 and the serious allegations which are nonetheless involved—

> 'Prima facie, the proper determination of a claim that an action was not brought in good faith would require the full investigation of the circumstances in which it was brought and of the knowledge and intentions of those who funded the litigation, which cannot fairly be made in the context of a summary application for costs.[2]'

Principle 6 of Balcombe LJ's principles[3] stresses that the judicial findings in the litigation are inadmissible as between a party and a stranger to the proceedings. The summary procedure was again considered in *Re Freudiana Holdings Ltd*[4] where it was emphasised that only where the connection of the non-party to the original proceedings is a close one, could a summary procedure be justified.

1   [1993] 4 All ER 792.
2   Ibid at p 811.
3   *Re Freudiana Holdings* [1994] NPC 89; affd (1995) Times, 4 December, CA and see *Symphony Group plc v Hodgson* above para **19.5**.
4   See above para **19.15**. Here the connection to the proceedings was found to be sufficiently close with respect to all respondents to the SCA 1981, s 51 applications.

SOLICITORS IN THEIR CAPACITY AS SOLICITORS

19.22   In *Symphony Group v Hodgson*[1], Balcombe LJ had said that the court had the ability to order a solicitor to a party to pay costs occasioned by his misconduct by exercising the inherent jurisdiction[2] over solicitors as officers of the court, a power regulated by the Rules of Court. *Hodgson v Imperial Tobacco Ltd*[3] took to the Court of Appeal the concern of solicitors acting under a CFA that SCA 1981, s 51 was wide enough to expose them to a non-party costs order. An application was made for an order that the defendants be debarred from seeking an order that the solicitors be liable for costs other than under s 51(6) (wasted costs). That application failed. The court held that solicitors were at no greater risk of a costs order when acting under a CFA than when acting under any other funding arrangement. The court then considered the jurisdiction to order a solicitor to pay costs and concluded that there were three heads of jurisdiction. A wasted costs order could be made, the inherent jurisdiction of the court with regard to solicitors could be exercised and s 51.

1   [1993] 3 WLR 830.
2   In *Nelson v Nelson* [1997] 1 All ER 970 the Court of Appeal quashed an order for costs which had been made in exercise of the inherent jurisdiction. The solicitors had acted for a client not knowing that he was a bankrupt. The court held that a solicitor in commencing proceedings on behalf of a client did not thereby represent that the client had a good cause of action, but merely that the client had authorised the proceedings. The solicitors in this case did have the authority of the client and that was all they had represented to the court. There was no breach of duty to the court.
3   [1998] 2 All ER 673.

19.23   In *Tolstoy v Aldington*[1] the trial judge had ordered solicitors to pay costs in an exercise of the general discretion conferred by s 51(1) and (3). The Court of Appeal held that the court had no jurisdiction under those sub-sections to make an order for costs against a legal representative when acting in their capacity as legal representatives. The court on the facts made a wasted costs order against the solicitors under s 51(6) and (7) on the grounds that the solicitors had acted unreasonably in instituting the litigation. The court made it clear however, that acting without fee was not sufficient to justify a wasted costs order even in a hopeless case[2] or where a case is struck out as an abuse of process.

1   [1996] 2 All ER 556.
2   See also *Harley v McDonald* (2001) Times, 15 May, PC where it was held that the pursuit of an apparently hopeless case was not of itself a breach of the duty to the court to maintain appropriate levels of confidence.

IMPECUNIOUS LITIGANTS

19.24   The *Tolstoy*[1] decision makes it clear that acting pro bono for an impecunious client is not of itself grounds for holding the legal representative liable for costs. Only where the conduct of the solicitors is itself negligent or unreasonable will there be a risk of a costs order. Thus in *Banks v Humphrey and Glasgow*[2] the Court of Appeal was faced with negligent non-action by the solicitors, the eventual discharge of a legal aid certificate and the replacement of the solicitors by other solicitors. The defendants were not informed of the discharge of legal aid.

Butler-Sloss LJ quoted from *Ridehalgh v Horsefield*[3] in respect of the meaning of 'unreasonable' in the context of s 51(7)—

> 'The expression aptly describes conduct which is vexatious, designed to harass the other side rather than advance the resolution of the case, and it makes no difference if the conduct is the product of excessive zeal and not improper motive. But conduct cannot be described as unreasonable simply because it leads in the event to an unsuccessful result or because other more cautious legal representatives would have acted differently. The acid test is whether the conduct permits of a reasonable explanation. If so, the course adopted may be regarded as optimistic and as reflecting on a practitioner's judgment, but it is not unreasonable.[4]'

1   *Tolstoy v Aldington* above at para **19.23**.
2   (24 May 1996, unreported).

3   [1994] 3 All ER 848.
4   Ibid n 2 at p 4 of the transcript.

19.25   The long running litigation in *Faryab v Smyth*[1] includes a Court of Appeal decision concerning an application under SCA 1981, s 51. A sum had been paid into court as security for costs, that sum having been provided by way of loans by four individuals. The loan agreements provided for the lenders to receive a premium which it was accepted would not be forthcoming save in the event of success. The s 51 application was made against those four lenders. The court dismissed the applications stating that to accede to them would be to give a larger layer of security than that which had been considered fit to order as security for costs.

1   [1998] CLY 411, CA, (Lord Woolf CJ).

Part 9

Risk Assessment

Chapter 20

Principles of Risk Assessment

INTRODUCTION

20.1 The introduction of Conditional Fee Agreements (CFAs) has led to an intensified interest in risk assessment and risk management in the context of litigation. Much of the work which has been done in relation to CFAs has necessarily concentrated on Personal Injury (PI), simply because it is here that the volume of work is significant and the number of solicitors firms conducting this work is relatively large. Thus although CFAs were permitted for fields other than PI when they were introduced in 1995[1], it has only been in PI that any real uptake of the method has occurred.

1   See Chapter 4.

20.2   Although CFAs have been available for PI work since July 1995, until April 2000 they ran alongside publicly funded litigation. The removal of legal aid from the vast majority of PI cases provides both an opportunity and a risk to the PI litigation department and practitioner. The risk arises because of the financial implications not only of cases which lose but perhaps rather more importantly from the effect of waiting for payment in cases which succeed. The opportunity arises not only to retain the client flow which existed under legal aid but further to increase the client flow by marketing litigation services to the potential client who would not have qualified for legal aid but who equally would not have contemplated funding litigation from their own resources.

   Outside the PI field, much the same opportunities and threats arise with the advent of CFAs. Many business related claims are no longer eligible for legal aid. The insolvency field lends itself to this form of funding now that success fees and insurance premiums are recoverable. Defamation and intellectual property disputes are further areas where good claims may exist but where the claimant cannot fund the litigation. The matters which have to be addressed are broadly similar whatever field of litigation is being considered.

20.3   Putting all of the issues together requires consideration by the legal practice of the following—

- The legal requirements for CFAs under the Courts and Legal Services Act 1990 (CLSA 1990) as amended by the Access to Justice Act 1999 (AJA 1999);

- The Rules of Professional Conduct of the Law Society – Rules 1, 8 and 15;
- Caseloads of the department, average time taken by a case, success rates and abandonment rates;
- Costs of running the average case and work in progress funding;
- The average level of disbursements – Funding disbursements;
- The market for the firm – joining referral schemes or going it alone?;
- Handling the litigation insurance needs of the client;
- Managing the decision to take a case on a CFA;
- Risk assessing the individual case;
- Success fees;
- Training;
- BACFA.

THE LEGAL REQUIREMENTS[1]

20.4   The statutory regime set up by the CLSA 1990 involves not only the statute but also Regulations, Orders and the CPR with its Practice Directions and the Pre-action Protocols. That scheme remains the same but the details of each element changed from 1 April 2000. From that date both the success fee and any insurance premium are recoverable from the opponent, subject to their challenge. The detailed rules are contained in the CPR and mostly in the Practice Direction About Costs (CPD). The CFA itself has changed from 1 April 2000 by virtue of the CFA Regulations 2000. The Law Society Model PI CFA[2] has been amended to take account of these changes. The documentation is available but there is no client guide as yet even though the regulations require the solicitor to explain the effect of a CFA to the client. A great deal of information must be given to the client orally and some both orally and in writing[3]. The information must be given to the client by the legal representative defined as 'the person providing the advocacy or litigation services to which the conditional fee agreement relates.' All of this then is in addition to the time needed to interview the client about their actual case. The issue of who covers the cost of all of this time really has to be addressed by the firm.

1   See Chapter 3 and generally Part 2.
2   See Chapter 7 and Appendix 2.
3   See Chapter 6.

THE LAW SOCIETY RULES OF PROFESSIONAL CONDUCT[1]

20.5   Rule 1 deals with the duty to act in the best interests of the client. Rule 8 permits the entering into of a CFA and Rule 15 requires compliance with the Solicitor's Costs Information and Client Care Code 1999. Complying with the CFA Regulations[2] will cover most of this. Client care letters can be used for the written information required by the regulations. Use of the old client guide to conditional fees is not in accordance with the Law Society's advice. Compliance with the Rules is therefore an essential part of the risk management which the firm must undertake.

1   See Chapter 2.
2   SI 2000/692.

CASELOAD HISTORY

20.6 Assuming that the cases which the new funding arrangements may bring into play will not differ dramatically from those that were in the system before CFAs were permitted it is important for the firm to know what case levels it has been handling, how long on average cases are taking to complete and in particular to know both the success rate and the rate of abandonment. A case which is abandoned under a CFA will in most cases be a case for which the firm receives no payment (it may even mean it has paid disbursements which are not recovered from the client). It is important to know how long cases run by the firm take to complete because the earliest that payment can be received will be on completion. It is important to know the success rate in order to know the extent of the firm's risk over the range of its CFA work. All of this relates to the risk for the firm rather than the risk in individual cases. Running litigation on a CFA basis is and must be a business decision taken with full knowledge of the financial exposure to which the firm will be subjected. Only with accurate information can proper use be made of the wide range of insurance and funding products now available[1].

1   See Part 7.

COST OF RUNNING CASES

20.7 The firm will be taking the risks mentioned in the previous section with respect to a level of costs. It is important to know what that level is. From the profile of cases run by the firm some estimation can be made as to the likely exposure in money terms of a year's caseload for the whole firm. The work in progress under the entire CFA workload has to be carried for the length of time the cases are open. There are insurance and funding products in the market to address this but it is clearly vital that the firm has a grasp of the likely figures involved and the period over which work in progress is likely to be carried. Once it is known how long, on average, cases of the type being considered take to close, decisions may well need to be taken to bring down that average time.

DISBURSEMENTS

20.8 Under CFAs the question must be addressed as to whether the client is to pay disbursements as they arise, whether the firm is going to carry that cost until completion, whether the firm will seek reimbursement from the client if the case loses and whether an insurance and funding solution is to be sought. Again, knowledge of the caseload of the firm will indicate the likely level at any one time of outstanding disbursements. If the firm is to carry disbursements then the financial exposure is all the greater. It is not necessary that one of these approaches to disbursements should be applied to all cases and all clients – it may well be practical to employ a selection of the approaches in accordance with suitability to the client and the case.

THE MARKET – REFERRAL SCHEMES OR NOT?

20.9   What market is the firm aiming at now that public funding will not be the basis for attracting clients and the new opportunity presented by CFAs is becoming known to potential clients? The number of referral schemes which aim to pool resources for marketing purposes has increased significantly in the last two years. Alternatively some firms are marketing themselves to the sector of the population they expect to be potential clients of the firm. Clearly there are business costs involved in each of these routes and there will be administrative demands in each. With referrals it is also the case that the work will not necessarily be geographically local to the firm. Working practices in such schemes must be appropriate to the circumstances and need to comply with the Professional Rules as well as the statutory regime. The strategies needed to ensure such compliance when dealing with clients at a distance must be carefully considered.

CLIENT INSURANCE NEEDS

20.10   Rule 15[1] and the CFA Regulations 2000[2] require the matter of insurance to be discussed with the client. In particular consideration needs to be given to whether a policy already exists (Legal Expenses Insurance) and whether an After-the-Event (AEI) policy would be available. The market provision of AEI is complex and ever growing with a multitude of options at widely differing premium levels. The Client Care Code does not require the solicitor to research this market in individual cases. The firm needs to give consideration, however, to whether it needs to be forming a relationship with a limited number of providers. With AEI insurance it is particularly important to remember that a policy is available for covering both sides' costs for cases where a CFA is not being used. Some of the referral schemes are based on this and do not use a CFA.

1   See Chapter 2 and Chapter 6.
2   Conditional Fee Agreements Regulations 2000, SI 2000/692 – See Chapter 6 and Appendix 1.

THE DECISION TO TAKE A CASE ON A CFA

20.11   Where, in view of the size of the firm it is possible, many use some form of internal review system so that the decision to accept instructions under a CFA is a firm's decision and not just an individual litigator's decision. The discipline of preparing for such a review is part of a risk assessment approach to litigation and does have the benefit of testing the litigator's opinion and providing fresh perspectives. Apart from the merits of the individual case such a process must have an overview of the exposure of the firm and how the proposed case fits in with workloads and funding requirements. The management of exposure to financial risk cannot be achieved without the knowledge which this approach provides.

RISK ASSESSING THE INDIVIDUAL CASE[1]

20.12   Risk assessment in the context of the individual case means that the factors which affect the success of litigation in the PI field must always be assessed and assessed as the case continues – it is not a once only task. What it does is to show up the real issues of the case and where the proof of those is to be found. The strengths and weaknesses on both sides will be illuminated and the structure of the case and the litigation process will be revealed. A Theory of the Case[2] is a crucial element as is an estimate of costs, the likelihood of settlement and the level at which the client is prepared to settle.

This is a complex discipline but it is one which is essential to the overall success of CFA work. The CFA Regulations[3] now require brief written reasons for setting the success fee to be given to the client as part of the CFA at the time it is made. Where there is a CFA with no success fee the process is equally important to the financial viability of the firm. In non-CFA cases risk assessment is important to the client and if insurance is being sought it is highly important to the success of the proposal.

1   See Chapter 21 below.
2   Dealt with fully in Chapter 21 below.
3   SI 2000/692. See Chapter 6 and Appendix 1.

SUCCESS FEES[1]

20.13   There is no legal requirement for a CFA to carry a success fee but in many cases it will be regarded by the firm as essential. The calculation[2] of the success fee has always been a subject of considerable and differing advice. The CFA Regulations[3] and the CPD clearly relate the level of the success fee to the perceived likelihood of success. That part of the success fee is also recoverable from the opponent. Any part referring to waiting for payment is only recoverable from the client. Success fees are to be expressed as a percentage increase, limited to 100%, over base costs. To relate prospects of success to such a figure it is necessary to express confidence levels as a percentage. The Legal Aid Board required a similar approach as do insurers. It is true to say, however, that there is no meaningful standard usage of commonly used percentage figures[4]. From a firm's point of view it is instructive for the litigators to agree a firm's standard for expressing confidence – an exercise which itself is illuminating for all involved in it. In terms of risk management it is crucial therefore that the success fee where used, is properly arrived at and capable of being defended should there be a challenge from the opponent. Very careful consideration needs to be given to the firm's approach where part of the success fee fails to be recovered at assessment or by negotiation. Equally the firm needs to consider whether the waiting for payment element is to be added and sought from the client – if it is not to be so recovered it has to be recognised that this becomes an overhead of the firm in carrying out such work.

1   See Chapter 8 and Chapter 22.
2   Dealt with fully in Chapter 22.
3   SI 2000/692. See Chapter 6 and Appendix 1.
4   A table of suggested meanings is given in Chapter 22.

TRAINING

20.14   The consideration of all of these factors necessarily calls for training. No firm can afford to have inconsistent and unmonitored use of the CFA as a funding mechanism and no system is going to be successful unless all using it know its principles and have had the opportunity to consider how it applies. The importance of training has been recognised by the Law Society's Training Committee which resolved in the year 2000 that members of the Personal Injury Panel should undertake risk assessment training.

BACFA

20.15   With apologies to Fisher and Ury[1] the entire approach to this new funding mechanism for litigation must be summed up by asking the question what is the Best Alternative to a CFA? What is the BACFA. This can be asked in respect of the firm and of the client – is a CFA right for this case, this client and this firm at this time? The consideration of the alternatives is important as is recognition that one of the alternatives for the firm will be to lose the client and for the client it will be not pursuing the case. The alternatives can then be looked at to determine which is the best one in the event that a CFA is not used.

1   Fisher and Ury *Getting to Yes* (New York, Penguin 1983) which uses the acronym BATNA – Best Alternative to a Negotiated Agreement.

AIMS OF RISK ASSESSMENT

20.16   Risk assessment is an approach to litigation and the process of litigating which aims to highlight the factors in an individual case that are most likely to affect the outcome. Having highlighted the factors through a rigorous method the issue or issues that will make or break the case can be clearly seen and can be the focus of attention. The central purpose then is to identify the issue – 'issue, issue or we all fall down!'[1] – and to enable the legal analysis.

There are other benefits from adopting the risk assessment approach.

1   See Goldrein and de Haas *Medical Negligence – Cost Effective Case Management* (Butterworths 1997).

Risk, costs and profit

20.17   Whatever method of risk assessment is to be used, the relationship between risk, the cost of litigating and ultimately the profitability of the work needs to be understood. There is a common interest between the client, the insurer and the litigation practice in assessing the risks involved in bringing and continuing the case. Risk assessment is not a once only process. A risk assessment method means that the case is kept under review against strict criteria that will provide the information for the decisions, which need to be made through the litigation process.

The funding of PI litigation has for a number of years involved risks to the firm. Legal Aid cases were funded differently according to success or failure but the major impact on the firm has been the introduction of CFAs. The virtual withdrawal of public funding from PI in April 2000 has profound implications for the balance of funding options in this field. The mix can now come from funders such as claims management companies (though many of these rely upon a CFA) or from clients who have Legal Expenses Insurance or from Membership Organisations such as Trade Unions and motoring organisations. For many firms this mix will be very limited with the vast majority of cases being funded by a CFA.

20.18   The financial implications arise not only from the fact that if a case loses the firm is not paid at all, but from the fact that under a CFA the firm is waiting for its fees until the case is concluded. In addition to the firm's own fees there arises a question over disbursements. Is the firm carrying the disbursements until conclusion and is it carrying liability if the case loses? So not only is there no income, there is a positive outgoing. It is clear that the link between risk, costs and profit must be understood. There is a cost to the firm in waiting for payment. There is a cost to the firm if it funds disbursements. Those costs can be recovered if the case wins. But the cost to the firm if the case loses includes of course the failure to earn fees. Clearly the concept of profit being an excess of income over expenditure when applied to this scenario will show exactly what the firm is up against. At the moment the risk in litigation is being transferred to the solicitor. It will remain to be seen whether the financial and insurance markets will eventually take over that risk. At present there are funding and insurance products available outside the use of CFAs which would enable a re-transfer of the risk away from the firm.

Assuming then that the firm is carrying the risk in a significant percentage of the caseload, there is a need for the firm to assess and manage the exposure to that risk. This involves a consideration at different levels from the control of decisions to an analysis of an individual case. Nonetheless, the principles behind risk assessment as a discipline are common – the purpose is to identify the risks and to organise the firm in the light of those risks. Not all of the risks can be avoided or transferred to others and therefore the firm is conducting its business knowing that a risk exists and being aware of the consequences. Risk assessed does not mean risk eliminated – it means that crucial information has been obtained on the basis of which business decisions can be made. There is also a common interest in risk assessment between the client, the insurer and the firm.

Client need

20.19   Risk assessment is based upon a methodical examination of the case being presented by the client. The claimant client may or may not be clear as to the real objective of the proposed litigation. Equally the defendant client may or may not be clear as to the basis upon which a settlement may be sought or the reasoning behind insisting on trial. Assessment in terms of the risk factors involved in the individual case and the necessary fact investigation and information gathering needed for that analysis provides an illumination for the client that better enables the lawyer to meet the needs of the client. Whilst good interviewing will lead to a sound grasp of client expectation, the process of risk analysis enables that initial position to be evaluated in terms of achievability, time and cost. In the context of CFAs, a risk assessment will satisfy the requirement to set out the reasons for the success fee[1]. Advice to the client presented as a result of a risk analysis will be instructive in explaining the legal context of the case and enable an informed decision to be taken as to its future conduct. If the case now is ready for negotiation the information marshalled during the analysis will be readily available for a sound negotiation plan.

1 Conditional Fee Agreements Regulations 2000, SI 2000/692, reg 4 requires brief written reasons to be given to the client, at the time the conditional fee agreement is made, for the level of the success fee. See Appendix 1.

Negotiation planning

20.20 Fisher and Ury[1] maintain that at the heart of successful legal negotiation lies the BATNA. A risk analysis will enable a realistic view to be taken as to what is the Best Alternative to a Negotiated Agreement and will avoid the common problem of assumptions being made as to the available options. If you know the risks involved in trial, a realistic appraisal can be made of any offer to settle and of the opportunity for making an offer to settle, be that as claimant or defendant.

1 Fisher and Ury *Getting to Yes* (New York, Penguin, 1983).

Lawyer need

20.21 The usefulness of risk analysis is by no means confined to CFA work. Nonetheless, in this funding field an accurate assessment of the chances of success is essential for the viability of this category of work. A risk assessment enables a refinement of the definition of success to be made. The definition of success lies at the centre of a CFA and indeed the viability of this funding mechanism. Without properly investigating client objectives no sensible agreement can be reached as to what success means for the funding agreement. Once that assessment has been made it also serves the purpose of setting the success fee and ensuring the viability of the work. Where the success fee is recoverable from the other side it establishes the reasons for the success fee. The written reasons given to the client at the time the CFA is made or amended are admissible at an assessment hearing and are highly relevant to the question of the reasonableness of the success fee[1].

1 AJA 1999, s 27 which inserts s 58A into the CLSA 1990 (in force from 1 April 2000). CPD, s 14.9 requires the party seeking to recover a success fee to make available to the court a copy of the risk assessment prepared at the time the CFA was made.

Insurer's need

20.22 Insurance products[1] are available to provide cover for other side's costs if the case is run on a CFA. Products are also available to provide cover for both sides' costs in conventionally funded cases. The essence of such cover is the risk of the case failing. The risk assessment process of the client's own lawyer will enable a clear picture for the insurer and enable a realistic assessment to be made of the level of costs involved and the appropriate premium level to be set. The level of case presentation and analysis displayed to insurers does have an influence on the decisions made in individual cases.

1 See Chapter 15.

20.23 The new litigation funding regime places great emphasis on a cost benefit approach and the ratio of costs, including any success fee and insurance premium, to quantum is a major consideration. The Legal Services Commission approach to cost benefit is to link the prediction of success with the ratio of costs to quantum. Thus where the prediction is 50%–60% the predicted damages must be at least double the predicted costs[1]. Under a CFA with a success fee the concern must be that the level of costs is not so disproportionate to the damages as to make it likely that costs will be disallowed in part. The strict CLS ratios may be viewed here as inappropriate. There are well known difficulties both in accurately estimating damages and in estimating costs. A risk assessment process will provide better information for the making of such estimates. A risk assessment will narrow the issues, which will incur work and therefore costs. It will identify the issues in quantum and how they are to be proved and the work involved in doing so. This information is critical to any costs benefit analysis.

1 The Funding Code – 5.7.3 (1 April 2000): If the claim is primarily a claim for damages by the client and does not have a significant wider public interest, full representation will be refused unless the following cost benefit criteria are satisfied:
   (i) If prospects of success are very good (80% or more), likely damages must exceed likely costs;
   (ii) If prospects of success are good (60%–80%), likely damages must exceed likely costs by a ratio of 2:1;
   (iii) If prospects of success are moderate (50%–60%), likely damages must exceed likely costs by a ratio of 4:1.

Identifying, eliminating, transferring and managing risk

20.24   These terms are commonly used when describing risk management as a process which will provide the information necessary for the proper management of whatever risk has been identified:

Risk

20.25   This really means uncertainty. A decision has to be made, the outcome of which is uncertain. In litigation there are many decisions to be made over a period of time with varying degrees of uncertainty as to outcome. Litigation involves people – crucially clients, judges and the litigation solicitors on each side. All of these people themselves will contribute to uncertainty. Put on top of that there is uncertainty through the facts of the case itself and in many other areas which will be discussed below. The only guarantee then is that there will be risk.

Identification

20.26   The whole process must of course begin with establishing where and what the risks are. In the subsequent pages are identified the main areas which give rise to risk in litigation in terms of what affects the success or failure of cases. It is important to identify also the consequences of the risks. In the previous section it has been shown that the consequences to the firm revolve around costs and profit. From the client's point of view the consequences being 'risked' are the damages which the client hopes to recover. The insurer has a risk of paying out on a claim on the policy – so the cover given under that policy is the measure of the risk.

Elimination

20.27   The ultimate in terms of an outcome of a risk assessment is of course being able to remove that risk entirely. In most instances that will not be possible. For example, there is a risk that the client will not turn up to court. Whilst measures can be taken to minimise the consequences of the client failing to appear, it is difficult to see how the risk itself can be removed. A written proof of evidence is a measure to reduce the impact of the risk but it still cannot remove the risk itself.

Transfer

20.28   Given that elimination will not be an option with most of the risks identified, the next best thing is to move that risk to a different party. The problem here of course is that by definition someone will still end up with that risk. Either the client or the solicitor or the insurer must bear the risk or of course there can be a sharing between them.

Management

20.29   Having identified the risks and failed to eliminate them they are being borne by someone. Whether the risks are being borne by the firm or its client or the insurer of the client, much of the responsibility involved in litigating is in managing the risks. Informing and advising both the client and the insurer of the changing risks and the decisions which need to be made in the light of the risks is the key to effective litigating. The solicitor has a duty to the client who will have a relationship with an insurer and of course the solicitor has obligations to the firm. Managing means therefore being able to give the advice needed by having in place a process which has as its aim the identification of the risks and the consequences so that surprises are kept to a minimum.

Risk management techniques

20.30   Possession of information is the vital factor in the management of risk. That information relates to costs, cash flow and caseloads where the financial risk to the firm is being addressed. With individual cases there is essential information which the firm needs in order to manage the decision to accept a client under a CFA.

Costs

20.31   The risk to the firm is in terms of the fees which would have been earned had the case won. A different perspective is to look at the marginal cost – ie the cost in terms of overheads which were expended in doing the work for no fee. It is this latter cost which will actually be incurred and which must then be carried by the firm through profits made elsewhere, either in success fees of successful cases or from different departments.

Is the expense of time[1] known to the firm and to the litigation team? Gross fees do not reveal the full picture since the real cost which must be covered consists of the outgoings of the business. In a large firm it may be sufficient to concentrate on the litigation department costs, assuming an accurate allowance is made for the firm's costs not attributable solely to individual departments. It is essential to know the cost to the firm for the work being done. Assuming that cost is known, it is then possible to calculate the exposure to costs risk over any period of time and according to the caseload of individuals and the entire department. If this cost is not known then assumptions will be made, often based on the premise – the department is busy so it must be making money – which are in fact seriously inaccurate.

1 See *The Expense of Time* (5th edn, Law Society publications).

Cash flow

20.32 Work done under a CFA will not be paid for until the conclusion of the case and indeed disputes over costs from the losing opponent can prolong receipt even beyond conclusion. A review of past cases, whether funded by CFA or not, will give some indication of how long the firm will be waiting for payment of its fees and reimbursement of disbursements in its typical caseload. The other element is the level of fees for which the firm is waiting. Looking at past cases of each member of the team will again give some indication of the level of fees incurred which, under a CFA, will not be paid until the end. Whilst the success fee can legitimately build in a percentage to cover this cost of waiting for payment, in cash-flow terms there is still a considerable impact to withstand. The cost of waiting for payment can be transferred via insurance products that fund disbursements and work in progress[1].

1 See Chapter 18.

Caseload

20.33 It may not be a practical matter to suggest that the number of cases taken on under a CFA can be monitored with a view to restricting them. Reality may well point to the policy that cases are not to be rejected on the grounds that the exposure of the firm is already at a particular (perhaps arbitrary) limit. Nonetheless, it is important that the exposure of the firm is known even if that knowledge is not going to prevent cases being taken on. It is important to know not only the predicted level of costs to the firm but also the predicted length of time that those costs will remain unpaid even if the case wins. This calls for predictions which may be unfamiliar but any management system must aim at this level of knowledge. It can of course be argued that over time, the revenue from completed cases will come in and can be used to carry the work in progress from then on. It must be remembered however, that not only has there been a cost involved before that revenue comes on stream, but there is an opportunity cost in applying that revenue to support new cases.

Summary

20.34

- What is this case going to cost to run? – include disbursements
- How much to date has this case cost the firm? – review periodically
- How long will the firm be waiting for payment?

Developing case selection criteria procedures

20.35   Assuming not all cases that come to the practice are run, and indeed from the point of view of all concerned, only cases which are viable are run, procedures can be put in place and criteria can be used in the selection process which aim to identify and manage the risks involved.

When in terms of time to enter into a CFA

20.36   Most practitioners in most fields of litigation are faced with the decision of whether to take a case or not at a time when very little is known. In the context of CFAs the issue arises as to when a decision can be made to accept the case on this basis. The rules[1] make this all the more important by requiring a written assessment to be given at the time the CFA is made. Procedure needs to include, therefore, a standard response to the question of when will a case be taken on under a CFA? In clinical negligence this may be after medical records have been obtained or only after a preliminary assessment by an expert. In PI the decision is likely to be made much earlier and possibly only on the basis of the client's own instructions. Whether the practice of these instructions being taken over the telephone is to be adopted needs careful thought. In the future consideration will need to be given to taking instructions via the Internet. In a commercial dispute it is likely that some preliminary investigation by the client is called for after interview.

1   Conditional Fee Agreements Regulations 2000, SI 2000/692, reg 3(1)(a).

What?

20.37   The factors regarded important in risk assessment show that the key to making a decision is the possession of information. This will continue to be the key throughout the litigation process, it is the level of information which changes over time but the procedure needs to decide for each stage what level is appropriate. That begins with the decision CFA or not.

Procedure

20.38   Much depends upon the size of the firm and the complexity and value of the case. What may be regarded as an essential for a complex clinical negligence case cannot be afforded in a more common road traffic case or tripping incident. Thus where the case justifies it, the procedure is likely to involve from day one, a written assessment and then a presentation of some kind to a group. This group may be a special committee appointed to consider CFAs. It may be a managing team in a department. It may be the whole department. The essence however is the same – to test the views of one against the views and experience of many.

Case selection procedure

20.39   Example for a personal injury matter

Stage	Minimum information needed	Obtained/comments
Initial inquiry	personal info type of injury circumstances – eg tripping in street witnesses	
First interview	client description of incident. details of witnesses. correspondence with defence other independent evidence when complaint first made employment details general health name of GP existing insurance	
CFA decision	medical records earnings/savings insurance cover needed estimate of costs estimate of quantum	

20.40   A similar approach can be continued for the stages of litigation once the case has been taken on. This is essentially a checklist of the minimum information needed before a relevant decision is taken. For the interview stage there may well be a firm's pro forma to ensure vital information is gathered as efficiently and early as possible. The CFA decision needs all of the information from the previous two stages.

The new litigation funding regime places great emphasis on a cost benefit approach and the ratio of costs, including any success fee and insurance premium, to quantum must be a major consideration. The Legal Aid Board approach to cost benefit is to link the prediction of success with the ratio of costs to quantum. Thus where the prediction is 50%–60% the predicted damages must be at least double the predicted costs. Under a CFA with a success fee the concern must be that the level of costs is not so disproportionate to the damages as to make it likely that costs will be disallowed in part. Proportionality under the CPR is to be applied separately to the base costs and to the success fee and not to the total[1]. Nonetheless it is likely that an impression will be given by the total which cannot be ignored by the practitioner faced with a decision as to the level of success fee to set. The strict LAB ratios may be viewed here as inappropriate.

1   CPD, s 11.5. See Chapter 8.

Planning

20.41   Clearly there are risks for the firm in conducting litigation in the new funding era. The taking on of clients with risk to the firm that it will not cover its costs, still less turn in an operating profit, must therefore be managed and in order to do so, vital information must be obtained in order to estimate the firm's exposure to risk in financial terms over a stated period:

- Likely duration from instruction to conclusion
- Likely level of disbursements
- Likely level of costs of each person working on the case
- Likely number of cases per fee earner over the average duration period

Management structures

20.42   Irrespective of the size of the firm or the litigation or PI department, the above knowledge is only useful if accurate monitoring of the actual exposure is going to take place. The plan for the firm will set out the exposure which it is thought the firm can withstand, both in terms of waiting for payment (cash flow) and in terms of unsuccessful cases. Having a plan means agreeing a forecast on the above information and taking a view of the financial strength of the firm. Assuming the figures are accurate a forecast can be made in liquidity terms. It is then possible to risk assess the financial exposure by calculating the effect of the figures being inaccurate by 10% to 30% and to see the effect of one case in 50 failing and of two cases in 50 and of the effect of an early case failing where there has not been a build up of success fees from successful cases to offset the loss. None of this can predict what is actually going to happen. Risk assessment is used to indicate the effects of possible events. It is crucial that the firm continues to monitor all of the actual information under the above headings. This means recording mechanisms and controlled decision making plus reporting of progress. A decision to take on an individual case can then be taken not only in the light of the risk assessment but also in the light of the real position overall at the time. BACFA[1] means 'Best Alternative to a CFA' not just for the client but also for the firm. Conditions in the firm's overall exposure must be known in order to be able to assess the risks of taking on another case on a CFA versus the risks of refusing it (eg the client goes elsewhere). Many firms use a committee for the decision to take on a case on a CFA so that the individual litigator dealing with the client does not have the decision. The litigator will make a proposal to the committee, which may or may not consist of other litigators or other litigators in the same field.

Transfer of risk in CFA work will also need to be managed as a firm. Insurance products are available to fund disbursements and to insure them in the event that the case loses. Hybrids between a CFA and a traditionally funded case are also possible to insure so that the firm is transferring some of the risk if the case loses. These must be decisions taken at a management level more than an individual case by case level.

1   See para **20.15** above.

Confluence of funding and risk

20.43   It is clear that solicitors are being expected to fund litigation and take the risk that the funding will not be recovered. Even where the funding is recovered it will inevitably be at a point later in time than has hitherto been experienced. There is therefore a confluence of funding and risk. There is a danger that both the reality of funding and the risk involved will be hidden if the firm has not carried out any analysis of the kind detailed in the previous pages. The cost of waiting for payment, of funding disbursements and of cases where the fees recovered are less than those expected[1] (and of course cases where no fees are paid at all) must be recognised and planned for. If the burden of all of this is to be carried by other parts of the firm the business plan needs to make that explicit and control must be exercised in just the same way that it would be exercised if the burden is transferred through insurance or borrowings.

1   In *Callery v Gray* (Chester County Court) Case No. MC002977 January 2001, the base costs were reduced on detailed assessment by 50% and the success fee was by concession reduced from 60% to 40% to remove the element for waiting for payment. The total fees recovered were in the region of £2000 whereas at the unreduced rates they would have exceeded £4000.

Chapter 21

Methods of Risk Assessment

21.1 Risk means uncertainty and in litigation the uncertainties create the need for a risk assessment. The risk assessment process is aimed at identifying and assessing the uncertainties. In most litigation there will need to be an assessment relating to liability and an assessment on quantum. The uncertainties arise under the same headings for both liability and quantum. Four methods are described below. Methods A, B and C are illustrated in the Case Studies (Chapter 28) and it is recommended that all least one case study be read in conjunction with the current chapter.

METHOD A – STRATEGIC ANALYSIS

Risk headings[1]

21.2
The Facts
The Law
The Client
The Opponent
The Costs
The Procedure

1   For a template of these headings see para **21.23** below.

The factual uncertainty

21.3 In many, but not all cases, there will be factual uncertainty which can affect the likelihood of success. Proving quantum requires the proof of facts in the same way that proof of liability depends upon proof of facts. Liability and quantum may also depend on expert opinion. For the purposes of risk assessment, expert opinion is regarded as a part of establishing facts. The risk assessment must show what has to be proved by expert opinion. From that analysis it is possible to identify the source of the evidence needed to prove the issue ie which expert will prove which issue. As with all evidence, proof may depend upon acceptance by the court of the evidence in the face of conflicting evidence called by the other side. This is true with respect to factual evidence and as to opinion evidence. 'The facts' refers to two levels –

direct facts and inferred facts. 'Did the barrel fall out of the window?' is a question of direct fact. 'Why did it fall?' may well be a matter for inference. (Did it fall due to the defendant's negligence is the ultimate inferential fact). Uncertainty can arise at the direct level but it often arises at the second, inferential level. An analysis aims to throw up these factual uncertainties so that a view can be taken as to how to remove or minimise the uncertainty or proceed with the uncertainty.

Proving the facts

21.4   It is necessary, and now possible, to assess how the facts can be proved. Areas of uncertainty will thus be highlighted against any evidence on either side already to hand and the gaps in the available evidence. The areas of uncertainty build up a picture which enables an assessment to be made of the objective of the client and the chances of success. It will highlight graphically where the gaps are and where the work needs to be done. Thus, consideration can be given to the source and reliability of evidence, be it documentary, oral or expert. Although English Law does not proceed on a basis of adding up the number of witnesses, it is crucial to know whether any particular issue depends for its proof on a single piece of evidence or a single witness. The risk assessment that shows that a major disputed fact in issue depends on the oral evidence of the client and that there are no other possible sources of evidence of that issue is a risk assessment which shows exactly what real risk is being run. Establishing the facts piece by piece will also throw up inconsistencies between evidence addressing the same fact and conflicts in the evidence of the opposing parties. Again this is essential analysis in order to assess the case.

An illustration of the effects of findings of fact comes from contributory negligence. Given a case where it is likely that the defendant will raise contributory negligence, a risk assessment can show the effect on outcome of a particular finding. It cannot show how likely the finding is – that will always be the area for professional judgement. The costs of the case set against the various outcomes will again place a value on the risk attached to the case going to trial.

Assuming loss of £20,000 can be proved

Contrib Neg	Effect on Damages	Predicted likelihood of finding
Nil	20,000	5%
25%	15,000	25%
50%	10,000	50%
75%	5,000	20%

The client would be advised if offered £5,000 that there was a very good chance of recovering more – indeed in this example an 80% chance. Were there to be an offer of £10,000 the advice changes since there is only a 30% chance of beating it.

21.5   The above table can be used to reflect the possibility of an overestimate of the likelihood factor. Suppose it were only 35% likely that the judge will find 50% contributory negligence and 30% likely that it will be found to be 75%. We then get—

Contrib Neg	Effect on Damages	Likelihood
Nil	20,000	5%
25%	15,000	25%
50%	10,000	35%
75%	5,000	35%

Here the change is not dramatic. At £5,000 there is still a 65% chance of a better outcome. At £10,000 there is still only a 30% chance of a better outcome. Looked at another way, it can be seen how wrong the calculation has to be before the risk changes dramatically, a good indication of the value of the risk in the litigation.

The uncertainty in the law

21.6   Assuming the facts are clear and can be proved, the question arises as to whether they establish a legal action. Two further questions are, 'would a judge agree' and 'why will the other side not agree?' Not all cases are going to raise potentially difficult points of law but a risk assessment must include a consideration of each case if only to determine that it is not one where the law is likely to be arguable.

Again, in these cases the risk assessment can be done to show the effects on the claimant's case of the various decisions on the law that could be made. At that stage some assessment has to be made as to the likelihood of one decision rather than another and clearly that is a matter for judgment. But, the isolation of that factor and its implications for the client are hugely useful for decision making and especially in identifying prospects of settlement. The other side is faced with the same uncertainty when it comes to the law – the difference will be the degree of likelihood which each side's lawyers are prepared to put on a favourable decision. In most cases each side will have a view that the prospects of success are favourable reflecting the difference in view as to the law.

Putting aside cases where one or even both of the parties wants a court to decide the law (test case situation), the true value of the case going to trial can be arrived at by seeing the area of difference in outcome according to each possible finding on the law. That value is what is at risk should the case proceed to trial.

Client risk

21.7   Risk assessment must include an assessment of the client. Assessment includes the client's commitment to the case, potential as a witness and whether the sympathy factor is likely to be positive or negative, why the client has decided to see a solicitor, whether they have seen another solicitor(s) already, whether they are the aggrieved or a relative of a deceased victim? Are they able to give a clear account of events? Do they add to their story at a later date? Do they contradict themselves? What is the level of their expectation as to outcome? Have they responded to advice or requests for further information? How emotionally involved in the case are they? Must they have 'their day in court'? Do they want revenge over the defendant/person they see as responsible? If the case reaches a trial, to what extent is the case dependant on the acceptance of the clients' version of events?

The requirement to give a written assessment to the client when entering a Conditional Fee Agreement (CFA) may cause some difficulty here. If the client is being taken on notwithstanding reservations about the client themselves, any recorded risk assessment ought to reflect that, but at the same time the client will need to be given advice in a sensitive manner.

Opponent risk

21.8 Assessing the other side in terms of solvency is likely to be standard. The potential for the opponent to become insolvent may mean that this risk should be reviewed periodically for the obvious reason that the client will receive nothing from the action against an insolvent defendant and the CFA will leave the solicitor unpaid if the client is unable to pay. The reputation of the other side, particularly as a litigant, may be of importance as indeed may the reputation of those representing them. In clinical negligence cases the individual medical practitioner may have anything from no part to play, to a very central part in the litigation decisions. It may be obvious that the other side is going to be difficult and therefore costly to deal with. The unrepresented opponent is likely to add to the time needed to proceed with the case. A risk assessment done at a time when crucial factors about the opponent (or even their identity) are unknown may leave the confidence level of success in the face of that uncertainty as no higher than 50%. If the opponent is from a category which ought by law for example to be insured is it known that this particular opponent is insured?

Procedural risk

21.9 Limitation periods are the firm favourite here but the Pre-action Protocols and indeed the whole of the Civil Procedure Rules (CPR) can give rise to uncertainty. With the protocols consideration needs to be given to the time period for completion and the time remaining. CPR Part 36 provides a staging point for reassessing risk. The risk assessment should point to the potential risk with an expression, as with all factors, of the confidence level of succeeding. It is abundantly clear form the law reports that Part 36 does remove the concept of certainty in cases where liability is not in issue. The risk in costs attached to Part 36 must be taken into the risk assessment process and will be reflected in the success fee where the case is run on a CFA basis.

Cost risk

21.10 Even outside CFAs, the costs risk is a factor to be assessed. Meeting the costs of Pre-action Protocols and fact investigation including potentially the need for experts raises questions for the client and the solicitor which may well have a bearing on the viability of the case for litigation. Proportionality of costs and the use and effect of CPR Part 36 offers are the regime in this respect. With the recoverability of insurance premiums and the success fee comes the need to assess the suitability of the funding mechanism, CFA or other, and the awareness of the ability of a losing opponent to challenge the recoverability of an additional liability.

Case analysis

Theory of the case

21.11 With the evidence and assertions available, what explanation(s) best deals with the material in a way which achieves the client objective? The material may, certainly early on, suggest more than one theory, but there is a danger in proceeding with conflicting theories. It is far better to proceed with a chosen theory and be prepared to abandon it later. Equally in the early stages it is important to keep open the possibilities for fresh theories.

The theory chosen will have an effect on the investigation and the formulation of negotiation strategy, the making of CPR Part 36 offers and right through to trial advocacy. The selection of evidence, the preparation of questions, the whole tenor of the case will wholly differ according to which of the theories you selected. Use of a theory also leads to effective analysis by seeing the evidence found as either in line with the theory or not. If not, then the decision has to made to proceed without the evidence or to reformulate the theory. Equally crucial is the need to consider the theory of the case from the point of view of the opponent and to construct the opponent's theory from the materials upon which they rely

21.12

Example–

Mrs B, a lady of 35, has suffered a dislocated hip having fallen over a wire shopping basket which was in the middle of the aisle in her local supermarket.

Even with these few facts it is possible to arrive at a theory of the case, an explanation of what happened which is consistent with Mrs B having a claim. The essence of a theory of the case is that it is as plausible as possible. The theory must fit the evidence and instructions already obtained and must anticipate as far as possible the evidence yet to be discovered. It has to provide a chronologically constructed account of the events which it is alleged must have happened and which give rise to a liability (if claimant) or deny liability (if defendant). No matter how complex the litigation there will be a chronology of events and omissions.

21.13

Theory–

Mrs B was distracted. The basket had been inadvertently left in the middle of the aisle by an employee (or had been seen by an employee). Mrs B fell over the basket and suffered injury.

Information is needed to establish why Mrs B did not see the basket (was there a special offer display on the top shelf?). Information is needed as to how the basket came to be where it was and how that relates to a breach of duty – hence the possibility that either an employee inadvertently put it there (perhaps they had been filling a shelf from it and were called away) or at least had seen it there and in the reasonable time available had not caused it to be removed.

Finding the theory requires investigation of facts – it does not lead to providing the client with evidence that does not exist. In essence the theory of the case proceeds on the basis that certain events did take place with certain consequences. There are many possible explanations – the theory of the case needs to be the most plausible explanation of facts that are known. Once the theory has been selected it is used as a tool for analysing the material which already exists, for gathering new material and for formulating questions which need to be answered. As the case proceeds with more material becoming available it may well prove necessary to revise the theory, or in some cases to wholly abandon it in favour of a different theory which the materials now suggest to be most plausible. Every step of the litigation process right through if it occurs, to examination of witnesses in court, should be informed by the theory of the case. Questions asked which cannot contribute to the establishment of the theory of the case must be regarded as inappropriate questions to ask. Quantum requires a similar approach – there needs to be a coherent factual explanation of what has happened and will in the future happen which supports a claim for damages.

Analysing the evidence

21.14 There will be critical stages throughout the litigation process at which an analysis of the evidence is vital. At first interview the purpose is to look for facts and assertions which suggest possible hypotheses. Prior to a CPR Part 36 offer there will have to be a very firm hypothesis to put to the other side with a clear assessment of the evidence in support. Again at the time of issue of proceedings. When information and rebuttal come from the other side there needs to be a re-assessment and finally before trial the purpose is to assess the evidence for trial performance.

At each stage the purpose of analysis must be kept in mind and the amount and quality of the evidence will vary over time so that the exercise is not a repeat but a true re-appraisal with new material. At each stage there must be a formulation or re-formulation of a theory of the case and a careful analysis of the evidence in the light of the theory.

The analysis is to a great extent a matter of information control and its mechanics are dealt with below. However, it is worth stating here that the analysis will, as the stages go on, increasingly include an evaluation exercise, that is, some estimate of how well the evidence will achieve its purpose at the relevant stage. The answer in evaluation at first interview needs only to be in terms of generating initial hypotheses and routes for investigation, whereas before trial the field has narrowed in terms of hypotheses and it is necessary to evaluate the likely effect of the evidence on the trier of fact.

METHOD B – FACT IN ISSUE ANALYSIS

21.15 In order to arrive at the uncertainties it is necessary to extract the factual issues from the materials available. Unless it is clearly established what facts are needed to establish liability or quantum and exactly what evidence is to be relied upon to establish those facts, the true strength of a case cannot be assessed. This process must begin with the identification of the facts in issue of the case. The substantive law lays down the facts in issue. Thus for any claim in negligence the following skeleton will always apply irrespective of how many issues have been conceded at the time of any risk assessment—

- Duty
- Breach

- Causation
- Lack of Contributory Negligence
- Damage

By analysing the case against that skeleton, the real issue(s) of the individual case will be found. The identification of the evidence needed to prove those real issues leads to the issues themselves being narrowed still further. This is the critical path analysis forming the basis of the conduct of the case through all the stages of litigation.

21.16 The legal action will set out the facts which must be established – the facts in issue. A good example is s 2(1) of the Misrepresentation Act 1967—

'Where a person has entered into a contract after a misrepresentation has been made to him by another party thereto and as a result thereof he has suffered loss, then, if the person making the representation would be liable to damages in respect thereof had the misrepresentation been made fraudulently, that person shall be so liable notwithstanding that the misrepresentation was not made fraudulently, unless he proves that he had reasonable ground to believe and did believe up to the time the contract was made that the facts represented were true.'

21.17 Here the facts in issue are—

- Contract
- Misrepresentation
- By a party
- Loss
- Lack of reasonable grounds

(The reference to fraud raises a question of law and not a fact in issue).

Against each fact in issue the evidence can be assessed and it would be possible to express confidence levels by a percentage figure against each fact in issue. It is essential that this rigorous approach is used in all cases and that no case is treated as a simple and obvious case of a particular type (if there is already an admission of liability then the process need only be applied to quantum). By insisting that all cases are subjected to this risk process all potential issues are looked at and the real issue or issues will be identified. There is great danger attached to an attempt to short cut the system. Thus even if the case appears to have no question on the matter of duty, the essence of a risk assessment approach is that the issue of duty is addressed and the means of proving it are recorded.

21.18 The FOUR categories of fact—

Facts known to your client which **support** your case – **CF**
Facts known to your client which are **adverse** to your case – **CU**
Facts which are not yet known but which would be **favourable** – **OF**
Facts which are not known but which would be **unfavourable** – **OU**

An analysis must be made against the facts in issue showing what evidence there is and is not, where it comes from and whether it is favourable or not.

21.19   Fact Analysis Form

KEY:	**CF** favourable facts known to your client
	CU unfavourable facts known to your client
	OF favourable facts known to opponent
	OU unfavourable facts known to opponent
	? facts as yet unknown

Claimant Evidence	Fact in Issue	Defendant Evidence
	Duty	
	Breach	
	Causation	
	Damage	
	Contrib	

21.20   The legal action will set out the facts that must be established – the facts in issue. Thus in a Personal Injury action the skeleton is Duty, Breach, Causation, Lack of Contributory Negligence, Damage. The facts in issue approach means that all elements are considered in all cases and no assumption is made as to where disputed issues will arise. The issues likely to be in dispute are only accurately identifiable after the fact in issue analysis has been completed.

Against each fact in issue the evidence can be identified and assessed and confidence levels can be expressed by a percentage figure. This analysis will identify gaps in evidence just as much as identifying the evidence which has already been obtained. This goes a long way to satisfying the requirement of a written assessment when entering a CFA. The following template can be used to display the material and reveal the strengths and weaknesses in the evidence.

21.21

Fact in issue	CF	CU	OF	OU
Duty				
Breach				
Causation				
Damage				
Contrib				

21.22   A systematic approach to the evidence and the *facts in issue* will lead to an orderly analysis of the evidence at the various stages. Each piece of evidence, and indeed each question asked, must aim at a fact in issue. A chart can be drawn up which allocates evidence, favourable and not, to the facts in issue which arise in the case. Gaps can be immediately seen and inconsistencies either between own evidence or between it and the other side will become clear. The litigator will know what they know *and* know what they do not.

Claimant evidence	Fact in issue	Def Evidence
List nature and source and gaps	See cause of action eg Personal injury negligence	Nature/source and gaps

Facts may be known/unknown, proved or yet to be proved.

Risk Assessment Template

21.23

Fact	Law
Client	Opponent
Costs	Procedure

Theory of the Case

METHOD C – FACTOR LIST ANALYSIS[1]

Risk factors

21.24   The uncertainties in litigation have been classified above into six areas – Fact, Law, Client, Opponent, Procedure and Costs from which a list of factors can be produced specific to the type of case, against which a case can be analysed. Whichever factor list is used[2], a profile of the case can be built by ranking the factors in order of importance to the case. Having ranked the factors it will be clear as to where, at the time the particular assessment is being made, the work has to be done. Thus, for example, if there were serious doubt as to the solvency of the opponent steps would have to be taken to address that factor before work and costs are put into other factors. With the example of Mrs B at para **21.12** it would be necessary to concentrate on how the basket came to be in the aisle before addressing other issues.

1   A fully worked example of this method is given in Chapter 25.
2   For personal injury cases two factor lists are given, either or both of which can be used for each case.

21.25   Factor lists can be constructed for any field of litigation. The method to be adopted in using them will be the same and is explained below.

Factor list for personal injury

21.26

1. Likely performance of client in court
2. Availability of witnesses
3. Availability of evidence
4. Existence of documents
5. Believability of client's story
6. Potentially difficult point of law
7. Time available before Limitation Period ends
8. Persuasiveness of other side's evidence
9. Quantum
10. Level of emotion in the claim/defence
11. Likely costs of bringing/defending action
12. Chances for settlement
13. This type of case is likely to win something for claimant
14. Likely view of judge on merits
15. Likely view of judge on sympathy factor
16. Level of dependency on oral evidence of fact
17. Client wants 'day in court'
18. Solvency of the other side

Fact in issue factor list for personal injury

21.27

1. Duty of care owed to claimant
2. Identity of party owing duty to claimant
3. Question of law involved in duty of care
4. Standard of care
5. Contributory negligence
6. Independent witness
7. Documentary evidence
8. Solvency of opponent
9. Likely performance of client as a witness
10. Reputation of the defendant
11. More than one prospective defendant
12. Quantum in relation to costs
13. Need for expert evidence
14. Limitation period
15. Causation in fact
16. Injury reported
17. Medical assistance given
18. Evidence of quantum

Factor list for non-personal injury civil claim

21.28

1.   Dependency on oral evidence of fact
2.   Available documents own side
3.   Available documents other side
4.   Limitation period
5.   Client's potential as a witness
6.   Arguable question of law
7.   Assessment of damages (Quantum)
8.   Solvency of opponent
9.   Ratio of costs to recovery value
10. Chances of settlement
11. Liability likely to be insured
12. Client wants 'day in court'
13. Number of alleged wrongs/breaches
14. Causation
15. Mitigation
16. Need for expert evidence
17. Reputation of opponent
18. Realism of client's case

Insolvency Factor List for Wrongful Trading

21.29

1.   Whether defendant governed by s 214
2.   Tracing of assets
3.   Question of law involved
4.   Date of insolvency
5.   Dispute as to defendant's knowledge of facts indicating insolvency
6.   Availability of documentary evidence
7.   Ability of opponent to meet liability and costs
8.   Likely performance of defendant as a witness
9.   Likely performance of witnesses
10. Quantum in relation to costs
11. Need for expert evidence
12. Proof of involvement of defendant in running business
13. Sympathy for defendant
14. Company's compliance with accounting and reporting requirements
15. Calculation of compensation order
16. Evidence of quantum
17. Accountancy advice to company
18. Settlement potential

Clinical negligence factor list

21.30

1. Complaint made as early as reasonably possible after the event.
2. Proximity of Limitation period
3. Client's word against that of health professional
4. Client believability/coherence
5. Level of client emotion in the claim
6. Field requires untried expert
7. Likely performance of client at trial
8. Quality of expert's report
9. Client's story not contradicted by medical notes
10. Bolitho needed to win
11. Ratio of investigation costs to quantum
12. No need for more than one expert for claimant
13. Ratio of damages to costs at trial
14. Multiplicity of issues in the case
15. Causation likely to be in dispute
16. Realistic client expectation
17. Liability likely to be disputed
18. This kind of claim likely to settle

Road traffic non-personal injury claims

21.31

1. Likely performance of client in court
2. Availability of witnesses
3. Availability of independent evidence
4. Police report
5. Believability of client's story
6. Pending prosecutions
7. Time available before Limitation Period ends
8. Persuasiveness of other side's evidence
9. Quantum
10. Photographic evidence
11. Likely costs of bringing/defending action
12. Chances for settlement/this type of case is likely to win something for claimant
13. Seat belts
14. Solvency/insurance of defendant
15. Road conditions
16. Level of dependency on oral evidence of fact
17. Pre-accident condition of vehicle
18. Contributory negligence

APPLYING THE FACTOR LISTS

Individual Factor List

Ranking Instructions

21.32   In the table below rank the factors from the appropriate factor list by putting the number corresponding to the chosen factor into the TOP box if it is the top choice and into the BOTTOM box if it is the last choice. This exercise is then repeated a further 8 times giving a total of 9 top and 9 bottom choices. Factors are ranked according to their significance to the case at the time of the assessment. This step in the risk assessment does not call for an evaluation of the strength or weakness of the factors.

   Example: If it is decided that the top factor is *existence of documents* and the least relevant factor is *level of emotion* the number 4 is put into the TOP box and the number 10 into the BOTTOM box for ranking round one. The exercise is then repeated with the remaining factors until all 9 rounds are complete.

Ranking round	Top	Bottom
1		
2		
3		
4		
5		
6		
7		
8		
9		

Analysis

21.33 The profile in terms of the most significant features at this stage and, therefore, the features which will require work, is given in the first five factors as ranked. This kind of profile will always benefit from the Theory of the Case technique[1]. The Theory of the Case must address these top five factors.

1 See above para **21.11**.

Weighting the risk

21.34 Whenever an expression of confidence is to be made the risk analysis is used to highlight exactly what factors it is which have been considered in arriving at that level of confidence. Where there is no information about a factor eg solvency, the expression of confidence must reflect that lack of knowledge. The final expression is to some extent then subjective to the individual litigator. It is important to recognise that the profile created will vary from litigator to litigator and that it is a reflection of how the individual litigator will run the litigation.

Confidence level

21.35 This sheet is to be completed after the ranking exercise has been completed.

From the ranking sheet enter the top five factors in the left hand column and give a %[1] to each to reflect the confidence in that factor.

Factor	Confidence level %
	Total % divided by 5[2] ....
	Success Fee[3] ....

1 The expression of confidence levels in percentage terms is dealt with in Chapter 22.
2 This provides an average confidence level but will not reflect the fact that a particular factor has been scored at below 50% indicating a negative confidence level. A different approach is to recognise the lowest confidence level given as being the overall confidence level on the basis that the case is never stronger than its weakest factor.
3 The calculation of the success fee is dealt with in Chapter 22.

METHOD D – CHECKLISTS

21.36 A much used form of risk assessment in personal injury cases, both road traffic and others, is the checklist which ensures that certain levels of information are achieved before an assessment is made. Some such lists provide a prior weighting to factors on the list and/or ask the user to enter a score for each factor within a pre-given range. In this weighted checklist system the designers of the list have already ranked to some extent the risk value of each factor.

21.37 A typical example of a weighted checklist is as follows;

Type of case – this factor will usually have been given a score by the designer of the list:

RTA	10%
Industrial accident	20%
Slip/Trip	25%

Liability issues

Causation –	0–20% indicating no difficulty up to high difficulty
Time since event	0–30% indicating length of time raises risk levels

Specific factors relating to the type of case – eg RTA

Police reports
Police attendance
Photographs
Weather conditions
Condition of client's vehicle
Seat belts

Such systems are similar in approach to Method C above but are often lacking in transparency as to how the weightings have been arrived at and what factors are really being taken into account. In some instances the number of factors identified exceed 40 with scoring systems in excess of 700 points all then averaged to a percentage figure. This makes for a difficult task in terms of assessment and particularly in terms of expression of confidence.

Unweighted checklists are used to ensure that the litigator is addressing factors which the firm has decided must be considered in all cases. The expression of confidence is then taken as one statement usually as a percentage figure. In such a system it will not be shown how the factors relate to the confidence levels. At their very basic level, lists such as these are in effect statements of the factors which will arise in litigation of the kind in question on a general basis but they do not indicate at all which factors apply to a particular individual case nor which have attracted a high confidence level and which have not. Whilst such a list if used literally as a checklist is a form of risk assessment, by not requiring more than a tick they do not constitute a discipline of risk assessment. It is submitted that they also fail to provide any insight into the reasons for a success fee in a CFA case since they do not highlight where the particular risks are in the individual case.

CHANCE FOR SETTLEMENT

21.38   Litigators assess risk, by whatever method they use, with a view to trial. That is, they are assessing the prospects of success on the assumption that the case goes to trial. It is true that the vast majority of cases do not go to trial but the assessment must be in terms of trial because all cases have a potential for trial and settlement depends upon preparedness to go to trial.

Whilst preparedness to go to trial may be an attitude of mind, risk assessing a case in terms of its prospects for settlement and establishing what is needed for settlement is a valid activity albeit under the CPR the decisions regarding trial may arrive quickly. The factors which affect success at trial will overlap with those giving a successful settlement but the latter will require other factors to be considered which the process of negotiation demands.

21.39   The factors affecting the chance of settlement[1]—

A   The law
B   The evidence
C   Value of possible recovery
D   Legal costs

Each side will have a view on A, B and C which is likely to differ and which will not be disclosed to the other side. It is more probable that the estimate of costs will be similar although estimates are notoriously difficult to produce with accuracy. From that A and B amount to the probability that liability will be imposed. C gives the value of the claim and D needs to be estimated right through to trial. Where the costs exceed the difference in values given by the parties then objectively there ought to be a settlement. The process of negotiation (and mediation) must aim at learning about each side's perceptions with regard to each of A – D if a settlement is to be facilitated.

1   See further Anderson and Twining *Analysing Evidence* (Sweet and Maxwell).

What causes a case to go to trial?

21.40   Other than the test case exception, the litigants' confidence, the perceived value of the claim and the information balance are critical factors.

The confidence which each litigant has in a favourable outcome should the case go to trial is clearly going to be a major influence over whether it does actually reach the court. That level of confidence can be represented in percentage terms and often risk assessment is expressed in that way. Whether or not such a method is effective, it is useful for illustrating the effect of confidence on this crucial question of what makes a case go to trial. The confidence level of each party will be a reflection in large measure of their own perception of factors A to D referred to above, rather than any objective state of those factors.

0% —————————————————50 —————————————————100%

Where the parties have levels of confidence which are not complimentary it is less likely to settle. Where the parties are at either end of the scale from each other, the pressure will be high to settle but it is likely that the parties will in any event be willing to settle such cases. In other words, where the parties roughly agree on the strength of the case there will be settlement. If both parties have confidence levels above 50% then clearly settlement will be more difficult. The level at which a settlement will be reached will also depend upon how far apart the parties are in their perceptions of the strength of their case and their perceptions of value.

Perceived value

21.41   A similar analysis may be made of the perceived value placed on the case by each party. The costs associated with trial and the potential for liability on costs makes sense only in the context of the value of the case to the party concerned. Where the parties put similar values on the case that is conducive to settlement. Where there is a wide divergence with the claimant's view much higher than defendant there is less likely to be settlement. Again, in preparing for negotiation, this factor must be kept in mind. If the parties are widely apart both on confidence level and value the settlement process will be all the more difficult. The risk assessment here is aimed at estimating the perceived value range of an opponent and estimating the opponent's confidence level in that value. See also Chapter 24—Decision Trees.

Information balance

21.42   The bird's eye view of the cases not likely to settle suggest that the parties do not have the same information. This situation is common and may lead to trial or protracted negotiations because one of the parties has an erroneous view. The problem is that neither party has the bird's eye view – they can only have their own view. Again, in the preparation for negotiation which ought to take place consideration needs to be given to this analysis. It is an example of risk assessing settlement as opposed to trial. It may be that where the case is subjected to a Case Management Conference[1] the bird's eye view will be disclosed and the work on settlement can proceed more effectively. Mediation can also be used as a process which will be informed by the bird's eye view gained by the mediator.

1   The Lord Chancellor's Department has commissioned research to examine case management under the Civil Justice Reforms.

Chapter 22

Risk and Success Fees

INTRODUCTION

22.1 The detailed statutory provisions relating to the recoverability of the success fee in a CFA are dealt with in Chapter 8. The calculation of the success fee will be influenced by that statutory regime and in particular regard must be had to the overriding principle that to be recoverable the success fee must be reasonable[1]. No statutory guidance is given as to the calculation of the success fee beyond the criteria which may be taken into account on an assessment. The Practice Direction about Costs (CPD)[2] refers to the risk of losing, the legal representative's liability for disbursements and other available methods of funding as three factors which a court may take into account in assessing the reasonableness of the success fee. The major part of the success fee will in nearly all cases be a reflection of the perceived level of risk that the case will fail. The complications arising from a definition of success which does not relate to a favourable costs order is dealt with in Chapter 5. It will be assumed for the purposes of the current chapter that success is defined in terms where a favourable costs order is to be expected. A further complication arises from the court's power to allow different percentage increases for different periods and for different items of costs[3]. The only other guidance to be found is in the provision[4] restricting the success fee to 100%[5] of basic costs. It is important to remember that the original limit to the success fee was made under a scheme where the client was to pay the success fee. With the change to recoverability of the success fee the 'consumer protection' element reflected in the limit of 100% was not removed[6]. The calculation of the success fee is, therefore, to be undertaken within the imposed limit of 100%.

1 See CPD, ss 11.5, 11.7 and 11.8. See Chapter 8.
2 CPD, s 11.8(1).
3 CPD, s 11.8(2).
4 Conditional Fee Agreements Order 2000, SI 2000/823, art 4.
5 No success fee at all is permitted in cases brought under s 82 of the Environmental Protection Act 1990 which are quasi criminal. Whilst the extension of CFAs to these proceedings was under consideration there was a concern that in criminal proceedings the legal representative ought not to be paid by results. The party using a CFA is prosecuting under the Act.
6 In the Government's consultation paper *Conditional Fees: Sharing the Risks of Litigation* (September 1999) views were sought as to the maximum level of the success fee. In its conclusions paper (February 2000) the Government stated that it had decided to leave the maximum at 100% except for cases in the Commercial, Admiralty and Technology and Construction Courts. The CFA Order 2000, SI 2000/823 however, limits the success fee in all cases to 100%. The reasoning for removing a limit in the specified cases was the perceived

sophistication of clients using those courts. It was not argued that success fees above 100% would be unreasonable, indeed the implication is that much higher fees would be expected. When it came to personal injury the 100% limit was said to be needed to protect the unworldly client, though it is not clear why such protection is needed where the success fee is to be recovered from the opponent. It was not argued that a success fee in excess of 100% in personal injury cases would always be unreasonable.

FACTORS AFFECTING SUCCESS FEES

22.2   The declared purpose of a success fee is to enable the lawyer to break even over a caseload funded by CFAs. The success fee is set at a percentage of base costs. It must not exceed 100%. The Practice Direction about Costs provides—
CPD, s 11.8(1)—

'In deciding whether a percentage increase is reasonable relevant factors to be taken into account may include—

(a)   the risk that the circumstances in which the costs, fees or expenses would be payable might or might not occur;
(b)   the legal representative's liability for any disbursements;
(c)   what other methods of financing the costs were available to the receiving party.'

Items (a) and (b) affect the calculation of the success fee. Additionally r 44.3B of the Civil Procedure Rules (CPR) pre-supposes that a success fee may include a percentage relating to the cost to the legal representative of the postponement of his fees and expenses albeit that element will not be recoverable from the opponent. Each of these three elements of the success fee is dealt with separately below.

EXPRESSIONS OF CONFIDENCE

22.3   In the context of CFAs one of the objectives of a risk assessment is to provide reasons for the level of the success fee. This pre-supposes that the level of confidence which the litigator has in the case can be translated into words with some consistency. Even if that can be done, ultimately there is a requirement to express that level of confidence as a percentage. In non-CFA cases it is not as necessary to express confidence in percentage terms but it is nonetheless common to do so. The Community Legal Service[1] calls for such expression within bands which are also the basis for the Bar Council's guidelines for advising on the merits for public funding applications and the risk assessment guidelines in the APIL/PIBA model CFA for use with counsel—

(a)   Very Good—80% chance or more of obtaining a successful outcome;
(b)   Good — 60%–80%;
(c)   Moderate — 50%–60%;
(d)   Borderline — this applies where the prospects of success are not poor, but, because there are difficult disputes of fact, law or expert evidence, it is not possible to say the prospects of success are better than 50%;
(e)   Poor — prospects of success are clearly less than 50% so that the claim is likely to fail;

(f) Unclear — the case cannot be put into any of the above categories because further investigation is needed.

1 Funding Code Guidance (November 2000), para 4.3.1.

22.4 The CLS Guidance summarises the concept of estimating the prospects of success as follows:

'Estimating prospects of success can never be an exact science, especially at the early stages of litigation. Therefore it is a matter of legal judgment and experience to decide which of the above categories applies to any particular case. Predictions of chances of success often vary during a case as new information comes to light.[1]'

1 Ibid note 1, para **22.3** above at para 4.3.2.

22.5 The APIL/PIBA guidelines use the same percentage bands but describe them in different terms:

A — Very good 80%
B — Good 60–80%
C — Reasonable 50–60%
D — Less than evens
E — Impossible to say

Using a mathematical basis for risk assessment is popular but it carries with it the danger, that by allotting a number and then adding to and subtracting from it, an appearance of precision or objectivity is given to what is in reality a subjective process[1]. Anderson and Twining[2] produce a probability table which illustrates mathematical expressions of a judgment of risk and non-mathematical equivalents—

Chance	Frequency	Wager	Belief support	Strength of	Marks
1.0	100%	No contest	I know	Beyond peradventure	A+
.7	70%	7–3	Confident	Strong	B+
.6	60%	6–4/3–2	I think	More likely than not	B
.5	50%	Evens	I wonder whether	evenly balanced	B-
.4	40%	4–6/2–3	I suspect	Not very likely	C+

The basis of risk assessment is to predict another's decision and evaluation of the evidence in terms of these expressions of confidence, be that either the opponent or a judge.

1 See further Chapter 23 – Probability and Chapter 24 – Decision Trees, in particular para **24.3**.
2 Anderson and Twining *Analysing Evidence* (Sweet and Maxwell).

THE USE OF PERCENTAGES

22.6 There is a clear convention in expressing confidence levels in percentage terms. In the case of CFAs the percentage confidence level may have been converted into a success fee in which case the CFA itself must contain brief written reasons for the success fee. The use of a methodical risk assessment at the time that the success fee is settled ought to prevent hurried and impressionistic decisions on assessment to reduce the fee. If the fee has been set in the first place on an impressionistic view with no real analysis then reduction is being invited. The following descriptions of commonly used percentages for CFA purposes may be used or the firm should adopt descriptions with which it feels confident—

A working definition of commonly seen percentages

%	Success Fee[1]	Narrative
85+	18	Excellent prospects on liability, causation and quantum. No real cause for concern on any factors. Good witness potential. Full documentation as appropriate to the case.
70	43	Very good prospects on primary liability. Some concerns over causation or contribution. Some weakness which will need to be addressed but likely to be overcome.
60	67	Serious risks involved – protocol stage may lead to withdrawal of claim. Client story believable but difficult. (Value of claim and client's funding ability will affect viability of continuing.)
55	82	High risk that the case will lose. Client believable but lack of evidence means difficult to prove.\n\n(example – client did not see GP at first reasonable opportunity, no independent evidence, no witnesses).
50	100	No independent evidence or witnesses. Client's own account inconsistent or missing detail – not easy to believe. Case will depend on client as witness – not a good court witness. Other side's explanation believable.

1   The success fee given here assumes that the costs ratio of won to lost cases is 1:1. See further below para **22.8**.

CALCULATION

Risk

22.7 The first published guidance on the calculation of success fees was made in the Law Society publication, *Conditional Fees – A Survival Guide*[1]. That publication contains a table of percentage chances of success (ie the chances of the circumstances needed for payment of fees not arising) and their mathematical reciprocal as expressions of the success fee. The same approach has been adopted in other places either in exactly the same way or as an expression in decimals. The effect is then the same. The assumption behind the mathematics is, however, that the costs incurred in a case which eventually loses will be the same as costs incurred in cases that win. The authors of the Law Society Guide recognised that there can be an overcharging where the fees in a case which wins far exceed those in cases which lose and accept that the converse is also possible.

1 Napier and Bawdon *Conditional Fees–A Survival Guide* (Law Society Publications, 1995).

22.8 There is no greater scientific basis, therefore, for assuming costs ratios of lost and won cases to be equal (ie a ratio of 1) than to assume that they are 2:1 in favour of lost cases (ie lost cases incur costs at double that in won cases), or indeed any other ratio. It is perhaps regrettable that the assumption of a ratio of 1 has been given prominence. To progress then to a different assumption is mathematically simple and this is reflected in the table below[1]. It may be argued however, that to move from an assumption of 1, to an assumption favouring a higher success fee can only be justified by showing that there really is a different ratio. It may also be argued that the ratio will differ according to the class of case concerned. Thus it may be asserted that the ratio in road traffic cases is likely to be nearer 1 whereas Repetitive Strain Injury cases might be nearer 3.

1 See para **22.11** below.

22.9 Regardless of whether the cost ratio of lost to won cases needs to be factored into any calculation, there is always a need to express the chances of winning before any conversion is made into success fees. This is the assumption behind the Practice Direction in its reference to the risk that the circumstances in which the costs would be payable might not occur[1]. Having assessed that risk[2] and expressed it in percentage terms[3] it is next necessary and possible to produce a success fee which reflects the level of confidence.

1 CPD, s 11.8(1)(a).
2 See Chapter 21 above.
3 See above para **22.6**.

22.10 The CFA Regulations 2000, reg 3(1)(a)[1], whilst requiring any CFA with a success fee to state briefly the reasons for setting the percentage increase, give no guidance on how the calculation should be done. CPR, r 44.3B(1) effectively provides for the court to require disclosure[2], at assessment, of the reasons for setting the success fee at the level stated in the CFA but nowhere in the CPR is there guidance on calculation. The Practice Direction factors, including the reference to the risk that the circumstances in which the costs would be payable might not occur, is not exclusive in terms of the factors which a court may take into account in assessing the reasonableness of a success fee. The risk that if the case loses, the loss to the firm will not be compensated by a simple ratio of lost cases to won cases of 1 is, it is submitted, a rational factor influencing the setting of the success fee, and is one of the reasons for setting it at the level stated in the CFA.

1 SI 2000/692.
2 SI 2000/692, reg 3(2)(a)(ii) requires the CFA to state that the legal representative can comply with a direction to disclose. CPD, s 14.9 requires the receiving party to have the risk assessment available for the court at the conclusion of proceedings.

22.11   The table below calculates the risk assessment part of the success fee according to the ratio of costs in lost cases to won cases. Thus a costs ratio of 1 means that it is assumed that the costs in a case which loses are equal to a case which wins. A ratio of 2 means that the assumption is that costs in a lost case will be double the costs in a case which wins. Percentages have been rounded up.

The shaded area of the table shows the levels of confidence needed to achieve a success fee below the statutory maximum of 100%. Allowance may still need to be made for disbursement liability and for waiting for payment, in which case the level of confidence will need to be higher.

Ratio of 1 – cut-off point

22.12   51% is the margin – out of 100 cases, 51 will win and 49 will lose (on average). With costs in losing cases being the same as the winning cases, there must be at least a 51% confidence of winning the case for the success fee to cover the losses.

This can be shown as follows: 51 cases win, at a success fee of 96% on £1,000.00 costs. Your total regained funds for these 51 cases are therefore 51 × 96% × 1000 = £48,960.00.

On the 49 cases that, on average, would lose, £49,000.00 would be paid out. The work just breaks even.

Ratio of 1.5 – cut-off point

22.13   61% confidence is your lowest possible limit. Recovered costs are 61 × 95.9% × 1000 = £59,000.00 and costs out are £39,000.00 × 1.5 = £59,000.00

At a ratio of 2 the same confidence level would give this result: costs recovered: 61 × 100% × 1000 = £61,000.00 whereas costs out are £39,000.00 × 2 = £78,000.00 leaving a deficit of £17,000.00.

Ratio of 2 – cut-off point

22.14   The cut-off point is now 67% confidence. Costs recovered will be £67,000.00 and costs going out will be £66,000.00. If the ratio went to 2.5 at that confidence level the following results: costs recovered £67,000.00 but costs going out are £82,500.00 giving a deficit of £15,500.00.

Success Fees Calculator

		Costs ratio	1	1.5	2	2.5	3	
Chance of winning			Success	Fee				
50			100%	150%	200%	250%	300%	
51			96%	144%	192%	240%	288%	
52			92%	138%	185%	231%	277%	
53			89%	133%	177%	222%	266%	
54			85%	128%	170%	213%	256%	
55			82%	123%	164%	205%	245%	
56			79%	118%	157%	196%	236%	
57			75%	113%	151%	189%	226%	
58			72%	109%	145%	181%	217%	
59			69%	104%	139%	174%	208%	
60			67%	100%	133%	167%	200%	
61			64%	96%	128%	160%	192%	
62			61%	92%	123%	153%	184%	
63			59%	88%	117%	147%	176%	
64			56%	84%	113%	141%	169%	
65			54%	81%	108%	135%	162%	
66			52%	77%	103%	129%	155%	
67			49%	74%	99%	123%	148%	
68			47%	71%	94%	118%	141%	
69			45%	67%	90%	112%	135%	
70			43%	64%	86%	107%	129%	
71			41%	61%	82%	102%	123%	
72			39%	58%	78%	97%	117%	
73			37%	55%	74%	92%	111%	
74			35%	53%	70%	88%	105%	
75			33%	50%	67%	83%	100%	
76			32%	47%	63%	79%	95%	
77			30%	45%	60%	75%	90%	
78			28%	42%	56%	71%	85%	
79			27%	40%	53%	66%	80%	
80			25%	38%	50%	63%	75%	
81			23%	35%	47%	59%	70%	
82			22%	33%	44%	55%	66%	
83			20%	31%	41%	51%	61%	
84			19%	29%	38%	48%	57%	
85			18%	26%	35%	44%	53%	
86			16%	24%	33%	41%	49%	
87			15%	22%	30%	37%	45%	
88			14%	20%	27%	34%	41%	
89			12%	19%	25%	31%	37%	
90			11%	17%	22%	28%	33%	
91			10%	15%	20%	25%	30%	
92			9%	13%	17%	22%	26%	
93			8%	11%	15%	19%	23%	
94			6%	10%	13%	16%	19%	
95			5%	8%	11%	13%	16%	
96			4%	6%	8%	10%	13%	
97			3%	5%	6%	8%	9%	
98			2%	3%	4%	5%	6%	
99			1%	2%	2%	3%	3%	

22.15 The following examples illustrate the effect of the costs ratio assumptions where the level of confidence is 75%—

Costs Ratio	Success fee %					
		Case Number	Costs	Success Fee	Loss	Net loss
1	33	1	1000	333.33	0	
		2	1000	333.33	0	
		3	1000	333.33	0	
		4	0	0	1000	
			1000	1000	1000	NIL
		Case Number	Costs	Success Fee	Loss	
1.5	50	1	1000	500	0	
		2	1000	500	0	
		3	1000	500	0	
		4	0	0	1500	
			1500	1500	1500	NIL
		Case Number	Costs	Success Fee	Loss	
2	66	1	1000	666.66	0	
		2	1000	666.66	0	
		3	1000	666.66	0	
		4	0	0	2000	
			2000	2000	2000	NIL
		Case Number	Costs	Success Fee	Loss	
2.5	83	1	1000	833.33	0	
		2	1000	833.33	0	
		3	1000	833.33	0	
		4	0	0	2500	
			2500	2500	2500	NIL
		Case Number	Costs	Success Fee	Loss	
3	100	1	1000	1000	0	
		2	1000	1000	0	
		3	1000	1000	0	
		4	0	0	3000	
			3000	3000	3000	NIL

22.16 All of the above calculations can be used where the CFA states that in the event of the case losing, no fee at all will be paid. In such a case the success fee reflects the risk of no payment. Where the CFA provides for some payment where the case loses[1], then the calculation of the success fee must reflect the fact that only part of the fees are being risked. One method of doing this is to calculate the success fee as above but provide that it is only to be applied to the part of the basic fees which would not be paid if the case loses.

Example assuming normal base fee is £1000—
    Case loses – 50% of normal fees payable – £500
    Case wins – 100% of normal fees payable £1000 plus success fee of 66%
    Success fee applied to 50% of basic fee is 66% × £500 = £330
The alternative method would be to reduce the ordinary success fee by the percentage of the basic fees being risked. In the above example, the success fee of 66% would be reduced by 50% to 33%. This reduced success fee when applied to normal basic costs gives the same result as the first method – ie 33% × £1000 = £330 but this does not reflect the risk assessment which should support a success fee at 66% and it is submitted that this method ought not to be used.

1   See above Chapter 13.

22.17   The statutory scheme regards risk of losing as a major part of the success fee to reflect the risk that fees will not be earned because the case fails. The CFA must contain brief reasons for setting this percentage[1]. A risk assessment of the individual case will provide the reasons for this element. The risk assessment needs to be expressed as a percentage level of confidence which can then be translated into a percentage success fee. The purpose of this element of the success fee is to recover from the successful cases sufficient funds to offset the losses incurred in unsuccessful cases. If the costs typically incurred in winning cases were the same as those typically incurred in cases which lose, an arithmetic conversion would be possible[2]. This conversion requires a simple mathematical formula as follows—

Express the confidence of success in percentage terms – eg 60%.
    Convert that to a two figure decimal by dividing the percentage figure by 100 –
    eg 60 : 100 =.6.
    Divide 1 by that decimal eg 1 ÷ .6 = 1.67. 1 represents the normal fee.
    To find the success fee, deduct 1 and multiply by 100. Eg 1.67 − 1 =.67 × 100 = 67%

1   SI 2000/692, reg 3(1)(a).
2   Such a conversion is produced in tabular form in Napier and Bawdon *Conditional Fees – A Survival Guide* (Law Society Publications, 1995).

Table of commonly used percentage success fees:

22.18

Confidence of success	Success fee	Confidence of success	Success fee
100	0	65	54
80	25	60	66
75	33.3	55	81
70	43	50	100

Such a conversion ratio cannot give an accurate reflection where costs incurred in a typical losing case exceed in a significant amount the costs typically incurred (and recovered) in successful cases. The conversion method can be used as a starting point in such an environment in that it shows the level of success fee which would be needed even where there is no differential in costs in won and lost cases. The table at para **22.11** provides for these differentials.

Waiting for payment element

22.19   The standard practice for a CFA is for payment of fees to be postponed until the (successful) outcome of the case. The payment of disbursements is less standard with some CFAs providing for payment before the conclusion of the case and others postponing this also. There is a cost attached therefore to this delay and it is carried by the solicitor. If a charge for this delay is to be included in the success fee then the percentage relating to waiting for payment must be separately stated in the CFA[1]. This element cannot form part of the additional liability to be recovered from an unsuccessful opponent[2]. It remains the liability of the client in the event that the case is successful. If the case is not successful then this cost to the firm is lost since the fees are not payable at all.

1   SI 2000/692, reg 3(1)(b).
2   CPR, r 44.3B (inserted by Civil Procedure (Amendment No 3) Rules 2000, SI 2000/1317).

22.20   The client can challenge the percentage of the success fee in the usual way under CPR, r 48. The percentage of the success fee relating to waiting for payment will on the face of the CFA apply to the base costs actually incurred in the litigation. Those costs will have been incurred over a period of time accumulating to a total to which the percentage of the success fee is then applied. Using the success fee as the mechanism for this recovery of cost will, therefore, have a tendency to inflate the amount recovered because base costs will have been incurred over a period of time and not all at the beginning. This tendency can be accounted for when setting the percentage figure. Where the case concludes after more than one year the tendency will be for the cost to be under-recovered. The difficulty in an individual case is accurately to predict the length of time during which the solicitor is waiting for payment.

   The use of the success fee as the mechanism for recovering the cost of waiting for payment calls for an accurate prediction of the length of time which will elapse before the conclusion of the case. The following table illustrates the percentage of a success fee which would be called for to obtain the annual interest rates in the table. There is nothing in the CFA Regulations 2000 nor elsewhere to preclude a CFA providing for the success fee to be calculated at the conclusion of the case, provided the CFA states what the calculation will be. A success fee could therefore be expressed as 75% for risk plus the following table's figures for waiting for payment. If it is thought that most of the costs will not be incurred early in the case the figure indicated in the table could be reduced by, for example, 50%, to reflect a likelihood of costs being fairly evenly distributed throughout the case.

Interest Rate (%)	6.0	8.0	10.0		6.0	8.0	10.0
Month				Month			
9	4.5	6.0	7.5	23	11.5	15.3	19.2
10	5.0	6.7	8.3	24	12.0	16.0	20.0
11	5.5	7.3	9.2	25	12.5	16.7	20.8
12	6.0	8.0	10.0	26	13.0	17.3	21.7
13	6.5	8.7	10.8	27	13.5	18.0	22.5
14	7.0	9.3	11.7	28	14.0	18.7	23.3
15	7.5	10.0	12.5	29	14.5	19.3	24.2
16	8.0	10.7	13.3	30	15.0	20.0	25.0
17	8.5	11.3	14.2	31	15.5	20.7	25.8
18	9.0	12.0	15.0	32	16.0	21.3	26.7
19	9.5	12.7	15.8	33	16.5	22.0	27.5
20	10.0	13.3	16.7	34	17.0	22.7	28.3
21	10.5	14.0	17.5	35	17.5	23.3	29.2
22	11.0	14.7	18.3	36	18.0	24.0	30.0

Liability for disbursements

22.21   CPD, s 11.8(1)(b)[1] expressly refers to the legal representative's liability for any disbursements as being a factor to be taken into account in assessing the reasonableness of the success fee. The success fee is applied to the fees charged and is not applied to disbursements. If the solicitor is carrying the liability for disbursements in the event that the case is unsuccessful, the only mechanism for reflecting that risk lies in increasing the percentage of the success fee. The increase attributable to this liability will be recoverable from a losing opponent and can therefore be challenged as being set at an unreasonable level. The test is whether the percentage increase was reasonable having regard to the circumstances as they reasonably appeared at the time the percentage was set[2]. As with the percentage for waiting for payment the difficulty is in accurately predicting the level of disbursements to be reflected in a percentage of the success fee which is a multiplier to the fees incurred throughout the life of the case. In order to calculate the percentage success fee to recover disbursement liability it is first necessary to express the disbursements as a percentage of costs. That percentage is then multiplied by the percentage figure representing the risk of the case losing since that is also the risk value in relation to losing the disbursements. This element of the success fee is vulnerable to inaccuracy in predicting the level of costs and/or disbursements with a risk of over or under estimating.

1   See Appendix 1.
2   CPD, s 11.7.

ILLUSTRATION OF THE CALCULATION OF THE DISBURSEMENT ELEMENT OF A SUCCESS FEE

22.22

A Disbursements	B Costs	C Ratio A to B	D % Confidence success fee	E Disbursement success fee %
£500	£10,000	5%	33.3%	1.66

The formula–

$A \div B \times 100 = C$
$C \times D \div 100 = E$

E is then added to the success fee (D).

ESTIMATES OF COSTS

22.23   It will be apparent that many of the figures needed for the proper calculation of the success fee will require an estimate of costs. The CPD[1] also contains requirements for the provision of a formal estimate of costs based upon Precedent H. However, the calculation of estimates of costs is known to be fraught with difficulty. Research of legal aid submissions where estimates were required has found that practitioners find this task difficult and the accuracy level is very low[2]. The implications for CFA's of the inaccuracy of estimates is serious given the financial viability of such a case load does depend upon success fees reflecting the financial exposure of the firm. Precedent H is set out below and requires an estimate of costs incurred and of costs to be incurred.

1   CPD, s 6. Estimates are required when filing an allocation questionnaire and a listing questionnaire. The court can order otherwise. The court can at any time order a party to file an estimate.
2   The Legal Aid Board Research Unit conducted research in 1999 (Pleasance, Buck and Christie *Testing the Case: Final Report*) and further research was conducted by Goriely – Institute of Advanced Legal Studies 2000. Both studies found significant inaccuracies in estimates of costs. Goriely found that only in 41% of cases were estimates of cost in the correct band for legal aid and that whilst most put the estimate into the middle band (£1500 – £2500) only 15% of cases actually fell into that band.

SCHEDULE OF COSTS PRECEDENTS – PRECEDENT H

22.24

IN THE HIGH COURT OF JUSTICE   2000 – B – 9999
QUEEN'S BENCH DIVISION
BRIGHTON DISTRICT REGISTRY
BETWEEN:

	AB	*Claimant*
	and	
	CD	*Defendant*

ESTIMATE OF CLAIMANT'S COSTS DATED 12TH APRIL 2001

The claimant instructed E F & Co under a conditional fee agreement dated
8th July 2000 in respect of which the following hourly rates are recoverable as
base costs

Partner – £180 per hour plus VAT
Assistant Solicitor – £140 per hour plus VAT
Other fee earners – £85 per hour plus VAT

Item No.	Description of work done	V.A.T.	Disbursements	Profit Costs
	PART 1: BASE COSTS ALREADY INCURRED			
	8th July 2000 – EF & Co instructed 7th October 2000 – Claim issued			
1	Issue fee 21st October 2000 – Particulars of claim served 25th November 2000 – Time for service of defence extended by agreement to 14th January 2001	—	£400.00	
2	Fee on allocation 20th January 2001 – case allocated to multi-track 9th February 2001 – Case management conference at which costs were awarded to the claimant and the base costs were summarily assessed at £400 (paid on 24th February 2001) 23rd February 2001 – Claimant's list of documents	—	£80.00	—
	ATTENDANCES, COMMUNICATIONS AND WORK DONE			
	Claimant			
3	0.75 hours at £180			£135.00
4	4.4 hours at £140			£616.00
	To Summary	£ —	£480.00	£751.00
	Witnesses of Fact			
5	3.8 hours at £140			£532.00
6	Paid travelling on 9th October 2000	£4.02	£22.96	
	Medical expert (Dr. IJ)			
7	1.5 hours at £140			£210.00
8	Dr. IJ's fee for report		£350.00	
	Defendant and his solicitor			
9	2.5 hours at £140		£350.00	
	Court (communications only)			
10	0.4 hours at £140			56.00
	Documents			
11	0.75 hours at £180 and 22.25 hours at £140			£3,250.00
	Negotiations			
12	2.75 hours at £140			385.00
13	VAT on solicitor's base fees	£968.45		
	To Summary	£972.47	£372.96	£4,783.00

Item No.	Description of work done	V.A.T.	Disbursements	Profit Costs
	PART 2: BASE COSTS TO BE INCURRED			
14	Fee on listing	—	400.00	
15	Attendance at pre-trial review 5 hours at £140			700.00
16	Counsel's base fee for pre-trial review		750.00	
17	Attendance at trial 20 hours at £140			£2,800.00
18	Counsel's base fee for trial including refresher		£3,000.00	
19	Fee of expert witness (Dr. IJ)		—	£1,000.00
20	Expenses of witnesses of fact	—	£150.00	
	ATTENDANCES, COMMUNICATIONS AND WORK TO BE DONE			
	Claimant			
21	1 hour at £180			£180.00
22	8 hours at £140			£1,120.00
	Witnesses of fact			
23	5 hours at £140			£700.00
	Medical expert (Dr. IJ)			
24	1 hour at £140			£140.00
	Defendant and his solicitor			
25	2 hours at £140			£280.00
	To Summary	£ —	£5,300.00	£5,920.00
	Court (communications only)			
26	1 hour at £140			£140.00
	Counsel (communications only)			
27	3 hours at £140			£420.00
	Documents			
28	1 hour at £180, 25 hours at £140 and 15 hours at £85			£4,995.00
	Negotiations			
29	5 hours at £140			£700.00
	Other work			
30	5 hours at £140			£700.00
31	VAT on solicitor's base fees	£2,253.13		
	To Summary	£2,253.13	£ —	£6,955.00

Item No.	Description of work done	V.A.T.	Disbursements	Profit Costs
	SUMMARY			
	Part 1			
	Page 1	£ —	£480.00	751.00
	Page 2	£972.47	£372.96	£4,783.00
	Total base costs already incurred	£972.47	£852.96	£5,534.00
	Part 2			
	Page 2	£ —	£5,300.00	£5,920.00
	Page 3	£2,253.13	£ —	£6,955.00
	Total base costs to be incurred	£2,253.13	£5,300.00	£12,875.00
	Total of base costs	£3,225.60	£6,152.96	£18,409.00
	Grand total			£27,787.56

Chapter 23

Probability

THE USE OF PROBABILITY IN RISK ASSESSMENT

23.1

'... a distinguished Soviet professor of statistics showed up in his local air-raid shelter. He had never appeared there before. "There are seven million people in Moscow," he used to say. "Why should I expect them to hit me?" His friends were astonished to see him and asked what had happened to change his mind. "Look," he explained, "there are seven million people in Moscow and one elephant. Last night they got the elephant."[1]'

---

1 Bernstein *Against The Gods* (Wiley 1996). For an in depth critique of the use of probability in the law see Cohen *The Probable and the Provable* (OUP 1977/ 1991 Gregg Revivals). See also Eggleston *Evidence, Proof and Probability* (Butterworths 1983).

23.2 If risk assessment in litigation means an assessment of the chances of a case succeeding, then what is being assessed is a future event. The case itself will revolve around past events when liability is being considered, and in some cases around future events when quantum is being considered. From one point of view the distinction between past event and future events may appear significant – a past event either did occur or it did not whereas a future event must by definition have no certainty. However, litigation will inevitably have to deal with uncertainty about an event which has occurred. That uncertainty can be expressed in terms of probability in exactly the same way as the uncertainty about a future event. After an event has occurred the attempt to find the explanation of what happened is the same as the attempt to predict the future. In terms of settlement the expression in probabilities of the chances of winning at trial can be used to analyse the level of monetary offer which is likely to lead to settlement[1]. A claimant can be advised in terms of the probability of winning at trial a stated level of damages. Probability theory will mean that the claim is worth the value at trial multiplied by the probability of winning at trial. Human nature may however reject that result. If probability is to be used at all in risk assessment then allowance must first be made for the inaccuracy of the information upon which probabilities are to be provided.

Illustration

Client amount	% chance win	% chance lose
£10,000	70%	30%

To the defendant there is a 70% chance of losing £10,000. A settlement at £7,000 buys that chance and any sum below that will be attractive. For the claimant there is a 70% chance of winning £10,000. £7,000 buys that chance. Anything above that will be attractive[2].

1 See Chapter 21.
2 The reality will be that the defendant and claimant will not have the same information and will not share the same prediction values. The effect of this asymmetry of information is dealt with in Chapter 21.

23.3 To attempt to make use of probabilities in risk assessing litigation is to embark upon a mathematical approach to limited amounts of real-life information. In the case of a dice it is known, beyond doubt, that there are six sides and each bears a different number. That perfect degree of information is never replicated nor even approached in the events which give rise to litigation nor to the litigation process itself. The essential characteristic of all litigation is that each case is a unique event[1]. There are similarities between cases but they are far removed from the kind of events which probability theory is used to predict. Given a sufficiently large number of cases of a type, sufficiently similar to a sample which is itself large, it is possible to show the probability of an individual case falling into that sample. If it is clear that the characteristics of the individual case are the same as the large sample it is possible to express the probability of that case performing to sample. What cannot be achieved however is knowledge that any particular case will in fact perform to sample. It should be immediately apparent that there will be difficulties in deciding how large the sample needs to be and similarly difficulty over how similar to the characteristics of the sample a case needs to be.

1 Even where the same event has affected more than one person, such as a car accident or a disaster, there will be a potential for significant unique characteristics to apply in each individual case thus affecting the litigation. For example, the injured passenger in the car may not have been wearing a set belt whereas the driver was wearing one.

PROBABILITY JUDGMENTS[1]

23.4 Statements such as (1) the chance of throwing double-six with a pair of true dice is one in 36; (2) that there is a slightly better than even chance that any given unborn infant will be a boy; and (3) that there is now little chance that Great Britain will leave the EU, are all probability expressions of judgment. Each statement, however, illustrates a different form of probability. (1) is a judgment of a prior probability, a mathematical calculation of chance; (2) is a statistical judgment estimating an actual frequency of a characteristic in a given class of subjects; (3) is a judgment of credibility, an expression of confidence in the occurrence or non-occurrence of an event. A statement that 97% of all personal injury cases are successful is an example of (2) and must not be confused with (3). A client may be interested in the fact that their case falls into a class with high success rates but they are vitally interested in knowing whether their particular case will form part of the 97% rather than the 3%. The solicitor acting on a CFA will take some comfort from knowing that a particular case falls into the class of case but again needs to know how many cases will actually succeed. For every girl that is born the chances were slightly higher that they would be a boy. A personal injury case as an individual matter can only use probability in the sense of (3) above. An expression of confidence that the case will fall into the 97% success field.

1   See Dowie and Lefrere *Risk and Chance* (Open University).

PREDICTING THE UNCERTAIN THROUGH PROBABILITY

23.5   One particular form of probability which has been debated in respect of litigation is Bayes' Theorem[1]. If two or more events must be combined, ie the probability of two events converging is required, then the probabilities of each event must be multiplied together. The result is the probability of convergence. For example, the probability of a head landing on two successive tosses of a coin is $.5 \times .5 = .25$. It may be objected however, that these two events are not in themselves connected, that the first event can have no effect upon the second, ie the probability of the coin landing heads the second time is not affected by the result of the first toss. Cohen[2] devotes six chapters of his book to the problems of using this form of probability in the legal arena. He argues that irrespective of how many issues need to be proved in order to succeed in a case the probability of proving them all is the same as the least likely issue.

1   Rev Thomas Bayes died in 1761. The theorem derives from his essay *Toward Solving a Problem in the Doctrine of Chances* published posthumously by the Royal Society. See Eggleston supra and Cohen supra.
2   Ibid.

23.6   Eggleston provides an example of the difference between these two approaches—

'Where a plaintiff seeks to prove a single fact in issue by a chain of inferences, he is arguing in the form ' from A infer B and from B infer C'. Assuming that A is certain, that the probability of B given A is 0.8, and that the probability of C given B and A is 0.7, the probability that C exists depends on whether A and B also exist,...what is the probability that A and B and C all exist? This probability is...$1 \times 0.8 \times 0.7 = 0.56$. Where a plaintiff has to prove more than one fact in issue in order to succeed (let us say facts D, E and F) the same consideration will apply. If D is established with certainty and (assuming them to be independent) E and F are established with a probability of 0.8 and 0.7 respectively, the plaintiff who must prove all three facts in order to succeed will likewise have a probability in his favour of 0.56...'

Cohen argues that in each case the probability of the conjunction of A, B and C is no lower than the probability of C, and that the conjunction of D, E and F has a probability no lower than that of F. The difficulty with using Bayes' Theorem can be illustrated by a simple personal injury case where it can be said that in order to win the claimant must prove A negligence and B causation and C damage. Suppose A has a probability of .65, B has .75 and C .6, the multiplication rule would produce a probability of winning of 0.29 or 29%. Cohen's approach would recognise the lowest probability as being .6 or 60%.

23.7 It is worth reconsidering the example of contributory negligence used in Chapter 21[1]—

Contrib Neg	Effect on Damages	Predicted likelihood of finding
Nil	20,000	5%
25%	15,000	25%
50%	10,000	50%
75%	5,000	20%

In Chapter 21 it is stated that the chances of winning compensation in excess of £5000 is 80%. Here the various findings are mutually exclusive. Probability theory in this case, again derived from Bayes' Theorem requires the individual probabilities to be added together. Thus the probability of recovering damages greater than £5,000 is found by adding 5%, 25% and 50% to give 80%. The probability of recovering more than £10,000 is found by adding the probabilities of 5% and 25% giving 30%.

1 See para **21.4**.

23.8 Cohen argues six difficulties[1] for the application of mathematical probabilities but it is the first of these with which civil litigation is primarily concerned. He argues that where the plaintiff's case conjoins several component points, which is often the case, the application of a mathematical probability places a severe constraint on the number of independent points that can be conjoined and the level of probability to which each must be proved. He also points out that to apply a mathematical probability method would permit a plaintiff to win even though one of the elements has been lost. Thus clearly the more elements which need to be conjoined the lower will be the product of the multiplication (which can be overcome only by individual probabilities being very high) and provided most elements carry high probabilities they can be combined with one which is below 0.5 and still give a positive product. Cohen rightly says that the legal system nowhere supports either of these results.

1 Ibid and see Chapter 19. Eggleston in *Evidence, Proof and Probability* (Butterworths 1983) summarises the six at p 35.

CONCLUSION

23.9 Whilst an insurer may have a sufficiently large number of cases to be able to apply probabilities, even very large law firms will be unable to proceed by such a method. The use of probability theory or method within an individual case is also fraught with difficulty and can be highly misleading. The expression of confidence levels in probability terms, for example as percentages, whilst common and helpful to an extent, cannot be permitted to progress into a mathematical analysis.

Chapter 24

Decision Trees

THE NATURE OF DECISION TREES

24.1 Decision trees are diagrammatic representations of complex, multifaceted problems. They are used to break down complex problems into a series of decisions and to highlight the effect of the factors of uncertainty. The use of decision trees in litigation is therefore one method of enabling all the issues and interrelated factors to be looked at systematically rather than attempting to analyse the problem as a whole. Decision trees are based upon probability values being given to the factors of uncertainty which the user has identified. As a method of risk assessment, therefore, they are likely to be used after one or more of the methods dealt with in previous chapters have been employed to identify the legal and factual issues to be examined.

PROBABILITY AND DECISION TREES

Objective probability

24.2 Objective probability is so called because whoever applies its methods will arrive at the same probability conclusion. There are two methods of calculating probability which come within the meaning of objective probability. Firstly, in classical probability theory, probability means the ratio of target outcomes to all outcomes. Thus the target outcome of throwing a six with a single die is one-sixth. The information 'out of 200 cases 80 failed' is expressed in probability terms as 80 (the number of target events) divided by 200 (the total number of events)—ie $80/200 = 0.4$—from which can be expressed the probability of any case failing as being 0.4 (or 40%). Secondly, a statistical method known as frequency of occurrence, or relative frequency of events, requires either an experiment repeated a large number of times or research into a large number of past events to produce the necessary statistics. Thus the life insurer has access to life statistics and can estimate the probability of an individual dying before a certain age. With this meaning and method the strength or weakness of the estimate will depend upon how specific the class of events which form the statistical record is and how close to that class the individual event is. In any use of probability it must be recognised that the purpose is to produce an estimated mathematical model and not to produce a definite knowledge of what will happen in any given single event. Thus, to the individual client, a probability-based answer will be of less comfort than it will be to the solicitor who will be taking many such cases and who may expect to produce a performance near to the probability if the event is repeated often enough.

Subjective probability

24.3 Lawyers are almost always looking at subjective probability, where they are expressing a degree of confidence or belief as to a unique event, either past or future. Such an expression is not capable of a mathematical proof in the same way that objective probability is. The expression of confidence, such as 'this case has a 75% chance of success' may well be influenced by a knowledge of similar cases and their historical performance, but it will not be based upon the statistical data needed for objective probability. Because such expressions are personal to the maker, different persons looking at the same information may express a different probability, hence this is labelled as subjective probability. Although there is a degree of variation in such expressions, it is usually the case that considerable changes in probability expressions will be required in order to indicate a change in decision. Thus the fact that there will be variations in the expression of confidence between litigators should not detract from the use of this method.

THE AIMS OF DECISION TREES

24.4 The branching structure of a decision tree provides a visual representation of the problem, puts uncertainties into perspective and requires those uncertainties to be taken into account in the decision-making process. By using a decision tree a litigator is aiming to identify all of the facts in issue, the potential defences and the possible levels of damage, and to display the inter relationship between these factors. In addition, the tree will call for the expression of confidence in probability terms which will enable clear communication of the professional judgment of the litigator, be that to the client, the opponent or the judge. The methods of risk assessment outlined in the previous chapters are therefore essential tools for the use of a decision tree since those other methods will enable the litigator to assemble the information which the tree will require.

CONSTRUCTING A DECISION TREE

24.5 A decision tree is made up of nodes and branches. A node represents either a decision point, a chance event or an outcome (terminal) . The branches from a decision node represent the choices open to the decision-maker. Branches from a chance node represent the possible outcomes of that chance event. Each type of node is represented by a symbol: □ represents a decision node; ○ represents a chance node; ▷ represents a terminal node. Branches from chance nodes must carry a probability value. The terminal node will then carry a payoff figure representing the known or estimated value of the outcome. In litigation a decision tree is likely to consist of a series of chance nodes representing the judge's potential findings or the action of the opponent. These are chance node events simply because they are not under the control of the litigator. The decision node will only be appropriate where decisions under the control of the litigator are to be analysed. A clear example of an analysis involving a decision node will be the response to be made to a Part 36 offer or payment, or a decision as to whether to make a Part 36 offer and if so at what level.

Figure 1 is a decision tree representing the following claim: it is alleged that the defendant is liable for professional negligence in that there was a failure to give advice to the claimant, that failure led to the claimant making an investment and that led to a loss of £100,000. The tree represents each element and the litigator's subjective probability expression as to the judge's findings.

CALCULATING THE DECISION TREE IN FIGURE 1

24.6   The calculation of a decision tree commences at the far right-hand side, with the terminal nodes and the payoffs to their right in the diagram. The terminal nodes display the values of £55k minus costs at £25k and £100k plus costs of £35k. Each branch leading to a node displays its probability. The calculation is therefore as follows:

(£30k × 40%) + (£135k × 60%)

=

£12k + £81k

=

£93k

The tree has then to be rolled back through the earlier chance nodes, which have to be overcome to reach the far right terminal nodes. Thus the probability of a favourable finding on the issue of causation (60%) must be added[1] to the probability of a favourable finding on the issue of the failure to give advice. The value of the terminal nodes must then be multiplied by that probability. Thus the value is 70% x £81k = £56.7k. With a payment in of £55k the decision as to whether to accept or reject the payment is clearly indicated.

1   The findings do not affect each other, ie the finding on the failure to give advice will not affect the finding as to causation.

24.7   The probability figures can then be altered to show the effect of under-estimation of the strength of the case. Thus if the probabilities of a favourable outcome were each reduced by 10%, the calculation would become:

(£30k × 50%) + (50% × £135k)

=

£15k + £67.5k

=

£82.5k × 60% = £49.5k

Figure 1

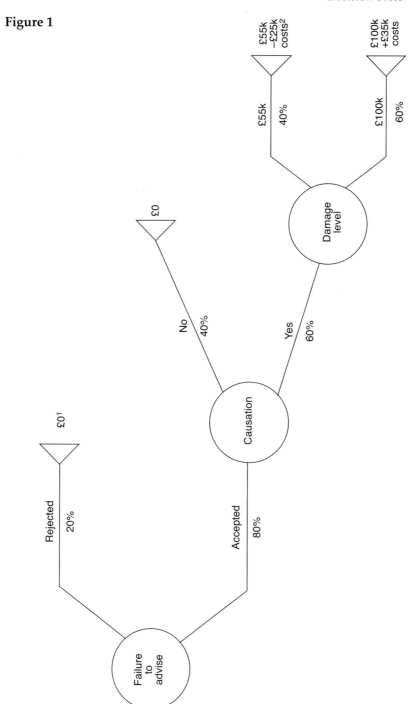

1 Assuming adverse costs are insured under a policy with deferred premium payable only in the event of success. If no such policy this figure will be a negative to reflect the adverse costs liability.

2 Assumes insurance policy gives cover only after damages have been exceeded by costs.

THE MEANING OF A DECISION TREE VALUE

24.8   The basis of decision trees is probability. The application of probability will produce a theoretical 'value' for a particular decision. That value is not being represented as a real option, it represents the mathematical value of the average result were the same case to be run many, many times. The analysis which the construction and calculation of a decision tree will require is seen as being a significant benefit in itself. In the above example the value arrived at of £56.7k is used to evaluate the possible alternative outcomes, which are uncertain, and the Part 36 payment, which is not uncertain. At an earlier stage in the case, before any offer or payment, the tree would be used to represent possible values to indicate where an offer might be made by the claimant and the tree value of any payment which might be made by the opponent.

Part 10

Case Studies

Chapter 25

Personal Injury Case Study

25.1
SINGLETON MEDICAL PRACTICE
Singleton Surgery   **Mark Prideaux**
Singleton, Berkshire SW35 3GP   **Anne Carpenter**
Singleton (01657) 675444   **Susan Brothers**

Ref: MB/MOBBS/AC

Miss Painter
Mobbs & Co
213 High Street
West Ashling
Berkshire SW 28 3LP

8.2.Yr 2

Dear Miss Painter

RE: Mr Martin Bishop DoB: 04.11.Yr.0 minus44
        6 Swan Way
        Singleton, Berkshire. 01657 413045

Thank you for asking me to consider the case of Mr Bishop with respect to
the onset of low back pain in June Yr.0.

Mr Bishop presented to the surgery on 17 June Yr.0 and saw Dr Prideaux,
a partner in the practice, in the emergency surgery for that day. The notes
from that consultation indicate that he was suffering from low back pain and
sciatica involving the left leg. The symptoms had started about 3 days before
and by the time he presented, the pain was worse on sitting or lying.
Examination showed that straight leg raising on the left was markedly
reduced (45 degrees) compared to the right (90 degrees). He was prescribed
Co-Dydromol for the pain.

Mr Bishop presented again 4 days later – 21 June Yr.0 and this time saw
myself in a routine surgery. The low back pain and left leg sciatica was worse
and the pain now radiated down to the ankle. His symptoms were such that
he was only just able to walk and completely unable to sit at all – not even to
go to the toilet. Examination revealed marked hyperrelexia in the left leg. I
prescribed a stronger pain killer – Dihydrocodeine, and a muscle relaxant –

Diazepam. I also organised an urgent referral to one of the local orthopaedic consultants – Mr Spring.

Mr Spring saw Mr Bishop the following week on 2 July Yr.0 and concluded that he was suffering from 'a very acute disc prolapse' and organised for him to be seen in the pain clinic as well as organising further investigations and discussing his management at home with myself over the telephone.

In the past Mr Bishop has suffered from low back pain on occasions. In Yr.0minus27 he had an episode of low back pain after lifting a heavy weight. He was referred to an orthopaedic surgeon and the pain settled with manipulation. The same occurred in Yr.0minus32 when he was referred again to an orthopaedic surgeon. It again settled with manipulation. In Yr.0minus4 he suffered another bout of low back pain with radiation down both legs after gardening. This time the pain settled on Diazepam and analgesia.

A story of acute low back pain is in my experience always preceded by an event of some sort. This might only be a minor event such as bending to pick something up, or it could be a major event such as a road traffic accident. Mr Bishop says that in Yr.0 the pain started after he had lifted some heavy roof trusses at work. The pain was at first not severe but became so over the next few days–when he decided to visit his GP.

Mr Bishop does not consult the doctor inappropriately. Over the years he has needed treatment for a number of conditions, and always with complete honesty and integrity. I have considered the onset of the pain in Yr.0 with Mr Bishop and it is quite clear to me that the pain started after having to lift some heavy roof trusses at work. This clearly follows the pattern that Mr Bishop's low back pain starts after doing some lifting involving bending and carrying weight on the low back.

I can see no reason to not believe Mr Bishop when he says that the pain started following the lifting of the trusses, indeed it appears to me that he is particularly genuine on this point. He appears to be an honest man who has never before tried to pursue a claim because of injury.

I am of the opinion that because Mr Bishop's pain started shortly after carrying heavy roof trusses, the pain and subsequent disability were due to the lifting of the roof trusses at work. I think he has a legitimate claim with respect to this.

Yours sincerely

Dr Anne Carpenter

INTERVIEW NOTES

25.2

Martin Bishop

DoB   4. 11. Yr.0minus44

Personal Injury

Mr Bishop was, at the time of the incident (13 June Yr.0), employed as a fork lift truck driver/general site labourer. He was working at a house building site at Harrogate Drive, Singleton for Opus Homes. He had started work for Opus some six weeks prior to his injury and had previously been employed by Hamilton Developments of Swinbridge for about two years again as a fork lift truck driver.

At the Harrogate Drive site he worked under the direction of Mr. Harold Gribble the site manager. On the day in question there were no other fork lift truck drivers on site. On 13 June he was instructed to lift roof trusses from the ground to the roof of a house nearing completion. These trusses are very large and made of soft wood. They are triangular in shape measuring 6 metres by 3 metres. As such they were too large for the fork lift truck to lift. Mr Bishop found himself to be the only workman on the ground, with two workmen on the roof. He would have expected the job of lifting these trusses to have involved four men – two on the ground and two on the roof. There were no others to ask for help – the site was generally under supplied with men. Mr Bishop felt forced therefore to lift these trusses on his own upwards towards the men on the roof. None of the other houses on this site had been constructed by the use of such trusses. This lifting caused considerable strain on his back. He spent a good part of the day lifting in this way. He felt pain whilst working but thought that given it was Friday he could rest over the weekend. He made no complaint to his employer on the day. The pain became progressively worse over the weekend. As a key holder to the site he reported for work on Monday morning but was in such pain that he told Mr Gribble that he could not work. He then took himself to his GP who referred him by ambulance to the local hospital – Springfield General. He saw a Mr Spring who diagnosed a prolapsed disc. Mr Bishop was sent home to rest in bed and was prescribed some pain killers. His pain was now in the lower back and the whole of the left leg. In February 1999 Mr Spring operated on Mr Bishop but found the disc to be attached to the sciatic nerve rendering removal too dangerous. Mr Bishop's condition has not responded to physiotherapy. He has not worked at all since the day in question. He cannot take long walks nor dance. He says his physical relationship with his wife has been badly affected and that he often feels very depressed.

His experience as a fork lift truck driver with Hamilton Developments was that he would move trusses around a site and that lifting was done by carpenters in teams of four. This appears not to be the case at Opus.

Date of interview: 7.12.Yr.1

COMPLETED RANKING SHEET FOR BISHOP

25.3

Ranking round	Top	Bottom
1	5	10
2	13	9
3	18	7
4	17	6
5	15	4
6	2	12
7	3	14
8	8	1
9	16	11

FACTOR LIST FOR PERSONAL INJURY IN RANKED ORDER

25.4

1 Believability of client's story

2 This type of case is likely to win something for claimant

3 Causation likely to be in issue

4 Contributory negligence likely to be raised

5 Quantum

6 Availability of independent witnesses

7 Evidence readily available

8 Persuasiveness of other side's evidence

9 Level of dependency on oral evidence of fact

10 Quantum ratio to costs

11 Likely performance of client in court

12 Likely view of judge

13 Chances for settlement

14 Existence of documents

15 Potentially difficult point of law

16 Time available before Limitation Period ends

17 Client expectation level

18 Level of emotion in the claim/defence

FACT ANALYSIS FORM

25.5

KEY:	**CF** favourable facts known to your client
	CU unfavourable facts known to your client
	OF favourable facts known to opponent
	OU unfavourable facts known to opponent
	? facts as yet unknown

Claimant Evidence	Fact in Issue	Defendant Evidence
Consistent with employee status **CF**	Duty	May claim independent contractor?
Claimant's account suggests unsafe system/no training **CF**	Breach	Expected experience worker to take care?
GP's note supports causal link from lifting trusses (**CF**) but also reports prior back problem (**CU**) Did not report incident on the day **CU**	Causation	No report of any incident **OU**
Has not worked since. Lack of mobility **CF**	Damage	May allege pre-existing injury/accelerated deterioration only
Experienced worker **CF**	Contrib	May allege that worker did not take reasonable care of own safety?

THEORY OF THE CASE

Claimant's theory

25.6
The claimant was an employee of the defendant. The claimant had not been provided with training in the lifting of the trusses. Insufficient workmen were provided by the employer. There was no supervision. The lifting caused the injury to his back which has prevented him from working.

Defendant's theory as estimated by claimant

25.7
The claimant was not an employee (possible argument). The claimant was an experienced worker and had a duty to take reasonable care for his own safety which he did not do. He was not told to lift the trusses in this manner. He suffered from back problems before this incident. His pre-existing condition was not made worse or if it was this was only a minor acceleration of inevitable deterioration of the pre-existing condition.

25.8
The following tables are the ranking results from an exercise involving 10 practitioners assessing this case study. After the first assessment (Table I) there was a group discussion followed by a second assessment producing the results in Table II. Although individuals produced changes for the second assessment, the overall rankings did not change significantly – only factor 2 was dropped from the top 5, to be replaced by factor 4. There was considerable agreement as to the top two ranked factors with less agreement thereafter. The exercise shows that risk assessment will produce different opinions amongst litigators assessing the same case. It is important to bear in mind that the litigator responsible for the case will run it in accordance with their view of it after an assessment except to the extent that the views of any mechanism such as a review committee can influence that litigator.

TABLE I

25.9

Ranking round	1	2	3	4	5	6	7	8	9	10	11	12	13	14	15	16	17	18	Rank
Factor 1	3	1			1	1	2	1			2		1	1					4
2		1	3	1		3	3												3
3	1					1			1	1	1						1		7
4		1		1			1	1	1	3	1		1	1		1			12
5	2	1			1	1			1			1			2	1	1		5
6					1		2	1	1	1		1			2	3	1	1	16
7	1			1				4					1	1	1	1			10
8											1	1	2		1	1			13
9											1	1		2		1	4	1	17
10												1					2	5	18
11		1	1	1		1		1	1	1	1	2	1		1				9
12			1	1		3		1				2	2	1					8
13		1			1				1	3	1	2			3				14
14	1		1	1	2						1		1	2	1		1	1	15
15				3	1				3	1		1	1	2				1	6
16	1	1	2	3	1		1		1						1	1			11
17	1	3	2				1											1	2
18	1				2				1										1

TABLE 2

25.10

Ranking round	1	2	3	4	5	6	7	8	9	10	11	12	13	14	15	16	17	18	Rank
Factor 1	1	1	2	1	1	1		2		1			1	2					3
2		1		1	1		1	2	1	2		1	1						8
3		2		1				2	2	2	2			1				1	6
4	4	2	2		1									1	1			1	5
5					1	1				1	1		2	1	1	2	1	1	2
6			1		3	1	2	1	2		1	4	1	1	1				16
7					1		2			2	1		1				7		7
8											1					1	1	1	12
9																4	1	5	17
10						1	1		1		2		1	2		1	1		18
11		1	1	1		1	1		1	1	2	1	1	1				1	9
12			1			2	1					1			4				13
13			1			1	1				1	1	1	2	1	1	1		14
14				1			1	1	1				2	1	1	1		1	15
15	1		2	1	1		1	1	2	1		2							11
16	1			2		3	1		1			2	1			1			9
17	1	3	2	1							1					1			4
18	3		1		1	3		1		1	1	1			1				1

Chapter 26

Clinical Negligence Case Study

26.1

Mrs Felicity McStea

DoB   4.11 Yr 0minus59

Clinical Negligence

21 June Yr1

Mrs Felicity McStea attended her GP surgery for necessary immunisations prior to a holiday to the Gambia. The holiday ran from 25 March to 1 April Yr 0. The visit for immunisation took place on 8 February Yr 0. Mrs McStea was seen by Dr Julia Hopper, a partner at the surgery. Mrs McStea was given mefloquine tablets. She states that she was given no information about possible side-effects.

Mrs McStea took one tablet 7 days before her flight to the Gambia. She awoke in the night feeling ill and in the morning had a severe headache and earache with a sore throat. She felt worse as the week went on and returned to her GP. Dr Hopper told her that her symptoms were caused by a virus and not anything to do with her tablets. Mrs McStea took a second tablet that evening.

Mrs McStea and her daughter went on holiday as planned but Mrs McStea became more ill as time went on. She suffered diarrhoea, depression and more headaches, earaches and stomach pains. She saw a doctor in the Gambia who prescribed a sleeping pill. Mrs McStea's holiday was ruined as a result of her symptoms.

When back in England she saw Dr Hopper again who referred her to Buckland Hospital. The consultant at the hospital diagnosed mefloquine toxicity. She was told that her symptoms may last as long as a year and very probably at least six months.

Mrs McStea was unable to work as a receptionist at a veterinary clinic upon returning from the Gambia. She worked part time before the holiday and had a take home pay of £98 per week. She eventually returned to her job on 1 November Yr 0, 7 months after returning from holiday.

Mrs McStea is still upset and angry that she was not told about the side effects especially when she returned to the surgery with symptoms. She says she stopped taking the tablets and worries that she would have been even more ill had she not been so careful. She is worried that other patients will not be so lucky.

MEDICAL NOTES

26.2
Mrs Felicity McStea
DoB   4.11.Yr 0minus59

Travel immunisations

26.3
Yr 0minus 2 – Barbados   Polio; Typhoid
Yr 0   Gambia Mefloquin

Clinical notes

26.4

5.4.Yr0minus2	Temp Abdo HS check urine for infectn Amoxycillin 75mg
15 .7 Yr 0 minus2	Dry cough since hol Spain – headache – exam- E/N/T norml – chest norml. Amoxycillin 25mg
8.2 Yr0	mefloquine 7 tabs
24.3.Yr0	worried about mefloquin side effects – sore throat, earache, headache nausea nervousness Advice
2.4.Yr0	bad reaction mefloquine – not sleeping, diarrhoea- nervousness. Saw Dr in Gambia – antibiotic – stop mefloquin – had only 2 tabs.
4.4.Yr0	home from Gambia – side effects – anxiety sleeplessness muscle aches mood wings- very angry – not told of side effects – ref to hosp
25.4.Yr0	poor sleep – confused – high anxiety – Temazepam – "you said it was not side effects but viral infection"
10.5.Yr0minus1	depressed – sleeplessness – headaches abdo pain
25 .8.Yr0	antidepressants – some effect
10.10.Yr0	much improved – driving,back to work 1.11

HOSPITAL NOTES

26.5

Mrs Felicty McStea

DoB   4.11.Yr0minus59

Buckland Hospital

9.4.Yr0	went to Gambia for hol – 25 Mar-1Ap started mefloquine 1 wk before – side effects sleeplessness, diarrhoea , headaches – diagnosed virus 2nd tab excessive thirst hallucinations poor concentration loss of appetite – diazepam to sleep
	OE – distressed Abdo NAD; CVS NAD; RS NAD
	Mefloquine toxicity
10 6.Yr0	some improvement – sleep without tablets – appetite still diarrhoea not driving not at work
3.8.Yr0	did some decorating at home – exhausted – depressed tearful –disturbed sleep
26.10.Yr0	return to work 1.11 – depression receded –
	She was very stressed when took first tablet of mefloquine – day before flying – terrified of flying

EXPERT REPORT

26.6

Mrs Felicity McStea

DoB   4.11.Yr 0minus59

(This is an extract of the main points and is not intended to indicate a poor standard of presentation. The expert is well qualified to give an opinion on the standard of care expected of a GP.)

Dates   medical events from Feb Yr0 to Nov Yr0

The side effects complained of to the GP after taking the first tablet are the recognised side effects of mefloquine as recorded in the manufacturer's data sheet.

The GP fell below the acceptable standard of medical care. She either did not know the side-effects of mefloquine or too readily dismissed the possibility that the symptoms presented were due to it.

Mrs McStea seems to have only taken two tablets.

Specialist advice may be needed to determine what effects can be attributed to the second tablet rather than the first, since Mrs McStea would have taken the first even had she been told of the possible side effects.

COMPLETED RANKING SHEET FOR MCSTEA

26.7

Ranking round	Top	Bottom
1	3	2
2	9	10
3	17	11
4	8	5
5	15	14
6	7	16
7	12	4
8	13	6
9	18	1

FACTOR LIST FOR CLINICAL NEGLIGENCE IN RANKED ORDER

26.8

1 Client's word against that of health professional

2 Client's story not contradicted by medical notes

3 Liability likely to be disputed

4 Quality of expert's report

5 Causation likely to be in dispute

6 Likely performance of client at trial

7 No need for more than one expert for claimant

8 Ratio of damages to costs at trial

9 This kind of claim likely to settle

10 Complaint made as early as reasonably possible after the event.

11 Field requires untried expert

12 Client believability/coherence

13 Realistic client expectation

14 Multiplicity of issues in the case

15 Level of client emotion in the claim

16 Ratio of investigation costs to quantum

17 Bolitho needed to win

18 Proximity of Limitation period

FACT ANALYSIS FORM

26.9

KEY: **CF** favourable facts known to your client **CU** unfavourable facts known to your client **OF** favourable facts known to opponent **OU** unfavourable facts known to opponent **?** facts as yet unknown		
Claimant Evidence	**Fact in Issue**	**Defendant Evidence**
Registered patient CF	Duty	Medical notes OF
No or no correct advice on side effects CF	Breach	Notes silent OF Diagnosed virus CU?
Side effects reported CF Medical expert CF		Notes no detail of advice OF?
Only two tablets CU Medical expert ambivalent? Possible CU	Causation	Notes no mention of cause of symptoms OF?
Unable to work CF	Damage	Hospital notes OF
Stopped taking tablets CF	Contrib	?

THEORY OF THE CASE[1]

Claimant's theory

26.10   Was prescribed mefloquine for her holiday but the GP gave no advice as to side effects – (would/would not have taken the tablet had she been told of possible side effects). The failure to advise was a breach of the duty of care. Complained of symptoms which are recognised as side effects of this drug but was told by the GP that the symptoms were of a virus. There was a further breach in the duty of care in not investigating the likelihood of the symptoms being caused as a side effect of the drug. The second tablet would not have been taken had the claimant been correctly diagnosed. The toxicity has led to loss of income as well as pain and discomfort and a ruined holiday.

Defendant's theory as estimated by claimant

26.11   Claimant would have been given the standard advice on the side effects. Claimant would have taken the first tablet in any event and had previously used the same drug without side effects. The assessment of the claimant after one tablet was not negligent. The symptoms were consistent with a viral infection. (May expect expert report in support?).

1   See Chapter 21, para **21.11**.

26.12   The analysis and the theory in this case have highlighted that the case will turn more on the second visit to the GP than on the original provision of the drug although if there was a failure to advise on side effects that may have contributed to the claimant taking a second tablet. There will need to be more material in order to assess the standard of care provided by the GP at the second visit and it seems likely that further expert evidence will be needed as to the effect of the second tablet in isolation from the first. Setting out the constituents of such as case assists in prioritising the work to be done as well as focussing on where the real risk lies. In this case causation is the major problem even assuming a breach of duty can be shown and as such the work needs to be concentrated on causation in the first instance.

Chapter 27

Insolvency Case Study

ADQ LIMITED IN LIQUIDATION V ANTHONY DAVID QUINTAN

27.1 This is part of a number of claims which the liquidator of ADQ Ltd is considering bringing not only against Mr Quintan but against fellow directors and against a company connected with ADQ. The case study considers only the claim against Mr Quintan.

BACKGROUND

27.2 ADQ was incorporated in Yr.0. It traded in the provision of hospitality services at major public sports fixtures both in the UK and abroad. The company went into voluntary creditors' liquidation in August Yr.3.

Mr Quintan had been in partnership with a Mr Chivers for some years before the company was formed. Both men have considerable experience in the provision of hospitality.

The event immediately giving rise to the liquidation was the failure to obtain tickets for the Olympics and the failure then to meet financial commitments made on the basis of that event.

Mr Quintan was not registered as a director of the company. There is substantial evidence that he took a day to day part in the running of the business and was indeed in the Olympics host country in June Yr.3 at the time of the Olympics. Mr Quintan was a 50% shareholder in the company.

THE FACTS

27.3 ADQ had advanced significant sums for the pre-payment of Olympics tickets which were not in the end supplied. ADQ's commitments to providing hospitality could not therefore be met and there was no income from those arrangements.

Documents exist showing payments in May and June Yr.3 by ADQ to another company, Park Lane Ltd, of which Mr Quintan was a director and shareholder. That company is also in liquidation. It has been claimed by Mr Quintan that these payments, totalling £560,000 were in respect of loans made by Park Lane to ADQ and in respect of sums expended by Park Lane in an attempt to purchase Olympics tickets on the 'secondary market'.

There were other payments made in June Yr.3 from ADQ to Mr Quintan amounting to £135,000. Mr Quintan has claimed that these were payments in respect of debts owed to Park Lane and were paid direct to him in repayment of loans he had made to Park Lane.

The bank statements of the ADQ show that on June 10 Yr.3 there was a credit balance of £75,000.

Generally the books of the company are regarded by the liquidator as being shoddy and the processes of the company show no regard to the possibility of insolvency. In particular there appear to be no records of the alleged loans between Park Lane and ADQ. No records have been offered from Park Lane in respect of the alleged loan from Mr Quintan to it.

Mr Quintan's personal resources are known to include not only a substantial house in England but also homes in Spain and Switzerland.

COMPLETED RANKING SHEET FOR ADQ

27.4

Ranking round	Top	Bottom
1	12	10
2	4	3
3	5	13
4	1	15
5	2	16
6	7	11
7	8	14
8	6	9
9	18	17

FACTOR LIST FOR INSOLVENCY IN RANKED ORDER

27.5

1 Proof of involvement of defendant in running business

2 Date of insolvency

3 Dispute as to defendant's knowledge of facts indicating insolvency

4 Whether defendant governed by s 214

5 Tracing of assets

6 Ability of opponent to meet liability and costs

7 Likely performance of defendant as a witness

8 Availability of documentary evidence

9 Settlement potential

10 Accountancy advice to company

11 Likely performance of witnesses

12 Company's compliance with accounting and reporting requirements

13 Need for expert evidence

14 Evidence of quantum

15 Calculation of compensation order

16 Sympathy for defendant

17 Question of law involved

18 Quantum in relation to costs

FACT ANALYSIS FORM

27.6

KEY:	**CF** favourable facts known to your client	
	CU unfavourable facts known to your client	
	OF favourable facts known to opponent	
	OU unfavourable facts known to opponent	
	? facts as yet unknown	

Claimant Evidence	Fact in Issue	Defendant Evidence
Shadow director Day to day running CF	S 214 person	Not a director – OU
June bank statement CF Non supply of tickets CF Vol Liq August	Knowledge of prospect of insolvency	Contract for tickets OU Prospect of finding alternative source of tickets?
Defendant previously in business poor records CF/OF	Reasonable/actual knowledge	?
Payments May/June to Park Lane Payment June to def.	Steps taken	Attempts to obtain alternative tickets?
In excess of £600,000	Compensation level	

THEORY OF THE CASE

Claimant's theory

27.7   At the time that significant payments were made to both Park Lane Ltd and the defendant it was evident that the tickets necessary to enable the company to meet its contractual obligations would not be forthcoming and that without those tickets the company would become insolvent. The bank statement of 10 June shows that the effect of the payments themselves was to hasten the insolvency.

Defendant's theory as estimated by claimant

27.8   There were reasonable prospects in May and June that the tickets would still be supplied and/or that an alternative source would be found. The payments made were not made at a time when the defendant ought reasonably to have concluded that there was no prospect of avoiding insolvency.

Chapter 28

Contractual Dispute Case Study

INITIAL INFORMATION

28.1   The client is a self-employed builder aged 46. Around January Yr.0 he went to R's premises and gave a verbal estimate to R of £15,000 for works to be done to the premises. There was to be a plan supplied by R to the client. The client says he forwarded to R a written estimate stating the cost to be £17,000 including VAT and that this was accepted. Work was done on the premises and payments on account were made by R amounting to £14,500. The client says that he was asked on several occasions to do extra works not included in the original estimate. During work the client told R that the roof tiles were not fit to be reused and that new tiles had to be ordered at extra cost. R told the client that she was in financial difficulties and that no further payments could be made. At this stage the roof was off. The client was eventually persuaded to complete the roof. No more payments were made and the client stopped work. Windows and doors had been made to fit the premises which the client says cannot be used elsewhere. The sum outstanding for additional works and materials is about £10,000.

FURTHER DETAILS

28.2   The following assertions are made by the builder in respect of the claim for unpaid work and materials.

1   In or around January Yr.0 John Makeit visited the premises of Celia Recard. The premises are a cottage. Makeit gave a verbal estimate of £15,000 (excluding VAT) for works to be carried out at the cottage. There was to be a plan provided by Recard. The work included replacing the roof, stripping out the inside, removing the back extension and disposing of old materials, putting in footings and drains and soakaways and constructing a new rear extension and a side extension up to the damp proof course and provide 14 new windows and two new doors.

2   Makeit forwarded to Recard an estimate setting out in more detail the works to be done and giving a price of £17,037.50 (including VAT). No copy can be found.

3   Recard accepted the estimate.

4   Makeit made it clear on various occasions that no carpentry, plumbing or electrical work was included in the estimate. Recard accepted this and said she had her own contractors for such work.

5   It was agreed that moneys would be paid periodically on account before work was carried out.

6   £8,000 was paid in advance of any work.

7   £2,500 was paid after a few weeks.

8   £2,000 was paid in May.

9   Makeit carried out the works listed in Document A1.

10   It was agreed from many conversations on site that more work was to be done- mainly carpentry and that additional payment would be made. This additional work is listed in Document A3.

11   It was specifically pointed out to Recard that the roof tiles could not be reused and that new tiles would have to be obtained. The original estimate covered the labour for replacing the roof but not the cost of new tiles.

12   In May when the roof was off, Recard said she had financial difficulties.

13   Makeit stopped work. Recard put pressure on Makeit to continue and eventually he did on receiving a promise that future payments would be made.

14   The roof was completed.

15   It became clear that no more payments would be made. Makeit stopped work again.

16   The relationship between the parties deteriorated rapidly. Recard told Makeit to leave the site until further funds were available.

17   Recard asked Makeit to remove hardwood doors and windows from the site because she feared they would be stolen.

18   The windows and doors were specially made for the cottage and cannot be reused. Recard has at no time since requested return of these items.

19   Nearly all of the originally quoted work and most of the additional work, including the roof, had been completed before Makeit left the site. Time consuming and costly preparation had also been done with respect to the damp course and foundations.

20   Works not done before leaving are given in Document A2.

21   Makeit removed materials from the site to use on another job once it was clear no more payments would be made. The value of these materials is £90.

22   By a verbal agreement in about March Yr.0 Makeit carried out building works at Recard's shop. Makeit submitted an invoice for this work but no payment has been made. This work is detailed in Document A4.

A1   Works carried out at Holly Cottage included in original quote

28.3

Stripping out old plaster boards and rendering. Disposing of old materials.

Digging out 8 footings for piers

Bricking up all piers putting on the girders in the old cottage.

Digging out the extension and bricking up to the site and putting in a concrete floor.

Brick laying the extension to the back and completing the extension on the side up to the damp proof course level.

Putting in all drains in and up to the damp proof and soakaways.

Supplying 14 windows and 2 doors specifically made for the cottage in hardwood.

Supplying lorry-load of bricks and three truck loads of blocks 4 tons of cement, butterflies and lintels.

Supplying the labour only for stripping off the roof and stacking the tiles on the site and putting the roof back on.

Supplying all steel girders for inside the piers.

Supplying 10 tons of sand and 10 tons of ballast.

Putting in large bricks to shore up the fireplace and bricking round the large blocks in Norfolk red brick.

Putting in a membrane throughout the cottage and the extension area (excluding rolling on top the damp proof course in the extension area)

A2   Works included in original quote which were not carried out (with approximate values)

28.4

Bricking up the rear extension from the damp proof course to 'plate height' including installing the interior walls to separate rooms. Installing the windows and doors.

Rolling the 4.5 inch damp proof course onto the rear extension.

Making up the side extension up to the damp proof course.

Total value of works Approximate

(including VAT) Approximately   £1,500

A3   Additional works carried out (not included in the original quote) but carried out with the agreement of Ms Recard and estimate of value

28.5

Putting new fascia boards at the front and back of the cottage.

Putting in new purlings.

Straightening up the old roof which was leaning.

Putting in new ridge boards in the roof.

Cutting new roof for the rest of the building in new timber

Supplying felt and tile batons and lead

Supplying 750 pantiles

Supplying the timber for the floors downstairs shaping the floor joists and stair trimmers to match the existing woodwork.

Approx value		£4,300.00
VAT		£752.50
	Total	£5,052.50

A4   Works carried out at Ms Recard's shop premises

28.6

Putting in two new door linings.

Supplying sand and cement.

Putting in one fire door and furnishings and supplying wood and finishing off the door.

Including labour		£971.59
plus VAT		£170.03
	Total	£1,141.62

PARTICULARS

Value of original quote		£17,037.50
Less value as in A2	£1,500	
Less value of bricks and blocks removed	£90	
Less monies paid on account	£12,500.00	£14,090.00
	Balance	£3,247.50
Value of additional works as in A3		£5.052.50
Value of works as in A4		£1,141.62
		£9,441.62

COMPLETED RANKING SHEET FOR MAKEIT

28.7

Ranking round	Top	Bottom
1	8	6
2	1	12
3	2	17
4	3	4
5	5	11
6	9	13
7	7	18
8	16	14
9	10	15

FACTOR LIST FOR CONTRACTUAL DISPUTE IN RANKED ORDER

28.8

1   Solvency of opponent

2   Dependency on oral evidence of fact

3   Available documents own side

4   Available documents other side

5   Client's potential as a witness

6   Ratio of costs to recovery value

7   Assessment of damages

8   Need for expert evidence

9   Chances of settlement

10 Mitigation

11 Causation

12 Realism of client's case

13 Number of alleged wrongs/breaches

14 Liability likely to be insured

15 Limitation period

16 Reputation of opponent

17 Client wants 'day in court'

18 Arguable question of law

FACT ANALYSIS FORM

28.9

KEY: **CF** favourable facts known to your client **CU** unfavourable facts known to your client **OF** favourable facts known to opponent **OU** unfavourable facts known to opponent **?** facts as yet unknown		
Claimant Evidence	**Fact in Issue**	**Defendant Evidence**
Oral evidence as to estimates given CF	Contract	Lack of written estimate? OU
Evidence of the completed work? CF Evidence that tiles unsuitable?	Performance	Allegation of sub-standard work? OU Challenge that tiles are suitable?
Failure to pay CF	Breach	Payments already made sufficient OU
Valuation of work?	Damage	Value of materials? OU

THEORY OF THE CASE

Claimant's theory

28.10   Under a contract between the claimant and defendant the claimant has performed considerable work without payment. The claim is in accordance with estimates given to the defendant before work began. All reasonable steps have been taken to mitigate the loss. The reason for non-payment is the defendant's claimed lack of funds. There has been no complaint as to the standard of work. The claim is based in contract and is for a reasonable price. The work at the shop has been completed to the contractual standard and a reasonable price is being claimed.

Defendant's theory as estimated by the claimant

28.11   At this stage any theory will be highly speculative given the lack of material from the defendant. The defendant may dispute that any estimates were given or dispute the figures. She may challenge the need for new roof tiles. She may challenge the claimant's assertion that the windows and doors cannot be used elsewhere. She may well produce a counterclaim as to the quality of work done. She may claim that the money already paid is sufficient to cover the work done. As to the shop work the defendant may claim that the work is not to contractual standard and the price is unreasonable. The factual theory would be that the claimant's work is not up to standard and that in any event the payments made discharge all liability.

Part 11

Non-Money Claims

Chapter 29

Conditional Fee Agreements and Risk Assessment in Non-Money Claims

INTRODUCTION

29.1 The statutory regime applicable to CFAs has been heavily influenced by personal injury litigation where the claim is for damages. Thus there is considerable consumer protection built into the regime. The recoverability provisions were introduced in order to protect the (usually small) level of compensation awarded. This same statutory regime applies however to all fields of litigation where CFAs are permitted and it applies irrespective of the remedy being sought or defended. With the exception of Collective CFAs, there is a considerable degree of advice[1] and information which must be given to any client, however well versed in litigation they may be. The CFA itself, or in the case of a CCFA a separate note, must also contain a brief risk assessment if a success fee is to be charged. None of the published model CFAs provide for cases where the remedy sought is not damages. It is with the definition of success that the particular difficulties will arise in non-money claims. The policy behind the recoverability of success fee and premium, the protection of damages, will have no application in non-money claims but both elements will still be subject to assessment if the opponent challenges them. The restriction on recovery of disallowed success fees from the client may also provide some difficulty given that the protection of the damages award is not in issue.

1 See Chapters 6 and 16.

INTERIM MATTERS

29.2 Where the CFA relates to a claim for damages it will usually include all necessary interim applications. The definition of success in such cases will be the award of damages, usually not specified in amount. Where however the CFA relates only to interim applications, either because that is expected to be the extent of the litigation or because the lawyer is not willing at this stage to enter into a CFA for later parts of the litigation, there needs to be a definition of success that relates to the application being made. It would seem appropriate to follow the example of the Law Society Personal Injury Model CFA[1] in using very general terms such as 'the court grants your application for….'. It should however be kept in mind that the statutory scheme assumes that the success fee will form part of a costs order made against the opponent.

In interim matters the risk that such an order may not be made must inform the decision to run the case on a CFA and must form part of the risk assessment.

1 See Appendix 2.

INJUNCTIVE RELIEF

29.3 Similar consideration will arise where the remedy being sought is injunctive relief. It will frequently be the case that a full trial of the merits of the case is not expected ever to take place and that the matter will be resolved one way or the other by some form of preliminary hearing with the prospect of an interim injunction. The CFA again needs to be drafted to ensure that the success fee is recoverable. The difficulty in the case of injunctions is that the final wording of an injunction , which itself will be subject to alteration in the event of a successful appeal, will in many instances vary from that proposed by the applicant. At the time the CFA is entered into it is highly unlikely that a form of words will be available for the purposes of the definition of success. It is likely therefore that that definition will again be in very general terms such as 'the court grants your application for injunctive relief'. Clearly as with interim matters, the issue of an adverse costs order must be kept in mind. The risk assessment must therefore include a careful consideration of the basis upon which an adverse costs order may be refused in the case of a successful application for injunctive relief. The CFA will provide that the client is liable for the success fee but it may be more likely that this will be the actual position in injunction cases than in claims for damages.

The wide variety of injunctive orders available in English Law necessarily means that the risk assessment criteria will differ according to the type of relief being sought. It is essential that the methods of risk assessment used clearly address the specific criteria applicable to the granting of the remedy being sought. It will then be necessary to assess the likelihood of a favourable costs order to include a success fee and insurance premium if any.

APPLICATIONS FOR SUMMARY JUDGMENT

29.4 The purpose behind the procedure for the obtaining of a summary judgment is to enable cases to be concluded where appropriate without the expense involved in proceeding to trial. The experience in costs only proceedings under CPR, Part 8 where again the case has been concluded at an early stage, does raise the possibility of costs orders to include additional liabilities. The summary judgment rules however are closely linked to the fixed costs regime albeit the court has power to order costs over and above the fixed costs provided. A risk assessment where an application is to be made for summary judgement must therefore consider the position on costs in the event that the application is successful. The prospects of success of the application itself call for an assessment not just of the merits of the case as would be required in respect of trial but also within the criteria for the granting of such an application – ie that there are no real prospects of the opponent succeeding.

29.5   CPR, r 24.2—

'The court may give summary judgment against a claimant or defendant on the whole of a claim or on a particular issue if—

(a)   it considers that—

    (i)   that claimant has no real prospect of succeeding on the claim or issue; or

    (ii)   that defendant has no real prospect of successfully defending the claim or issue; and

there is no other compelling reason why the case or issue should be disposed of at a trial.'

The Practice Direction about Costs (CPD)

29.6   CPD, s 1.3—

'An application for summary judgment under rule 24.2 may be based on:

(1)   a point of law (including a question of construction of a document),
(2)   the evidence which can reasonably be expected to be available at trial or the lack of it, or
(3)   a combination of these.'

Costs

29.7   CPD, s 9—

'9.1 Attention is drawn to Part 45 (fixed costs).

9.2 Attention is drawn to the Costs Practice Direction and in particular to the court's power to make a summary assessment of costs.

Attention is also drawn to rule 44.13(1) which provides that if an order does not mention costs no party is entitled to costs relating to that order.'

Fixed costs

29.8   CPR, r 45.1—

'(1) This Part sets out the amounts which, unless the court orders otherwise, are to be allowed in respect of solicitors' charges in the cases to which this Part applies.

(The definitions contained in Part 43 are relevant to this Part)

(2) This Part applies where—

(a)   the only claim is a claim for a specified sum of money and—

    ...

    (iv)   summary judgment is given under Part 24.'

JUDICIAL REVIEW

29.9   This is another field in which defining success will need to be done in the general terms of the granting of a judicial review application. Success would clearly not be defined in terms of any change in decision by the body whose decision has been judicially reviewed. Again the matter of costs must be carefully considered with respect to the recoverability of the success fee from the opponent.

CFAS FOR DEFENDANTS

29.10   From the point of view of a defendant entering into a CFA all cases are in effect non-money claims in terms of the difficulty of defining success. Clearly one level of success will be the dismissal of the claim with costs in favour of the defendant. However, in many cases the defendant will be seeking to minimise the damages and costs liability and has no realistic case for avoiding liability altogether. Apart from the effect of a successful Part 36 offer, there is little likelihood of a costs order in favour of the defendant. The statutory regime relating to CFAs has been written with claimants as the model which may cause difficulty in the case of defendants with a CFA which has a success fee. Assuming the defendant has not obtained a favourable costs order but has achieved the aim in terms of limiting its overall liability, the CFA remains a fee agreement between the client and solicitor, and subject to own client assessment, the success fee is payable by the client.

PART 12

Questions and Answers

Chapter 30

Questions and Answers

A CONDITIONAL FEE AGREEMENTS

30.1

1 Q What is the difference between a conditional and a contingency fee?

A The phrase 'contingency' fee is used to refer to an agreement whereby the fee is calculated as a direct share of the damages award. Such an agreement in relation to litigation (contentious business) is contrary to the Law Society Rules. A conditional fee is defined and governed by the Courts and Legal Services Act 1990 (CLSA 1990) and is lawful and complies with the Law Society Rules. Such an agreement provides for the fees (or part of them) to be payable only in certain circumstances. Other than in housing disrepair cases under the Environmental Protection Act 1990, a success fee can be charged up to a maximum of 100%. See generally Chapter 13.

2 Q Can I still refer to *'Thai Trading'* agreements?

A No. This was a briefly recognised non-statutory form of conditional fee agreement. The case has been doubted by the Court of Appeal. Since 1 April 2000 a lawful CFA must comply with the statute – CLSA 1990, s 58. See Chapter 1 for *Thai Trading* and Chapter 4 for the statute.

3 Q What happens if a CFA fails to comply with the statute?

A Under CLSA 1990, s 58 as substituted by Access to Justice Act 1999 (AJA 1999), s 27, any CFA made after 1 April 2000 which fails to comply with the statute and the CFA Regulations 2000, SI 2000/692 is unenforceable. See Chapter 4.

4 Q Are there any types of case where a CFA cannot be used?

A CFAs cannot be used in criminal proceedings (except Environmental Protection Act 1990) nor in family proceedings. See Chapter 4 – 'prescribed proceedings'.

5 Q Can a blanket success fee of 100% be applied to all CFAs which the firm takes on?

A No. The CFA Regulations 2000, SI 2000/692 make it clear that there must be a written risk assessment. The Practice Direction about Costs goes on to refer to the risk that the case will lose as being one of the criteria for assessing the reasonableness of the success fee at an assessment hearing. A blanket success fee would fail to comply with these provisions. See Chapter 8.

6 Q How is a success fee to be calculated?

A The Practice Direction about Costs lays down the criteria against which the reasonableness of a success fee will be judged. The initial calculation should address these criteria. In particular a risk assessment must be done. See Chapter 22.

7 Q What is the significance of the date 1 April 2000?

A Important provisions of AJA 1999 came into force. Success fees and insurance premiums were made recoverable. A new CLSA 1990, s 58 came into force making the statutory regime compulsory for all CFAs. See Chapter 3.

8 Q Can a CFA be made today which is retrospective to before 1 April 2000?

A If this was the first CFA in the matter it would be legal if it complied with the statutory scheme but it would not attract the advantages of the Access to Justice Act in relation to the pre-1 April work. If however this CFA sought to replace a pre 1 April CFA the advantages of the 1999 Act would not apply to any of the work pre or post 1 April 2000. See Chapter 11.

9 Q Has Maintenance and Champerty gone?

A Any funding agreement with a lawyer which might previously have fallen within this doctrine will now either be valid by complying with CLSA 1990, s 58 or will be unenforceable because it fails so to comply. The doctrine is in this respect therefore irrelevant today. As far as third parties are concerned the recent case law suggests strongly that s 51 of the Supreme Court Act 1980 will be used where it is thought right to make a costs order against a third party. A stay of proceedings on grounds of Maintenance and Champerty would not be granted. See Chapter 19.

B RECOVERABILITY

30.2

10 Q Is the entire success fee recoverable from the losing opponent?

A Any element relating to waiting for payment cannot be recovered. The remainder is recoverable subject to assessment where the issue is one of reasonableness. See Chapter 8.

11 Q   Is any shortfall in recovery of the success fee from the opponent then recoverable from the client under the CFA?

 A   Such a recovery will require the leave of the court. Where the shortfall is due to the disallowance by the court of part of the success fee. The CFA itself must state that leave of the court is needed.

12 Q   What kind of insurance premium is recoverable?

 A   The premium for an after the event legal expenses policy. Such a policy may be linked to a CFA or may provide both sides' cover where there is no CFA at all or where the CFA makes provision for the payment of some fees in the event the case loses. See Chapter 17.

13 Q   Is the entire insurance premium recoverable from the losing opponent?

 A   The premium is recoverable subject to assessment. There are criteria laid down in the Practice Direction about Costs by which the reasonableness of the decision of the client to purchase the insurance is to be judged. See Chapter 17.

14 Q   Does Rule 15 require a solicitor to review all insurance products in the market and advise as to the best policy in each case?

 A   Rule 15 requires the question of insurance to be raised. It does not require 'best advice'. See Chapter 16.

C   GIVING NOTICE

30.3

15 Q   When must the opponent be informed of a CFA?

 A   Only if the CFA carries a success fee need notice be given. Notice has to be given at the time proceedings are issued. If the CFA with success fee is entered into after proceedings are issued then notice must be given within 7 days. See Chapter 8.

16 Q   When must the opponent be informed about an insurance policy?

 A   If it exists when proceedings are issued then notice must be given at that time. If insurance is taken after proceedings have been issued then notice must be given within 7 days. See Chapter 17.

17 Q   Is the opponent told the level of success fee/cost of insurance?

 A   This information is not required to be given until an assessment of costs.

D   RISK ASSESSMENT

30.4

18   Q   What is risk assessment?

  A   It is a methodical and disciplined approach to litigation which requires consideration of the factors in any individual case which give rise to a risk that the case will not succeed. See Chapter 20.

19   Q   Is risk assessment necessary?

  A   The CFA Regulations 2000, SI 2000/692 and the CCFA Regulations 2000, SI 2000/2988 require risk assessment to be in writing. There are many benefits of adopting a risk assessment approach to litigation in addition to complying with those regulations. See Chapter 20.

20   Q   How can a risk assessment be carried out?

  A   There are several methods for conducting a risk assessment. In some cases it will be beneficial and cost effective to use more than one method. See Chapter 21.

Appendix 1

Statutory Materials

Civil Procedure Rules 1998, SI 1998/3132

COURT'S DISCRETION AND CIRCUMSTANCES TO BE TAKEN INTO ACCOUNT WHEN EXERCISING ITS DISCRETION AS TO COSTS

Rule 44.3

(1) The court has discretion as to—

    (a) whether costs are payable by one party to another;
    (b) the amount of those costs; and
    (c) when they are to be paid.

(2) If the court decides to make an order about costs—

    (a) the general rule is that the unsuccessful party will be ordered to pay the costs of the successful party; but
    (b) the court may make a different order.

(3) The general rule does not apply to the following proceedings—

    (a) proceedings in the Court of Appeal on an application or appeal made in connection with proceedings in the Family Division; or
    (b) proceedings in the Court of Appeal from a judgment, direction, decision or order given or made in probate proceedings or family proceedings.

(4) In deciding what order (if any) to make about costs, the court must have regard to all the circumstances, including—

    (a) the conduct of all the parties;
    (b) whether a party has succeeded on part of his case, even if he has not been wholly successful; and
    (c) any payment into court or admissible offer to settle made by a party which is drawn to the court's attention (whether or not made in accordance with Part 36).

(Part 36 contains further provisions about how the court's discretion is to be exercised where a payment into court or an offer to settle is made under that Part)

(5) The conduct of the parties includes—

    (a) conduct before, as well as during, the proceedings and in particular the extent to which the parties followed any relevant pre-action protocol;
    (b) whether it was reasonable for a party to raise, pursue or contest a particular allegation or issue;
    (c) the manner in which a party has pursued or defended his case or a particular allegation or issue; and
    (d) whether a claimant who has succeeded in his claim, in whole or in part, exaggerated his claim.

(6)   The orders which the court may make under this rule include an order that a party must pay—

    (a)   a proportion of another party's costs;
    (b)   a stated amount in respect of another party's costs;
    (c)   costs from or until a certain date only;
    (d)   costs incurred before proceedings have begun;
    (e)   costs relating to particular steps taken in the proceedings;
    (f)   costs relating only to a distinct part of the proceedings; and
    (g)   interest on costs from or until a certain date, including a date before judgment.

(7)   Where the court would otherwise consider making an order under paragraph (6)(f), it must instead, if practicable, make an order under paragraph (6)(a) or (c).

(8)   Where the court has ordered a party to pay costs, it may order an amount to be paid on account before the costs are assessed.

(9)   Where a party entitled to costs is also liable to pay costs the court may assess the costs which that party is liable to pay and either—

    (a)   set off the amount assessed against the amount the party is entitled to be paid and direct him to pay any balance; or
    (b)   delay the issue of a certificate for the costs to which the party is entitled until he has paid the amount which he is liable to pay.

COSTS ORDERS RELATING TO FUNDING ARRANGEMENTS

Rule 44.3A

(1)   The court will not assess any additional liability until the conclusion of the proceedings, or the part of the proceedings, to which the funding arrangement relates.

("Funding arrangement" and "additional liability" are defined in rule 43.2)

(2)   At the conclusion of the proceedings, or the part of the proceedings, to which the funding arrangement relates the court may—

    (a)   make a summary assessment of all the costs, including any additional liability;
    (b)   make an order for detailed assessment of the additional liability but make a summary assessment of the other costs; or
    (c)   make an order for detailed assessment of all the costs.

(Part 47 sets out the procedure for the detailed assessment of costs)

LIMITS ON RECOVERY UNDER FUNDING ARRANGEMENTS

Rule 44.3B

(1)   A party may not recover as an additional liability—

    (a)   any proportion of the percentage increase relating to the cost to the legal representative of the postponement of the payment of his fees and expenses;

    (b)   any provision made by a membership organisation which exceeds the likely cost to that party of the premium of an insurance policy against the risk of incurring a liability to pay the costs of other parties to the proceedings;

    (c)   any additional liability for any period in the proceedings during which he failed to provide information about a funding arrangement in accordance with a rule, practice direction or court order;

    (d)   any percentage increase where a party has failed to comply with—

        (i)   a requirement in the costs practice direction; or

        (ii)   a court order,

        to disclose in any assessment proceedings the reasons for setting the percentage increase at the level stated in the conditional fee agreement.

(2)   This rule does not apply in an assessment under rule 48.9 (assessment of a solicitor's bill to his client).

(Rule 3.9 sets out the circumstances the court will consider on an application for relief from a sanction for failure to comply with any rule, practice direction or court order)

CASES WHERE COSTS ORDERS DEEMED TO HAVE BEEN MADE

Rule 44.12

(1)   Where a right to costs arises under—

    (a)   rule 3.7 (defendant's right to costs where claim struck out for non-payment of fees);

    (b)   rule 36.13(1) (claimant's right to costs where he accepts defendant's Part 36 offer or Part 36 payment);

    (c)   rule 36.14 (claimant's right to costs where defendant accepts the claimant's Part 36 offer); or

    (d)   rule 38.6 (defendant's right to costs where claimant discontinues),

    a costs order will be deemed to have been made on the standard basis.

(2)   Interest payable pursuant to section 17 of the Judgments Act 1838 or section 74 of the County Courts Act 1984 on the costs deemed to have been ordered under paragraph (1) shall begin to run from the date on which the event which gave rise to the entitlement to costs occurred.

PROVIDING INFORMATION ABOUT FUNDING ARRANGEMENTS

Rule 44.15

(1)   A party who seeks to recover an additional liability must provide information about the funding arrangement to the court and to other parties as required by a rule, practice direction or court order.

(2)   Where the funding arrangement has changed, and the information a party has previously provided in accordance with paragraph (1) is no

longer accurate, that party must file notice of the change and serve it on all other parties within 7 days.

(3)   Where paragraph (2) applies, and a party has already filed—(a) an allocation questionnaire; or (b) a listing questionnaire,

he must file and serve a new estimate of costs with the notice.

(The costs practice direction sets out—

- the information to be provided when a party issues or responds to a claim form, files an allocation questionnaire, a listing questionnaire, and a claim for costs;
- the meaning of estimate of costs and the information required in it).

(Rule 44.3B sets out situations where a party will not recover a sum representing any additional liability)

ADJOURNMENT WHERE LEGAL REPRESENTATIVE SEEKS TO CHALLENGE DISALLOWANCE OF ANY AMOUNT OF PERCENTAGE INCREASE

Rule 44.16
Where–

(a)   the court disallows any amount of a legal representative's percentage increase in summary or detailed assessment proceedings; and
(b)   the legal representative applies for an order that the disallowed amount should continue to be payable by his client,

the court may adjourn the hearing to allow the legally represented party to be notified of the order sought.

(Regulation 3(2)(b) of the Conditional Fee Agreements Regulations 2000 provides that a conditional fee agreement which provides for a success fee must state that any amount of a percentage increase disallowed on assessment ceases to be payable unless the court is satisfied that it should continue to be so payable. Regulation 5(2)(b) of the Collective Conditional Fee Agreements Regulations 2000 makes similar provision in relation to collective conditional fee agreements).

Practice Direction about Costs

DIRECTIONS RELATING TO PART 44

GENERAL RULES ABOUT COSTS

SECTION 9 COSTS ORDERS RELATING TO FUNDING ARRANGEMENTS: RULE 44.3A

*9.1   Under an order for payment of "costs" the costs payable will include an additional liability incurred under a funding arrangement.

*9.2   (1) If before the conclusion of the proceedings the court carries out a summary assessment of the base costs it may identify separately the amount allowed in respect of: solicitors' charges; counsels' fees; other disbursements; and any value added tax (VAT). (Sections 13 and 14 of this Practice Direction deal with summary assessment.)

(2) If an order for the base costs of a previous application or hearing did not identify separately the amounts allowed for solicitor's charges, counsel's fees and other disbursements, a court which later makes an assessment of an additional liability may apportion the base costs previously ordered.

SECTION 10 LIMITS ON RECOVERY UNDER FUNDING ARRANGEMENTS: RULE 44.3B

*10.1   In a case to which rule 44.3B(1)(c) or (d) applies the party in default may apply for relief from the sanction. He should do so as quickly as possible after he becomes aware of the default. An application, supported by evidence, should be made under Part 23 to a costs judge or district judge of the court which is dealing with the case. (Attention is drawn to rules 3.8 and 3.9 which deal with sanctions and relief from sanctions).

*10.2   Where the amount of any percentage increase recoverable by counsel may be affected by the outcome of the application, the solicitor issuing the application must serve on counsel a copy of the application notice and notice of the hearing as soon as practicable and in any event at least 2 days before the hearing. Counsel may make written submissions or may attend and make oral submissions at the hearing. (Paragraph 1.4 contains definitions of the terms "counsel" and "solicitor".)

SECTION 11 FACTORS TO BE TAKEN INTO ACCOUNT IN DECIDING THE AMOUNT OF COSTS: RULE 44.5

11.1   In applying the test of proportionality the court will have regard to rule 1.1(2)(c). The relationship between the total of the costs incurred and the financial value of the claim may not be a reliable guide. A fixed percentage cannot be applied in all cases to the value of the claim in order to ascertain whether or not the costs are proportionate.

11.2   In any proceedings there will be costs which will inevitably be incurred and which are necessary for the successful conduct of the case. Solicitors are not required to conduct litigation at rates which are uneconomic. Thus in a modest claim the proportion of costs is likely to be higher than in a large claim, and may even equal or possibly exceed the amount in dispute.

11.3   Where a trial takes place, the time taken by the court in dealing with a particular issue may not be an accurate guide to the amount of time properly spent by the legal or other representatives in preparation for the trial of that issue.

*11.4   Where a party has entered into a funding arrangement the costs claimed may, subject to rule 44.3B include an additional liability.

*11.5   In deciding whether the costs claimed are reasonable and (on a standard basis assessment) proportionate, the court will consider the amount of any additional liability separately from the base costs.

*11.6   In deciding whether the base costs are reasonable and (if relevant) proportionate the court will consider the factors set out in rule 44.5.

*11.7   Subject to paragraph 17.8(2), when the court is considering the factors to be taken into account in assessing an additional liability, it will have regard to the facts and circumstances as they reasonably appeared to the solicitor or counsel when the funding arrangement was entered into and at the time of any variation of the arrangement.

*11.8   (1) In deciding whether a percentage increase is reasonable relevant factors to be taken into account may include:

(a)   the risk that the circumstances in which the costs, fees or expenses would be payable might or might not occur;
(b)   the legal representative's liability for any disbursements;
(c)   what other methods of financing the costs were available to the receiving party.

(2) The court has the power, when considering whether a percentage increase is reasonable, to allow different percentages for different items of costs or for different periods during which costs were incurred.

*11.9   A percentage increase will not be reduced simply on the ground that, when added to base costs which are reasonable and (where relevant) proportionate, the total appears disproportionate.

*11.10   In deciding whether the cost of insurance cover is reasonable, relevant factors to be taken into account include:

(1)   where the insurance cover is not purchased in support of a conditional fee agreement with a success fee, how its cost compares with the likely cost of funding the case with a conditional fee agreement with a success fee and supporting insurance cover;

(2)   the level and extent of the cover provided;

(3)   the availability of any pre-existing insurance cover;

(4)   whether any part of the premium would be rebated in the event of early settlement;

(5)   the amount of commission payable to the receiving party or his legal representatives or other agents.

*11.11   Where the court is considering a provision made by a membership organisation, rule 44.3B(1) (b) provides that any such provision which exceeds the likely cost to the receiving party of the premium of an insurance policy against the risk of incurring a liability to pay the costs of other parties to the proceedings is not recoverable. In such circumstances the court will, when assessing the additional liability, have regard to the factors set out in paragraph 11.10 above, in addition to the factors set out in rule 44.5.

SECTION 17 COSTS-ONLY PROCEEDINGS: RULE 44.12A

*17.1   A claim form under this rule should be issued in the court which would have been the appropriate office in accordance with rule 47.4 had proceedings been brought in relation to the substantive claim. A claim form under this rule should not be issued in the High Court unless the dispute to which the agreement relates was of such a value or type that had proceedings been begun they would have been commenced in the High Court.

*17.2   A claim form which is to be issued in the High Court at the Royal Courts of Justice will be issued in the Supreme Court Costs Office.

*17.3   Attention is drawn to rule 8.2 (in particular to paragraph (b)(ii)) and to rule 44.12A(3). The claim form must:

(1)   identify the claim or dispute to which the agreement to pay costs relates;

(2)   state the date and terms of the agreement on which the claimant relies;

(3)   set out or have attached to it a draft of the order which the claimant seeks;

(4)   state the amount of the costs claimed; and,

(5)   state whether the costs are claimed on the standard or indemnity basis. If no basis is specified the costs will be treated as being claimed on the standard basis.

*17.4   The evidence to be filed and served with the claim form under Rule 8.5 must include copies of the documents on which the claimant relies to prove the defendant's agreement to pay costs.

*17.5   A costs judge or a district judge has jurisdiction to hear and decide any issue which may arise in a claim issued under this rule irrespective of the amount of the costs claimed or of the value of the claim to which the agreement to pay costs relates. A court officer may make an order by consent under paragraph 17.7, or an order dismissing a claim under paragraph 17.9 below.

*17.6   When the time for filing the defendant's acknowledgement of service has expired, the claimant may by letter request the court to make an order in the terms of his claim, unless the defendant has filed an acknowledgement of service stating that he intends to contest the claim or to seek a different order.

*17.7   Rule 40.6 applies where an order is to be made by consent. An order may be made by consent in terms which differ from those set out in the claim form.

*17.8   (1) An order for costs made under this rule will be treated as an order for the amount of costs to be decided by a detailed assessment to which Part 47 and the practice directions relating to it apply. Rule 44.4(4) (determination of basis of assessment) also applies to the order.

(2) In cases in which an additional liability is claimed, the costs judge or district judge should have regard to the time when and the extent to which the claim has been settled and to the fact that the claim has been settled without the need to commence proceedings.

*17.9   A claim will be treated as opposed for the purposes of rule 44.12A(4)(b) if the defendant files an acknowledgement of service stating that he intends to contest the proceedings or to seek a different remedy. An order dismissing it will be made as soon as such an acknowledgement is filed. The dismissal of a claim under rule 44.12A(4) does not prevent the claimant from issuing another claim form under Part 7 or Part 8 based on the agreement or alleged agreement to which the proceedings under this rule related.

*17.10   (1) Rule 8.9 (which provides that claims issued under Part 8 shall be treated as allocated to the multi-track) shall not apply to claims issued under this rule. A claim issued under this rule may be dealt with without being allocated to a track.

(2) Rule 8.1(3) and Part 24 do not apply to proceedings brought under rule 44.12A.

*17.11   Nothing in this rule prevents a person from issuing a claim form under Part 7 or Part 8 to sue on an agreement made in settlement of a dispute where that agreement makes provision for costs, nor from claiming in that case an order for costs or a specified sum in respect of costs.

SECTION 19 PROVIDING INFORMATION ABOUT FUNDING ARRANGEMENTS: RULE 44.15

*19.1   (1) A party who wishes to claim an additional liability in respect of a funding arrangement must give any other party information about that claim if he is to recover the additional liability. There is no requirement to specify the amount of the additional liability separately nor to state how it is calculated until it falls to be assessed. That principle is reflected in rules 44.3A and 44.15, in the following paragraphs and in Sections 6, 13, 14 and 31 of this Practice Direction. Section 6 deals with estimates of costs, Sections 13 and 14 deal with summary assessment and Section 31 deals with detailed assessment.

(2) In the following paragraphs a party who has entered into a funding arrangement is treated as a person who intends to recover a sum representing an additional liability by way of costs.

(3) Attention is drawn to paragraph 57.9 of this Practice Direction which sets out time limits for the provision of information where a funding arrangement is entered into between 31 March and 2 July 2000 and proceedings relevant to that arrangement are commenced before 3 July 2000.

Method of giving information

*19.2   (1) In this paragraph, 'claim form' includes petition and application notice, and the notice of funding to be filed or served is a notice containing the information set out in Form N251.

(2)—

(a) A claimant who has entered into a funding arrangement before starting the proceedings to which it relates must provide information to the court by filing the notice when he issues the claim form.

(b) He must provide information to every other party by serving the notice. If he serves the claim form himself he must serve the notice with the claim form. If the court is to serve the claim form, the court will also serve the notice if the claimant provides it with sufficient copies for service.

(3) A defendant who has entered into a funding arrangement before filing any document:

(a) must provide information to the court by filing notice with his first document. A 'first document' may be an acknowledgement of service, a defence, or any other document, such as an application to set aside a default judgment.

(b) must provide information to every party by serving notice. If he serves his first document himself he must serve the notice with that document. If the court is to serve his first document the court will also serve the notice if the defendant provides it with sufficient copies for service.

(4) In all other circumstances a party must file and serve notice within 7 days of entering into the funding arrangement concerned.

(5) There is no requirement in this Practice Direction for the provision of information about funding arrangements before the commencement of proceedings. Such provision is however recommended and may be required by a pre-action protocol.

Notice of change of information

*19.3 (1) Rule 44.15 imposes a duty on a party to give notice of change if the information he has previously provided is no longer accurate. To comply he must file and serve notice containing the information set out in Form N251. Rule 44.15(3) may impose other duties in relation to new estimates of costs.

(2) Further notification need not be provided where a party has already given notice:

(a) that he has entered into a conditional fee agreement with a legal representative and during the currency of that agreement either of them enters into another such agreement with an additional legal representative; or

(b) of some insurance cover, unless that cover is cancelled or unless new cover is taken out with a different insurer.

(3) Part 6 applies to the service of notices.

(4) The notice must be signed by the party or by his legal representative.

Information which must be provided

*19.4 (1) Unless the court otherwise orders, a party who is required to supply information about a funding arrangement must state whether he has—

entered into a conditional fee agreement which provides for a success fee within the meaning of section 58(2) of the Courts and Legal Services Act 1990;

taken out an insurance policy to which section 29 of the Access to Justice Act 1999 applies;

made an arrangement with a body which is prescribed for the purpose of section 30 of that Act;

or more than one of these.

(2) Where the funding arrangement is a conditional fee agreement, the party must state the date of the agreement and identify the claim or claims to which it relates (including Part 20 claims if any).

(3) Where the funding arrangement is an insurance policy the party must state the name of the insurer, the date of the policy and must identify the claim or claims to which it relates (including Part 20 claims if any).

(4) Where the funding arrangement is by way of an arrangement with a relevant body the party must state the name of the body and set out the date and terms of the undertaking it has given and must identify the claim or claims to which it relates (including Part 20 claims if any).

(5) Where a party has entered into more than one funding arrangement in respect of a claim, for example a conditional fee agreement and an insurance policy, a single notice containing the information set out in Form N251 may contain the required information about both or all of them

*19.5 Where the court makes a Group Litigation Order, the court may give directions as to the extent to which individual parties should provide information in accordance with rule 44.15. (Part 19 deals with Group Litigation Orders.)

SECTION 20 PROCEDURE WHERE LEGAL REPRESENTATIVE WISHES TO RECOVER FROM HIS CLIENT AN AGREED PERCENTAGE INCREASE WHICH HAS BEEN DISALLOWED OR REDUCED ON ASSESSMENT: RULE 44.16

*20.1 Attention is drawn to Regulation 3(2)(b) of the Conditional Fee Agreements Regulations 2000, which provides that any amount of an agreed percentage increase, which is disallowed on assessment, ceases to be payable under that agreement unless the court is satisfied that it should continue to be so payable. Rule 44.16 allows the court to adjourn a hearing at which the legal representative acting for the receiving party applies for an order that a disallowed amount should continue to be payable under the agreement.

*20.2 In the following paragraphs 'counsel' means counsel who has acted in the case under a conditional fee agreement which provides for a success fee. A reference to counsel includes a reference to any person who appeared as an advocate in the case and who is not a partner or employee of the solicitor or firm which is conducting the claim or defence (as the case may be) on behalf of the receiving party.

Procedure following Summary Assessment

*20.3 (1) If the court disallows any amount of a legal representative's percentage increase, the court will, unless sub-paragraph (2) applies, give directions to enable an application to be made by the legal representative for the disallowed amount to be payable by his client, including, if appropriate, a direction that the application will be determined by a costs judge or district judge of the court dealing with the case.

(2) The court that has made the summary assessment may then and there decide the issue whether the disallowed amount should continue to be payable, if:

(a) the receiving party and all parties to the relevant agreement consent to the court doing so;

(b) the receiving party (or, if corporate, an officer) is present in court; and

(c) the court is satisfied that the issue can be fairly decided then and there.

Procedure following Detailed Assessment

*20.4 (1) Where detailed assessment proceedings have been commenced, and the paying party serves points of dispute (as to which see Section 34 of this Practice Direction), which show that he is seeking a reduction in any percentage increase charged by counsel on his fees, the solicitor acting for the receiving party must within 3 days of service deliver to counsel a copy of the relevant points of dispute and the bill of costs or the relevant parts of the bill.

(2) Counsel must within 10 days thereafter inform the solicitor in writing whether or not he will accept the reduction sought or some other reduction. Counsel may state any points he wishes to have made in a reply to the points of dispute, and the solicitor must serve them on the paying party as or as part of a reply.

(3) Counsel who fails to inform the solicitor within the time limits set out above will be taken to accept the reduction unless the court otherwise orders.

*20.5 Where the paying party serves points of dispute seeking a reduction in any percentage increase charged by a legal representative acting for the receiving party, and that legal representative intends, if necessary, to apply for an order that any amount of the percentage disallowed as against the paying party shall continue to be payable by his client, the solicitor acting for the receiving party must, within 14 days of service of the points of dispute, give to his client a clear written explanation of the nature of the relevant point of dispute and the effect it will have if it is upheld in whole or in part by the court, and of the client's right to attend any subsequent hearings at court when the matter is raised.

*20.6 Where the solicitor acting for a receiving party files a request for a detailed assessment hearing it must if appropriate, be accompanied by a certificate signed by him stating:

(1) that the amount of the percentage increase in respect of counsel's fees or solicitor's charges is disputed;

(2) whether an application will be made for an order that any amount of that increase which is disallowed should continue to be payable by his client;

(3)   that he has given his client an explanation in accordance with paragraph 20.5; and,

(4)   whether his client wishes to attend court when the amount of any relevant percentage increase may be decided.

*20.7   (1) The solicitor acting for the receiving party must within 7 days of receiving from the court notice of the date of the assessment hearing, notify his client, and if appropriate, counsel in writing of the date, time and place of the hearing.

(2) Counsel may attend or be represented at the detailed assessment hearing and may make oral or written submissions.

*20.8   (1) At the detailed assessment hearing, the court will deal with the assessment of the costs payable by one party to another, including the amount of the percentage increase, and give a certificate accordingly.

(2) The court may decide the issue whether the disallowed amount should continue to be payable under the relevant conditional fee agreement without an adjournment if:

(a)   the receiving party and all parties to the relevant agreement consent to the court deciding the issue without an adjournment,

(b)   the receiving party (or, if corporate, an officer or employee who has authority to consent on behalf of the receiving party) is present in court, and

(c)   the court is satisfied that the issue can be fairly decided without an adjournment.

(3) In any other case the court will give directions and fix a date for the hearing of the application.

DIRECTIONS RELATING TO PART 48

COSTS—SPECIAL CASES

SECTION 57 TRANSITIONAL ARRANGEMENTS:

57.1   In this section 'the previous rules' means the Rules of the Supreme Court 1965 ('RSC') or County Court Rules 1981 ('CCR'), as appropriate.

General Scheme of Transitional Arrangements concerning Costs Proceedings

*57.2   (1) Paragraph 18 of the Practice Direction which supplements Part 51 (Transitional Arrangements) provides that the CPR govern any assessments of costs which take place on or after 26th April 1999 and states a presumption to be applied in respect of costs for work undertaken before 26th April 1999.

(2) The following paragraphs provide five further transitional arrangements:

(a)   to provide an additional presumption to be applied when assessing costs which were awarded by an order made in a county court before 26th April 1999 which allowed costs 'on Scale 1' to be determined in accordance with CCR Appendix A, or 'on the lower scale' to be determined in accordance with CCR Appendix C.

(b)   to preserve the effect of CCR Appendix B Part III, paragraph 2;

(c)   to clarify the approach to be taken where a bill of costs was provisionally taxed before 26th April 1999 and the receiving party is unwilling to accept the result of the provisional taxation.

(d)   to preserve the right to carry in objections or apply for a reconsideration in all taxation proceedings commenced before 26th April 1999.

(e)   to deal with funding arrangements made before 3 July 2000.

Scale 1 or lower scale costs

57.3   Where an order was made in county court proceedings before 26th April 1999 under which the costs were allowed on Scale 1 or the lower scale, the general presumption is that no costs will be allowed under that order which would not have been allowed in a taxation before 26th April 1999.

Fixed costs on the lower scale

57.4   The amount to be allowed as fixed costs for making or opposing an application for a rehearing to set aside a judgment given before 26th April 1999 where the costs are on lower scale is £11.25.

Bills provisionally taxed before 26th April 1999

57.5   In respect of bills of costs provisionally taxed before 26th April 1999:

(1)   The previous rules apply on the question who can request a hearing and the time limits for doing so; and

(2)   The CPR govern any subsequent hearing in that case.

Bills taxed before 26th April 1999

57.6   Where a bill of costs was taxed before 26th April 1999, the previous rules govern the steps which can be taken to challenge that taxation.

Other taxation proceedings

*57.7   (1) This paragraph applies to taxation proceedings which were commenced before 26th April 1999, were assigned for taxation to a Taxing Master or District Judge, and which were still pending on 26th April 1999.

(2) Any assessment of costs that takes place in cases to which this paragraph applies which is conducted on or after 26th April 1999, will be conducted in accordance with the CPR.

(3) In addition to the possibility of appeal under rules 47.20 to 47.23 and Part 52 any party to a detailed assessment who is dissatisfied with any decision on a detailed assessment made by a costs judge or district judge may apply to that costs judge or district judge for a review of the decision. The review shall, for procedural purposes, be treated as if it were an appeal from an authorised court officer.

(4) The right of review provided by paragraph (3) above, will not apply in cases in which, at least 28 days before the date of the assessment hearing, all parties were served with notice that the rights of appeal in respect of that hearing would be governed by Part 47 Section VIII (Appeals from Authorised Court Officers in Detailed Assessment Proceedings) and Part 52 (Appeals).

(5) An order for the service of notice under sub-paragraph (4) above may be made on the application of any party to the detailed assessment proceedings or may be made by the court of its own initiative.

Transitional provisions concerning the Access to Justice Act 1999 sections 28 to 31

*57.8   (1) Sections 28 to 31 of the Access to Justice Act 1999, the Conditional Fee Agreements Regulations 2000, the Access to Justice (Membership Organisations) Regulations 2000, and the Access to Justice Act 1999 (Transitional Provisions) Order 2000 came into force on 1 April 2000. The Civil Procedure (Amendment No.3) Rules come into force on 3 July 2000.

(2) The Access to Justice Act 1999 (Transitional Provisions) Order 2000 provides that no conditional fee agreement or other arrangement about costs entered into before 1 April 2000 can be a funding arrangement, as defined in rule 43.2 The order also has the effect that where an conditional fee agreement or other funding arrangement has been entered into before 1 April 2000 and a second or subsequent funding arrangement is entered into on or after 1 April 2000, the second or subsequent funding arrangement does not give rise to an additional liability which is recoverable from a paying party.

*57.9   (1) Rule 39 of the Civil Procedure (Amendment No 3) Rules 2000 applies where between 1 April and 2 July 2000 (including both dates)—

a funding arrangement is entered into, and
proceedings are started in respect of a claim which is the subject of that agreement.

(2) Attention is drawn to the need to act promptly so as to comply with the requirements of the Rules and the Practice Directions by 31 July 2000 (ie within the 28 days from 3 July 2000 permitted by Rule 39) if that compliance is to be treated as compliance with the relevant provision. Attention is drawn in particular to Rule 44.15 (Providing Information about Funding Arrangements) and Section 19 of this Practice Direction.

(3) Nothing in the legislation referred to above makes provision for a party who has entered into a funding arrangement to recover from another party any amount of an additional liability which relates to anything done or any costs incurred before the arrangement was entered into.

Courts and Legal Services Act 1990

Miscellaneous

58 Conditional fee agreements

(1) A conditional fee agreement which satisfies all of the conditions applicable to it by virtue of this section shall not be unenforceable by reason only of its being a conditional fee agreement; but (subject to subsection (5)) any other conditional fee agreement shall be unenforceable.

(2) For the purposes of this section and section 58A—

(a) a conditional fee agreement is an agreement with a person providing advocacy or litigation services which provides for his fees and expenses, or any part of them, to be payable only in specified circumstances; and

(b) a conditional fee agreement provides for a success fee if it provides for the amount of any fees to which it applies to be increased, in specified circumstances, above the amount which would be payable if it were not payable only in specified circumstances.

(3) The following conditions are applicable to every conditional fee agreement—

(a) it must be in writing;

(b) it must not relate to proceedings which cannot be the subject of an enforceable conditional fee agreement; and

(c) it must comply with such requirements (if any) as may be prescribed by the Lord Chancellor.

(4) The following further conditions are applicable to a conditional fee agreement which provides for a success fee—

(a) it must relate to proceedings of a description specified by order made by the Lord Chancellor;

(b) it must state the percentage by which the amount of the fees which would be payable if it were not a conditional fee agreement is to be increased; and

(c) that percentage must not exceed the percentage specified in relation to the description of proceedings to which the agreement relates by order made by the Lord Chancellor.

(5) If a conditional fee agreement is an agreement to which section 57 of the Solicitors Act 1974 (non-contentious business agreements between solicitor and client) applies, subsection (1) shall not make it unenforceable.

[This section is reproduced as amended by the Access to Justice Act 1999, s 27.]

58A Conditional fee agreements: supplementary

(1) The proceedings which cannot be the subject of an enforceable conditional fee agreement are—

(a)   criminal proceedings; and
(b)   family proceedings, apart from proceedings under section 82 of the Environmental Protection Act 1990.

(2) In subsection (1) 'family proceedings' means proceedings under any one or more of the following—

(a)   the Matrimonial Causes Act 1973;
(b)   the Adoption Act 1976;
(c)   the Domestic Proceedings and Magistrates' Courts Act 1978;
(d)   Part III of the Matrimonial and Family Proceedings Act 1984;
(e)   Parts I, II and IV of the Children Act 1989;
(f)   Part IV of the Family Law Act 1996; and
(g)   the inherent jurisdiction of the High Court in relation to children.

(3) The requirements which the Lord Chancellor may prescribe under section 58(3)(c)—

(a)   include requirements for the person providing advocacy or litigation services to have provided prescribed information before the agreement is made; and
(b)   may be different for different descriptions of conditional fee agreements (and, in particular, may be different for those which provide for a success fee and those which do not).

(4) In section 58 and this section (and in the definitions of 'advocacy services' and 'litigation services' as they apply for their purposes) 'proceedings' includes any sort of proceedings for resolving disputes (and not just proceedings in a court), whether commenced or contemplated.

(5) Before making an order under section 58(4), the Lord Chancellor shall consult—

(a)   the designated judges;
(b)   the General Council of the Bar;
(c)   the Law Society; and
(d)   such other bodies as he considers appropriate.

(6) A costs order made in any proceedings may, subject in the case of court proceedings to rules of court, include provision requiring the payment of any fees payable under a conditional fee agreement which provides for a success fee.

(7) Rules of court may make provision with respect to the assessment of any costs which include fees payable under a conditional fee agreement (including one which provides for a success fee).

Access to Justice Act 1999

Costs

28   Litigation funding agreements

In the Courts and Legal Services Act 1990, after section 58A (inserted by section 27 above) insert—

'58B   Litigation funding agreements

(1)   A litigation funding agreement which satisfies all of the conditions applicable to it by virtue of this section shall not be unenforceable by reason only of its being a litigation funding agreement.

(2)   For the purposes of this section a litigation funding agreement is an agreement under which—

   (a)   a person ("the funder") agrees to fund (in whole or in part) the provision of advocacy or litigation services (by someone other than the funder) to another person ("the litigant"); and

   (b)   the litigant agrees to pay a sum to the funder in specified circumstances.

(3)   The following conditions are applicable to a litigation funding agreement—

   (a)   the funder must be a person, or person of a description, prescribed by the Lord Chancellor;

   (b)   the agreement must be in writing;

   (c)   the agreement must not relate to proceedings which by virtue of section 58A(1) and (2) cannot be the subject of an enforceable conditional fee agreement or to proceedings of any such description as may be prescribed by the Lord Chancellor;

   (d)   the agreement must comply with such requirements (if any) as may be so prescribed;

   (e)   the sum to be paid by the litigant must consist of any costs payable to him in respect of the proceedings to which the agreement relates together with an amount calculated by reference to the funder's anticipated expenditure in funding the provision of the services; and

   (f)   that amount must not exceed such percentage of that anticipated expenditure as may be prescribed by the Lord Chancellor in relation to proceedings of the description to which the agreement relates.

(4)   Regulations under subsection (3)(a) may require a person to be approved by the Lord Chancellor or by a prescribed person.

(5)   The requirements which the Lord Chancellor may prescribe under subsection (3)(d)—

(a)   include requirements for the funder to have provided prescribed information to the litigant before the agreement is made; and

(b)   may be different for different descriptions of litigation funding agreements.

(6)   In this section (and in the definitions of "advocacy services" and "litigation services" as they apply for its purposes) "proceedings" includes any sort of proceedings for resolving disputes (and not just proceedings in a court), whether commenced or contemplated.

(7)   Before making regulations under this section, the Lord Chancellor shall consult—

(a)   the designated judges;

(b)   the General Council of the Bar;

(c)   the Law Society; and

(d)   such other bodies as he considers appropriate.

(8)   A costs order made in any proceedings may, subject in the case of court proceedings to rules of court, include provision requiring the payment of any amount payable under a litigation funding agreement.

(9)   Rules of court may make provision with respect to the assessment of any costs which include fees payable under a litigation funding agreement.'

[This section was not in force at the time of going to press.]

29   Recovery of insurance premiums by way of costs

Where in any proceedings a costs order is made in favour of any party who has taken out an insurance policy against the risk of incurring a liability in those proceedings, the costs payable to him may, subject in the case of court proceedings to rules of court, include costs in respect of the premium of the policy.

30   Recovery where body undertakes to meet costs liabilities

(1) This section applies where a body of a prescribed description undertakes to meet (in accordance with arrangements satisfying prescribed conditions) liabilities which members of the body or other persons who are parties to proceedings may incur to pay the costs of other parties to the proceedings.

(2) If in any of the proceedings a costs order is made in favour of any of the members or other persons, the costs payable to him may, subject to subsection (3) and (in the case of court proceedings) to rules of court, include an additional amount in respect of any provision made by or on behalf of the body in connection with the proceedings against the risk of having to meet such liabilities.

(3) But the additional amount shall not exceed a sum determined in a prescribed manner; and there may, in particular, be prescribed as a manner of determination one which takes into account the likely cost to the member or other person of the premium of an insurance policy against the risk of incurring a liability to pay the costs of other parties to the proceedings.

(4) In this section 'prescribed' means prescribed by regulations made by the Lord Chancellor by statutory instrument; and a statutory instrument

containing such regulations shall be subject to annulment in pursuance of a resolution of either House of Parliament.

(5) Regulations under subsection (1) may, in particular, prescribe as a description of body one which is for the time being approved by the Lord Chancellor or by a prescribed person.

31   Rules as to costs

In section 51 of the Supreme Court Act 1981 (costs), in subsection (2) (rules regulating matters relating to costs), insert at the end 'or for securing that the amount awarded to a party in respect of the costs to be paid by him to such representatives is not limited to what would have been payable by him to them if he had not been awarded costs.'

Conditional Fee Agreements Regulations 2000, SI 2000/692

1 Citation, commencement and interpretation

(1) These Regulations may be cited as the Conditional Fee Agreements Regulations 2000.

(2) These Regulations come into force on 1st April 2000.

(3) In these Regulations—

'client' includes, except where the context otherwise requires, a person who—

(a) has instructed the legal representative to provide the advocacy or litigation services to which the conditional fee agreement relates, or

(b) is liable to pay the legal representative's fees in respect of those services; and

'legal representative' means the person providing the advocacy or litigation services to which the conditional fee agreement relates.

2 Requirements for contents of conditional fee agreements: general

(1) A conditional fee agreement must specify—

(a) the particular proceedings or parts of them to which it relates (including whether it relates to any appeal, counterclaim or proceedings to enforce a judgment or order),

(b) the circumstances in which the legal representative's fees and expenses, or part of them, are payable,

(c) what payment, if any, is due—

(i) if those circumstances only partly occur,

(ii) irrespective of whether those circumstances occur, and

(iii) on the termination of the agreement for any reason, and

(d) the amounts which are payable in all the circumstances and cases specified or the method to be used to calculate them and, in particular, whether the amounts are limited by reference to the damages which may be recovered on behalf of the client.

(2) A conditional fee agreement to which regulation 4 applies must contain a statement that the requirements of that regulation which apply in the case of that agreement have been complied with.

3 Requirements for contents of conditional fee agreements providing for success fees

(1) A conditional fee agreement which provides for a success fee—

(a)   must briefly specify the reasons for setting the percentage increase at the level stated in the agreement, and

(b)   must specify how much of the percentage increase, if any, relates to the cost to the legal representative of the postponement of the payment of his fees and expenses.

(2) If the agreement relates to court proceedings, it must provide that where the percentage increase becomes payable as a result of those proceedings, then—

(a)   if—

(i)   any fees subject to the increase are assessed, and

(ii)   the legal representative or the client is required by the court to disclose to the court or any other person the reasons for setting the percentage increase at the level stated in the agreement,

he may do so,

(b)   if—

(i)   any such fees are assessed, and

(ii)   any amount in respect of the percentage increase is disallowed on the assessment on the ground that the level at which the increase was set was unreasonable in view of facts which were or should have been known to the legal representative at the time it was set,

that amount ceases to be payable under the agreement, unless the court is satisfied that it should continue to be so payable, and

(c)   if—

(i)   sub-paragraph (b) does not apply, and

(ii)   the legal representative agrees with any person liable as a result of the proceedings to pay fees subject to the percentage increase that a lower amount than the amount payable in accordance with the conditional fee agreement is to be paid instead,

the amount payable under the conditional fee agreement in respect of those fees shall be reduced accordingly, unless the court is satisfied that the full amount should continue to be payable under it.

(3) In this regulation 'percentage increase' means the percentage by which the amount of the fees which would be payable if the agreement were not a conditional fee agreement is to be increased under the agreement.

4   Information to be given before conditional fee agreements made

(1) Before a conditional fee agreement is made the legal representative must—

(a)   inform the client about the following matters, and

(b)   if the client requires any further explanation, advice or other information about any of those matters, provide such further explanation, advice or other information about them as the client may reasonably require.

(2) Those matters are—

(a)   the circumstances in which the client may be liable to pay the costs of the legal representative in accordance with the agreement,

(b)   the circumstances in which the client may seek assessment of the fees and expenses of the legal representative and the procedure for doing so,

(c)   whether the legal representative considers that the client's risk of incurring liability for costs in respect of the proceedings to which agreement relates is insured against under an existing contract of insurance,

(d)   whether other methods of financing those costs are available, and, if so, how they apply to the client and the proceedings in question,

(e)   whether the legal representative considers that any particular method or methods of financing any or all of those costs is appropriate and, if he considers that a contract of insurance is appropriate or recommends a particular such contract—

    (i)   his reasons for doing so, and

    (ii) whether he has an interest in doing so.

(3) Before a conditional fee agreement is made the legal representative must explain its effect to the client.

(4) In the case of an agreement where—

(a)   the legal representative is a body to which section 30 of the Access to Justice Act 1999 (recovery where body undertakes to meet costs liabilities) applies, and

(b)   there are no circumstances in which the client may be liable to pay any costs in respect of the proceedings,

paragraph (1) does not apply.

(5) Information required to be given under paragraph (1) about the matters in paragraph (2)(a) to (d) must be given orally (whether or not it is also given in writing), but information required to be so given about the matters in paragraph (2)(e) and the explanation required by paragraph (3) must be given both orally and in writing.

(6) This regulation does not apply in the case of an agreement between a legal representative and an additional legal representative.

5   Form of agreement

(1) A conditional fee agreement must be signed by the client and the legal representative.

(2) This regulation does not apply in the case of an agreement between a legal representative and an additional legal representative.

6   Amendment of agreement

Where an agreement is amended to cover further proceedings or parts of them—

(a)   regulations 2, 3 and 5 apply to the amended agreement as if it were a fresh agreement made at the time of the amendment, and

(b)   the obligations under regulation 4 apply in relation to the amendments in so far as they affect the matters mentioned in that regulation.

7   Revocation of 1995 Regulations

The Conditional Fee Agreements Regulations 1995 are revoked.

8   Exclusion of Collective Conditional Fee Agreements

These Regulations shall not apply to collective conditional fee agreements within the meaning of regulation 3 of the Collective Conditional Fee Agreements Regulations 2000.

Conditional Fee Agreements Order 2000,

SI 2000/823

1 Citation, commencement and interpretation

(1) This Order may be cited as the Conditional Fee Agreements Order 2000 and shall come into force on 1st April 2000.

(2) In this Order 'the Act' means the Courts and Legal Services Act 1990.

2 Revocation of 1998 Order

The Conditional Fee Agreements Order 1998 is revoked.

3 Agreements providing for success fees

All proceedings which, under section 58 of the Act, can be the subject of an enforceable conditional fee agreement, except proceedings under section 82 of the Environmental Protection Act 1990, are proceedings specified for the purposes of section 58(4)(a) of the Act.

4 Amount of success fees

In relation to all proceedings specified in article 3, the percentage specified for the purposes of section 58(4)(c) of the Act shall be 100%.

The Access to Justice Act 1999 (Transitional Provisions) Order 2000, SI 2000/900

1

(1) This Order may be cited as the Access to Justice Act 1999 (Transitional Provisions) Order 2000 and shall come into force on 1st April 2000.

(2) In this Order a reference to a section by number alone means the section so numbered in the Access to Justice Act 1999.

2

(1) Section 58A(6) and (7) of the Courts and Legal Services Act 1990 shall not apply, as regards a party to proceedings, to:

(a) any proceedings in relation to which that party entered into a conditional fee agreement before 1st April 2000; or

(b) any proceedings arising out of the same cause of action as any proceedings to which sub-paragraph (a) refers.

(2) The coming into force of section 27 (Conditional fee agreements) shall not affect the validity of any conditional fee agreement entered into before 1st April 2000, and any such agreement shall continue to have effect after that date as if section 27 had not come into force.

(3) In paragraphs 1(a) and (2) 'conditional fee agreement' has the same meaning as in section 58 of the Courts and Legal Services Act 1990 as that section stands immediately before the coming into force of section 27 of the Access to Justice Act 1999.

3 Section 29 (Recovery of insurance premiums by way of costs) shall not apply, as regards a party to proceedings, to:

(a) any proceedings in relation to which that party took out an insurance policy of the sort referred to in section 29 before 1st April 2000; or

(b) any proceedings arising out of the same cause of action as any proceedings to which sub-paragraph (a) refers.

4 Section 30 (Recovery where body undertakes to meet costs liabilities) shall not apply, as regards a party to proceedings, to:

(a) any proceedings in relation to which that party gave an undertaking before 1st April 2000 which, if it had been given after that date, would have been an undertaking to which section 30(1) applied; or

(b) any proceedings arising out of the same cause of action as any proceedings to which sub-paragraph (a) refers.

Access to Justice (Membership Organisations) Regulations 2000, SI 2000/693

1   Citation, commencement and interpretation

(1) These Regulations may be cited as the Access to Justice (Membership Organisations) Regulations 2000.

(2) These Regulations come into force on 1st April 2000.

2   Bodies of a prescribed description

The bodies which are prescribed for the purpose of section 30 of the Access to Justice Act 1999 (recovery where body undertakes to meet costs liabilities) are those bodies which are for the time being approved by the Lord Chancellor for that purpose.

3   Requirements for arrangements to meet costs liabilities

(1) Section 30(1) of the Access to Justice Act 1999 applies to arrangements which satisfy the following conditions.

(2) The arrangements must be in writing.

(3) The arrangements must contain a statement specifying—

(a)   the circumstances in which the member or other party may be liable to pay costs of the proceedings,
(b)   whether such a liability arises—

  (i)   if those circumstances only partly occur,
  (ii)   irrespective of whether those circumstances occur, and
  (iii)   on the termination of the arrangements for any reason,

(c)   the basis on which the amount of the liability is calculated, and
(d)   the procedure for seeking assessment of costs.

(4) A copy of the part of the arrangements containing the statement must be given to the member or other party to the proceedings whose liabilities the body is undertaking to meet as soon as possible after the undertaking is given.

4   Recovery of additional amount for insurance costs

(1) Where an additional amount is included in costs by virtue of section 30(2) of the Access to Justice Act 1999 (costs payable to a member of a body or other person party to the proceedings to include an additional amount in respect of provision made by the body against the risk of having to meet the member's or other person's liabilities to pay other parties' costs), that additional amount must not exceed the following sum.

(2) That sum is the likely cost to the member of the body or, as the case may be, the other person who is a party to the proceedings in which the costs order is made of the premium of an insurance policy against the risk of incurring a liability to pay the costs of other parties to the proceedings.

The Collective Conditional Fee Agreements Regulations 2000, SI 2000/2988

1 Citation, commencement and interpretation

(1) These regulations may be cited as the Collective Conditional Fee Agreements Regulations 2000, and shall come into force on 30th November 2000.

(2) In these Regulations, except where the context requires otherwise—

'client' means a person who will receive advocacy or litigation services to which the agreement relates;

'collective conditional fee agreement' has the meaning given in regulation 3;

'conditional fee agreement' has the same meaning as in section 58 of the Courts and Legal Services Act 1990;

'funder' means the party to a collective conditional fee agreement who, under that agreement, is liable to pay the legal representative's fees;

'legal representative' means the person providing the advocacy or litigation services to which the agreement relates.

2 Transitional provisions

These Regulations shall apply to agreements entered into on or after 30th November 2000, and agreements entered into before that date shall be treated as if these Regulations had not come into force.

3 Definition of 'collective conditional fee agreement'

(1) Subject to paragraph (2) of this regulation, a collective conditional fee agreement is an agreement which—

(a) disregarding section 58(3)(c) of the Courts and Legal Services Act 1990, would be a conditional fee agreement; and

(b) does not refer to specific proceedings, but provides for fees to be payable on a common basis in relation to a class of proceedings, or, if it refers to more than one class of proceedings, on a common basis in relation to each class.

(2) An agreement may be a collective conditional fee agreement whether or not—

(a) the funder is a client; or
(b) any clients are named in the agreement.

4 Requirements for contents of collective conditional fee agreements: general

(1) A collective conditional fee agreement must specify the circumstances in which the legal representative's fees and expenses, or part of them, are payable.

(2) A collective conditional fee agreement must provide that, when accepting instructions in relation to any specific proceedings the legal representative must—

(a) inform the client as to the circumstances in which the client may be liable to pay the costs of the legal representative; and
(b) if the client requires any further explanation, advice or other information about the matter referred to in sub-paragraph (a), provide such further explanation, advice or other information about it as the client may reasonably require.

(3) Paragraph (2) does not apply in the case of an agreement between a legal representative and an additional legal representative.

(4) A collective conditional fee agreement must provide that, after accepting instructions in relation to any specific proceedings, the legal representative must confirm his acceptance of instructions in writing to the client.

5   Requirements for contents of collective conditional fee agreements providing for success fees

(1) Where a collective conditional fee agreement provides for a success fee the agreement must provide that, when accepting instructions in relation to any specific proceedings the legal representative must prepare and retain a written statement containing—

(a) his assessment of the probability of the circumstances arising in which the percentage increase will become payable in relation to those proceedings ('the risk assessment');
(b) his assessment of the amount of the percentage increase in relation to those proceedings, having regard to the risk assessment; and
(c) the reasons, by reference to the risk assessment, for setting the percentage increase at that level.

(2) If the agreement relates to court proceedings it must provide that where the success fee becomes payable as a result of those proceedings, then—

(a) if—

(i) any fees subject to the increase are assessed, and
(ii) the legal representative or the client is required by the court to disclose to the court or any other person the reasons for setting the percentage increase at the level assessed by the legal representative,

he may do so,

(b) if—

(i) any such fees are assessed by the court, and
(ii) any amount in respect of the percentage increase is disallowed on the assessment on the ground that the level at which the increase was set was unreasonable in view of facts which were or should have been known to the legal representative at the time it was set

that amount ceases to be payable under the agreement, unless the court is satisfied that it should continue to be so payable, and

(c)   if—

(i)   sub-paragraph (b) does not apply, and

(ii) the legal representative agrees with any person liable as a result of the proceedings to pay fees subject to the percentage increase that a lower amount than the amount payable in accordance with the conditional fee agreement is to be paid instead,

the amount payable under the collective conditional fee agreement in respect of those fees shall be reduced accordingly, unless the court is satisfied that the full amount should continue to be payable under it.

(3) In this regulation 'percentage increase' means the percentage by which the amount of the fees which would have been payable if the agreement were not a conditional fee agreement is to be increased under the agreement.

6   Form and amendment of collective conditional fee agreement

(1) Subject to paragraph (2), a collective conditional fee agreement must be signed by the funder, and by the legal representative.

(2) Paragraph (1) does not apply in the case of an agreement between a legal representative and an additional legal representative.

(3) Where a collective conditional fee agreement is amended, regulations 4 and 5 apply to the amended agreement as if it were a fresh agreement made at the time of the amendment.

7   Amendment to the Conditional Fee Agreements Regulations 2000

After regulation 7 of the Conditional Fee Agreements Regulations 2000 there shall be inserted the following new regulation:

8   Exclusion of collective conditional fee agreements

These Regulations shall not apply to collective conditional fee agreements within the meaning of regulation 3 of the Collective Conditional Fee Agreements Regulations 2000.

Courts and Legal Services Act 1990

58

(1) In this section 'a conditional fee agreement' means an agreement in writing between a person providing advocacy or litigation services and his client which—

(a) does not relate to proceedings of a kind mentioned in subsection (10);

(b) provides for that person's fees and expenses, or any part of them, to be payable only in specified circumstances;

(c) complies with such requirements (if any) as may be prescribed by the Lord Chancellor; and

(d) is not a contentious business agreement (as defined by section 59 of the Solicitors Act 1974).

(2) Where a conditional fee agreement provides for the amount of any fees to which it applies to be increased, in specified circumstances, above the amount which would be payable if it were not a conditional fee agreement, it shall specify the percentage by which that amount is to be increased.

(3) Subject to subsection (6), a conditional fee agreement which relates to specified proceedings shall not be unenforceable by reason only of its being a conditional fee agreement.

(4) In this section 'specified proceedings' means proceedings of a description specified by order made by the Lord Chancellor for the purposes of subsection (3).

(5) Any such order shall prescribe the maximum permitted percentage for each description of specified proceedings.

(6) An agreement which falls within subsection (2) shall be unenforceable if, at the time when it is entered into, the percentage specified in the agreement exceeds the prescribed maximum permitted percentage for the description of proceedings to which it relates.

(7) Before making any order under this section the Lord Chancellor shall consult the designated judges, the General Council of the Bar, the Law Society and such other authorised bodies (if any) as he considers appropriate.

(8) Where a party to any proceedings has entered into a conditional fee agreement and a costs order is made in those proceedings in his favour, the costs payable to him shall not include any element which takes account of any percentage increase payable under the agreement.

(9) Rules of court may make provision with respect to the taxing of any costs which include fees payable under a conditional fee agreement.

(10) The proceedings mentioned in subsection (1)(a) are any criminal proceedings and any proceedings under—

(a)   the Matrimonial Causes Act 1973;
(b)   the Domestic Violence and Matrimonial Proceedings Act 1976;
(c)   the Adoption Act 1976;
(d)   the Domestic Proceedings and Magistrates' Courts Act 1978;
(e)   sections 1 and 9 of the Matrimonial Homes Act 1983;
(f)   Part III of the Matrimonial and Family Proceedings Act 1984;
(g)   Parts I, II or IV of the Children Act 1989; or
(h)   the inherent jurisdiction of the High Court in relation to children.

[This section is reproduced in its original form prior to the amendments made by the Access to Justice Act 1999, s 27.]

The Conditional Fee Agreements Order 1995, SI 1995/1674

1 Citation and commencement

This Order may be cited as the Conditional Fee Agreements Order 1995 and shall come into force on the day after the day on which it was made.

2 Specified proceedings

(1) The proceedings specified for the purpose of section 58(4) of the Courts and Legal Services Act 1990 (conditional fee agreements in respect of specified proceedings not to be unenforceable) are the following:

(a) proceedings in which there is a claim for damages in respect of personal injuries or in respect of a person's death, and 'personal injuries' includes any disease and any impairment of a person's physical or mental condition;

(b) proceedings in England and Wales by a company which is being wound up in England and Wales or Scotland;

(c) proceedings by a company in respect of which an administration order made under Part II of the Insolvency Act 1986 is in force;

(d) proceedings in England and Wales by a person acting in the capacity of—

    (i) liquidator of a company which is being wound up in England and Wales or Scotland; or

    (ii) trustee of a bankrupt's estate;

(e) proceedings by a person acting in the capacity of an administrator appointed pursuant to the provisions of Part II of the Insolvency Act 1986;

(f) proceedings before the European Commission of Human Rights and the European Court of Human Rights established under article 19 of the Convention for the Protection of Human Rights and Fundamental Freedoms opened for signature at Rome on 4th November 1950, ratified by the United Kingdom on 8th March 1951, which came into force on 3rd August 1953,

provided that the client does not have legal aid in respect of the proceedings.

(2) Proceedings specified in paragraph (1) shall be specified proceedings notwithstanding that they are concluded without the commencement of court proceedings.

(3) In paragraphs (1)(b) and (1)(d) 'company' means a company within the meaning of section 735(1) of the Companies Act 1985 or a company which may be wound up under Part V of the Insolvency Act 1986.

(4) Where legal aid in respect of the proceedings to which a conditional fee agreement relates is granted after that agreement is entered into the proceedings shall cease to be specified from the date of the grant.

(5) In this article, 'legal aid' means representation under Part IV of the Legal Aid Act 1988.

3   Maximum permitted percentage increase on fees

For the purpose of section 58(5) of the Courts and Legal Services Act 1990 the maximum permitted percentage by which fees may be increased in respect of each description of proceedings specified in article 2 is 100%.

The Conditional Fee Agreements Order 1998, SI 1998/1860

1 Citation, commencement and interpretation

(1) This Order may be cited as the Conditional Fee Agreements Order 1998 and shall come into force on the day after the day on which it is made.

(2) In this Order 'the Act' means the Courts and Legal Services Act 1990.

2 Revocation of 1995 order

The Conditional Fee Agreements Order 1995 is revoked.

3 Specified proceedings

(1) All proceedings are proceedings specified for the purposes of section 58(3) of the Act (conditional fee agreements in respect of specified proceedings not to be unenforceable).

(2) Proceedings specified in paragraph (1) shall be specified proceedings notwithstanding that they are concluded without the commencement of court proceedings.

4 Maximum permitted percentage increase on fees

For the purposes of section 58(5) of the Act the maximum permitted percentage by which fees may be increased in respect of any proceedings designated by article 3 as proceedings specified for the purposes of section 58(3) of the Act is 100%.

The Conditional Fee Agreements Regulations 1995, SI 1995/1675

1 Citation, commencement and interpretation

(1) These Regulations may be cited as the Conditional Fee Agreements Regulations 1995 and shall come into force on the day after the day on which they are made.

(2) In these Regulations—

'agreement', in relation to an agreement between a legal representative and an additional legal representative, includes a retainer;

'legal aid' means representation under Part IV of the Legal Aid Act 1988;

'legal representative' means a person providing advocacy or litigation services.

2 Agreements to comply with prescribed requirements

An agreement shall not be a conditional fee agreement unless it complies with the requirements of the following regulations.

3 Requirements of an agreement

An agreement shall state—

(a) the particular proceedings or parts of them to which it relates (including whether it relates to any counterclaim, appeal or proceedings to enforce a judgment or order);

(b) the circumstances in which the legal representative's fees and expenses or part of them are payable;

(c) what, if any, payment is due—

(i) upon partial failure of the specified circumstances to occur;

(ii) irrespective of the specified circumstances occurring; and

(iii) upon termination of the agreement for any reason;

(d) the amount payable in accordance with sub-paragraphs (b) or (c) above or the method to be used to calculate the amount payable; and in particular whether or not the amount payable is limited by reference to the amount of any damages which may be recovered on behalf of the client.

4 Additional requirements

(1) The agreement shall also state that, immediately before it was entered into, the legal representative drew the client's attention to the matters specified in paragraph (2).

(2) The matters are—

(a)   whether the client might be entitled to legal aid in respect of the proceedings to which the agreement relates, the conditions upon which legal aid is available and the application of those conditions to the client in respect of the proceedings;

(b)   the circumstances in which the client may be liable to pay the fees and expenses of the legal representative in accordance with the agreement;

(c)   the circumstances in which the client may be liable to pay the costs of any other party to the proceedings; and

(d)   the circumstances in which the client may seek taxation of the fees and expenses of the legal representative and the procedure for so doing.

5   Application of regulation 4

Regulation 4 shall not apply to an agreement between a legal representative and an additional legal representative.

6   Form of agreement

An agreement shall be in writing and, except in the case of an agreement between a legal representative and an additional legal representative, shall be signed by the client and the legal representative.

7   Amendment of agreement

Where it is proposed to extend the agreement to cover further proceedings or parts of them regulations 3 to 6 shall apply to the agreement as extended.

Appendix 2

Model Agreements

Law Society Model Conditional Fee Agreement

For use in personal injury cases, but not clinical negligence

This agreement is a binding legal contract between you and your solicitor/s. Before you sign, please read everything carefully. Words like 'our disbursements', 'basic charges', 'win' and 'lose' are explained in condition 3 of the Law Society Conditions which you should also read carefully.

Agreement date

[ ]

I/We, the solicitor/s You, the client

[ ]

[ ]

What is covered by this agreement

- Your claim against [ ] for damages for personal injury suffered on [ ].

- Any appeal by your opponent.

- Any appeal you make against an interim order during the proceedings.

- Any proceedings you take to enforce a judgment, order or agreement.

What is not covered by this agreement

- Any counterclaim against you.

- Any appeal you make against the final judgment order.

Paying us

If you win your claim, you pay our basic charges, our disbursements and a success fee. The amount of the success fee is not based on or limited by the damages. You are entitled to seek recovery from your opponent of part or all of our basic charges, our disbursements, a success fee and insurance premium.

Please also see conditions 4 and 6.

It may be that your opponent makes a Part 36 offer or payment which you reject and, on our advice, your claim for damages goes ahead to trial where you recover damages that are less than that offer or payment. We will not add our success fee to the basic charges for the work done after we received notice of the offer or payment.

If you receive interim damages, we may require you to pay our disbursements at that point and a reasonable amount for our future disbursements.

If you receive provisional damages, we are entitled to payment of our basic charges our disbursements and success fee at that point.

If you win but on the way lose an interim hearing, you may be required to pay your opponent's charges of that hearing. Please see conditions 3(*h*) and 5.

If on the way to winning or losing you win an interim hearing, then we are entitled to payment of our basic charges and disbursements related to that hearing together with a success fee on those charges if you win overall.

If you lose, you pay your opponent's charges and disbursements. You may be able to take out an insurance policy against this risk. Please also see conditions 3(*j*) and 5. If you lose, you do not pay our charges but we may require you to pay our disbursements.

If you end this agreement before you win or lose, you pay our basic charges. If you go on to win, you pay a success fee. Please also see condition 7(*a*).

We may end this agreement before you win or lose. Please also see condition 7(*b*) for details.

Basic charges

These are for work done from now until this agreement ends.

How we calculate our basic charges

These are calculated for each hour engaged on your matter [from now until the review date on [ ]]. Routine letters and telephone calls will be charged as units of one tenth of an hour. Other letters and telephone calls will be charged on a time basis. The hourly rates are:

- Solicitors with over four years' experience after qualification £ [ ]

- Other solicitors and legal executives and other staff of equivalent experience £ [ ]

- Trainee solicitors and other staff of equivalent experience £ [ ]

[We will review the hourly rate on the review date and on each anniversary of the review date. We will not increase the rate by more than the rise in the Retail Prices Index and will notify you of the increased rate in writing.]

Success fee

This is [ ]% of our basic charges

The reasons for calculating the success fee at this level are set out in Schedule 1 to this agreement.

You cannot recover from your opponent the part of the success fee that relates to the cost to us of postponing receipt of our charges and disbursements (as set out at paragraphs (*a*) and (*b*) at Schedule 1). This part of the success fee remains payable by you.

Value added tax (VAT)

We add VAT, at the rate (now [ ]%) that applies when the work is done, to the total of the basic charges and success fee.

Law Society Conditions

The Law Society Conditions are attached because they are part of this agreement. Any amendments or additions to them will apply to you. You should read the conditions carefully and ask us about anything you find unclear.

Other points

Immediately before you signed this agreement, we verbally explained to you the effect of this agreement and in particular the following:

(*a*)   the circumstances in which you may be liable to pay our disbursements and charges;

(*b*)   the circumstances in which you may seek assessment of our charges and disbursements and the procedure for doing so;

(*c*)   whether we consider that your risk of becoming liable for any costs in these proceedings is insured under an existing contract of insurance;

(*d*)   other methods of financing those costs, including private funding, Community Legal Service funding, legal expenses insurance, trade union funding;

(*e*)   (i)   In all the circumstances, on the information currently available to us, we believe that a contract of insurance with [ ] is appropriate. Detailed reasons for this are set out in Schedule 2.

(ii)   In any event, we believe it is desirable for you to insure your opponent's charges and disbursements in case you lose.

(iii)   We confirm that we do not have an interest in recommending this particular insurance agreement.

Signatures

Signed for the solicitor/s

Signed by the client

I confirm that my solicitor has verbally explained to me the matters in paragraphs (*a*) to (*e*) under 'Other points' above.

Signed .... (Client)

I specifically confirm that I verbally explained to the client the matters in paragraphs (*a*) to (*e*) under 'Other points' and confirm the matters at (*e*) in writing in Schedule 2.

Signed .... (Solicitors)

This agreement complies with the Conditional Fee Agreements Regulations 2000 (SI 2000/692)

SCHEDULE 1

The Success Fee

The success fee is set at [ ]% of basic charges and cannot be more than 100% of the basic charges.

The percentage reflects the following:

(a) the fact that if you win we will not be paid our basic charges until the end of the claim;
(b) our arrangements with you about paying disbursements;
(c) the fact that if you lose, we will not earn anything;
(d) our assessment of the risks of your case. These include the following:
(e) any other appropriate matters.

The matters set out at paragraphs (a) and (b) above together make up [ ]% of the increase on basic charges. The matters at paragraphs (c), (d) [and (e)] make up [ ]% of the increase on basic charges. So the total success fee is [ ]% as stated above.

SCHEDULE 2

The Insurance Policy

In all the circumstances and on the information currently available to us, we believe, that a contract of insurance with [ ] is appropriate to cover your opponent's charges and disbursements in case you lose.

This is because

We are not, however, insurance brokers and cannot give advice on all products which may be available.

LAW SOCIETY CONDITIONS

1. Our responsibilities

We must:

- always act in your best interests, subject to our duty to the court;
- explain to you the risks and benefits of taking legal action;
- give you our best advice about whether to accept any offer of settlement;
- give you the best information possible about the likely costs of your claim for damages.

2. Your responsibilities

You must:

- give us instructions that allow us to do our work properly;
- not ask us to work in an improper or unreasonable way;
- not deliberately mislead us;
- co-operate with us;
- go to any medical or expert examination or court hearing.

3. Explanation of words used

(a) *Advocacy*

Appearing for you at court hearings.

(b) *Basic charges*

Our charges for the legal work we do on your claim for damages.

(c) *Claim*

Your demand for damages for personal injury whether or not court proceedings are issued.

(d) *Counterclaim*

A claim that your opponent makes against you in response to your claim.

(e) *Damages*

Money that you win whether by a court decision or settlement.

(f) *Our disbursements*

Payment we make on your behalf such as:

- court fees;
- experts' fees;
- accident report fees;
- travelling expenses.

(g) *Interim damages*

Money that a court says your opponent must pay or your opponent agrees to pay while waiting for a settlement or the court's final decision.

379

(h) *Interim hearing*

A court hearing that is not final.

(i) *Lien*

Our right to keep all papers, documents, money or other property held on your behalf until all money due to us is paid. A lien may be applied after this agreement ends.

(j) *Lose*

The court has dismissed your claim or you have stopped it on our advice.

(k) *Part 36 offers or payments*

An offer to settle your claim made in accordance with Part 36 of the Civil Procedure Rules.

(l) *Provisional damages*

Money that a court says your opponent must pay or your opponent agrees to pay, on the basis that you will be able to go back to court at a future date for further damages if:

- you develop a serious disease; or

- your condition deteriorates; in a way that has been proved or admitted to be linked to your personal injury claim.

(m) *Success fee*

The percentage of basic charges that we add to your bill if you win your claim for damages and that we will seek to recover from your opponent.

(n) *Win*

Your claim for damages is finally decided in your favour, whether by a court decision or an agreement to pay you damages. 'Finally' means that your opponent:

- is not allowed to appeal against the court decision; or

- has not appealed in time; or

- has lost any appeal.

4. What happens if you win?

If you win:

- You are then liable to pay all our basic charges, our disbursements and success fee—please see condition 3(n).

- Normally, you will be entitled to recover part or all of our basic charges, our disbursements and success fee from your opponent.

- If you and your opponent cannot agree the amount, the court will decide how much you can recover. If the amount agreed or allowed by the court does not cover all our basic charges and our disbursements, then you pay the difference.

- You will not be entitled to recover from your opponent the part of the success fee that relates to the cost to us of postponing receipt of our charges and our disbursements. This remains payable by you.

- You agree that after winning, the reasons for setting the success fee at the amount stated may be disclosed:

  (i) to the court and any other person required by the court;
  (ii) to your opponent in order to gain his or her agreement to pay the success fee.

- If the court carries out an assessment and disallows any of the success fee percentage because it is unreasonable in view of what we knew or should have known when it was agreed, then that amount ceases to be payable unless the court is satisfied that it should continue to be payable.

- If we agree with your opponent that the success fee is to be paid at a lower percentage than is set out in this agreement, then the success fee percentage will be reduced accordingly unless the court is satisfied that the full amount is payable.

- It may happen that your opponent makes an offer that includes payment of our basic charges and a success fee. If so, unless we consent, you agree not to tell us to accept the offer if it includes payment of the success fee at a lower rate than is set out in this agreement.

- If your opponent is receiving Community Legal Service funding, we are unlikely to get any money from him or her. So if this happens, you have to pay us our basic charges, disbursements and success fee.

You remain ultimately responsible for paying our success fee. You agree to pay into a designated account any cheque received by you or by us from your opponent and made payable to you. Out of the money, you agree to let us take the balance of the basic charges; success fee; insurance premium; our remaining disbursements; and VAT. You take the rest.

We are allowed to keep any interest your opponent pays on the charges.

Payment for advocacy is explained in condition 6.

If your opponent fails to pay

If your opponent does not pay any damages or charges owed to you, we have the right to take recovery action in your name to enforce a judgment, order or agreement. The charges of this action become part of the basic charges.

5. What happens if you lose?

If you lose, you do not have to pay any of our basic charges or success fee. You do have to pay:

- us for our disbursements;

- your opponent's legal charges and disbursements.

If you are insured against payment of these amounts by your insurance policy, we will make a claim on your behalf and receive any resulting payment in your name. We will give you a statement of account for all money received and paid out.

If your opponent pays the charges of any hearing, they belong to us.
Payment for advocacy is dealt with in condition 6.

6. Payment for advocacy

The cost of advocacy and any other work by us, or by any solicitor agent on our behalf, forms part of our basic charges. We shall discuss with you the identity of any barrister instructed, and the arrangements made for payment.

Barristers who have a conditional fee agreement with us

If you win, you are normally entitled to recover their fee and success fee from your opponent. The barrister's success fee is shown in the separate conditional fee agreement we make with the barrister. We will discuss the barrister's success fee with you before we instruct him or her. If you lose, you pay the barrister nothing.

Barristers who do not have a conditional fee agreement with us

If you win, then you will normally be entitled to recover all or part of their fee from your opponent. If you lose, then you must pay their fee.

7. What happens when this agreement ends before your claim for damages ends?

(a) Paying us if you end this agreement

You can end the agreement at any time. We then have the right to decide whether you must:

- pay our basic charges and our disbursements including barristers' fees when we ask for them; or

- pay our basic charges, and our disbursements including barristers' fees and success fees if you go on to win your claim for damages.

(b) Paying us if we end this agreement

(i) We can end this agreement if you do not keep to your responsibilities in condition 2. We then have the right to decide whether you must:

  - pay our basic charges and our disbursements including barristers' fees when we ask for them; or
  - pay our basic charges and our disbursements including barristers' fees and success fees if you go on to win your claim for damages.

(ii) We can end this agreement if we believe you are unlikely to win. If this happens, you will only have to pay our disbursements. These will include barristers' fees if the barrister does not have a conditional fee agreement with us.

(iii) We can end this agreement if you reject our opinion about making a settlement with your opponent. You must then:

  - pay the basic charges and our disbursements,

  including barristers' fees;

  - pay the success fee if you go on to win your claim for damages.

  If you ask us to get a second opinion from a specialist solicitor outside our firm, we will do so. You pay the cost of a second opinion.

(iv) We can end this agreement if you do not pay your insurance premium when asked to do so.

(c)   Death

This agreement automatically ends if you die before your claim for damages is concluded. We will be entitled to recover our basic charges up to the date of your death from your estate.

If your personal representatives wish to continue your claim for damages, we may offer them a new conditional fee agreement, as long as they agree to pay the success fee on our basic charges from the beginning of the agreement with you.

8.   What happens after this agreement ends

After this agreement ends, we will apply to have our name removed from the record of any court proceedings in which we are acting unless you have another form of funding and ask us to work for you.

We have the right to preserve our lien unless another solicitor working for you undertakes to pay us what we are owed including a success fee if you win.

NOTES for Accident Line Protect cases

- For Accident Line Protect cases, you need to annex the following clause to the agreement

'Accident Line Protect insurance (ALP)

Accident Line Protect is an insurance policy only made available to you by solicitors who have joined the Accident Line Protect scheme.

You agree to pay a premium of £[ ] for Accident Line Protect Insurance when you sign this agreement. We undertake to send this to the broker on your behalf. If you lose after proceedings have been issued, Accident Line Protect will cover our disbursements and your opponent's charges and disbursements. It will not cover fees to your barristers or advocates. The maximum cover is £100,000.

If this agreement ends before your claim for damages ends, Accident Line Protect ends automatically at the same time.'

© The Law Society, July 1995

CONDITIONAL FEES—CHECKLIST FOR USE WITH MODEL CONDITIONAL FEE AGREEMENT

The following is a non-exhaustive list of issues which should be considered *before* signing the conditional fee agreement.

HAVE YOU.........

1. TAKEN into account the overriding objective and proportionality in considering the potential net benefit of the case to your client?

2. CONSIDERED whether the case could be allocated to the Small Claims Track and the costs implications if that occurred?

3. CHECKED that you have the correct model agreement for this type of case?

4. UNDERTAKEN a thorough risk assessment?

5. APPLIED your risk assessment to your success fee, taking account of:

- the prospects of success/failure

- payments on account/financial subsidy

- the risk that losing cases often have higher costs than winning ones and when setting your success fee,

- considered the element of the success fee relating to financial subsidy separately.

- recorded your reasons in writing and provided a copy to your client?

6. CONSIDERED the possibility of achieving success on liability but failure on enforceability?

7. DISCUSSED with your client whether a barrister will be used ? If so, have you discussed:

- whether the barrister will be instructed on a conditional fee agreement?

- whether the conditional fee agreement with the barrister will be on the same terms as the conditional fee agreement with the client eg success fee?

8. EXPLAINED to your client the information required by the Conditional Fee Regulations:

- the circumstances which will make them liable to pay your costs or disbursements and discussed how the client will fund these amounts;

- when they can seek assessment of your costs and the procedure for doing so;

- the circumstances which will make them liable to pay the costs of any other party;

- whether their risk of becoming liable for costs is insured under an existing contract of insurance;

- other methods of financing costs;

- whether you believe a particular contract of insurance is appropriate (this should be confirmed in writing);

- the requirement of their consent to disclose to the court or opponent at the end of the case the reasons for setting the success fee?

9. CHECKED whether your client's proposed insurance will meet the other side's costs, if a Part 36 offer or payment is not beaten?

10. THOUGHT through the different clauses which can be used regarding Part 36 offers and payments? (There are two possible options if ALP insurance is used. Other insurers may have different approaches. Check the requirements of your AEI—they may specify the approach you must take.)

11. EXPLAINED to your client the information on costs required by the Solicitors' Costs Information and Client Care Code 1999?

Remember the Code imposes a duty on you to:

- give to your client the best costs information possible—paragraphs 4 (a) and (c)

- keep your client updated about costs as the matter progresses— paragraph 6.

12. EXPLAINED to your client that the agreement prevents the client from instructing you to accept an offer to settle which does not provide for your full success fee?

13. MADE SURE the agreement:

- specifies the proceedings to which it relates;

- will be signed by you and your client;

- specifies the reasons for setting the success fee, and specifies how much of the success fee, if any, relates to the cost of financial subsidy;

- deals with appropriate funding methods and the insurance position?

APIL/PIBA 5

CONDITIONAL FEE AGREEMENT

INDEX TO PARAGRAPHS

Counsel's entitlement to fees on termination of the agreement:

23   Fees on termination

24   Challenge to fees

25   Return of work

Assessment and payment of fees:

26   Costs Assessment

27   Solicitors obligation to pay

28   Interest

29   Challenge to Success Fee

Disclosing the reasons for the success fee

30   Disclosing the reasons for the success fee

Counsel's fees in the event of assessment or agreement:

31   Reduction on assessment

32   Agreement of fees

NOTES: These paragraphs need to be completed by counsel or counsel's clerk: 1; 2; 3; 10(10); 16; 17(1), (2) & (3); 25(1).

CONDITIONAL FEE AGREEMENT

between

SOLICITORS AND COUNSEL

THE NATURE OF THE AGREEMENT

1.   In this agreement:

"Counsel means: _____

and any other counsel either from Chambers or recommended by counsel in accordance with clause 25 who signs this agreement at any time at the solicitors request;

"the solicitor" means the firm:

Messrs: _____

"the client means: _____

[acting by his Litigation Friend _____]

"Chambers" means members of chambers at _____

2.   This agreement forms the basis on which instructions are accepted by counsel from the solicitor to act on a conditional fee basis for the client in his/her claim against: _____ ("the Opponent(s)") for damages for personal injuries suffered on: _____ until

(1)   the claim is won, lost or otherwise concluded or

(2)   this agreement is terminated.

3.   This agreement relates to

(1)   issues of jurisdiction;

(2)   issues of breach of duty;

(3)   issues of causation;

(4)   issues of limitation

(5)   issues of damages;

(6)   any appeal by the client's opponent(s);

(7)   any appeal by the client against an interim order;

(8)   any appeal by the client advised by counsel;

(9)   any proceedings to enforce a judgment or order.

It does not cover:

(10) any other appeal by the client;

(11) any counterclaim or defence by way of set-off;

(12) any part 20 claim

(13) part only of the proceedings unless specifically incorporated in this agreement.

[NOTE: delete those parts of the proceedings to which the agreement does NOT relate]

4.   This agreement is not a contract enforceable at law. The relationship of counsel and solicitor shall be governed by the Terms of Work under which barristers offer their services to solicitors and the Withdrawal of Credit Scheme as authorised by the General Council of the Bar as from time to time amended and set out in the Code of Conduct of the Bar of England and Wales, save that where such terms of work are inconsistent with the terms of this agreement the latter shall prevail.

5.   Counsel has been provided with:

(1)   A copy of the conditional fee agreement between the solicitor and the client and the Law Society's Conditions as they apply to the claim;

(2)   written confirmation that "after the event" or other similar insurance is in place, or a written explanation why it is not; and

(3)   where more than one defendant is sued, copies of correspondence between the solicitor and the "after the event" insurers clarifying whether and when defendants costs are to be covered if the claimant does not succeed or win against all of the defendants; and

(4)   all relevant papers and risk assessment material, including all advice from experts and other solicitors or barristers to the client or any Litigation Friend in respect of the claim, which is currently available to the solicitor.

(5)   Any offers of settlement already made by the client or the defendant.

6.   The solicitor confirms that:

(1)   he/she has complied with Regulation 4 of the Conditional Fee Agreements Regulations 2000 no 692 and the client has confirmed by signing the solicitor/client agreement that Regulation 4 has been complied with; and

(2)   the client or any Litigation Friend has consented to the terms and conditions set out in this agreement insofar as they relate to the client.

(3)   Either:

    (a)   there are no other methods of financing costs available to the client, or

    (b)   Notwithstanding there are other methods of financing costs available to the client, namely ....
............., the client has reasonably decided to fund this claim with conditional fees.

7.   Counsel is not bound to act on a conditional fee basis until he/she has signed this agreement.

OBLIGATIONS OF COUNSEL

8.   Counsel agrees to act diligently on all proper instructions from the solicitor subject to paragraph 9 hereof.

9.   Counsel is not bound to accept instructions:

(1)   to appear at an interlocutory hearing where it would be reasonable

    (a)   to assume that counsel's fees would not be allowed on assessment or

    (b)   to instruct a barrister of less experience and seniority, provided that counsel has first used his/her best endeavours to ensure that an appropriate barrister will act for the client on the same terms as this agreement;

(2)   to draft documents or advise if a barrister of similar seniority would not ordinarily be instructed so to do if not instructed on a conditional fee basis;

(3)   outside the scope of this agreement.

OBLIGATIONS OF THE SOLICITOR

10.   The solicitor agrees:

(1)   promptly to supply a copy of this agreement to the client or any Litigation Friend;

(2)   to comply with all the requirements of the CPR, the practice direction about costs supplementing parts 43 to 48 of the CPR (PD Costs), the relevant pre-action protocol and any court order relating to conditional fee agreements and in particular promptly to notify the Court and the opponent of the existence and any subsequent variation of the CFA with the client and whether he/she has taken out an insurance policy or made an arrangement with a membership organisation and of the fact that additional liabilities are being claimed from the opponent.

(3) promptly to apply for relief from sanction pursuant to CPR part 3.8 if any default under part 44.3B(1)(c) or (d) occurs and to notify counsel of any such default.

(4) to act diligently in all dealings with counsel and the prosecution of the claim;

(5) to consult counsel on the need for advice and action following:

    (a) the service of statements of case and if possible before the allocation decision; and

    (b) the exchange of factual and expert evidence;

(6) to deliver within a reasonable time papers reasonably requested by counsel for consideration;

(7) promptly to bring to counsel's attention:

    (a) any priority or equivalent report to insurers;

    (b) any Part 36 or other offer to settle;

    (c) any Part 36 payment into Court;

    (d) any evidence information or communication which may materially affect the merits of any issue in the case;

    (e) any other factor coming to the solicitor's attention which may affect counsel's entitlement to success fees whether before or after the termination of this agreement.

(8) promptly to communicate to the client any advice by counsel:

    (a) to make, accept or reject any Part 36 or other offer;

    (b) to accept or reject any Part 36 payment in;

    (c) to incur, or not incur, expenditure in obtaining evidence or preparing the case;

    (d) to instruct Leading counsel or a more senior or specialised barrister;

    (e) that the case is likely to be lost;

    (f) that damages and costs recoverable on success make it unreasonable or uneconomic for the action to proceed;

(9) promptly to inform counsel's clerk of any listing for trial;

(10) to deliver the brief for trial not less than .... weeks/days before the trial;

(11) if any summary assessment of costs takes place in the absence of counsel, to submit to the court a copy of counsel's risk assessment and make representations on counsel's behalf in relation to his/her fees;

(12) to inform counsel in writing within 2 days of any reduction of counsel's fees on summary assessment in the absence of counsel and of any directions given under PDCosts 20.3(1) or alternatively to make application for such directions on counsel's behalf;

(13) where points of dispute are served pursuant to CPR part 47.9 seeking a reduction in any percentage increase charged by counsel on his fees, to give the client the written explanation required by PDCosts 20.5 on counsel's behalf;

(14) where more than one defendant is sued, the solicitor will write to the "after the event" insurers clarifying whether and when defendants costs are to be covered if the claimant does not succeed or win against all of the defendants, and send that correspondence to counsel.

(15) When drawing up a costs bill at any stage of the case to include in it a claim for interest on counsel's fees.

TERMINATION OF THE AGREEMENT BY COUNSEL

11.   Counsel may terminate the agreement if :

(1) Counsel discovers that the solicitor is in breach of any obligation in paragraph 10 hereof;

(2) the solicitor client or any Litigation Friend rejects counsel's advice in any respect set out in paragraph 10(8) hereof;

(3) Counsel is informed or discovers the existence of any set-off or counter-claim which materially affects the likelihood of success and/or the amount of financial recovery in the event of success;

(4) Counsel is informed or discovers the existence of information which has been falsified or knowingly withheld by the solicitor client or any Litigation Friend, of which counsel was not aware and which counsel could not reasonably have anticipated, which materially affects the merits of any substantial issue in the case;

(5) Counsel is required to cease to act by the Code of Conduct of the Bar of England and Wales or counsel's professional conduct is being impugned;

provided that counsel may not terminate the agreement if so to do would be a breach of that Code, and notice of any termination must be communicated promptly in writing to the solicitor.

TERMINATION OF THE AGREEMENT BY THE SOLICITOR

12.   The solicitor may terminate the agreement at any time on the instructions of the client or any Litigation Friend.

AUTOMATIC TERMINATION OF THE AGREEMENT

13.   This agreement shall automatically terminate if:

(1) Counsel accepts a full-time judicial appointment;

(2) Counsel retires from practice;

(3) the solicitor's agreement with the client is terminated before the conclusion of the case;

(4) Legal Services Commission funding is granted to the client;

(5) the client dies;

(6) The court makes a Group Litigation Order covering this claim.

CLIENT BECOMING UNDER A DISABILITY

14.   If the client at any time becomes under a disability then the solicitor will:

(1)   consent to a novation of his Conditional Fee Agreement with the client to the Litigation Friend and

(2)   where appropriate, apply to the Court to obtain its consent to acting under a conditional fee agreement with the Litigation Friend.

Thereafter, the Litigation Friend shall, for the purposes of this agreement, be treated as if he/she was and has always been the client.

COUNSEL TAKING SILK

15.   If counsel becomes Queen's Counsel during the course of the agreement then either party may terminate it provided he/she does so promptly in writing.

COUNSEL'S NORMAL FEES

16.   (1) Counsel's fees upon which a success fee will be calculated (the normal fees) will be as follows:

(a)   Advisory work and drafting
In accordance with counsel's hourly rate obtaining for such work in this field currently £.................... per hour.

(b)   Court appearances

    (i)   Brief fee

        (a)   Trial

        For a trial whose estimated duration is up to 2 days (including— hours of preparation) £.................... , 3 to 5 days (includ- ing—hours of preparation) £.................... , 5 to 8 days (in- cluding—hours of preparation) £.................... , 8 to 12 days (including—hours of preparation), £.................... , and 13 to 20 days (including—hours of preparation) £.................... .

        (b)   Interlocutory hearings

        For an interlocutory hearing whose estimated duration is up to 1 hour (including—hours of preparation), £.................... , 1 hour to 1/2 day (including—hours of preparation) £.................... , 1/2 day to 1 day (including hrs of preparation) £.................... , over 1 day (including—hours of preparation) will be charged as if it was a trial.

    (ii)   Refreshers

In accordance with counsel's daily rate obtaining for such work in this field, currently £.................... , per day.

    (iii)   Renegotiating counsel's fees

        (a)   To the extent that the hours of preparation set out above are reasonably exceeded then counsel's hourly rate will apply to each additional hour of preparation.

(b)   If the case is settled or goes short counsel will consider the solicitor's reasonable requests to reduce his/her brief fees set out above.

(2)   The normal fees will be subject to review with effect from each successive anniversary of the date of this agreement but counsel will not increase the normal fees by more than any increase in the rate of inflation measured by the Retail Prices Index.

COUNSEL'S SUCCESS FEE

17.   (1) The rate of counsel's success fee will be ....% of counsel's normal fees;

(2) The reasons, briefly stated, for counsel's success fee are that at the time of entry into this agreement:

(i)   the prospects of success are estimated by counsel as .... (X)% as more fully set out in counsel's risk assessment, and a percentage increase of .... (Y)% reflects those prospects
(ii)   the length of postponement of the payment of counsel's fees and expenses is estimated at ... year, and a further increase of .... (Z)% relates to that postponement

[Note: the success fee at paragraph 17(1) must be the sum of Y% and Z%]

(3) The reasons for counsel's success fee are more fully set out in counsel's risk assessment which is*/ is not*(*please delete as appropriate) attached to this agreement.

COUNSEL'S EXPENSES

18.   If a hearing, conference or view takes place more than 25 miles from counsel's chambers the solicitor shall pay counsel's reasonable travel and accommodation expenses which shall:

(1)   appear separately on counsel's fee note;

(2)   attract no success fee and

(3)   subject to paragraph 21 be payable on the conclusion of the claim or earlier termination of this agreement.

COUNSEL'S ENTITLEMENT TO FEES—WINNING AND LOSING

[IF THE AGREEMENT IS NOT TERMINATED]

19.   (1) "Success" means the same as "win" in the Conditional Fee Agreement between the solicitor and the client.

(2) Subject to paragraphs 20, 23 & 26 hereof, in the event of success the solicitor will pay counsel his/her normal and success fees.

(3) If the client is successful at an interim hearing counsel may apply for summary assessment of solicitors basics costs and counsels normal fees.

20.   If the amount of damages and interest awarded by a court is less than a Part 36 payment into Court or effective Part 36 offer then:

(1)   if counsel advised its rejection he/she is entitled to normal and success fees for work up to receipt of the notice of Part 36 payment into Court or offer but only normal fees for subsequent work;

(2)   if counsel advised its acceptance he/she is entitled to normal and success fees for all work done.

21.   Subject to paragraph 22(1) hereof, if the case is lost or on counsel's advice ends without success then counsel is not entitled to any fees or expenses.

ERRORS AND INDEMNITY FOR FEES

22.   (1) If, because of a breach by the solicitor but not counsel of his/her duty to the client, the client's claim is dismissed or struck out:

(a)   for non-compliance with an interlocutory order; or

(b)   for want of prosecution, or

(c)   by rule of court or the Civil Procedure Rules; or becomes unenforceable against the MIB for breach of the terms of the Uninsured Drivers Agreement:

the solicitor shall (subject to sub paragraphs (3)–(6) hereof) pay counsel such normal fees as would have been recoverable under this agreement.

(2) If, because of a breach by counsel but not the solicitor of his/her duty to the client, the client's claim is dismissed or struck out:

(a)   for non-compliance with an interlocutory order; or

(b)   for want of prosecution, or

(c)   by rule of court or the Civil Procedure Rules

counsel shall (subject to sub paragraphs (3)–(6) hereof) pay the solicitor such basic costs as would have been recoverable from the client under the solicitor's agreement with the client.

(3) If, because of non-compliance by the solicitor but not by counsel of the obligations under sub-paragraphs (2), (3), (11), (12) or (13) of paragraph 10 above, counsel's success fee is not payable by the Opponent or the client then the solicitor shall (subject to sub-paragraphs (5) to (7) hereof) pay counsel such success fees as would have been recoverable under this agreement.

(4) No payment shall be made under sub paragraph (1), (2) or (3) hereof in respect of any breach by the solicitor or counsel which would not give rise to a claim for damages if an action were brought by the client;

Adjudication on disagreement

(5) In the event of any disagreement as to whether there has been an actionable breach by either the solicitor or counsel, or as to the amount payable under sub paragraph (1), (2) or (3) hereof, that disagreement shall be

referred to adjudication by a panel consisting of a Barrister nominated by PIBA and a solicitor nominated by APIL who shall be requested to resolve the issue on written representations and on the basis of a procedure laid down by agreement between PIBA and APIL. The costs of such adjudication shall, unless otherwise ordered by the panel, be met by the unsuccessful party.

(6) In the event of a panel being appointed pursuant to sub paragraph (5) hereof:

(a)   if that panel considers, after initial consideration of the disagreement, that there is a real risk that they may not be able to reach a unanimous decision, then the panel shall request APIL (where it is alleged there has been an actionable breach by the solicitor) or PIBA (where it is alleged that the has been an actionable breach by counsel) to nominate a third member of the panel;

(b)   that panel shall be entitled if it considers it reasonably necessary, to appoint a qualified costs draftsman, to be nominated by the President for the time being of the Law Society, to assist the panel;

(c)   the solicitor or counsel alleged to be in breach of duty shall be entitled to argue that, on the basis of information reasonably available to both solicitor and barrister, the claim would not have succeeded in any event. The panel shall resolve such issue on the balance of probabilities, and if satisfied that the claim would have been lost in any event shall not make any order for payment of fees or costs.

Cap

(7) the amount payable in respect of any claim under sub paragraph (1) or (2) or (3) shall be limited to a maximum of £25,000.

COUNSEL'S ENTITLEMENT TO FEES ON TERMINATION

OF THE AGREEMENT

23.   (1) Termination by counsel If counsel terminates the agreement under paragraph 11 then, subject to sub-paragraphs (b) and (c) hereof, counsel may elect either:

(a)   to receive payment of normal fees without a success fee which the solicitor shall pay not later than three months after termination: ("Option A"), or

(b)   to await the outcome of the case and receive payment of normal and success fees if it ends in success: ("Option B").

(2) If counsel terminates the agreement because the solicitor, client or Litigation Friend rejects advice under paragraph 10(8)(e) hereof counsel is not entitled to any fee.

(3) If counsel terminates the agreement because the solicitor, client or Litigation Friend rejects advice under paragraph 10(8)(f) counsel is entitled only to "Option B".

(4) Termination by the solicitor If the solicitor terminates the agreement under paragraph 12, counsel is entitled to elect between "Option A" and "Option B".

(5) Automatic Termination and counsel taking silk

(a) If the agreement terminates under paragraph 13(1) (judicial appointment) or 13(2) (retirement) or 15 (counsel taking silk) counsel is entitled only to "Option B".

(b) If the agreement terminates under paragraph 13(3) (termination of the solicitor/client agreement) then counsel is entitled to elect between "Option A" and "Option B" save that:

   (i) if the solicitor has ended the solicitor/client agreement because he considers that the client is likely to lose and at the time of that termination counsel considers that the client is likely to win, and the client goes on to win, the solicitor will pay counsel's normal and success fees;

   (ii) if the solicitor has ended the solicitor/client agreement because the client has rejected the advice of the solicitor or counsel about making a settlement the solicitor will pay counsel's normal fee in any event and, if the client goes on to win the case, will also pay counsel's success fee.

(c) If the agreement terminates under paragraph 13(4) (Legal Services Commission) or paragraph 13(5) (death of client) or paragraph 13(6) (group litigation order) counsel is entitled only to "Option B".

24. If the client or any Litigation Friend wishes to challenge:

(a) the entitlement to fees of counsel or the level of such fees following termination of the agreement or

(b) any refusal by counsel after signing this agreement to accept instructions the solicitor must make such challenge in accordance with the provisions of paragraphs 14 and 15 of the Terms of Work upon which barristers offer their services to solicitors (Annex D to the Code of Conduct of the Bar of England and Wales).

RETURN OF WORK

25. If counsel in accordance with the Bar's Code of Conduct is obliged to return any brief or instructions in this case to another barrister, then:

(1) Counsel will use his/her best endeavours to ensure that an appropriate barrister agrees to act for the client on the same terms as this agreement;

if counsel is unable to secure an appropriate replacement barrister to act for the client on the same terms as this agreement counsel will

   *(a) be responsible for any additional barristers' fees reasonably incurred by the solicitor or client and shall pay the additional fees to the solicitor promptly upon request and in any event within 3 months of such a request by the solicitor

   *(b) not be responsible for any additional fee incurred by the solicitor or client.

(2)   Subject to paragraph 25(3) hereof, if the case ends in success counsel's fees for work done shall be due and paid on the conditional fee basis contained in this agreement whether or not the replacement barrister acts on a conditional fee basis; but

(3)   if the solicitor or client rejects any advice by the replacement barrister of the type described in paragraph 10(8) hereof, the solicitor shall immediately notify counsel whose fees shall be paid as set out in paragraph 23(1) hereof.

[NOTE: delete 25(1)(a) or 25(1)(b)]

ASSESSMENT AND PAYMENT OF COSTS / FEES

26.   (1)   If:

(a)   a costs order is anticipated or made in favour of the client at an interlocutory hearing and the costs are summarily assessed at the hearing; or

(b)   the costs of an interlocutory hearing are agreed between the parties in favour of the client; or

(c)   an interlocutory order or agreement for costs to be assessed in detail and paid forthwith is made in favour of the client:

then

> (i)   the solicitor will include in the statement of costs a full claim for counsel's normal fees; and
> (ii)   the solicitor will promptly conclude by agreement or assessment the question of such costs; and
> (iii)   within one month of receipt of such costs the solicitor will pay to counsel the amount recovered in respect of his/her fees, such sum to be set off against counsel's entitlement to normal fees by virtue of this agreement.

27.   (1)   The amounts of fees and expenses payable to counsel under this agreement

(a)   are not limited by reference to the damages which may be recovered on behalf of the client and

(b)   are payable whether or not the solicitor is or will be paid by the client or opponent.

(2) Upon success the solicitor will promptly conclude by agreement or assessment the question of costs and within one month after receipt of such costs the solicitor will pay to counsel the full sum due under this agreement.

28.   The solicitor will use his best endeavours to recover interest on costs from any party ordered to pay costs to the client and shall pay counsel the share of such interest that has accrued on counsel's outstanding fees.

29.   (1) The solicitor will inform counsel's clerk in good time of any challenge made to his success fee and of the date, place and time of any detailed costs assessment the client or opponent has taken out pursuant to

the Civil Procedure Rules and unless counsel is present or represented at the assessment hearing will place counsel's risk assessment, relevant details and any written representations before the assessing judge and argue counsel's case for his/her success fee.

(2) If counsel's fees are reduced on any assessment then:

(a) the solicitor will inform counsel's clerk within seven days and confer with counsel whether to apply under Regulation 3(2)(b) of the CFA Regulations 2000 for an order that the client should pay the success fee and make such application on counsel's behalf;

(b) subject to any appeal, counsel will accept such fees as are allowed on that assessment and will repay forthwith to the solicitor any excess previously paid.

30. Disclosing the reasons for the success fee

(1) If

(a) a success fee becomes payable as a result of the client's claim and

(b) any fees subject to the increase provided for by paragraph 17(1) hereof are assessed and

(c) Counsel, the solicitor or the client is required by the court to disclose to the court or any other person the reasons for setting such increase as the level stated in this agreement,

he/she may do so.

31. Counsel's fees in the event of assessment or agreement If any fees subject to the said percentage increase are assessed and any amount of that increase is disallowed on assessment on the ground that the level at which the increase was set was unreasonable in view of the facts which were or should have been known to counsel at the time it was set, such amount ceases to be payable under this agreement unless the court is satisfied that it should continue to be so payable.

32. If the Opponent offers to pay the client's legal fees at a lower sum than is due under this agreement then the solicitor:

(a) will calculate the proposed pro-rata reductions of the normal and success fees of both solicitor and counsel, and

(b) inform counsel of the offer and the calculations supporting the proposed pro-rata reductions referred to in paragraph (a) above, and

(c) will not accept the offer without counsel's express consent.

If such an agreement is reached on fees, then counsel's fees shall be limited to the agreed sum unless the court orders otherwise.

Dated: _____

Signed by counsel _____

or by his/her clerk [with counsel's authority] _____

*[Additional interlocutory counsel _____]

*[Additional interlocutory counsel _____]

*see paragraph 1

Signed by : _____

Solicitor/employee in Messrs: _____

The solicitors firm acting for the client:

By signing and today returning to counsel the last page of this agreement by fax the solicitor agrees to instruct counsel under the terms of this agreement and undertakes to furnish counsel within 14 days of today with hard copies of the signed agreement together with any documents under paragraph 5 of this agreement which are not already in counsel's possession.

PART 7: COUNSEL'S RISK ASSESSMENT

to help counsel make a Risk Assessment *(1)* and give a Statement of Reasons *(2)* for Conditional Fees in Personal Injury Cases

	Ready Reckoner	
1. **Parties**: Csl's Ref: .... Sol's Ref:		
Names of Client (*& Litigation Friend)	**Prospects of**	**Basic**
	"Success"	**Uplift**
and Defendant(s)	100%	0%
(*actual/intended)	95%	5%
2. **Proceedings**: Date of injury	90%	11%
Nature of claim	80%	25%
If the proposed CFA is intended to apply to part only of the proceedings, specify to which	75%	33%
part(s):	70%	43%
....	67%	50%
3. **"Success"** is achieving, by final judgment or	60%	66%
agreement, the entitlement to damages for the claimant[3]. Specify any alternative definition of	50%	100%
success that might be intended:		
....		
4. **Information on which assessment based**[4]: Instructing solicitor ("Sol") provided Csl with instructions, see copy attached, date stamped		
....		
and the documents listed there.		

5. The prospects of success *(5)* are estimated by Csl as ....

6. Csl's Success Fee will be a % increase on his/her normal fees. The % increase in this case will be ....% which comprises the following elements:

a.   An element to reflect the prospects of success (see Ready Reckoner) ....%

b.   An element relating to the cost to Csl of the postponement of the payment of fees & expenses *(6)* ....%

....

Total: ....%

[Sol's uplift. ....%]

7. Statement of Reasons*(7)* Csl's reasons for setting the % increase at the level stated are: (here state the particular risks identified in the risk assessment. N.B. The ordinary risks of litigation are deemed to be incorporated into this statement of reasons and do not need to be repeated here unless a particular risk is heightened on the facts of this case)

[Continue on a separate sheet or attach another document if necessary]

8. Further considerations: Current APIL/PIBA 5 Agreement?   y/n Case requiring screening? Y/n   Csl has reason to believe the client is/may be, a child or patient y/n A leader is likely to be needed y/n This Statement of Reasons is to be attached to the CFA? y/n   [see para. 17(3) of A/P5]

Csl's decision: *Accepted at ....% increase / Rejected &/or advised alternative funding *(8)* / ADR

Csl's note of the next step due to be taken (if instructed on conditional fees) & any comment: ....

....

11. Screened by .... on ....

Signed .... Dated ....

[PIBA Risk Assessment—18/01/2001 Adapted for use with APIL/PIBA 5]

THIS IS NOT AN ADVICE

Read the Notes Over [They form part of the statement of reasons]

NOTES (These form part of the Statement of Reasons)

(1) This risk assessment ("RA") was made by Csl for his own purposes deciding whether or not to accept instructions upon a conditional fee basis and, if so, upon what percentage increase (ie success fee). It is RA material for the purposes of para 5(4) of the APIL/PIBA 5 Model Agreement of .... ("A/P5") for use between solicitors and Csl whether or not a CFA is subsequently entered into. It also constitutes Csl's statement of reasons [referred to in Reg 3(2)(a) of the CFA Regulations 2000/692 ("the CFA Regs")] for the % increase which are to be briefly stated in para 17 of A/P5. It is not an advice to the client or the solicitor. Csl will advise as appropriate in the course of proceedings only after he has accepted instructions. Csl is referred to the Bar Council's "Conditional Fee Guidance" of February 2001 (available on www.barcouncil.org.uk) and may also contact the CFA Panel Helpline via the Bar Council.

(2) This statement of reasons for setting the % increase will be relied upon by the Costs Judge when deciding whether it is reasonable (see paras. 14.9(3) and 32.5(1)(b) of the Costs PD supplementing CPR Parts 43–48). Keep it, and any attachments, safely.

(3) Under para 19(1) of A/P5 "success" means the same as "win" in the CFA between Solicitor and Client, which defines "win" to mean: "Your claim for damages is finally decided in your favour, whether by a court decision or an agreement to pay you damages …" [Law Society Conditions, 3(n)]. Other relevant circumstances are referred to in paras 20, 23 and 26—see para 19(2) of A/P5.

(4) The reasons for Csl's % increase will be reviewed in light of the information then available (para 11.7 of the Costs PD). It is therefore essential to record what information was before counsel when the risk assessment was undertaken. This is best done by attaching a copy of the instructions and noting thereon any further information or documents subsequently received. Csl should have all the documents listed under para 5 of A/P5. Other documents to ask for include witness statements (name them and state if dated and/or signed), key documents such as police report/accident report/form/book/photos/sketch plan/GP records/Medical report(s) (give dates), pre-action protocol correspondence with details of any issues raised and offers of settlement already made by either party.

(5) Prospects of success: RA is not a science but the application of knowledge and experience to the facts as known at the time. Try to assess the prospects of success as either: A very good (80%); B Good (60–80%); C Reasonable (50–60%); D Less than evens; or E Impossible to say. These are taken from the Bar Council's guidelines for Csl's advice on the merits for legal aid. In assessing the prospects of success, have regard particularly to the definition of success applicable to this case, any identified risk that the CFA may be terminated without achieving success (eg if finely balanced whether reasonable and economic for the action to proceed under para 10(8)(f) of A/P5), and the prospects of beating any Part 36 payment or offer already made. Do not make any allowance in the percentage increase for the extra costs of CFA work in general or for the risk assessment/screening carried out in this case. See further note 7 below.

(6) This element of the percentage increase is permissible but must be specified as a separate element (Reg 3(1)(b) of the CFA Regs 2000 & see para 17(2)(ii) of A/P5). It cannot be recovered from the paying party as an additional liability (CPR 44.3B(1)(a)) and is not one of the factors listed in Costs PD11.8. The Bar Council continues to recommend $3\frac{1}{2}$% pa of expected postponement.

(7) The statement of reasons should be short and to the point, concisely recording the main risk factors influencing the risk assessment. State any perceived difficulties with jurisdiction or limitation, establishing a relevant duty, proving breach of duty, causation or quantum. State any perceived risk of adverse findings on contributory negligence, any counterclaim, set off or other likely defence. Specify the reasons why you think the claim may not end in success and otherwise why the circumstances in which Csl's normal or success fees become payable might not arise (see note 5 above). There is no need to state the obvious underlying risks which apply to all claims, some of which are set out below, because these are the ordinary risks of litigation which are relevant and which are deemed to have been included in your RA without specific mention. But state any special factor increasing such risks in this case. Ordinary risks of litigation common to all claims include: (a) the client may not pursue the claim for any reason (eg moves abroad, dies, loses

interest), is or becomes a person under a disability and the litigation friend and/or the Court does not consent to funding the action under this Agreement; (b) the claim may not be pursued to a successful conclusion if Csl advises it is likely to lose or if it becomes uneconomic or unreasonable for the action to proceed (eg the defendant or his insurer may become insolvent in the course of proceedings, eg an adverse order for costs may be made at an interlocutory hearing, eg the cost of obtaining medical evidence to prove the claim may become disproportionately high); (c) the client's or other witnesses' account of the facts may prove to be inaccurate or they may not come up to proof; (d) further evidence may come to light which is adverse to the claim (e) material evidence may be lost; (f) the Court may err in law or fact; (g) the claim may be dismissed or struck out for non-compliance with any rule.

(8) The solicitor may prefer to treat Csl's fees as a disbursement and to use after the event insurers who allow this. There are clear advantages for client, solicitor and Csl.

[Guidance Notes updated 18/01/2001]

[Extract taken from The Bar Council CFA Guidance 2001.]

Terms of engagement for preliminary work where retainer on a conditional fee basis is contemplated

This document is to be completed and used in conjunction with the covering letter to Heads of Chambers from the Vice Chairman of the Chancery Bar Association dated 21st July 2000.

1.   This agreement contains the terms and conditions upon which Counsel agrees to undertake investigation and provide advice prior to deciding whether to accept instructions on a conditional fee basis. [This agreement is/is not a contract enforceable at law.] The relationship between Counsel and Solicitor shall be governed by the Terms of Work under which barristers offer their services to solicitors and the Withdrawal of Credit Scheme as authorised by the General Council of the Bar as from time to time amended and set out in the Code of Conduct of the Bar of England and Wales, save that where such terms of work are inconsistent with the terms of this agreement the latter shall prevail.

2.   In this agreement the following expressions have the meanings set out in this paragraph:

(1)   The Action means *the action, the short title and reference to the record of which is … /*the proposed action between the Client and … for … /*the following part or parts of the action, the short title and reference to the record of which is …/*the following part or parts of the proposed action between the Client and … for … *[delete as appropriate and specify in addition whether any counterclaim and/or appeal and/or proceedings to enforce a judgment are included within the definition]*

(2)   CFA means a conditional fee agreement.

(3)   The Client means .... [acting by his/her litigation friend]

(4)   The Costs Insurance means the policy or policies of insurance providing cover against the Opposing Party's costs of the Action.

(5)   Counsel means the barrister named above as Counsel who is party to this agreement.

(6)   The Opposing Party means the defendants or proposed defendants to the Action or, where there is an issue between the Client and any other party or parties to proceedings, the determination of which is covered by the definition of success referred to in paragraph 20 below, that other party or parties.

(7)   Other acceptable counsel means other counsel who the Solicitor has agreed or does agree is acceptable for the purpose of this agreement.

(8)   The Solicitor means the solicitor or firm of solicitors who or which is party to this agreement.

(9)   The Solicitor's Conditional Fee Agreement means the Conditional Fee Agreement entered into between the Solicitor and the Client.

3.   The Solicitor will, as soon as practicable, provide Counsel with, or make available to Counsel, the following material so far as it is available (and which may in accordance with the Code of Conduct of the Bar of England and Wales be reviewed by other counsel):

(1)   Copies of all documents relevant to the Action which are reasonably available to the Client and/or to the Solicitor.

(2)   Reasonably detailed statements on the subject matter of the Action from witnesses whose evidence is available to the Client and/or the Solicitor.

(3)   Any documents containing or recording the advice or opinion of the Solicitor (and any other solicitors or other Counsel who are or have been instructed in the Action, or approached to consider entering into a conditional fee arrangement) on or relevant to the Action.

(4)   Any other documents or information relevant to the Action which Counsel reasonably requests and which are available to the Client and/or the Solicitor.

(5)   A copy of the Solicitor's Conditional Fee Agreement and the rate of uplift on the Solicitor's normal fees provided for in the Solicitor's Conditional Fee Agreement [(or as a minimum) the rate of uplift on the Solicitor's normal fees provided for in the Solicitor's Conditional Fee Agreement].

(6)   A copy of the Costs Insurance (including all relevant schedules, slips or documents containing the terms of the Costs Insurance) or, if none, an explanation as to why there is none and an explanation as to how any interlocutory or final costs orders will be met.

4.   Counsel will thereafter advise whether s/he requires to see the Client or any witnesses whose evidence is available to the Client or the Solicitor in conference, and, if s/he does, the Solicitor will arrange such conference or conferences to take place. Such conferences may be attended by other acceptable counsel.

5.   After being provided with the material described in paragraph 3 above and after any conference required under paragraph 4 above, Counsel will:

(1)   advise either in writing or in conference on the merits of the action;

(2)   indicate whether s/he is prepared, subject to agreeing the terms to be included in a CFA, to act in the Action on a conditional fee basis.

6.   Counsel's fees in respect of work carried out pursuant to this agreement shall be calculated in accordance with his/her hourly rate for the type of work involved, namely £ per hour.

7.   In the event that Counsel and the Solicitor do not enter into a CFA:

(1)   the Solicitor shall pay to Counsel his/her fees for work carried out pursuant to this agreement within [3 months of receiving a fee note] and regardless of whether the Solicitor is paid by the Client; and

(2)   the Solicitor is free to request Counsel to continue to act in the Action other than on a conditional fee basis. If the Solicitor does so request, Counsel will agree to continue to act on a normal fee basis under the Terms of Work referred to in paragraph 1 hereof.

8.   In the event that Counsel and the Solicitor do enter into a CFA:

*Counsel shall not be entitled to any fees in respect of the work done pursuant to this agreement

*the Solicitor shall pay to Counsel his/her fees in respect of work done pursuant to this agreement in any event at the rate specified in this agreement, such fees to be paid within 3 months of delivery of the fee note.

*the Solicitor shall pay to Counsel his/her fees in respect of work done pursuant to this agreement in accordance with the terms of the CFA, save that that in the event that Counsel is entitled to be paid fees at the Base Rate or the Reduced Rate in any event during the course of the Action the fees to which Counsel is entitled to be paid pursuant to this agreement shall be paid within 3 months of the delivery of the fee note in respect of those fees.

*the Solicitor shall, but only in the event that the action ends in success (as that term is defined in the CFA), pay to Counsel his/her fees in respect of work done pursuant to this agreement at the rate specified in this agreement.

*[*Delete three of the above as appropriate. The third option is appropriate only if the CFA includes paragraph 18 of the draft CFA.]*

CHANCERY BAR ASSOCIATION

TERMS OF ENGAGEMENT FOR USE WHERE COUNSEL IS TO BE RETAINED ON A CONDITIONAL FEE BASIS

This document is to be completed and used in conjunction with the covering letter to Heads of Chambers from the Vice Chairman of the Chancery Bar Association dated 21st July 2000.

INDEX OF PARAGRAPHS

15. The Uplifted Rate.

16. The Reduced Rate.

17. Disclosure of reasons for Uplift.

Payment of Counsel's fees

18. Fees in respect of the Preliminary Agreement.

19. Payment of fees in the event of Success and Counsel's retainer is not terminated.

20. Meaning of Success.

21. Part 36 offers.

22. Payment of fees in the event of Failure.

23. Payment of fees in the event of Failure as a result of breach by the Solicitor.

24. Payment of costs to the Solicitor in the event of Failure as a result of breach by Counsel of his/her duty to the Client.

25. Payment of fees in the event of termination by Solicitor before determination of the Action: General.

26. Payment of fees in the event of termination by Solicitor before determination of the Action: termination without cause or as a result of breakdown of relationship.

27. Payment of fees in the event of termination by Solicitor before determination of the Action: Counsel becoming unavailable for the trial.

28. Payment of fees in the event of termination by Solicitor before determination of the Action: good reason to believe that Counsel manifested incompetence.

29. Payment of fees in the event of termination by Counsel: termination under paragraph 11.

30. Payment of fees in the event of termination by Counsel: termination under paragraph 12.

31. Payment of base rate fees in any event.

32. Repayment of base rate fees in the event of failure.

33. Information and further payment.

34. Interim payment: Immediate Payment of base rate fees.

35. Interim payment: payment of fees in the event of success.

36. Interim payment: repayment of base rate fees in the event of failure.

37. Interlocutory costs award: Immediate payment of fees.

38. Effect of reduction of fees payable by reason of assessment.

39. Effect of reduction of fees payable by agreement.

40. Interest.

41. Disbursements.

42. Payment of fees whether or not Solicitor is paid.

Rights to challenge and dispute resolution

43. Right to refer dispute to arbitration.

44. Costs of arbitrators/umpire.

45. Counsel's right to argue causation.

46. Time limit for reference to arbitration.

This document records the terms of engagement ("this agreement") between .... ("Counsel") of [Address] and .... ("Solicitor")

1. This agreement contains the terms and conditions upon which Counsel agrees to act in the Action on behalf of the Client. [This agreement is/is not a contract enforceable at law.] The relationship between Counsel and Solicitor shall be governed by the Terms of Work under which barristers offer their services to solicitors and the Withdrawal of Credit Scheme as authorised by the General Council of the Bar as from time to time amended and set out in the Code of Conduct of the Bar of England and Wales, save that where such terms of work are inconsistent with the terms of this agreement the latter shall prevail.

[NOTE: this form of agreement is not intended for use where Counsel is instructed directly by a BarDIRECT client]

Definitions

2. In this agreement the following expressions have the meanings set out in this paragraph:

(1) The Action means *the action, the short title and reference to the record of which is … /*the proposed action between the Client and … for … /*the following part or parts of the action, the short title and reference to the record of which is …/*the following part or parts of the proposed action between the Client and … for … *[delete as appropriate and specify in addition whether any counterclaim and/or appeal and/or proceedings to enforce a judgment are included within the definition]*

(2) The Base Rate means the rates of Counsel's fees described in paragraph 14 below, which are Counsel's normal rates.

(3) The Client means.....[acting by his/her litigation friend]

(4) The Costs Insurance means the policy or policies of insurance providing cover against the Opposing Party's costs of the Action.

(5) Counsel means the barrister named above as Counsel who is party to this agreement.

(6) Failure has the meaning described in paragraph 22 below.

(7) Normal Litigation Practice means the normal practice adopted in litigation in the [Chancery Division/Commercial Court/Queen's Bench Division] which is not carried out under a conditional fee agreement.

(8)   The Opposing Party means the defendants or proposed defendants to the Action or, where there is an issue between the Client and any other party or parties to proceedings, the determination of which is covered by the definition of Success referred to in paragraph 20 below, that other party or parties.

(9)   Other acceptable counsel means other counsel who the Solicitor has agreed or does agree is acceptable for the purpose of this agreement.

(10) Preliminary Agreement means the agreement date [....................] made between Counsel and the Solicitor relating to investigation carried out and advice given by Counsel as a preliminary to entering into this agreement.

(11) The Reduced Rate means the rate of Counsel's fees specified in paragraph 16 below.

(12) The "Returned Brief, Counsel's Clerk's letter" is the letter a draft of which is at Annex 1 to this agreement.

(13) The Solicitor means the solicitor or firm of solicitors who or which is party to this agreement.

(14) The Solicitor's Conditional Fee Agreement means the Conditional Fee Agreement entered into between the Solicitor and the Client.

(15) Success has the meaning set out in paragraph 20 below.

(16) The Uplift means the difference between Counsel's fees at the Base Rate and Counsel's fees at the Uplifted Rate.

(17) The Uplifted Rate means the rate of Counsel's fees specified in paragraph 15 below.

Counsel's obligations

3.   Counsel will (subject to paragraph 5 below) diligently perform in accordance with his/her instructions any tasks in or related to the Action which in Normal Litigation Practice would be performed by a barrister of his/her seniority.

4.   In particular, Counsel is not bound:

(1)   to appear at any interlocutory hearing for which s/he reasonably believes that:

(a)   counsel of lesser experience and seniority would ordinarily be instructed; or
(b)   the court would conclude that the hearing was not fit for the attendance of one or, in a case where two or more counsel are instructed, two or more, counsel;

Provided that in the case set out in paragraph 4(1)(a) above, s/he has first used his/her best endeavours to ensure that other acceptable counsel are willing to represent the client at such hearing [on an agreed conditional fee basis] [who has agreed to act in accordance with the terms of the "Returned Brief. Counsel's Clerk's letter" (see Annex I hereto)].

(2)   to draft documents such as schedules, letters, summonses or witness statements or to advise orally or in writing or perform any other task if such would not be expected of counsel in Normal Litigation Practice;

(3)   to accept instructions outside the scope of this agreement;

(4)   to accept any brief or instructions where s/he is required or permitted to refuse such brief or instructions.

5.   If Counsel is, in accordance with the Bar's Code of Conduct, obliged or permitted to return any brief or instructions in this Action to another barrister or not to accept any brief or instructions in the Action then :

(1)   S/he will endeavour to ensure that other acceptable counsel will accept the brief and agree to act [on a conditional fee basis] [in accordance with the terms of the "Returned Brief, Counsel's Clerk's letter"]. However, neither Counsel nor Counsel's Chambers warrants or guarantees that they will be able to arrange for any alternative counsel to accept the brief or instructions or to act [on a conditional fee basis] [in accordance with the terms of the "Returned Brief, Counsel's Clerk's letter"];

(2)   If replacement Counsel cannot be found or does not agree for whatever reason to act [on a conditional fee basis] [in accordance with the terms of the "Returned Brief, Counsel's Clerk's letter"] that will not be a breach by Counsel of this agreement or retainer.

(3)   In the event of Success, Counsel's fees for his/her work, whether or not replacement counsel acted [on a conditional fee basis] [in accordance with the terms of the "Returned Brief, Counsel's Clerk's letter"], shall be due and paid in accordance with this agreement at the Uplifted Rate.

The Solicitor's Obligations

6.   The Solicitor will (subject to paragraph 7(5) below) perform any tasks in or related to the Action which in Normal Litigation Practice would be performed by a solicitor.

7.   The Solicitor confirms that s/he has brought the terms of this agreement to the attention of the Client [or any Litigation Friend] and has explained to the Client [or Litigation Friend] the Client's responsibilities and liabilities under this agreement, and that the Client [or any Litigation Friend] has consented to the terms and conditions set out in this agreement insofar as they relate to the Client. The Solicitor will (without limiting the generality of paragraph 6 above)

(1)   prosecute and prepare the Action promptly, diligently and carefully and take all necessary procedural steps in time;

(2)   provide Counsel with, or make available to Counsel, copies of all documents relevant to the Action as soon as possible after they become available to the Client or the Solicitor;

(3)   inform Counsel of all material developments and information relevant to the action as soon as possible after they become known to the Client or the Solicitor;

(4) acquire and provide Counsel with or make available to Counsel any other documents or information relevant to the Action which Counsel reasonably requests and which are available to or known to the Client or Solicitor;

(5) consider with Counsel the need for Counsel to advise on evidence, merits and quantum or to perform any other tasks and the need for any further procedural steps which Counsel may consider necessary at, at least, each of the following stages of the action:

   (a) on first instructing Counsel;
   (b) upon service of any statement of case or application by the Opposing Party;
   (c) upon completion of disclosure and inspection of documents;
   (d) upon exchange or service of any witness statement or affidavit;
   (e) upon exchange or service of any expert's report;
   (f) at any other time when Counsel considers it expedient;

   and shall instruct Counsel to advise or to act accordingly, provided that such advice or task would be given or performed by Counsel in Normal Litigation Practice;

(6) communicate Counsel's advice on at least the following matters to the Client forthwith at whatever stage the Action has reached:

   (a) advice by Counsel on the merits or quantum of the Action, including in particular that the Action is not likely to end in Success;
   (b) advice by Counsel about the appropriate terms, if any, under which the Action ought to be settled, and on whether any Part 36 payment into court or any analogous type of offer should be made or accepted;
   (c) advice that the Financial Recovery together with the costs recoverable on Success are such that they are not likely to exceed the Client's legal costs and disbursements likely to be allowed following a conventional (non-conditional fee basis) solicitor and own client taxation;
   (d) advice that expenditure should or should not be incurred in instructing Leading Counsel or a more senior or specialised barrister, or instructing experts or otherwise obtaining evidence or preparing the Action.

(7) inform Counsel's clerk in good time of the date, place and time of any hearing fixed in the Action and instruct Counsel and provide all necessary papers for the hearing within a reasonable time before the hearing or, where appropriate, within a reasonable time before the date that Counsel's skeleton argument is due to be lodged and/or or exchanged;

(8) deliver the brief (and, where appropriate, agree stage accrual of brief fees) for any hearing within a reasonable time before the hearing;

(9) forthwith upon receipt of any Part 36 or other offer to settle the Action or any issues in it communicate immediately the terms of the offer to Counsel and seek his/her advice on whether to accept or reject the offer or as to the appropriate terms, if any, under which the Action or issues ought to be settled;

(10) forthwith upon receipt of notice of a Part 36 payment into court, inform Counsel immediately of such payment in and seek his/her advice on whether to accept or reject that Part 36 payment;

(11) give to any other party to the Action information relating to this agreement required by the Civil Procedure Rules and/or any practice direction; and

(12) in any case where the amount of Counsel's fees falls to be assessed by the court, take such steps as may reasonably be necessary to ensure that Counsel is entitled to be paid fees at the Base Rate/Reduced Rate and, where applicable, the Uplifted Rate specified in this agreement, including:

    (a) notifying Counsel immediately of any appointment or hearing when Counsel's fees fall to be assessed;

    (b) taking reasonable steps to assist Counsel in preparation of argument in support of his/her fees, including obtaining information reasonably required by Counsel for that purpose; and

    (c) where Counsel is not present at any hearing or appointment relating to the assessment of his/her fees, acting for Counsel at that hearing or appointment.

Termination of the Agreement

Termination by the Solicitor

8. Subject to paragraph 10 below the Solicitor may terminate Counsel's retainer at any time without cause, in which case the provisions of paragraph 26 apply.

9. Subject to paragraph 10 below, the Solicitor may terminate Counsel's retainer with cause in any of the following circumstances :

(1) Counsel becomes unavailable for the trial of the Action, in which case the provisions of paragraph 27 apply; or

(2) the Solicitor has good reason to believe that the relationship of trust between the Solicitor and Counsel has irretrievably broken down, in which case the provisions of paragraph 26 apply; and/or

(3) the Solicitor has good reason to believe that Counsel has in breach of his/her duty to the Client manifested incompetence so as to justify the termination of his/her retainer, in which case the provisions of paragraph 28 apply.

10. The Solicitor shall not have the right to terminate Counsel's retainer on any ground once Counsel has fully performed all his/her obligations under this agreement.

Termination by Counsel

11. Counsel may terminate his/her retainer in any of the following circumstances:

(1) s/he reasonably believes that the relationship of trust between the Solicitor and Counsel [or between Counsel and other Counsel instructed in the Action] has irretrievably broken down;

(2)   the Solicitor and/or the Client and/or more senior Counsel instructed in the case rejects Counsel's advice about the appropriate terms under which the Action ought to be settled and/or any Part 36 payment into court should be made, accepted or rejected or on any other material matter;

(3)   the Solicitor has failed to comply with any obligation under this agreement;

(4)   Counsel is informed of or discovers the existence of an actual or likely set-off or counterclaim or of information which has been falsified or withheld by the Client or the Solicitor which s/he reasonably believes materially affects the likelihood of Success in the Action and/or the amount of Financial Recovery in the event of Success but of which s/he was not aware and which s/he could not reasonably have anticipated from the information before him/her at the date of his/her entry into this agreement;

(5)   Counsel is required to cease to act by the Code of Conduct of the Bar of England and Wales or Counsel's professional conduct is being impugned;

(6)   [Counsel becomes Queen's Counsel during the course of this agreement];

[Optional—delete as required]

(7)   the Client dies;

(8)   in the case of an individual client, the Client goes bankrupt or an individual voluntary arrangement is approved in respect of the Client; or

(9)   in the case of a corporate client, a winding up order is made against the Client or a resolution is passed for the voluntary winding up of the Client, or an administration order is made against the Client or administrative receivers are appointed over the property of the Client or a company voluntary arrangement is approved in respect of the Client;

provided that Counsel may not terminate the agreement if to do so would be a breach of the Code of Conduct of the Bar of England and Wales.

12.   Counsel must terminate his/her retainer in the following circumstances:

(1)   Funding is granted to the Client by the Legal Services Commission in respect of the Action;

(2)   the Solicitor's Conditional Fee Agreement is terminated before the conclusion of the case;

(3)   Counsel accepts a full time judicial appointment; or

(4)   Counsel ceases to practise as a barrister.

Provided that Counsel must in the circumstances referred to in sub-paragraph (3) or (4) endeavour to arrange that other acceptable counsel will agree to take over and act on a conditional fee basis. However, neither Counsel nor Counsel's Chambers warrants that it will be able to arrange for alternative counsel to take over. If replacement counsel does not agree for whatever reason to act on a conditional fee basis that will not be a breach of this agreement or retainer by Counsel.

Exercise of termination in writing

13.   Both the Solicitor and Counsel must give notice of termination in writing giving the reason, if any, relied upon.

The amount of Counsel's fees

The Base Rate

14.   The Base Rate for Counsel's fees to which the Uplift for the Uplifted Rate is to be applied will be as follows :

(1)   Advisory work and drafting

   In accordance with his/her hourly rate applicable to the type of work involved in the claim, currently £..... per hour

(2)   Court Appearances.

(a)   Trial

The brief fee will be—

   *[based upon the number of days which Counsel reasonably considers are required for the preparation charged at a daily rate of £..... to include the first day of trial] or

   *[£.....for a hearing whose estimated duration is 1 day;

   £.....for a hearing whose estimated duration is up to 2 days;

   £.....for a hearing whose estimated duration is 3–4 days;

   £.....for a full hearing whose estimated duration is 5 days;

   £.....for a full hearing whose estimated duration is 6–8 days;

   £.....for a full hearing whose estimated duration is 8–10 days;

   £.....for a hearing whose estimated duration is 11–15 days;

   £.....for a hearing whose estimated duration is 16–20 days;

   £....., plus £.... for each additional week or part of a week, for a hearing whose estimated duration is more than 4 weeks]

(*delete one or other of the above two alternatives as appropriate)

(b)   Interlocutory hearings

   For an interlocutory hearing the fee will be

   *[based upon the number of hours which Counsel considers are required for the preparation charged at an hourly rate of £..... plus the hourly rate for the number of hours the hearing is due to last]

     *[£…..for a hearing whose estimated duration is up to 1 hour;

     £….for a hearing whose estimated duration is 1 hour to $\frac{1}{2}$ day;

     £…..for a hearing whose estimated duration is $\frac{1}{2}$ day to 1 day;

     for hearings estimated to last more than 1 day the fee will be the same as for a trial]

(*delete one or other of the above two alternatives as appropriate)

(c)   Refreshers

In accordance with his/her daily rate obtaining for the type of work involved in the claim, currently £….. per day.

(d)   Re-reading Fees

In the event of a trial being adjourned for more than one month, a re-reading fee based on the hourly/daily rate specified in paragraph 14(1) above will be charged.

(3) Counsel's rates referred to in (1) and (2) of this paragraph 14 will be subject to review with effect from each successive anniversary of the date of this agreement but s/he will not increase the rates by more than any increase in the rate of inflation measured by the Retail Prices Index, unless s/he has in the meantime become a Queen's Counsel.

The Uplifted Rate and the Reduced Rate

15.   The Uplifted Rate which is to apply to Counsel's fees is […]. The reasons for setting the Uplifted Rate at this level are […specify briefly the reasons]. [Where any part of the Uplifted Rate relates to the cost to Counsel of the postponement of the payment of his/her fees and expenses state how much of the Uplifted Rate so relates].

16.   The Reduced Rate which is to apply to Counsel's fees is […]

17.   Where the Uplifted Rate becomes payable then if

(1)   any fees subject to the Uplifted Rate are assessed, and

(2)   Counsel or the solicitor or the Client is required by the court to disclose to the court or any other person the reasons for setting the Uplifted Rate at the level stated in this agreement,

he or she may do so.

Payment of Counsel's fees

18.   The fees to which Counsel is entitled pursuant to this agreement (whether at the Base Rate, the Uplifted Rate or the Reduced Rate) shall include the fees incurred in respect of the Preliminary Agreement.

[Note: delete this paragraph as appropriate and so as to be consistent with the terms of the Preliminary Agreement]

Fees in the event of Success and Counsel's retainer is not terminated

19.   Upon Success the Solicitor will, subject to paragraph 21 below, pay Counsel his/her fees at the Uplifted Rate or, where such fees have already

been paid at the Base Rate [or the Reduced Rate], the difference between those fees at the Base Rate [or the Reduced Rate] and at the Uplifted Rate, within [... months of delivery of a final fee note].

20. Success means:

(1) the Client becomes entitled, whether pursuant to a decision of the court or agreement between the parties, to the relief specified in the Annex marked [....] to this Agreement; *and*

(2) where the Client's entitlement to that relief is pursuant to a decision of the court, the Opposing Party or (in the case of multi-party litigation) any Opposing Party is not allowed to appeal against the court decision or has not appealed in time or has entered into a settlement agreement.

21. If the amount of damages and interest awarded by a court is less than a Part 36 payment into Court or effective Part 36 offer then:

(1) If Counsel advised its rejection s/he is entitled to fees at the Base Rate [or the Reduced Rate] and at the Uplifted Rate for the work done up to the receipt of the notice of Part 36 payment into Court or offer but fees at the Base rate [or the Reduced Rate] only for subsequent work;

(2) If Counsel advised its acceptance, or did not advise whether it should be accepted or rejected, s/he is entitled to fees at the Base Rate [or the Reduced Rate] and at the Uplifted Rate for all work done.

Fees where the Action ends in Failure and this Agreement is not terminated.

22. In the event that the Action ends in Failure (other than in the circumstances referred to in paragraph 23 or paragraph 24 below) and this Agreement has not been terminated then, without prejudice to Counsel's entitlement to be paid in respect of Disbursements in accordance with paragraph 41 below,

no fees will be payable to Counsel.*

Counsel will be entitled to his/her fees only at the Reduced Rate*

[*NOTE: delete as appropriate. The second option is appropriate where Counsel agrees to a reduced rate, which is lower than his/her normal fees, but is payable in any event, with an uplift in the event of success.]

Failure means that the Action is concluded without qualifying under the heading of Success.

23. If the action is dismissed for want of prosecution or because the Client fails to provide security for costs or otherwise ends in Failure as a result of the breach by the Solicitor but not by Counsel of any of the terms of this agreement or a procedural default by the Solicitor and/or the Client but not by Counsel, the Solicitor shall pay Counsel's fees within three months of the date of dismissal or ending of the Action at the [Base Rate/Reduced Rate/Uplifted Rate].

24. If, because of a breach by Counsel but not the Solicitor of his/her duty to the Client, the action is dismissed for want of prosecution or otherwise ends in Failure Counsel shall, subject to sub-paragraphs (1) to (3) below, pay the Solicitor such basic costs, excluding any element of uplift, as would have

been recoverable from the Client under the Solicitor's agreement with the Client.

(1)   No payment shall be made under this paragraph 24 in respect of any breach by Counsel which would not give rise to a claim for damages if an action were brought by the Client.

(2)   In the event of a disagreement as to whether there has been an actionable breach by Counsel, or as to causation, or as to the amount payable under this paragraph 24, that disagreement shall be referred to arbitration pursuant to the procedure set out in paragraphs 43 to 46 below.

(3)   The amount payable in respect of any claim under this paragraph 24 shall be limited to a maximum of [£25,000].

Fees in the event of termination by the Solicitor

25.   If Counsel's retainer is terminated by the solicitor and thus before it can be determined whether the Action has ended in Success, the fees (if any) payable to Counsel will depend on the nature of the termination. In all cases the Solicitor has the right to challenge Counsel's fees [although not the agreed rates] in accordance with the Terms of Work referred to in paragraph 1 above.

26.   If the Solicitor terminates the retainer under paragraph 8 above without cause, or under paragraph 9(2) above as a result of the Solicitor having good reason to believe that the relationship of trust and confidence between the Solicitor and Counsel has irretrievably broken down,

(1)   the Solicitor shall immediately upon termination pay to Counsel his/her fees accrued to the date of the termination at the Base Rate [or Reduced Rate]; and

(2)   in addition, in the event of Success, the Solicitor shall pay to Counsel the difference between his/her fees at the Base Rate [or Reduced Rate] and at the Uplifted Rate.

27.   If the Solicitor terminates the retainer under paragraph 9(1) above as a result of Counsel becoming unavailable for the trial of the Action the Solicitor shall:

(1)   only where Counsel is entitled pursuant to paragraph 22 above to be paid his/her fees at the Base Rate [or Reduced Rate] in the event of Failure, pay his/her fees at the Base Rate [or Reduced Rate] to the date of termination.

(2)   in the event of Success:

    (a)   where (1) above applies, pay to Counsel the difference between his/her fees at the Uplifted Rate and the amount paid pursuant to (1) above; or

    (b)   in any other case, pay to Counsel his/her fees at the Uplifted Rate.

28.   If the Solicitor terminates the retainer under paragraph 9(3) above as a result of the Solicitor having good reason to believe that Counsel has in breach of his/her duty to the Client manifested incompetence the Solicitor shall:

(1) only where Counsel is entitled pursuant to paragraph 22 above to be paid his/her fees at the Base Rate [or Reduced Rate] in the event of Failure, pay his/her fees at the Base Rate [or Reduced Rate] to the date of termination.

(2) in the event of Success:

(a) where (1) above applies, pay to Counsel the difference between his/her fees at the Uplifted Rate and the amount paid pursuant to (1) above; or

(b) in any other case, pay to Counsel his/her fees at the Uplifted Rate.

Fees in the event of termination by Counsel

29. If Counsel terminates his/her retainer upon any of the grounds specified in paragraph 11 above:

(1) the solicitor shall immediately pay to Counsel his/her fees accrued to the date of the termination at the Base Rate [or Reduced Rate]; and

(2) in addition, in the event of Success, the Solicitor shall immediately pay to Counsel the difference between his/her fees at the Base Rate [or Reduced Rate] and at the Uplifted Rate.

30. If the termination is by Counsel on the grounds specified in paragraph 12 above, the Solicitor shall pay to Counsel:

(1) only where Counsel is entitled pursuant to paragraph 22 above to be paid his/her fees at the Base Rate [or Reduced Rate] in the event of Failure, his/her fees at the Base Rate [or Reduced Rate] to the date of termination.

(2) in the event of Success:

(a) where (1) above applies, the difference between his/her fees at the Uplifted Rate and the amount paid pursuant to (1) above; or

(b) in any other case, his/her fees at the Uplifted Rate.

Payment of Base Rate [or Reduced Rate] Fees in any event

31. The Solicitor will every [3 months] during the Action pay Counsel's fees for work done to that date at the Base Rate [or the Reduced Rate]. In the event of Success, the Solicitor shall pay to Counsel the difference between his/her fees at the Base Rate [or the Reduced Rate] and at the Uplifted Rate.

[NOTE: this is likely to be appropriate only where (1) Counsel is, pursuant to the terms of the CFA Agreement, entitled to be paid his fees at a reduced rate upon Failure, and/or (2) Counsel is requested to act on a conditional fee basis otherwise than by reason of the impecuniosity of the Client.]

32. [In the event of Failure, save where Counsel is in any event entitled pursuant to paragraph 22 above to be paid his/her fees at the Reduced Rate upon Failure, Counsel shall repay to the Solicitor the fees paid pursuant to paragraph 31 above.]

Information and Further Payment

33. In the event that Counsel may be entitled (including after termination) to [further] payment in the event of Success, the Solicitor must keep Counsel

reasonably informed of the progress of the Action, must promptly inform Counsel of Success if it occurs, and must pay Counsel the further payment within [3 months of the delivery of a final fee note].

Payment of fees when the Client is awarded an interim payment

34.   In the event that the Client is awarded an interim payment in the Action, whether by Court Order or agreement with the Opposing Party, the Solicitor will pay Counsel's fees for work done to the date of the order for interim payment at the Base Rate [or the Reduced Rate].

35.   In the event of Success, the Solicitor shall pay to Counsel the difference between his/her fees at the Base Rate [or the Reduced Rate] and at the Uplifted Rate.

36.   In the event of Failure, save where Counsel is in any event entitled to be paid at the Base Rate [or the Reduced Rate] upon Failure, Counsel shall repay to the Solicitor the fees paid pursuant to paragraph 34 above.

Payment of fees in respect of costs awarded or agreed in respect of an interlocutory hearing

37.   If:

(1)   A costs order is made in favour of the Client at any interlocutory hearing and the costs are summarily assessed at the hearing; or

(2)   The costs of an interlocutory hearing are agreed between the parties in favour of the Client; or

(3)   An interlocutory order or agreement for costs to be assessed in detail and paid forthwith is made in favour of the Client;

then the Solicitor will, where sub-paragraphs (2) or (3) above apply, promptly conclude by agreement or assessment the question of such costs and, in each case, within one month after receipt of such costs the Solicitor will pay to Counsel the amount recovered in respect of his/her fees, such sum to be set-off against Counsel's entitlement to normal and success fees by virtue of this agreement.

Counsel's entitlement to fees in the event of assessment

38.   If any fees subject to the Uplifted Rate are assessed and any amount in respect of the Uplifted Rate is disallowed on assessment on the ground that the level at which the Uplifted Rate was set was unreasonable in view of the facts which were or should have been known to Counsel at the time it was set, such amount ceases to be payable under this agreement, unless the court is satisfied that it should continue to be so payable.

39.   In any case where fees subject to the Uplifted Rate are not assessed, if Counsel agrees with any person liable as a result of the Action to pay fees subject to the Uplifted Rate that a lower amount than the amount payable in accordance with this agreement is to be paid instead, then the amount payable under this agreement in respect of those fees shall be reduced accordingly, unless the court is satisfied that the full amount should continue to be payable under it.

Interest

40.   In the event that Counsel's fees are not paid in due time under this agreement, the Solicitor will pay Counsel interest on those fees at the rate of …

Disbursements

41.   The Solicitor will, regardless of whether the Action ends in Success or not, pay Counsel any disbursement costs incurred by Counsel. Such costs are to be paid by the Solicitor to Counsel [within … months of the costs being incurred by Counsel]. Such costs include, but are not limited to the following:

(1)   Counsel's reasonable travel costs incurred in connection with the Action;

(2)   Counsel's reasonable accommodation and reasonable subsistence costs incurred in connection with the Action;

(3)   Counsel's reasonable legal research costs incurred in connection with the Action, including the cost of computer data base research.

Payment of Counsel's fees in any event

42.   The Solicitor will pay Counsel's fees in accordance with this agreement whether or not the Solicitor is or will be paid by the Client or the Opposing Party.

RIGHTS TO CHALLENGE AND DISPUTE RESOLUTION

43.   Any dispute arising out of or in connection with this agreement shall be referred to arbitration by a panel consisting of a Barrister nominated by the Chairman of the Bar Council and a solicitor nominated by the President of the Law Society, who shall act as arbitrators in accordance with the Arbitration Act 1996. The arbitrators so appointed shall have power to appoint an umpire.

44.   The arbitrators so appointed and, where applicable, the umpire, will be entitled to act with or without charge. In the event that any one or more of them choose to charge for their services, the fees and expenses of such arbitrator(s) and/or umpire shall be paid by one or both of the parties as the panel, in their discretion, shall direct. The panel shall not have power to make any order in respect of the costs of the parties.

45.   In the event of a reference to arbitration pursuant to paragraph 43 above, Counsel alleged to be in breach of duty shall be entitled to argue that the claim would not have succeeded in any event. The panel shall resolve such issue on the balance of probabilities, and if satisfied that the claim would have been lost in any event shall not make any order for payment of the Solicitor's fees or costs incurred in relation to the Action.

46.   The right to refer any dispute to arbitration must be exercised promptly by either Solicitor or Counsel. In the event of termination it must be exercised at the latest within 3 months of (i) receipt of notice of such termination or (ii) receipt of the fee note for the fee being subjected to challenge, failing which the right of challenge will become irrevocably barred.

Appendix 3

Forms

Notice of Funding of Case or Claim

Notice of funding by means of a conditional fee agreement, insurance policy or undertaking given by a prescribed body should be given to the court and all other parties to the case:

- on commencement of proceedings
- on filing an acknowledgement of service, defence or other first document; and
- at any later time that such an arrangement is entered into, changed or terminated

In the	
Claim No.	
Claimant (include Ref.)	
Defendant (include Ref.)	

Take notice that in respect of [all claims herein] [the following claims   ] the case of   *(specify name of party)*

[is now] [was] being funded by:
(Please tick those boxes which apply)

☐ a conditional fee agreement dated   which provides for a success fee;

☐ an insurance policy issued on *(date)*   by *(name of insurers)*

☐ an undertaking given on *(date)*   by *(name of prescribed body)*   in the following terms

The funding of the case has now changed:

☐ the above funding has now ceased

☐ the conditional fee agreement has been terminated

☐ a conditional agreement dated   which provides for a success fee has been entered into

☐ the insurance policy dated   has been cancelled

☐ an insurance policy has been issued *(name of insurer)* on *(date)*

☐ the undertaking given on *(date)*   has been terminated

☐ an undertaking has been given on *(date)*   by *(name of prescribed body)* in the following terms

Signed   **Date**
Solicitor for the (claimant) (defendant) (Part 20 defendant) (respondent) (appellant)

The court office at

is open between 10 am and 4 pm Monday to Friday. When corresponding with the court, please address forms or letters to the Court manager and quote the claim number.

N251 Notice of funding of case or claim (7.00)   *The Court Service Publications Unit*

427

Notice of commencement of assessment of bill of costs

In the	
Claim No.	
Claimant (include Ref.)	
Defendant (include Ref.)	

To the claimant (defendant)

Following an . . . . *(insert name of document eg order, judgment)* dated . . . . (copy attached) I have prepared my Bill of Costs for assessment. The Bill totals *£. . . . . If you choose to dispute this bill and your objections are not upheld at the assessment hearing, the full amount payable (including the assessment fee) will be £. . . . . (together with interest *(see note below)*). I shall also seek the costs of the assessment hearing

Your points of dispute must include

- details of the items in the bill of costs which are disputed

- concise details of the nature and grounds of the dispute for each item and, if you seek a reduction in those items, suggest, where practicable, a reduced figure

You must serve your points of dispute by . . . . *(insert date 21 days from the date of service of this notice)* on me at:— *(give full name and address for service including any DX number or reference)*

You must also serve copies of your points of dispute on all other parties to the assessment identified below *(you do not need to serve your points of dispute on the court)*.

I certify that I have served the following person(s) with a copy of this notice and my Bill of Costs:— *(give details of persons served)*

If I have not received your points of dispute by the above date, I will ask the court to issue a default costs certificate for the full amount of my bill *(see above*)* plus fixed costs and court fee in the total amount of £ . . . .

Signed . . . .   **Date** . . . .
(Claimant)(Defendant)('s solicitor)

Note: Interest may be added to all High Court judgments and certain county court judgments of £5,000 or more under the Judgments Act 1838 and the County Courts Act 1984.

The court office at

is open between 10 am and 4 pm Monday to Friday. When corresponding with the court, please address forms or letters to the Court manager and quote the claim number.

N252 Notice of commencement of assessment of bill of costs (12.99)   *The Court Service Publications Unit*

Statement of Costs (summary assessment)

In the	
	Court
Case Reference	

Judge/Master

Case Title

[Party]'s Statement of Costs for the hearing on *(date)*

(interim application/fast track trail)

Description of fee earners*

    (a) *(name) (grade) (hourly rate claimed)*

    (b) *(name) (grade) (hourly rate claimed)*

Attendances on   *(party)*

(a) *(number)*	hours at £		£	0.00
(b) *(number)*	hours at £		£	0.00

Attendances on opponents

(a) *(number)*	hours at £		£	0.00
(b) *(number)*	hours at £		£	0.00

Attendance on others

(a) *(number)*	hours at £		£	0.00
(b) *(number)*	hours at £		£	0.00

Site inspections etc

(a) *(number)*	hours at £		£	0.00
(b) *(number)*	hours at £		£	0.00

Work done on negotiations

(a) *(number)*	hours at £		£	0.00
(b) *(number)*	hours at £		£	0.00

Other work, not covered above

(a) *(number)*	hours at £		£	0.00
(b) *(number)*	hours at £		£	0.00

Work done on documents

(a) *(number)*	hours at £		£	0.00
(b) *(number)*	hours at £		£	0.00

Attendance at hearing

(a) *(number)*	hours at £		£	0.00
(b) *(number)*	hours at £		£	0.00
(a) *(number)*	hours travel and waiting at £		£	0.00
(b) *(number)*	hours travel and waiting at £		£	0.00

                                 Sub Total £   0.00

Index

Index

Index

440